Scattering the Seed

Scattering the Seed

*A Guide through Balthasar's Early Writings on
Philosophy and the Arts*

Aidan Nichols OP

THE CATHOLIC UNIVERSITY OF AMERICA PRESS

Published by T&T Clark
A Continuum imprint
The Tower Building, 11 York Road, London SE1 7NX
80 Maiden Lane, Suite 704, New York, NY 10038

www.continuumbooks.com

This edition published under license from T&T Clark, an imprint of Continuum International Publishing Ltd, by The Catholic University of America Press 620 Michigan Avenue, N.E., Washington, D.C. 20064

British Library Cataloguing-in-Publication Data
A catalogue record for this book is available from the British Library

Typeset by YHT Ltd, London
Printed on acid-free paper in Great Britain by
MPG Books Ltd, Bodmin, Cornwall.

Contents

Preface   vii

1. BEGINNING FROM MUSIC   1

2. FRIENDS AND RIVALS: ART AND RELIGION   9

3. BALTHASAR'S FIRST THEOLOGICAL PROGRAMME   17

4. EXPLORING ULTIMATES: ESCHATOLOGY AND THE GERMAN SOUL   33

5. FROM LESSING TO FICHTE   45

6. FROM SCHELLING TO GOETHE   69

7. FROM JEAN PAUL TO NIETZSCHE   109

8. FROM BERGSON TO DOSTOEVSKY   133

9. FROM THE WAR POETS TO SCHELER   179

10. FROM HEIDEGGER AND RILKE TO BARTH   203

11. MYTH, UTOPIA, KAIROS   231

12. THE TASKS OF CATHOLIC PHILOSOPHY IN BALTHASAR'S TIME   245

13. A VERY SUMMARY CONCLUSION   253

Index of Names   255

Index of Subjects   259

Preface

My *Introduction to Hans Urs von Balthasar* – three books out of five have already appeared (*The Word Has Been Abroad: A Guide through Balthasar's Aesthetics* [Edinburgh 1998]; *No Bloodless Myth: A Guide through Balthasar's Dramatics* [Edinburgh 2000]; *Say It Is Pentecost: A Guide through Balthasar's Logic* [Edinburgh 2001]) – continues with this survey of his early writings, which are predominantly philosophical in character. So far they have received very little attention. Indeed, it is doubtful whether more than a handful of people have read them throughout. But they are not only of considerable interest in and for themselves. More than this, they provide an indispensable clue to the genesis and development of Balthasar's thought.

Above all, *Apokalypse der deutschen Seele*, the vast three-volume work which dominated Balthasar's life and work as a young man, furnishes numerous concepts and images that proved indispensable to the crafting of his trilogy and the rest of his theological work. In its light the scope and implications of his theology look markedly different. It is easier to see how he sifted late modern thought for its possible contributions to orthodox theology as well as its snares and tripwires. It also emerges how presciently he trod. These chapters are investigations of a doctor of the Church for the post-modern age.

Blackfriars, Cambridge
Memorial day of St Ephrem, 2005

1

❧

Beginning from Music

The aim of the initial chapters of this book is not to give the reader a more historically precise *entrée* to Balthasar's life and work. Hopefully, enough has been said for the purposes of general orientation in the opening pages of the first volume of my 'Introduction to Hans Urs von Balthasar', *The Word Has Been Abroad*.[1] What I want to investigate here is, rather, Balthasar's own introduction to the labour of writing: the earliest essays by which he began in a modest way to make his name known as, first, layman and then young Jesuit in the Switzerland (and the wider German-speaking world) of the 1920s and 30s. The rubric under which his earliest contributions are most readily brought is a triple one: 'music, art-and-religion, theology'.

A Musical Project

We can assume that Balthasar's aesthetic sense was awakened above all by music – not only the Romantics whose piano pieces he practised as a child at home in Lucerne but also, and above all, music heard in the visual setting of the central European Baroque – the abbey church of Engelberg where his schooling began.[2] When, as a precocious twenty year old, he embarks on the brief book which opens his writing career, it will be devoted to an 'attempt at a synthesis of music' by way of an account of the 'unfolding of the musical idea'.[3]

This is, surely, a title – and a sub-title – that could never have occurred to anyone not already committed to the systematic project of distinctively Teutonic philosophical thinking! But what were the embryonic cultural – and metaphysical – allegiances Balthasar was forming?

The opening of the work shows unmistakably, and even alarmingly to the tutored theological eye, the extent of Balthasar's commitment, at this early stage, to a rather naïve version of Christian Romanticism. What all the arts have in common is their capacity to mediate the divine. This is asserted in so

1 A. Nichols, OP, *The Word Has Been Abroad: A Guide through Balthasar's Aesthetics* (Edinburgh 1998), pp. ix–xx.
2 For his own description of his musical passion, consult the autobiographical remarks in *Unser Auftrag. Bericht und Entwurf* (Einsiedeln 1984). His occasional writings in praise of Mozart were published in the year of his death as *Bekenntnis zu Mozart* (Einsiedeln 1988).
3 *Die Entfaltung der musikalischen Idee. Versuch einer Synthese der Musik* (Braunschweig 1925).

unqualified a fashion that one wonders what work of divine disclosure might remain for Incarnation and Atonement to perform! However, as we shall see, when Balthasar begins to draw this essay to an end he strikes a far more realistic note, recognizing the inevitable failure of art – and therefore of music – as a mediation of the plenitude of meaning on earth. Still, his ultimate conclusion will be theologically 'upbeat': 'Music ... is, like all art, logical – indeed, perhaps more so than any other art. It is a limit point of the human, and on this boundary begins the divine. It is an everlasting monument to the fact that human beings can surmise (*ahnen*) what God is: eternally simple, manifold and dynamically fluent in himself and as Logos in the world.'[4]

The Origins of Music

Despite these words, Balthasar's study of music is as much anthropology as theology or, better, religious philosophy. It is also cosmology, since Balthasar places human music in continuity with the animal world, and the world of nature at large, quite as much he does with the world of God. 'There is in nature no silence.'[5] That is a statement justified by, among other things, the roar of the ocean, the rushing of waterfalls, the ceaseless 'voices' of insects and reptiles in the woods.

But is any of this music? Or is it simply sound? Whatever may be said of 'dead' nature, the inorganic elements, Balthasar cannot accept that the world of the animals is bereft of musical values. 'With the animals we see the most basic stage in the employment of the phenomenon of sound as the expression of some kind of function in the sphere of life.'[6] Theirs is a primitive expression of meaning which, being instinctive, is at best semi-conscious. Precisely the lack of reflexive consciousness of the animal explains the permanence of this level in the emergence of music: there is as yet no stimulus to go further. Birdsong, for example, confronts us with a stage in the 'unfolding of the musical idea' which lacks all possibility of further development. And yet how it compels our attention! We already find in it, through the interruption of sound and the variation of tone, two key elements of all music: rhythm and melody.[7]

In this sense, the first members of the human species found music already to hand, not only in the 'symphony of nature' around them but also as something that was given in the functions they shared with the animal realm. (That is how Balthasar would explain the early ascription of music's origin to the gods.) Humankind wanted to second this divine creativity by another creativity all their own. Hence their practice of music, originally by imitation of the proto-musical cries of bird and beast.

---

4 Ibid., pp. 37–38.
5 Ibid., p. 8.
6 Ibid.
7 Olivier Messiaen was still to do his fieldwork when Balthasar wrote, but musicologically relevant scientific interest in birdsong went back to the late nineteenth century – e.g. C.A. Witchell, *The Evolution of Bird Song* (London 1896), just as numerous composers – beginning, it seems, with Clément Jannequin (born *c.* 1485) and Nicholas Gombert, pupil of Josquin des Prés (died 1521) – had, in the charming words of a standard encyclopaedia, 'recalled or imitated their bird colleagues', P.A. Scholes (ed.), *The Oxford Companion to Music* (London, 9th edn, 1955), p. 109.

Rhythm and Order

Even more important a factor, Balthasar considers, was the continuous struggle to wrest a living from nature, whence the employment of rhythm in laborious work. And so a spiritual (*geistig*) factor enters in to complement an organic one – for the human heartbeat, as Aristotle had noticed, must always have provided man with a fundamental sense of the pairing quick/slow, essential as this is to rhythmic sound. But in the genesis of rhythm, the first fundament of music (Balthasar accepts Claus von Bülow's dictum, 'In the beginning was rhythm'), a sense of *cosmic order* was more important still.

> The order of the cosmic event is one of rhythmic symmetry. The alternation of day and night, ebb and flow, summer and winter, life and death, advises us that the manifestation of spirit in the bodily, i.e. the law of order, is, at any rate for our world and our thinking – inseparable from the law of rhythm, the heartbeat of the universe.[8]

Man made labour rhythmic because he was himself the world in microcosm. The philosophic Balthasar sees man *cosmically*. We have an indication here that the future theological Balthasar will not stay content with any mere Existentialism, or lightly accept a basically anthropocentric presentation of faith. Faintly, we can discern the possibility of his attraction, one day, to the Greek Father for whom ideas of microcosm were key, St Maximus the Confessor.[9]

Of more immediate concern, though, is the thought that the 'primordial cell' of art is 'the organic-psychic feeling for order' whence come (he proposes) language, dance and music itself. So Balthasar would like to define music, on this basis, as the 'desire-accompanied drive for order in the realm of the acoustic'.[10]

In the beginning-times, melody – soon to engage Balthasar's attention – is so bound to rhythm as hardly to enjoy a life of its own. When it begins to do so it needs at first the help of stamping, clapping and so forth to make its presence felt. A music almost exclusively rhythmic need not, however, be primitive in a pejorative sense, for the peoples who practise it may develop a 'polyrhythmia' or intercalation of rhythms which ears attuned to later developments can barely follow.

This leads Balthasar to raise for the first time the question of the *principle* of musical development. In his introduction to this short treatise, he had made good use of the Scholastic concept of *materia signata*. That phrase refers to matter specifically as ready to enter the field of communication – which it can do through the appropriate *form* whereby something comes to actual expression. Now what Balthasar proposes is this. The *materia prima* of all art is sensuously embodied meaning, *der Sinn*. The arts – as the composer-librettist Richard Wagner saw – differ 'only in their forms. In their deepest

8 *Die Entwicklung der musikalischen Idee*, op. cit., p. 10.

9 *Kosmische Liturgie. Das Weltbild Maximus des Bekenners* (Einsiedeln, 2nd edn, 1961; the first edition was subtitled more dramatically *Höhe und Krise des griechischen Weltbilds bei Maximus Confessor* (Freiburg 1941). For the importance of the microcosm concept, see L. Thunberg, *Microcosm and Mediator: The Theological Anthropology of Maximus the Confessor* (Lund 1965).

10 *Die Entwicklung der musikalischen Idee*, op. cit., p. 11.

ground, they are rooted in the same foundation.'[11] But the *materia prima* in question is always *materia signata:* from the first it is 'modified' by its reference to some determinate form. What strikes us about any artwork worth the name is the expressive unity by which significance and physical medium are bonded together in a single (in effect 'hylomorphic' – matter-and-form) substance.

But here Balthasar has to register a further complication. When we think of the arts as a whole, we see how their semantic matter is differently 'signed' for each of, say, dramatic acting, music, poetry. But the 'matter' of just one of the arts is also differently 'signed' in the various cultures where that art is practised. The inhabitants of a culture take up different angles of view on an art; they make different demands on it; and so they shape it after different fashions. For the Arabs music is intoxication; for the Chinese it is encouragement to sober, rational thought. For Romanticism music consists of feeling equivalents; for the Hellenes it was ethical formation.

Balthasar doubts – understandably – that any synthesis of such approaches is feasible. What, though, can be noted is the way that, when a culture comes to ripeness, it often opens itself with a new confidence to other cultures and learns from them. That is a concession which distances Balthasar from mainstream Romantic theory about cultures as organic wholes. It has relevance, too, for the debate in the Catholicism of his last years about the 'inculturation' of faith: it is not necessarily wicked for the Church to introduce one culture to another!

For Balthasar's immediate purposes in the essay on music, even this qualified acceptance of a *de iure* as well as *de facto* cultural pluralism creates a problem. How can it be possible to speak of the *general development* of the musical idea when criteria of judgment about music are so (appropriately) disparate? This is a puzzle that will exercise him in the concluding section of *Die Entwicklung.*

Melody, Dionysian and Apollonian

Meanwhile, what does he have to say about melody, the second great element, after rhythm, of musical sound? He finds it the most mysterious of the three musical elements (harmony will be the last). We have seen how rhythm is rationally explicable – and harmony Balthasar will regard as essentially the result of numerical relationships. But melody is something else again. Resistant to rational analysis, it makes itself sensuously evident in an immediately effective way. It is a classic example, in fact, of a *Gestalt* – a formal whole that cannot be satisfactorily analysed by decomposition into parts. And yet, as the Greeks discovered, this form can house, paradoxically, relative formlessness in the – frenzied and unmeasured – Dionysian experience of melody. Hence the need many Greeks felt to limit its potential wildness in some more Apollonian – calm and measured – 'eurhythmy'.

Balthasar treats the melodic as a peg on which to hang his earliest reflections on a theme that will remain central to his account of the human: the contrast of Dionysian and Apollonian (as is well known, the terms are Friedrich Nietzsche's) in both psyche and culture. 'Apollo' here represents a

11 Ibid., p. 4.

striving for 'peaceful detachment'; 'Dionysus' the drive towards 'fantastic self-stupefaction'.[12]

The Greek ideal was Apollonian. But the gifts of Apollo – measure, order – could be lost in the vortex of Dionysus: the measureless, the amorphous, the a-rhythmic. Hence the hostility of philosophers and pedagogues to melody. However, just as the instinctive life must be temperately ordered and not simply denied (or more troubles will come), so also melody must be united with rhythm if music is to attain its optimal flowering. It was the Greek fear of the Dionysian that rendered the ground of ancient Hellas less than propitious soil for the growing together of melody with rhythm. To the Grecian ideal of perfected form the medium of stone, not sound, was the better suited. Hence the genius of Greece can be found more readily in the plastic arts – the construction of the Parthenon, the sculpting of the Venus de Milo.

Harmony: Acoustics in Proportion

And so at last to harmony, the final building block of the musical. Balthasar treats harmony as the key discovery of Western music. The awareness of acoustic proportions which underlies the discovery of the musical possibilities of simultaneously sounding tones implies a sense for the relational which was, he would contend, alien to the Greek genius.

This is an extraordinary generalization for which the evidence adduced – the lack of perspectival sense in the fine arts and the weak development of historical sense (Herodotus?, Thucydides?) among the Greeks – scarcely seems probative.[13] Be that as it may, this 'vertical' dimension of sound opened up further possibilities of musical expression even as, by its own mathematical character, it could also come in time to all but suppress the melodic (as in the mid to late nineteenth century, the age of *Lebensmathematisierung*, the 'mathematicization of life'). This was a mistake because: 'Only melody can bring off the highest flights, though harmony is its unavoidable support, for melody draws strength from harmony, through harmony soars weightlessly upward; in harmony finds fulfilment.'[14]

Progressive Development?

Despite the heterogeneity of the factors Balthasar has identified in the history of music, he wants to say that the development of music has always had its goal within it (it is teleological), and that its unity is of a kind best compared to that of a living thing (it is organic). The production of musical forms is really an 'eduction': such forms are drawn out according to the exigencies of a 'higher lawfulness'.

Not, however, that an earlier stage of musical development is only of interest for the light it can throw on a later stage. Each form can be an

---

12 Ibid., p. 17.
13 On the former, for an interesting test-case, see C.A. Mango, 'Antique Statuary and the Byzantine Beholder', *Dumbarton Oaks Papers* 17 (1963), pp. 53–75, and for the latter, very generally, C. Fornara, *The Nature of History in Ancient Greece and Rome* (Berkeley and Los Angeles 1983).
14 *Die Entwicklung der musikalischen Idee*, op cit., p. 23.

'authentic fulfilment of a part of the total idea of music', just as one leaf of a tree is not only beautiful but contains the tree's whole 'entelechy' – Aristotle's term for developing purposive form – in itself. The history of music, accordingly, is not just a history of pure types but of confluence and mingling. Gregorian chant is melodic; so, essentially, is Renaissance music; so are the operas of Verdi; Baroque music is basically harmonic, as are the operas of Wagner. But on the spectrum melodic/harmonic are many subtle colours shading off one into another. That is what we would expect if music is organic, for organism is life, not mathematics, and to assert this Balthasar uses the vocabulary not only of vitalism and existentialism but also of the 'dialectic' of Proclus and Hegel.[15]

Extraneous Association and Intrinsic Form

For Balthasar, music is both a form for the metaphysical, the 'higher', and an expression of the imaginable world, the 'lower'. Because it is both of these, neither the 'programme music' so popular around the turn of the nineteenth and twentieth centuries (think of the many 'nature effects' in Richard Strauss) nor the neo-classicist 'back to Bach' school will serve our turn. If it is the second that comes closest to 'absolute music' – the reflection in sound of the 'dynamically metaphysical' (itself the manifestation in creation of the living God), the high altitude of such 'associationless' music has air too thin for us to breathe for long. And so we need the support of the first which, at its best, expresses in refined fashion our experience of the sensuous world. Not everything incorporated into music is simply musical – there is Wagner trying to philosophize, Richard Strauss exploring the emotional world of Nietzsche's *Thus spake Zarathustra*, Beethoven setting out, in the Pastoral Symphony, to capture the sounds of the Rhenish countryside.

But if music is of metaphysical interest insofar as it attempts to express a truth that lies beyond not only the verbal and visual but the conceptual as well, it can still draw on these other resources – whether consciously or not – for aid in this task. (Balthasar compares the kind of music that depends for its effect on extra-musical associations to a heat-haze which, in glaring light, may actually *assist* viewing.) Still, Balthasar is inclined to think that his own time, typified as it is by a healthy reaction to an earlier, excessively anti-metaphysical age, will not be content with an impressionist art but will once again seek form as a 'revelation from above'.

This emphasis on formal values surely reflects the new wave in both theory and practice in the music of the 1920s that is forever linked to the name of Igor Stravinsky. In the middle of that decade, Stravinsky at last abandoned the Russian Romantic style he had learned from Rimsky-Korsakov and did so to the point that he claimed to have discarded all extra-musical influences on his work. 'Absolute' music as opposed – and antithetically so – to 'programme' music left off any attempt to represent the sounds of nature or human living, or the emotions suggested by an image or text. 'Proper' musical form is found when that which has been composed can be

15 Ibid., p. 26.

considered *only* as music.[16] For Balthasar, however, 'form' can never be a purely formal value. It is a value, all right, but a downright metaphysical one.

The individualism of the era that, in the 1920s, was passing, had focused attention on the artist's subjectivity. To Balthasar's mind, indeed, artistic subjectivity is only of interest inasmuch as through the artwork it brings before us something universally valid for humanity. How should such universal validity be understood? In a passage heavily indebted to the 'Objective Idealism' tradition in classical German philosophy, Balthasar proposes that form encapsulates aspects of 'idea' in the latter's evolution as a whole. It is by forwarding that process in some way that an artwork can betoken 'progress'. If we ask what on earth, in these comments, the word 'idea' might signify, he gives us our answer by paraphrasing his own statement about the work of art. In the artwork of the hypothetical example, 'the divine has gone a step further into the world'.[17]

As Balthasar uses them, terms like 'progress' (*Fortschritt*) or even 'development' (*Entwicklung, Evolution*) must not be over-deterministically misunderstood. To read this essay in a theologically benign way: Balthasar is using nineteenth-century vocabulary to express what is, basically, a Hellenic metaphysic of the real: central to his thinking is the Aristotelian notion of 'entelechy' or the goal-orientation in things. As he recognizes, there are entire periods, whole cultural epochs, in which matters may stand still or go backwards. In some ways he treated his own period as an example, finding the neo-Romantic neglect of melody (Schönberg) sterile, the subsequent love-affair of the avant-garde with a-tonalism destructive. These are symptoms of regression. Nonetheless, the overall drive is to fulfilment, to flowering, and this in itself does not fail.

Conclusion

Balthasar leaves us, in this impressive *juvenilium*, with an antinomy. On the one hand, forms combine in multifarious ways, approximating the more closely as they do so to the 'ideal total form of the musical idea'. On the other hand, form is inevitably narrowing, since that *Gesamtidee* is never fully present in it. The optimism of the first observation seems cancelled out by the tragic implications of the second. The antinomy brings home to us the provisional quality of the revelation of being that is music, and fills us with new longing for the eternal.

The treatise is pullulating with ideas: too many, from the standpoint of coherence, for its own good. Still, the first seedlings of some of his later ideas and works have begun to sprout. In debt to a number of philosophical

16 'In the course of [the] quest ... for a place in music's universal concert, even at the price of anonymity, ... the only abiding place for him was convention, the "immutable mould", ... for convention both frees the music from any connotation, or subjection to feeling, and also rids words themselves of their meaning in the musical text, restoring them as "pure feeling" ', A. Boucourechliev, *Stravinsky* (ET London 1987), p. 166. Stravinsky had himself remarked, 'In borrowing a form already established and consecrated, the creative artist is not in the least restricting the manifestation of his personality. On the contrary, it is more detached and stands out better when it moves within the definite limits of a convention', *An Autobiography* (ET London 1975), p. 132.

17 *Die Entwicklung der musikalischen Idee*, op. cit., p. 32.

schools, it is the work of a brilliant mind that has not yet reached intellectual integration. In particular – and Balthasar's subsequent essays on the relation of art and religion will reinforce this point – we have here a thinking that has not yet reached the theological level properly so called, where the ideas of creation and salvation, nature and grace, Trinity and Incarnation crucial to all baptized thought are brought into play in the service of a Christian understanding of reality at large.

None the less, the musical impulse will stay with Balthasar throughout, and not just in the sense that he devoted hours to musical listening (or performance) of the kind that the French writer Albert Béguin noted during Balthasar's years as a University chaplain in Basle (1938–1945).[18] Comparison with musical form and manner was for him a way of understanding his sources of theological inspiration, for in music freedom streams through – and over – structure and laws. That will be, for example, not only central to his understanding of Augustine in the theological aesthetics,[19] but a key also to his grasp of theological time as held together by the divine freedom in his essays on time and history, *Das Ganze im Fragment*.[20] Under the entire confusing music of world time a *basso profundo*, consisting of the divine Word and the divinely enabled answer to that Word, is *sostenuto*. Here Balthasar's musicology – and musicality – begins to be placed at the service of doctrinal vision. He will find in divine revelation a music of freedom where the Spirit gives free play to dramatic developments and yet shows himself sovereign as the music ends.[21] Grasping how to integrate his artistic insights into his theological project will be a protracted process.

18 A. Béguin, 'Préface', in *La théologie de l'histoire* (French translation, Paris, 2nd edn, 1970).
19 *Herrlichkeit. Eine theologische Ästhetik*, II.1 (Einsiedeln, 3rd edn, 1984), p. 22.
20 *Das Ganze im Fragment. Aspekte der Geschichtstheologie* (Einsiedeln 1963), p. 36.
21 See on this C. Dumont, SJ, 'Ein musikalisches Genie', in K. Lehmann – W. Kasper (ed.), *Hans Urs von Balthasar Gestalt und Werk* (Cologne 1989), pp. 223–36.

2

Friends and Rivals: Art and Religion

The Values of Aesthetics and Religion

The 1927 essay 'Kunst und Religion' was originally a lecture to the literature section of *Logos*, the Viennese society of Catholic intellectuals. In it the young Balthasar asked how the *values* – this was a term favoured by the then fashionable phenomological philosopher, Max Scheler[1] – of art and religion may be said to be embodied in *personality* – the lives of individuals, as well as in *making* or artistic production. Useful background is provided by the editors of *Volkswohl*, the journal where this essay first appeared, who explain that the rationale of the research group Balthasar had addressed consisted in 'clarification of the chief questions of German [i.e. Germanophone] Catholic literary life'.[2] This is not simply a theoretical enquiry, then, as the essay on music could be said to be. It is a contribution to helping along the active relations of culture and faith. The person and the work, these are to be the *idées clefs*, and indeed they name the two sides, subjective and objective, of all artistic labour.

Balthasar's initial description of the artistically beautiful seems perilously close to absorbing the religious into the aesthetic. Aesthetic enjoyment, he explains, combines what is concretely given with reference to an 'idea' – the 'eternal, ideal and essential' lying behind it, glimpsed as though through glass. Indeed: 'precisely in this oscillation between concreteness and idea, this suspension between two realms, lies art's bliss-making quality [*das Beseligende der Kunst*]'.[3] In its ordered freedom, the artwork has 'fallen from heaven' (a remark that is only partly tongue-in-cheek). It is a making present of the demands of eternity. But Balthasar then surprises us by insisting on the irreducibility of the aesthetic to the religious. Art and religion are 'qualitatively different'. So how are we to categorize the 'religious' attitude properly so called?

---

1 M. Scheler, *Der Formalismus in der Ethik und die materiale Wertethik* (Halle 1916). It should be noted that by 'material' Scheler means objective values inhering in things in their value-qualities. In emotional stormy weather, Scheler abandoned Christian practice, and even, it would seem, theism in the years immediately preceding his death in 1928. Thus 'A Note on the Author' by I.M. Bochenski [Innozent Bochenski, OP], in M. Scheler, *On the Nature of the Eternal in Man* (ET London 1960), pp. 471–78.
2 Editorial note in 'Kunst und Religion', *Volkswohl* 18 (1927), p. 354.
3 Ibid., p. 355.

Balthasar wants to make *conscience* the key to that attitude – not, however, conscience in the narrowly conceived moral sense which the German word *das Gewissen* tends to connote, but what he terms (in, he thinks, a fashion indebted to John Henry Newman) 'that paradoxical function in us ... [by which] we experience here our own deepest law and simultaneously that, at its deepest, it is strange (*fremd*) to us'. The feeling for beauty has no particular relation to the personal, whereas *law-giving* cannot but be a personal work. So understood, conscience points directly to a highest Lawgiver and, while it is for us a 'last frontier and fulfilment', it is also an 'ordering of definitive values', of 'final, irrevocable validities and antinomies' – good and evil, gracing and reprobation.

As with aesthetic experience, these decisive – nay, ultimate – contrasts strike us at particular moments. But those moments create, through our response to them, the sense of responsibility that is crucial to authentic 'piety' (*Frömmigkeit*). There may well be other proofs of the existence of God. Balthasar is no doubt thinking of the 'five ways' of Thomas Aquinas, widely taken up as these were in the apologetics and philosophical theology of Catholicism in the inter-war years. But, he holds, such proofs do not bring one to God without the 'bridge' of some such understanding of conscience as the one now offered.

So, far from being scarcely indistinguishable, then, the aesthetic and the religious stand sharply contrasted. Aesthetic experience is this-worldly in its mastery of concrete things, its delight in finding their inner norms. Religious experience is other-worldly, experienced as given from without, though it also tells us of an ultimate destiny and thus decants the meaning of our lives.

Aesthetic and Religious Values in Persons

In what fashion, then, may both 'the aesthetic' and 'the religious' be present as values in subjects (persons) and in objects (works)? This has to be Balthasar's next question.

The difficulty of combining the aesthetic and religious attitudes in *personal existence* leads Balthasar to name (after Newman, and Scheler – whose presence is inferred) a third major intellectual influence on this essay. And that is Søren Kierkegaard. The Danish father of Christian Existentialism was afraid that man-before-God would be robbed of the 'fear and trembling' necessary to all decision-making for or against the saving good – robbed of it by the clamant alternative pretensions of the aesthetic in the form of Romantic poetics and their philosophical accompaniment. Kierkegaard, one might be tempted to think, furnishes the over-optimistic art-lover of *Die Entwicklung der musikalischen Idee* with a healthy corrective.

To situate Kierkegaard's problem more broadly, however, Balthasar stands back to consider the terrain. He points out that things around us do not present themselves to us in a homogeneous way – as though they were, fundamentally, all alike. Rather, they show themselves arranged in strata and orders (*Schichten und Ordnungen*). Correspondingly, when we look at how people scan, and come to know, the world about them, there is in the human subject no one all-purpose brand of perception. Rather is there a 'plurality of attitudinal possibilities' (*eine ... Mehrheit von Einstellungsmöglichkeiten*). The adequate grasp of a determinate object in its own order means the actualizing of the appropriate correlative potentiality in human beings.[4]

One aspect of this is especially thought-provoking. The higher and more value-laden an object, the deeper its entry into the subject, the perceiver. And the greater the demand placed on the subject in this way, the more that perceiving subject finds herself at once liberated and yet bound – *liberated* in that what is best in the subject becomes actual, *bound* owing to the 'height and breadth', the sublimity and amplitude, of the object. Just so the legendary *Dornröschen* (the German original of Sleeping Beauty), in the kiss that awoke her, was freed yet bound by love. Now, claims Balthasar, *only personal and religious values can achieve this*. This is not to say that other values are dispensable. The pillars of an aqueduct in mountain country are of unequal length, yet all are needed to carry the water of life.

Balthasar proposes that the various 'strata' of the experienced world are unified in the person, in personal agency. But how well they are grasped in their differentiated unity turns on the standpoint the acting subject adopts. In another Alpine metaphor, only the walker who climbs to a mountain top can see not just the outlines of distant ranges but the valleys in between. Now anything and everything *can* be looked at from the standpoint of the beautiful – that is, by exclusive attention to its form. (Even, says Balthasar, the text of Kant's *Critique of Pure Reason*, or a vaccuum cleaner!) The aesthetic attitude may thus discover certain aspects of religious value. But it will never reach the latter's heart.

Here Kierkegaard could not be more correct. The religious attitude need not deny anything of the aesthetic. But, like the mountaineer, it will see further. In the meanness of poverty it may see inner beauty shine out, or in Socrates' plain features love of humankind and the desire to give others truth. Or in the 'horrors and meaninglessness' of a war (Balthasar's original Austrian hearers were only a few years away from the carnage of 1914–1918), it may be the case that, quite suddenly, 'great metaphysical facts and continuities light up'.[5] And this tells us how through deeper insight into a new stratum, a new beauty (unknown to the aesthetic attitude as such) can be born. That is how Balthasar understands the Scholastic axiom, *Pulchrum quasi splendor veritatis*: 'the beautiful is, as it were, the splendour of truth'. Is it going, interpretatively, too far to say that here Balthasar has already divined something of the kenotic or cruciform shape of beauty? That 'shape' to

---

4 We note in passing how the specific vocabulary, and even conceptuality, Balthasar uses in this essay is eclectic. It belongs to no one philosophical school. It enjoys, though, an affinity with the thought of Aquinas whose 'analectic' philosophical method it parallels. Such 'eclecticism with a Thomist core' is prophetic of what Balthasar's mature philosophical theology will look like. Cf. B. Lakebrink, *Perfectio omnium perfectionum* (Vatican City 1984, = *Studia Thomistica* 24), p. 9: 'a natural and uncoerced attitude of a well-balanced kind toward the cosmos, the renunciation of everything extreme, the view of the whole, prior to all its parts, no matter how tense and differentiated the internal relations of the whole may be – this method of simultaneous contemplation of everything that is, this feeling for the network-like inter-relatedness of all things and the organicity of beings within the whole, the continuous attempt to draw out the primordial centre in these so different things; this thinking that overlooks nothing but preserves every thing in what is its own and proceeds in a way that does being justice ... this we name "analectic"'.

5 Ibid.

which, in *The Glory of the Lord*, he will devote his *theological* aesthetics – at once discontinuous yet continuous with aesthetics normally so called – of the Incarnation and the Cross?

Be that as it may, the practical corollary Balthasar draws is that religious 'energy' can be expended on an artwork *without leaving the ground of authentic religion behind*. The lower stratum of the aesthetic is subsumed – in the Hegelian tag, *aufgehoben* – under the higher. For example, whereas aesthetic empathy with 'cosmos, all, and man' – a religion-substitute – makes a false absolute of aesthetics-with-a-dash-of-ethics-thrown-in, real religion can nonetheless take up such empathy and give it, fulfilled, its proper place in a person's life. Balthasar is of the opinion that Kierkegaard (like Plato and the later Tolstoy) gave disproportionate attention to the difficulties attendant on such religious subsuming of aesthetics. They were too personally tempted, he suggests, by the imperialist pretensions of beauty to give a serene answer to the question in hand.

The overall conclusion leads to an imperative. 'Absolutized aesthetics' can never understand religion, but religion can actualize potencies of the soul that give rise to new values in art. In that case, says Balthasar, *give* religion primacy. There is here a basic philosophical axiom at stake, which Balthasar formulates as 'whoever affirms more, is right'. That is not a recipe for maximizing ill-considered assertions about all and sundry. It is an early expression of the foundational principle of Balthasar's apologia for Catholic Christianity. The true faith is the one that can incorporate, and illuminate, all lesser truths within itself, while itself remaining inexplicable by reference to them.

Religious and Aesthetic Values in Works

We now have a good idea of how Balthasar saw art and religion coming together in the *person*. But what about in the *work*?

When we are considering the religious aspects of an artwork we need to bear in mind, says Balthasar, the difference between objective and subjective value in religion. Religion steps forth in the world as an 'order of objectivities [*Gegenständlichkeiten*]' but it also appears in subjective values in the soul. This distinction explains how one work of art may represent the Nativity (an objectively religious topic) and do so without a shred of real religious sense, while another can so depict landscape or the human figure as to be (in terms of its suffusion by a holy subjectivity) eminently religious in character. Of course, even when an artwork is *both* objectively and subjectively religious the continuity between the aesthetic and religion must not be overstated, for it lies in the realm of signification (merely). Such art is neither God nor grace, and yet as the opportunity for 'religious self-actualization' it is nevertheless a great deal. To this end, the religious painter makes use of means both 'primary' and 'secondary'. *Primary* means are ones which, phenomenologically, are inseparably linked to the articulation of religious experience. An example might be the motif of light as Lorrain exploits it in his classical landscapes or Rembrandt in his dramatic portraits. From the Upanishads to St John's Gospel that motif in its further significance really does seem a cross-cultural given. *Secondary* means are more variable, convention-bound and culturally limited (even if, as Balthasar freely admits, the borderline between secondary and primary is not always plain). We detect the constancy of the 'primary' means in the artistic canon whenever religiously alerted viewers agree in finding in an artwork that uses such 'means' a religious dimension of which the original artist was unaware. (I suggest as an example the early nine-teenth-century English painter Turner, notably in his use of, precisely, light.[6])

The means in question, we recall, are means to the expression of objective and subjective values. The apprehension of value is, otherwise expressed, *valuation* – that is, a measuring of value and a doing so by tacit reference to some standard of absolute value. In the last analysis, this is ontological in character. It is in the *God* who said he was 'the Truth' and 'the Life' – and could just as well have described himself as 'the Beauty' – that being and value are one. Those Johannine titles will be crucial to Balthasar's later *Theologik* or theological logic which tries, precisely, to show all metaphysics in a Christological and Trinitarian light.

Naturally, opponents of all talk of a divine Absolute reject this. Such an Absolute, they say, is simply a conceptual extrapolation from our experience, an experience that in any case – so the variety of taste proves – is far from easy to construe as disclosive of a scale of perfection of *any* kind. In reality (atheists go on), is it not our experience – that is, humankind itself – that is the measure of things? Somewhat surprisingly, Balthasar replies he can agree to this (historically, Sophist) position *if* it is made plain that the man who is the measure is man 'the striver' (*der Strebende*) and none other than he. Balthasar can say this because he thinks such striving will always *eventually* prove to be a striving for what mounts higher, for what journeys deeper inward, and *therefore* for the ultimate beauty. *That* is what guarantees the possibility of an appreciation of art that is at once objective and shared.

But then, taking the argument one final step further, that very striving *is only carried on by beings blessed with a conscience oriented toward the Absolute.* Essentially, these words comprise the young Balthasar's resolution of the question, How, positively, can we understand the art/religion relationship? It is, concludes Balthasar, the 'highest duty' of Catholics to point out the channel that lies between the Scylla of aestheticism on the one hand, and the Charybdis of puritanism on the other. Why the *highest* duty? Because the human openness to transcendence is here at stake. One has to say, however, that, except by interpretation formed in the light of his later thought, Bal-thasar does not really rise, in this essay, above the level of a religious theory of culture. As in his book on music, it is only by the eloquence of its absence that the dogmatic theology proper to revelation and its vehicle, the Church, makes itself felt.

Pros and Cons of Catholic Art

A great step forward was taken in this regard when Balthasar returned to the subject the same year in 'Katholische Religion und Kunst'. Writing for the

---

6 See my comments on the choice of a title in A. Nichols, OP, *Epiphany: A Theological Introduction to Catholicism* (Collegeville 1998), p. 5.

Einsiedeln journal *Schweizerische Rundschau*, Balthasar broaches his topic in a severely a priori manner.[7] A religion capable of bonding with art, he says, would have to show four features.

First, it would need to unite reason with intuition – as Catholicism does, for instance, in its Christology which is at once apologetic-rational and mystical-dogmatic. Secondly, it would need to unite the objective with the subjective – and Catholicism's most fundamental feature is its objectivism, but this is a devotion to the objective precisely out of concern for the subjective, the inner life. Thirdly, a religion that would co-exist happily with art must supply the person with enough room for development – and certainly Catholicism, with its conviction that the divine Trinity is the model of personhood, does this. Lastly, a religion altogether friendly to art would have to stress the principle of *Formung*, 'formation', the high importance of 'matter' finding its form. And indeed Pure Act, God himself, forms material into a cosmos, an ordered work of art of global dimensions. On the fourth and final 'pro', so much is obvious, we might think, for the very idea of a Creator carries with it some such notion. More original is Balthasar's suggestion that, in Catholic Christianity, salvation is itself such 'formation'. 'The triumph of formative power [*die Formkraft*] is Christ, for in him the wholly formless has itself achieved a form, and in his Church he penetrates like a leaven the whole historical world with his forming power, and only rests when all is leavened by him through and through.'[8] This short text from the 1920s could almost be a summary of the theological aesthetics of half a century later.

What of possible objections to Balthasar's sanguine view of the innate congruence of the Catholic Church and art? There is no trouble in finding some. To begin with, the Church is, surely, limited, whereas the arts are unlimited. But Balthasar denies that the Church is limited. Is she not filled with the *plêrôma*, the 'fullness', of the risen Lord in whom the whole divinity dwells bodily?[9] Once the dogmas of the Church are conceded, they become a spacious home that people can inhabit in multifarious fashion. A second objection has it that the Church, unlike the arts, is concerned with the *Jenseits* – what lies beyond this world. But, says Balthasar, with Christ the *Jenseits* has entered this world to transform it. The whole creation – according to Paul again, this time in Romans – groans with longing for that outcome.[10] Nature is on the way to God. It is to be divinized and so is already holy, mysteric, love-worthy. In a striking confession, Balthasar declares 'aesthetic panentheism' to be perfectly capable of union with Catholicism.[11] (Compare the remarks on how religion can subsume aesthetic feeling for the world in the essay described above.) A third objection takes a parallel course. Does not faith induce in many Catholics a quietism of withdrawal, not least from the issues that engage contemporary art? If so, says Balthasar, they stand condemned, since being a member of the Church carries obligations to help, carry, serve. Actually, what is likely to press the Catholic forward is not doubt (as the objection might be supposed to imply) but wonderment –

7 H.U. von Balthasar, 'Katholische Religion und Kunst', *Schweizeriche Rundschau* 27 (1927), pp. 44–54.
8 Ibid., p. 47.
9 Ephesians 1.23; Colossians 2.9.
10 Romans 8.22.
11 Balthasar, 'Katholische Religion und Kunst', p. 50.

admiratio – which is also the case with the true artist. More probingly, Balthasar points out that the Church gives full weight to tragedy while avoiding 'pantragism' – the secular dogma that would make of tragedy the final word. Here, with the benefit of hindsight, we can glimpse far ahead Balthasar's exploration of the soteriological significance of such dramatic analogies for life before God in his *Theodramatik* or theological dramatics.

Two fine passages counterpose here the Church's tragic sense with her sense that the tragic is *not* the end. On the one hand: 'The suffering of a guiltless God on the Cross, the existence of an eternal Hell, show how deep in the heart of Catholicism the tragic dwells.' On the other hand: 'The ultimately reconcilable quality of the world's ground, its final harmony, always has the upper hand, and decisively so, when compared with the transitory level [*Durchgangsstufe*] of the tragic.'[12]

Returning, then, to the list of objections: is not, fourthly, the ethics of Catholicism an external ethics, one imposed on things from without by divine decree, and is not this, then, inimical to the concerns of art? Yet what can be more inborn than natural law, which draws the artist's attention to the inner form (again) of actual things? Of course the Church tells the artist to be concerned for morality. But why should that be deemed anti-aesthetic? Morality is the *style* of life, as, for example, the great eighteenth-century German dramatist, aesthetician and ethicist Friedrich Schiller would readily have recognized. Finally, does not Church authority, and a revealed religion generally, endanger the autonomy which is essential to art? Balthasar's response to this comes in two parts. First, he points out that conscience is, for Catholics too, the first and last court of appeal in human affairs. But secondly, just as the education of the artist is made possible by learning the discipline of surrender (*Hingabe*) to an objectivity beyond him, so the Catholic receives his *entrée* into truth unending through dogma – which is a surrender to heteronomy, if you like, but a *heteronomy of means*, not ends. Conscience builds its inner world not through a process of centring on self but, on the contrary, by surrender to, precisely, the law of what is other – to, in fact, the heteronomous. The key is, in fact, that word *Hingabe*, 'surrender', increasingly prominent in the Balthasarian vocabulary as this term will be.

> The person who has grasped that the source of all religious and artistic experience is *Hingabe* – in religious experience, surrender to the Absolute, to the 'Wholly Other', and in aesthetic experience, surrender to the object and to beauty – that person has understood the capacity of the two to be united and has conceded the ultimate possibility of Catholic art.[13]

So Catholicism is not an aesthetes' religion but it *is* a religion for artists. It can be, not an obstacle to their efforts, but the very fulfilment of their project. Here once again Balthasar looks ahead to the great scheme of a theological aesthetics. As yet, the cloud is no bigger than a man's hand. For first he must clarify his basic approach not only to theology but to the 'message' of his own culture, to the voices of German philosophy and literary art.

12 Ibid., p. 51.
13 Ibid., pp. 53–54.

3

Balthasar's First Theological Programme

Balthasar's Starting-point

As is well known, the pre-theological formation of young Jesuits is a lengthy one, since the Society of Jesus owes to its Renaissance origins a great respect for *litterae humaniores*. But Balthasar had already completed higher studies in literature and philosophy as a layman. By the later 1930s, then, Balthasar was thoroughly immersed in theological waters, at a time when a gathering mood of dissatisfaction with neo-Scholasticism, above all in France, was beginning to signal a coming storm, which would break over the post-War Church under the name of the 'crisis of the *nouvelle théologie*'. Balthasar evidently found it necessary to work out his own position, and a substantial essay, published by the Viennese journal *Theologie der Zeit* on the eve of the Second World War, sets out to do just that under the title 'Patristics, Scholasticism and ourselves'.[1]

He begins from a pessimistic evaluation of the state of Christian culture and its prospects of survival in the modern world. After all, 1939 was a year of imminent cataclysm for France and many other parts of Europe, if not for Switzerland. Thinking no doubt of Bolshevism, Fascism and the crisis of the political Liberalism inherited from the nineteenth century as well as the spread of agnosticism in the educated class, Balthasar writes that the leaves on the tree of Christian civilization are falling. Historic forms (*Wohnungen*, 'dwellings') are crumbling – but that must make the Christian enquire after Christianity's 'own living essence and kernel which, as the creative ground of those forms, cannot simply be identical with them'.[2] That is a question which naturally makes us look back to the origins, *der Ursprung*, lying behind all subsequent cultural forms of expression as these do.

At the hands of some (Balthasar clearly has in mind the – by later standards, mildly – radical spirits of the Church of his day, proponents of *la nouvelle théologie*), that enquiry proceeds in something like the following way. Renaissance and Baroque Scholasticism were the work of mere epigones – second-rate commentators and scribes. So perhaps we should go back to the Scholastic wellspring of the High Middle Ages. But even that Scholasticism is

---

1 Balthasar, 'Patristik, Scholastik und wir', *Theologie der Zeit* 3 (1939), pp. 65–104. (There is an English translation of this essay: 'The Fathers, the Scholastics, and Ourselves', *Communio* 24 [1997], pp. 347–96.)
2 Ibid., p. 65.

questionable – was it not excessively rationalistic in its approach to dogma, conceptually over-subtle, and far too ready to adopt 'secular' (read: 'pagan') philosophical modes? Balthasar's tone becomes ironic as he piles on the objections to Christian Scholasticism as a pedagogy for faith. If only the *philosophia perennis* were assimilable in the time taken by a quick coach tour. But no, years are needed, and all that Latin! Surely, then, it is *patristic* theology – so much closer to the apostles – that is the need of the hour. At least in its (more important) Greek segment, the realm of patristic thought has many advantages for us: its powerful sense of transcendence, its feeling for the Church as a 'mystical-liturgical community', its character as a 'pneumatic' Christianity where the primordial experiences of the Gospel were still existentially lived. Quite a case! If any one theologian is in mind it is probably his fellow-Jesuit Jean Daniélou.

In what follows Balthasar makes it clear that he is not going to throw in his lot entirely with the 'new theologians'. For he asks, is there not an 'almost Romantic nostalgia [that] draws theologians quite as much as laypeople back to this forgotten Paradise'?[3] And anyhow, how are the faithful at large supposed to get there? Not, one supposes, by mastering the serried ranks of the volumes of 'Migne' – the vast, ramifying set of patristic collections in various Oriental languages (as well as Latin) founded by an enterprising mid-nineteenth-century French cleric. Perhaps with the help of the modern Eastern Orthodox one can overleap the centuries, synthesizing Greco-Slav liturgy, Russian neo-Gnosis and the mysticism of the Christian East in a combined gesture against the clericalised Latin liturgy, theological rationalism and psychologizing mysticism of an over-bureacratic Western Church.[4]

Where will it all lead? Apparently – one might be forgiven for thinking – to Constantinople, or at any rate to the cathedral of the Russian diaspora in *chic* Parisian exile on the Rue Daru – Mecca of the intelligentsia of the Russian Orthodox Church in the West. Be that as it may, Balthasar is clear that no Catholic could accept this narrative. No one who holds that the Paraclete accompanies all epochs of the life of the Church in communion with the see of Rome could buy into this account of ever-accelerating deviation from the Gospel. And while the authentically Catholic (*das Katholische*) is indeed 'a constant looking back after Tradition', the concrete form such 'looking back' should take is not that of an adolescent desire to flee from the demands of our own time but 'an interpretation of the past from out of the present in its highest power'.[5]

Moreover, there is no knowing a priori, says Balthasar, which period of post-apostolic Christianity will turn out to be the most normative or ideal. There is no possible aprioristic ranking, but another method *is* possible and it can advance us in evaluating the relative claims of neo-mediaeval, neo-patristic and, for that matter, self-consciously modern theology.

The method Balthasar advises is to discern in the properties of each epoch of Church history the 'inner structural law' of each, and then to compare this

3 Ibid., p. 67.
4 The rather rude reference to 'Russian neo-Gnosis' probably had in mind the then fashionable, French-based Russian Orthodox philosopher Nikolai Berdyaev.
5 Balthasar, 'Patristik, Scholastik und wir', p. 68. The thought came to him, he says, from his reading of Nietzsche.

with the 'structural law' of what is Christian *tout court*. And just what might *that* – the structural law of Christianity – be? Not, explains Balthasar, an abstract 'general law' to be inferred from scanning all periods indifferently, for the structural law of Christianity comes to its fulfilment in history in ever new forms. In this respect, the manner of its fulfilment differs not at all from what the wider conditions of existence – 'the law of space and time' we live by as ordinary human beings – might lead us to expect. There too 'being other', non-identity, is the condition of earthly fulfilment in a human world where people differ so much that they can hardly be called simply examples of a type. (This is the sort of remark, with its uncanny anticipation of the Post-Structuralist language of 'alterity', which has made some treat Balthasar as a forerunner of Post-Modernism.)

A Mini-dogmatics

This could be a recipe for 'fudge' or 'wool', those somewhat ill-assorted English metaphors for vagueness, did not Balthasar take as his point of reference in the search for the 'structural law' (*Strukturgesetz*) of Christianity something solid and fixed – the 'fundamental law' (*Grundgesetz*) of revelation as given in the doctrines of Incarnation and Atonement and the continuation of the grace of these mysteries in the mission of the Church. In effect what Balthasar will be offering us here is a mini-dogmatics, so shaped, however, as to enable him to answer his basic question, What period in the history of Christian thought – if any one such may be singled out – should we take as our lodestar in the reorientation of Catholic theology today? The fundamental law of Christianity consists in two principal clauses: it is being 'in Christ' and being 'in the Church'. These simple phrases, so it turns out, stand for a much more complex pattern of thought in which the Fathers and three particular names, on whom more anon: Aquinas, Barth and Przywara – will prove to be the preponderant influences.

The Originality of Sin

In the dogmatic section of this essay, Balthasar sets out from a characterization of original sin, understood not as the primordial fact about humanity (our creation is *that*) but as the necessary condition for understanding what has gone wrong with that God-directedness which is in other respects our glory. In a statement saturated with Romanticism, our 'deepest nostalgia' (*tiefste Sehnsucht*) is to be like God – freed from the constraints of the narrow self, mastering the flow of events in their transience and fatefulness. In this, our 'most inner drive' (*innerstes Trieb*) shows evident signs of the poison spewed by the serpent in the Garden of Eden. Such a desire to become spirit, wise, a mystic, perfect, however religious it seems and in one sense quite reasonably seems, is in fact revolt against God. It is a rebellion against the Creator who made us in a mode of existence for which earth, the body–soul composite, community, and space and time (*die irdische, leib-seeleische, gemeinschaftliche, zeiträumliche Existenzweise*) are crucial.[6]

Rather than serve God, man wants to be like God on his own human terms

6 Ibid., p. 69.

which, in the post-Paradise situation, take the typical form of a denial of creatureliness in its God-dependent character. Rather neatly, Balthasar puts together a classical ontological theology of creaturehood, emphasizing its distinctive *being*, with a 'modern' psychological theology of the same that lays the stress on its characteristic consciousness or *feeling*. The upshot of sin, says Balthasar, is to push into the background:

> that which makes the creature, innerly, formally, what it is – a creature: the consciousness, with its entire ontic condition, which is to stand under the creative will, the good pleasure and disposition of the Creator; and withal the consciousness likewise that over against the creature there is an absolute Being, whose essence consists, in a fashion beyond conceiving, in its being through itself – which is something that could never ever be true of creaturely essence . . .[7]

Being through itself, *aseitas*, is for Thomist ontology the root metaphysical concept in the theology of God. This awareness, which 'expresses the primary truth of being', is now displaced by the Fall to the margins of life.[8] The refusal to accept the most basic truth we can know about ourselves – namely, that we are not God – leads to the false mysticism and spiritual delusion by which erroneous thinking treats man as, in some aspect or dimension of his being, already divine.

It would appear to be an early sign of Balthasar's indebtedness to the Swiss Evangelical theologian Karl Barth that he locates the symptoms of original sin in, first and foremost, human religiosity.[9] Typically, post-lapsarian existence fails to inscribe the idea of humanity's imagehood of God within the even more foundational truth of the creature's not being itself divine. The more we know God, the more we realize that we are not God – and we can only know God (the term used, *erkennen*, implies cognitive communion and not merely a well-founded belief in God's existence) through the gracious action of God himself.

The True Mysticism

Shortly, however, Balthasar alters the inflexion of his voice to take on the tones less of Barth than of his Jesuit mentor Erich Przywara.[10] The message of the mystics is that the more we know God the more we realize how little we know him, since there is shown to us how much greater than our

7 Ibid., p. 70.
8 Ibid.
9 The note of combined admiration and criticism was already struck in his earliest essay on Barth, contemporary with 'Patristik, Scholastik und wir', namely: 'Karl Barth und der Katholizismus', *Theologie der Zeit* 3 (1939), pp. 126–32. I discuss this essay along with Balthasar's other Barth writings in the final volume of my 'Introduction to Hans Urs von Balthasar': *Divine Fruitfulness. Balthasar's Later Theology: Beyond the Trilogy* (forthcoming).
10 One of his earliest articles was devoted to this figure: 'Die Metaphysik Erich Przywaras', originally published in the Einsiedeln *Schweizerische Rundschau* 6 (1933), pp. 489–99. Balthasar held firm to his view of Przywara's significance as is plain from the republication of the piece as an introduction to the Johannes Verlag reprinting of Przywara's works: L. Zimny (ed.), *Erich Przywara. Sein Schrifttum* (Einsiedeln 1963), pp. 5–18, and again as 'Erich Przywara', in H.-G. Schulz (ed.), *Tendenzen der Theologie im 20. Jahrhundert. Eine Geschichte in Porträts* (Stuttgart 1966), pp. 354–59.

comprehension his mystery is. In this context, if light increases by arithmetical progression then darkness grows by geometrical progression – that is to say, in duly proportioned leaps and bounds. Moreover, this dizzyingly accelerating distance is precious, because non-identity – the sense of which grows in the experience – is precisely what makes love possible. Who, even in human love, would want the beloved to possess one's own 'measure and format'? Nor is this an unjustifiable analogy in context, as the revelation of God as Trinity makes clear.

> In the relation between God and ourselves 'reciprocal being other' [*gegenseitige Anderssein*] does not solely signify what is 'strange' and 'distant' in the situation of the servant vis-à-vis the Lord but also harbours within itself the deeper mystery of love. That is something we surmise from the revelation of the trinitarian God, in which precisely the highest unity and communality of the Essence demands and grounds the diversity of the Persons.[11]

'Likeness in radical difference' is the formula of our creaturely nature in its relation to God, and it is *this* that grace does not destroy but perfects and exalts. But exactly that 'formula' – likeness in radical difference between God and ourselves – is what original sin – as Balthasar defines it – would obliterate, by a contemptuous misconstrual that leads ultimately into a realm of anguish and spiritual-physical disintegration.

The Nature of Redemption

If this be true, then the compass of all possible redemption is plain. The Redeemer must restore, in a human life, the right fundamental relation between humanity and God as the way to an incomprehensibly great elevation of humankind to divine communion. At the Incarnation, the union of divinity and humanity in the person of the Logos takes place in – to cite Chalcedon – the 'unconfusion' of the natures – and even, so Balthasar adds, going beyond the text of the Fourth Ecumenical Council, 'their greatest distance'. He interpolates that phrase in order to prepare us for what follows. In the Redemption, God saved us from our own striving to denature ourselves for the most deceptively plausible of spiritual reasons, and he did so by pinpointing *the weakness of the flesh* as the very wellspring of saving grace for us. He chose what was natural and carnal in us, our bodily being, as the place of his saving revelation so as to put us to shame in the (pseudo-)spiritual and 'pneumatic' status we would claim for ourselves. For man becomes authentically spirit (*Geist*) and 'pneuma' only as he 'remains rooted in his fundamental truth, the truth of his nature'.[12] Balthasar's comments here are strongly redolent of such early patristic authors as Tertullian and Irenaeus.

Verbum caro factum est, 'The Word was made flesh': this axiom of Balthasar's last major theological work, *Theologik*, completed in 1987, is already crucial in this his first (genuinely) theological essay, published in 1939. Notice, however, that here at least it is not used to deny the validity of the Romantic search, but rather to assert the need utterly to reorient that search if

11 Balthasar, 'Patristik, Scholastik und wir', p. 71.
12 Ibid., p. 73.

it is ever to reach its goal. The longing for divinization is not an illusion. That longing *can* be fulfilled, but only if we accept the Redeemer's extreme accentuation of the difference between man and God. From crib to Cross that was the Saviour's way. Accepting the 'impotence' and 'feebleness' that reached their lowest pitch in the death of Christ is necessary if the creature is to be emptied of pretension – and it is also the means to filling it with the real thing, God's glory. Just this reversal of expectations is what makes the order of redemption the 'inversion' (*Umkehrung*) of the order of original sin.

So much has the later Balthasar been (mis)understood as the prophet of a nature whose contours are obliterated by the force of grace – one who would elide, then, the nature/grace distinction – that it comes as a shock to see just what emphasis he lays on how all this reconciled us to our *nature* – not, as he says, 'naturalistically understood' (nature in its brute facticity, that would be) but that 'unpathetic' nature best seen in 'simple folk' who give the harshness as well as the opportune joys of existence their due. His account of such folk, with their 'few words' and unwillingness to find in their own self-sacrificing dutifulness anything out of the ordinary, might be based, one supposes, on observation (or idealization) of the peasantry of the region of Lake Lucerne, the 'Lake of the Four Forest Cantons', in the time of his childhood. A hard enough life small farmers would have had of it in the years when Balthasar was growing up there. Be that as it may, it was 'natural' life, thus with deliberate *naïveté* defined, that was made in Bethlehem of Judah the site of our redemption, the place where the divine was seen and handled. That nature, once shown its utter difference from the 'Godness of God', became the locus of epiphany.

> The Resurrection of Christ is indeed the fulfilment of created being that is hollowed out, burnt out, through the glory of the incomparable God, but it is this precisely as a final emphasising of nature: insofar as it is resurrection in the flesh, to that extent do a new heaven and new earth arise, and these signify the completing of nature just inasmuch as they stand forth distinct from God.[13]

And Balthasar went on:

> The new aeon is the proof of the definitive validity of the greater difference between God and creature – precisely in the intimacy of a communion than which nothing closer and more blessed can be thought.[14]

Any suggestion that we are to be 'as gods' should be countered by the report that *the more grace calls us to divine friendship, the deeper grows the awareness that we are only servants*. Only in the moment of highest engracing does the graced creature grasp the truth of our Lady's self-description, 'Behold, the *handmaid* of the Lord' (Luke 1.38).

And what all this boils down to is the truth of the axiom, Grace does not destroy nature, it perfects it. It is *man* who destroys his own nature when he strives to rise up to a purely spiritual realm – as such non-Christian religions as Buddhism and Gnosticism urge and all the great Christian heresies from Docetism to Origenism in the ancient world through Joachimism in the

13 Ibid., p. 74.
14 Ibid.

Middle Ages to Protestant Spiritualism in the modern period in one way or another concur. All these heresies in effect *abolish the law of the Incarnation*. Whether this be because the flesh is thought unworthy of God, or because in Christ's saving deed nature itself is regarded as an enemy now conquered, overcome, these heretical modes of thought reintroduce the structure of original sin into Christianity. This they do inasmuch as they refuse to allow the law of being – fundamental ontology – its role as the basis of the fulfilment of the world. They fail to see that the directness of approach to God they advocate goes clean counter to the law of the Incarnation which has established nature as the basis and measure of grace, with the Cross and the Tomb the place of nature's resurrection. Kierkegaard was right when he wrote in his *Journals* that with every forward step man takes, God becomes more sublime – and so man smaller. This is no indignity for man. It is the law of all true love.

Redemptive Continuation in the Church

Balthasar has said, then, that the fundamental law of Christianity consists in two primary clauses – being in Christ and being in the Church. Having now dealt with being in Christ and shown how Christ's Incarnation must be understood as the highest union of man with God through the accentuation of the greater difference between them, he now needs to turn to the second primary clause: being in the Church. The fundamental law of the Incarnation continues to work itself out in Christ's mystical body, in the Church. In that body, the Head is hypostatically one with the divine Logos; the members of the body are *not* hypostatically one with him. The Head is sinless and redeeming; the members are sinful and redeemed. Thus a distance between body and Head mirrors the distance between creature and God. The Church is not Christ. When she speaks, she does not speak on her own authority but *as representing him*, transmitting and interpreting his revelation in such a way as not to alter it. She proclaims what she has heard. This must at all times be borne in mind when we are speaking of the outworking of the law of Christ in the Church and especially when we offer, as Balthasar is about to do, a high doctrine of the Church's life and mission.

This caveat entered, we can now go on to affirm that the Church is, in Balthasar's words, 'the obedient co-fulfilment of Christ's movement of descent into the world, right down to the decisive "natural realities" of Cross and Death'. In this very movement of descent, *diese Abstiegsbewegung*, the Church is 'the place where the divine epiphanises [in the world], the locus of the most elevated unification of God and creature'.[15] And yet once again, this means no abolition of the natural but its highest preservation and sanctioning.

As the Father sends Christ, so Christ sends the apostolic heads of the Church – sends them, Balthasar stresses, *into the world*. This journey has its ultimate source and justification in the Son's inner divine journey from the Father in his eternal mission, that mission (more commonly called his *procession*) which is the root of Christ's historical mission in the public time of this world. So precisely when we are placed by God in our determinate place in the world, whatever that place be, we become sharers in the Church's

15 Ibid., p. 77.

inner-Trinitarian life: another example of the prosaic lifted up to the heights. For Balthasar, it is precisely when this seems all too human, and especially when the 'little ship' of the Church seems lost in the storms of this world, that we are most decisively one with the servant form of the Redeemer and, in and through that, one with God himself.

So the more we recognize the Church as a supernatural community founded from above, the more we ought to see her as a natural, authentically human and visible society, just as Christ, the Son of God, was a natural and visible human being. There is a duo of terms here – community/society, *Gemeinschaft/Gesellschaft, communio/societas*, which played a major part in contemporary Catholic ecclesiology at the time of Balthasar's writing, and, through the documents of the Second Vatican Council which drew on them, still do today. Such representatives of that ecclesiology as the Dominican Yves Congar realized, like Balthasar, that the two – the invisible, mystical communion and the visible, institutional society – must be held together. More specifically they must be held together, as Congar declared in his book *Christ, our Lady and the Church*, in a forthrightly Chalcedonian fashion.[16] Two 'natures', though unconfused, are inseparably united. Balthasar is saying exactly the same thing. In the Church we find the visibility of cultic life in the hierarchy and the liturgy; we find the rationality of theology and the humanity of ethics. And yet for all that, the Church is not the world, faith is not reason, the theological virtues not mere human dispositions. No more does Christ because he is man cease to be God. In fact, Balthasar goes on, and putting it provocatively, the Church can only be the instrument of redemption in the world if she stresses the human, the natural, the non-divine. Only this allows her to be the place of encounter between the world and God. Only so can she be the epiphany of the Word made flesh.

Balthasar emphasizes, however, that the visible frontiers of the Church must not be identified with the invisible boundaries of the total extensiveness of the grace of Christ. The Church has a mission to preach salvation to the world, to mediate salvation sacramentally, and through her presence to represent visibly the invisible presence of redeeming grace. But not for a moment can she substitute herself for the source of salvation. And just this makes her in an excellent way the continuator of her Master as he whom Isaiah prophesied in the Songs of the Servant, the *ebed YHWH*, 'the Servant of the Lord'. To what extent humankind *is* dying and rising with Christ, that being the rhythm of salvation – to what extent, then, humanity *is being saved*, remains God's secret. But we know that salvation *can* only come about in that way. In dying to sin with Christ, the basic pattern of creatureliness is restored, and in rising with Christ to newness of life the inherent being – *das In-sich-sein* – of the creature is wonderfully fulfilled as now a form of being in God – *In-Gott-sein*. Thinking of this death-and-resurrection rhythm of salvation helps us to see how the Church can be not only a Church turned towards the world, an *active* Church, but also a Church turned away from the world, like the disciples in the Fourth Gospel 'not of the world', a *contemplative* Church. As contemplative Church, the Church lives out her own death to this age of the world as she moves from the old aeon to the new; as active Church she takes hold of the potencies of the new aeon and sets them

16　Y.M.-J. Congar, OP, *Le Christ, Marie et l'Eglise* (Paris 1952).

to work in the field of this world. Both sides of the Church's life express mission. Both are a function of the Church's world-redeeming task. We see this in the great Religious Orders. A Benedictine monastery is in an eminent sense a city set on a hilltop, withdrawn from the world yet ordering and educating the world around it. St Teresa of Avila founded her contemplative monasteries as bulwarks against Protestantism. St Dominic intended his friars to seal with the supernatural all areas of human discourse and thought. These are typical manifestations of ecclesial being.

The Major Theological Epochs

The starting-point of this whole enquiry by Balthasar was how we should evaluate the respective claims on us of the Fathers, the Scholastics and the moderns. That question now becomes: the fundamental law of Christianity, as Balthasar has just expounded it, how well is it expressed in these three epochs? In each epoch, the Church, living in some distinctive cultural space, has to take into her life and proclamation certain natural, worldly elements – and these will of course be affected by original sin. That is so even though, as Catholic Christians, we do not regard humankind's natural capacities as utterly perverted by sin nor do we exclude the touching of nature by the order of grace prior to and outside the Church. (The first of those denials would be, rather, characteristic of the Reformers of the sixteenth century; the second, of seventeenth-century Jansenism). Evidently, expressing the fundamental law in any epoch is going to have its problems as well as opportunities. To evaluate these, in large terms, by reference to the age of the Fathers, the age of the Schoolmen, and the age of the moderns, will occupy Balthasar for the rest of 'Patristik, Scholastik und wir'.

The Age of the Fathers

First, then, the patristic epoch, the first great epoch in the history of ideas in the Church.[17] The Church enters the pagan world 'with a maximum of direct, glowing Christian life and instinctive assurance about what is true and determinative for the Christian reality'.[18] This would seem to set Balthasar straightaway on the side of the pure neo-patristic theologians in the incipient debate over 'la nouvelle théologie' already beginning in the later 1930s. But in point of fact, he draws up a balance-sheet of loss and gain in a very unpartisan fashion. Emerging as the predominant factor on the debit side is what he perceives as the threat posed by the Platonism of the Fathers to the

---

17 Balthasar had by this date already written the first versions of two of the three works in his miniature trilogy on the Greek Fathers (Origen, Nyssa, Maximus): thus 'Le Mystérion d'Origène', *Recherches de science religieuse* 26 (1936), pp. 513–62, and 27 (1937), pp. 38–64, and 'Présence et pensée. La philosophie religieuse de Grégoire de Nysse', *Recherches de science religieuse* 29 (1939), pp. 513–49. In the year of appearance of 'Patristik, Scholastik und wir' he had also begun his exploration of the Evagrian corpus in two Innsbruck journals: 'Die Hiera des Evagrius', *Zeitschrift für katholische Theologie* 63 (1939), pp. 86–106; 181–206, and 'Metaphysik und Mystik des Evagrius Ponticus', *Zeitschrift für Aszese und Mystik* 14 (1939), pp. 31–47. I investigate these together with Balthasar's later patristic writings in the final volume of my introduction to Balthasar, *Divine Fruitfulness. Balthasar's Later Theology: Beyond the Trilogy* (forthcoming).
18 Balthasar, 'Patristik, Scholastik und wir', p. 84.

'fundamental law'. There are lesser warnings too about the undesirability of an over-enthusiastic embrace of the early Fathers and ecclesiastical writers. Many authors in the ante-Nicene period (i.e., before 325) used formulae which should be regarded as quite *dépassé* and even, in the light of later standards, heterodox. The struggle with the great heresies – Gnosticism, Montanism, Arianism, Nestorianism, Monophysitism, Manichaeanism, Donatism – led the Church of this epoch to restrict the arena for acceptable speculation ever more tightly. Yet, on the credit side, let us not overlook the positive greatness of a period to which all subsequent generations in the Church are in permanent debt. With the help of the early Ecumenical Councils, spiritual building goes on that provides foundations for all later Christian theology, and, to change the metaphor from architectural to aquatics, with a fullness from the source that will never be attained again. Nourished by Scripture, patristic doctrine takes on the character of 'an almost direct unfolding and continuation of revelation itself'.[19] This is the springtime of the Church in the world, a *Jugendzeit* when immediacy of response allows a 'more open and instinctual reaction' to the truth to be conserved. In Athanasius, Basil, Cyril, Chrysostom, Ambrose, Augustine, life and teaching were one reality. And so the first, the greatest and the most taxing struggle with the spiritual-intellectual powers of paganism was won. All successing generations of thinkers, preachers, mystics, must go back to the fountains of the Fathers, to drink and be strengthened.

So where's the rub? As already indicated, it lies – shades here of Barth – with the very religiosity of the Hellenistic culture into which the Church stepped forth. It lies with the seemingly already supernatural and world-transcending character of that culture. It lies in the way a by no means altogether benign 'atmosphere' or 'method' entered the Church from Hellenism: not so much false doctrines (these, when present, were soon identified and eliminated) as age-old customary manners of thought. Here we must be careful not to exaggerate, after the fashion of the late nineteenth-century historian of dogma Adolf von Harnack. As the example of Origen of Alexandria shows, what is happening may be no more than the clothing of the Gospel in borrowed means of expressions – means of expression which enable it to step forth, re-embodied, with cultural efficacy yet leave its soul essentially untouched, intact, as integrally itself as ever before. 'Behind the Neoplatonist words, we hear the true Christian pathos.'[20]

But there remains a real problem. Balthasar identifies it in the first place with the way the concept of *participation* was used in the Platonist school. For a common scheme of thought in Hellenism, the ultimate divine reality is taken as the participated-in, and the world does the participating as the potencies of divine, primordial being find expression in a series of descending levels which divide up among them the total range of reality from fullest being to nothing. The divine goes out of itself through being participated in by ever decreasing degrees. True, this scheme was corrected in the context of formal Trinitarian doctrine. In the course of the controversies about the being of the Son and the Spirit in the fourth and fifth centuries, the Church rejected the view that the Son's nature is on a lower level than the

19 Ibid.
20 Ibid., p. 86.

Father's, participating (only) in his being, and likewise for the Spirit in relation to the Son. But the defeat of such philosophically originated Subordinationism did not leave Christian consciousness unharmed. We can see the harm, thinks Balthasar, in the continuing difficulties of the Greek Orthodox, even today, with the *Filioque*, the double procession of the Spirit from Father *and Son*, for the *Filioque* 'locates' the Spirit as substantial Love *between* the Father and the Son – something that appears, to this mind-set, very odd indeed. We can see it too in the slowness with which a thoroughgoingly Trinitarian mysticism developed in the patristic period, and in the recurring tendencies of the ascetical and mystical tradition to describe the movement toward Christian perfection in terms of spiritualization understood as de-corporealization: something that goes quite against the grain of the 'fundamental law'.

To some extent here, the issue is one of decoding language. To a degree, the whole trajectory of 'from matter to spirit' in ancient Christian piety is meant as a symbol of the more primordial trajectory 'from creature to God'. All the great Fathers knew quite well that deification is a question of participation in grace, not the abolition of the contours of human nature – and in any case both St Paul and St John had called God 'Spirit' and treated 'flesh' and 'pneuma' as symbols for, respectively, the old and the new aeons. And anyway every worthwhile asceticism has to respect the truth Augustine summed up in the fomula 'the body below the soul, the soul below God'. The Platonism of the Fathers, and its disadvantages, can indeed be exaggerated, both by failing to realize how much of it is biblicism in Platonic dress and by not noticing how, in the development of the Platonist school, such large chunks of Aristotelean and Stoic thought were swallowed that the organism took a rather different shape. Not just for the Antiochenes but even for the Alexandrians, commonly regarded as the most Platonist of patristic age Christians, the outcome was far less at odds with the law of Incarnation than is sometimes alleged.

With so many concessions made and qualifications entered, what remains of Balthasar's original criticism of Platonic thought? It comes down to this. The particular use to which Platonist participation language was set conveyed the impression that the graced creature now exists, precisely through being graced, by participation in the divine nature. This fails to do justice to the undergoing continuing realities of the *natures* involved – God's which is divine, and ours, which is human. Patristic participation language for life in Christ speaks only, Balthasar alleges, of a gracious relationship, not of the realities that in this relationship are re-related. Created being falls into the background or off the stage as, in this context, a relative nothing. Thus christianized Platonism treats the God-creature relation too simplistically, and it is from this simplification that all the 'dangers' of patristic theology and spirituality arise. To wish to return to a form of Christian Platonism, perhaps out of admiration for the richness of its doctrine of the exemplary causality whereby the divine life is mirrored in the universe, is to risk the return of the tendency of the age of the Fathers toward a unilateral spiritualism and supernaturalism. Here, though his language betrays how he felt the attraction he spurned, Balthasar was slapping down the claims of one kind of neo-patristic theologian in his own time.

That is why, then, we cannot exclusively 'return to the sources' as the neo-

patristically minded would have us do. We cannot bypass the Scholastics
without whom the nature-grace relationship remains unclarified. The most
damaging Platonizing presuppositions of patristic thought would only
return to haunt us.

The Age of the Schoolmen

Balthasar looks to the mediaeval Schoolmen for what he calls 'a necessary
clarification of basic structures'. The Schoolmen – the thirteenth century
Dominican St Thomas is chiefly in mind – realized that the participation
schema could not be allowed to stand alone. The chief theological point of
their appeal to Aristotle lay in the realization that to do justice to the natural
element in the relation between God and the graced creature (and in that way
indeed to do justice to the grace that builds on and elevates, precisely, nature), it was necessary to set alongside *metochê*, 'participation', the equally
important *energeia*, 'activity', and/or *entelecheia*, which we could paraphrase
as the purposeful flowering of a nature in such *energeia* or activity. God's
creative activity is not the progressive depotentialization of being as emanation declines from angelic intelligences to what W.S. Gilbert called in *The
Mikado* 'a primordial protoplasmic atomic globule'. God's creative activity is
precisely the bringing into being of the other, another reality with its own
inner self-possession and therefore positivity: an intrinsic positive value all
its own. Thomas's notion of primary and secondary causality is all-important
for doing justice to created natures in their God-given consistency. Thomas is
for Balthasar *the* 'theologian of nature' – that is, of what is presupposed by all
gracious participation in God, the 'ownness' or 'being itself-ness', *Eigen-
ständigkeit*, of created being in all its kinds. This alone can make sense of what
engracing divine activity is actually *about*. The God-relatedness of the creature stands on the ground of a mutual otherness between God and the created, and only this foundation suffices to make possible the highest union
between them. Just why that is so Balthasar thinks he has already shown in
expounding the fundamental law.

For Thomas, God as Creator stands for the same distancedness yet nearness to all creatures indifferently and only against this background can a
special relation with self-conscious created spirit be delineated. Moreover, for
Thomas again, the closer such a creature is to God the more thoroughly is it
capable of self-movement. In this sense, its autonomy grows with its God-
likeness. Does not, then, an opposite danger to that endemic in the Fathers
arise – the threat not of supernaturalism but of naturalism? Balthasar does not
deny it. But when we speak of the 'great' Scholastics, we are speaking of those
who seek neither pure philosophy nor pure theology but the integration of
nature and supernature into a total vision of reality, and who, moreover, see
this total vision of reality as itself divinely offered to human thought. We are
dealing here with a unitary philosophical-theological thinking (we might call
it 'sapiential'), not with a merely immanent 'system' of rigorously defined
concepts as in much modern Scholasticism – no doubt the sort Balthasar
remembered with a shudder from the Bavarian Jesuit studentate.

But what of the possibility that this insistence on clarifying the foundational structure of the nature/grace relation will produce a 'two storey'
picture of the resultant edifice, with grace slapped on as a kind of dormer

extension to the family home? This was the 'extrinsicism' combated at the time of Balthasar's writing by the French Jesuit theologian-philosopher Henri de Lubac, even though the advent of the Second World War and de Lubac's role in the French resistance delayed the publication of *Surnaturel* – his work on this topic – till 1946. For Balthasar, the great Scholastics were never guilty of this theological crime, nor will be anyone who grasps with them the absolute singularity of the ultimate, supernatural goal of the world, a goal furnishing the finality that 'leads' or 'orientates' everything in the natural order. It is the highest nobility of the created to be, by its essence and existence, an instrument disposed for the praise and service of God. Its *disponibilité*, what the Scholastics call its *potentia oboedientalis*, and the subjective attitude that corresponds to this, entrusting oneself to God, self-abandonment to him, is what best expresses the ultimate reality of creatureliness. It is the most perfect manifestation of the creaturely attitude there can be. When this being at the disposition of the Creator is raised up into gracious participation in the divine nature, supernature writes itself into the very foundations of nature. There is, then, no extrinsicism here. The union could not be more intimate despite, or rather because of, the objective differentiation.

So: is the answer to the question, What should we be, neo-patristics, neo-mediaevals or moderns, that we should be neo-mediaevals? Not entirely. Where Balthasar differs from Thomas in all this and goes his separate way is when the *potentia oboedientalis* is treated as a *potentia naturalis* – in the famous phrase, a 'natural desire for the vision of God': something implanted in human nature rather than in the human person. And this criticism, which is more symptomatic of the weaknesses of Christian Scholasticism than might at first appear, is what brings him to the merits (and otherwise) of his third great epoch, that of the moderns.

The Epoch of the Moderns

Characterizing modernity – even Christian modernity, defined as the period from the fifteenth-century European Renaissance onwards – is not the easiest of tasks. Balthasar sees two principal lines of development. The first he describes as leading from the intellectual – some would say, abstract – universalism of Scholasticism towards an ever greater discovery and appreciation of the concrete, the unique and the historical. Put Thomistically: in place of the notion of individuation by reason of matter – counting up instances of things, whether oranges or people, what we increasingly find is the tendency to treat individuation as by reason of form – treating individuals as more than just *numerically* unique. Such form would include of course the bodily form which enthused the Renaissance and was turned by the Baroque to the service of representing the transcendent. This line of development in European thought also produced its own difficulties – empiricism, materialism, historicism prominent among them.

The second line Balthasar takes as an Ariadne's thread through a complex maze of phenomena is related in fairly obvious guise to the first. Setting out from the Scholastic concept of nature, thinkers sought to develop the rather underemployed Scholastic idea of the 'suppositum': the metaphysical subject of a natural entity. In the case of a *spiritual* natural entity – one endowed with powers of intelligence and will – this 'suppositum' is a person. Just as mediaeval Nominalism to some extent anticipated the later shift of focus to the concrete, unique, historical, so another mediaeval thought pattern, Scotism, anticipated this later tendency to highlight the personal and with that personal agency and so the significance – and even the primacy – of *will*. Balthasar finds that later tendency in the founder of his own Order, Ignatius Loyola, and in secularized form in much nineteenth-century irrationalism, not least in Kant. When writing his own theological anthropology, Balthasar would discover in the Vienna theologian Anton Günther a lucid exposition of the difference between spiritual being and personhood. But Günther's belief that what personality adds to the spiritual powers of human nature is nothing other than the supernatural itself was thoroughly mistaken. It trapped him in a version of Idealism which – so the implication runs – the magisterium of the Catholic Church did well to warn against.[21]

The ideological dead-ends to which these lines of development from the high Scholastic 'clarification' of the patristic achievement can lead may not seem encouraging. But for Balthasar these two lines of development, *when governed by the sense of faith*, in fact served the Church well. They had the effect of bringing what is 'decisively' or 'distinctively' Christian to fuller expression than had been the case heretofore. Enhanced appreciation of the individually concrete meant a better grasp of the 'authentic worldliness of the world' – that is, of the natural structure of creatures in all their distinctive individuality. More emphasis on the personal dimension meant a more complete understanding of the fact that, by virtue of their particular natural structure, human beings are created as *subjects* and not just as objects. The two together had the effect of finally expunging the residue of what was unhelpful in the Platonist inheritance – the false assertion of the primacy of the universal over the singular and the false direction of Godward aspiration as a turning from material and particular realities to spiritual and general ones.

To illustrate the advantages of Christian modernity thus conceived, Balthasar brings together rather strange bedfellows – the modern concern with the person of Jesus in his earthly, human, facticity, set over against the cosmic image of Christ in the patristic period, and the dogmatic definition in 1870 of the infallibility of the pope, with its underlining of the positive value of the hierarchy in the Church. The first underscores the unexpected and unpredictable character of the personal self-disclosure of God in the historical order of salvation, and the consequent need for attitudes of submission and self-surrender, faith and service. The second is cognate with this because it concerns the need for obedience to the particularity of the manner of divine revelation *as actually received*. One thinks of Newman's words in *The Dream of Gerontius*: 'And I hold in veneration/for the love of him alone/Holy Church as his creation/and her teachings as his own.'[22]

So the world into which the divine saving initiative comes in revelation cannot now in the modern period be construed as a shadow world, a symbolist replica of a higher spiritual world beyond. Rather is it a world consisting of uniquely selved persons and situations in genuine history, all embedded in the bodily and essentially finite shape of things. It is into this

21 Balthasar, *Man in History* (ET London 1967), p. 72, note.
22 Tillotson (ed.), *Newman. Prose and Poetry* (London 1957), pp. 814–15.

world and no other that God comes to take possession. Consequently, it becomes more difficult to experience one key form of post-lapsarian temptation – namely, the attempt to divinize oneself by taking leave of one's own nature. In the modern period it becomes easier to see, as Christians, that such divinization can only come about through co-achievement with Christ in 'descending' into what is most natural and seemingly ungodly in nature – the unglamorous grind of poverty, the blindness of obedience (is this a Jesuit emphasis, by any chance?), the abandoned condition of a creature at once miserable yet full of compassion on the Cross. No longer can the human spirit be mistaken for the Holy Spirit. When we realize that our union with the divine nature comes about through these means and no other, we can only give glory to God not to ourselves. Balthasar puts this in very strong language which risks blurring the distinction between renunciation and masochism.

The progressive clarification of the decisively Christian can go astray in a whole variety of ways: into, for example, a sheer actualism which regards being as no more than action (there is a criticism here of Karl Barth); or a personalism that is no more than a camouflage for becoming a libertine (anything is all right so long as it expresses my personality); or a Christian humanism that has ceased to be God-centred and just writes 'man' in large letters; or again tragic Existentialism, the 'theology of crisis' and other fashionable substitutes (in the 1930s) for the real thing. If we ask what the 'real thing' is, Balthasar replies that it is the full transcendence of the Christian reality over against nature and at the same time its complete immanence within nature. The more complete our union with God, the more divine does he appear. Pure Przywara.

Conclusion

For Balthasar, what is attractive about the modern period is that it completes the Scholastic clarification of what the Fathers achieved. It makes it plain that God's sovereignty and indeed totality is not won at the cost of the world. God is so much God that he can be himself in everything that is not he. The patristic sense of the objectivity of divine revelation in its representation of God does not become in Christian modernity subjectivism and anthropocentrism as some would have it. (Balthasar was thinking there of the criticisms made of theological modernity both by exclusively neo-patristic theologians and by Thomists of the strict observance.) On the contrary, this patristic sense of objectivity and representation comes to its climax in the modern Christian sense of subjectivity wherever – and this is a vital qualification – this sense is properly contextualized by a consciousness of Christian mission. It is a mistake to think that the Fathers have a theocentric, ontological, liturgical piety and the moderns an anthropological, subjective, psychological one. (Here Balthasar will most likely have in mind the Benedictine theologians of the school of Maria Laach.) The difference between them lies really only in this: the Fathers, owing to Platonically originated limitations, did not yet understand subjectivity as itself a function of the total Christian representation.

Over against the erroneous naturalism of our times – here now at last Balthasar formulates his programme – we have to make the fundamental law of dying into the new redeemed world of Christ tangible to our contemporaries. For this the Fathers and the patristic ethos will always remain our most lively image. We shall never have a better model to follow – once we have been tutored by Thomas in how to appreciate this best. But we must carry out this same dying specifically as a personal – in the fullest sense – mission into a world affirmed in its humanity and 'worldliness', a world which is the locus of epiphany of the ever-greater and ever more incomprehensible God.

In these phrases, Balthasar foreshadowed, without knowing it, his literary oeuvre and even the Secular Institute he was to found with the woman he met during the following year: Adrienne von Speyr. Here are marching orders for a lifetime of dogmatic work. What remained before Balthasar could dive into the depths was a reckoning with his own cultural tradition, the world of *Germanistik*.

4

Exploring Ultimates: Eschatology and the German Soul

The Major Pre-War Project

At the time Balthasar brought out his programmatic essay 'Patristik, Scholastik und wir', he was seeing through the press a much more grandiose project in three hefty volumes. This was 'Apocalypse of the German Soul', a wide-ranging survey of German or German-language philosophers and poets (with the occasional extra-Teutonic sport thrown in). It had emerged from his doctoral thesis on the 'eschatological problem in modern German literature', but this was now expanded to several times its original length and went into the wider doctrine of the writers concerned at considerably greater depth. Later in his life, Balthasar had some difficulty in coming to terms with this work. He called it his 'giant child', almost as though he had given birth to a monster and confessed looking quizzically at it lying on his shelves and wondering what on earth its purpose had been. He refused to allow it to be re-published in his lifetime, and until very recently it was extremely difficult, at any rate in the United Kingdom, to lay one's hand on a set.

Philosophers and poets. Putting those two classes of people together now sounds rather odd in English. Anglo-Saxon analytic philosophy certainly bears some relation to ancient philosophy with its concern for definitional clarity. But its predominantly logical interests in the formalization of propositions make it a curious bedfellow for poetry. It was not ever thus, even in England. S.T. Coleridge, J.H. Newman, Matthew Arnold are not perhaps in the first rank of philosophers but they held philosophic and poetic modes of writing in a close unity. In the Germany of the eighteenth and nineteenth centuries, the great age of classical German philosophy, this was even more the case. In German, the same word *Dichter* does duty both for poet and for writers of fine philosophical prose, and part of the reason for that dual usage is presumably that philosophers in the German tradition are willing to advance their thought by the deployment of images and symbols, considering the exploration of reality by imagistic and symbolic modes of thinking to be congruent with, and not opposed to, more strictly rational procedures. So when at the beginning of the Romantic movement, the French belles-lettriste Madame de Staël called Germany 'the land of philosophers and poets', either she wasn't thinking of two fully separate groups of people or she shouldn't have been.

But why, though, should Balthasar, as his burgeoning mind is revealed to us in his first attempt at theology, have wanted to invest so much continuing time and attention in the German philosophers or poets, or, as they often appear from Herder to Nietzsche, philosopher-poets? The conclusion of 'Patristik, Scholastik und wir' was that we should be neither neo-patristic nor neo-mediaeval. Though treating the mind and ethos of the Fathers as our best guide to biblical revelation and the high mediaeval Scholastics as a necessary help to us in clarifying that mind and ethos, we should in fact situate ourselves quite consciously in the sphere of *modern* thought – understood as that kind of thinking which developed out of the mediaeval theological and philosophical universe to gain maturity by at any rate the late eighteenth century along two distinct yet convergent lines. One of these, we discovered, emphasizes the worldliness of the world as a complex composite of things that are concrete, singular and set in an historical process. The other underlines the fact that, as persons and not simply natures, human beings are above all *subjects*, bearers of subjectivity, which (so Balthasar assured us) does not consign us to wallowing in a subjectivist morass but is in the context of the Church an essential dimension of the total representation of divine revelation. To anticipate a later stage of enquiry: he would come to see such subjective representation supremely in the saints who as subjects – unique, irreplaceable selves – initiate a personal manner of responding to revelation by their minds, imaginations, passions, and often succeed thereby in bringing out objective facets of that revelation hitherto unnoticed. Compare St Francis of Assisi and the mystique of poverty; compare St Thérèse of Lisieux and the little way of spiritual childhood.

Now if one is looking for philosophical, or philosophical-poetic, attempts in the modern period to think through rationally and imaginatively a world entertained by personal subjects after the fashion modernity 'at its highest power' considers it to be (namely, a complex composite of things that are concrete, singular and set in an historical process), then the German philosophy of the eighteenth and nineteenth centuries – broadly, Idealism, perhaps better called 'Real-Idealism', along with Romanticism – is by no means the worst place to begin. And this is so precisely owing to that philosophy's joint interest in cosmology on the one hand and on the other subjectivity, whether the latter be universal and transcendental (pertaining to the human subject as such) or merely culturally corporate or even simply individual and personal.

But all the same we need to bear in mind, when approaching this material, Balthasar's clear statement that Thomas Aquinas is *the* philosopher of nature, and not just of nature but of the entire God-world relationship – the fundamental ontology of the Creator God in his relation to creation – as that underlies nature's transformation by grace. The desire to incorporate into a Christian philosophy those elements of modernity that do greater justice to the concrete, particular, historical dimensions on the one hand, and subjectivity on the other, is not to be seen as overthrowing or abandoning the *philosophia perennis* but as weaving new factors into it and thus enriching its texture. And just as Balthasar's appeal to Thomas is to Thomas as, essentially, the clarifier of the foundational structure of being presupposed by the patristic continuation of biblical revelation, this means at the same time that Balthasar's fundamental commitment is to a combined philosophical-theological thinking in which the philosophical elements are not fully separated out from the theological but united with them in a total Christian sacramental-metaphysical vision.

When in 1947 Balthasar writes his study *Wahrheit*, 'Truth', which will turn out to be the largely philosophical opening volume of the theological logic, all this will be confirmed. What we shall see is a version of the *philosophia perennis* of Thomist Scholasticism into which has been woven a more acute sense of both the concrete particularity of things and, above all, their inwardness: an inwardness which begins to be the case quite far down the scale of being but only achieves full vigour with the emergence of personal subjects. And for these additional elements – which, if found in Thomas, are not found in the same way or to the same extent – Balthasar is indebted to the classical German philosophers.

Another way of putting this is to say Balthasar realized he needed a wider 'instrumentarium' of concepts than that provided by Thomism if he was to do justice to the theological vision he was beginning to develop – a bit like a composer who realizes he needs a greater variety of instruments in the orchestra than he had earlier supposed. Although that theological vision at its most comprehensive – in the trilogy – is structured around the trans-cendentals (the beautiful, the good, the true) and in that sense is based on mediaeval Scholastic thought, the concepts Balthasar deploys in order to show how the saving revelation is supremely beautiful (the aesthetics), good (the dramatics) and true (the logic) come from many sources, prominent among them the classical German thinkers from Goethe to Hegel and beyond. These concepts act as aids or midwives (the Germans call them *Hilfsmittel*) that enable philosophical-theological insights of a congruently Catholic kind to be expounded more fully than could otherwise be the case.

What we have in 'Apocalypse of the German Soul' is a large number of miniature monographs on a variety of philosophers and poets in which Bal-thasar runs through their work for the light they can throw on ideas of ultimate reality or final destiny – on what he terms 'eschatology', a word he uses in a very broad sense that is unconfined to discussion of 'the Four Last Things', death, judgment, Heaven, Hell, though these are not excluded. In one sense, these volumes can be read as an encyclopaedic history of German thought and literary culture. But for the student of Balthasar's theology, their chief interest lies in ideas subsequently brought into play in the ambit of Christian doctrine – either positively, by assisting in the demonstration of what that doctrine is, or negatively, by helping to show what it is not. Often, Balthasar will be describing fallacious world-views, in contrast to which the orthodox Christian view of God, the world and the self can be made to stand out the more clearly. Often again, he will be expounding philosophies that can furnish certain conceptual elements to complement Christian Scholasticism and thus serve more fully the vision of the Fathers, re-expressed for a modern setting.

In his first book-length work (and *what* a length, here is great literary ambitiousness), Balthasar explained that his interest in German thought and letters lay in what it revealed of the 'ultimate attitudes' of the authors con-cerned.[1] For, as he put it, by way of explanation of the overall title of

---

1 Cited in the second, renamed but otherwise unaltered edition: *Prometheus. Studien der Geschichte des deutschen Idealismus* (Heidelberg 1947), p. v. Cited below as '*Apokalypse I*' since the original title, *Apokalypse der deutschen Seele. Studien zu einer Lehre von letzten Haltungen, I. Der deutsche Idealismus*, has been restored in the posthumous republication of this work.

Apokalypse der deutschen Seele: 'Eschatology can be defined as a teaching about the relation of the soul to its eternal destiny, whose attainment (fulfilment, assimilation) is its apocalypse.'[2] It is important to note that in this work Balthasar does not use the word 'soul' in its psychological sense – not even in the sense of the classical philosophical psychology or metaphysics of soul found in Plato, Aristotle or Aquinas. For him 'soul' is what is at once most concrete and most ultimate about persons – and by extension in the world of things which is their living environment. Moving in this widest possible context, he found himself simultaneously attracted and repelled by German Idealism and its transformed continuation in Romanticism.

In the second chapter of this study, we saw how by the later 1920s Balthasar was already a confirmed disciple of the eighteenth-century philosopher-poet and moralist Goethe. The notion of beauty as sensuous form, the epiphany of the realm of essence in a world of concrete things, is what attracted Balthasar to Goethe as one key representative of German classical philosophy. And that school – in the widest sense – was the departure-point of a number of influential Catholic writers of the first half of the nineteenth century: Romantic theologians and those of the *katholische Tübinger Schule* – as well as the posthumously condemned Günther. From Classicism through Idealism to Romanticism, a process that might be summed up in three names – Goethe, Schelling and Novalis – a certain theological posterity had already descended. Within it Balthasar was tempted to count himself. How, then, was he to situate his nascent thought in relation to these predecessors and also, indeed, contemporaries?

A General Orientation

A few remarks by way of general orientation may be in place before we take a deep breath and launch into the great sea of this massive work. For the Balthasar of *Apokalypse*, aesthetic experience – the subject of his earliest essays – only leads into religious experience by way of a radical purification. The chief point of such purification is to ensure that aesthetic appreciation does not lead in the contrary direction to religion, by an incongruous exaltation of the 'I'. 'Patristik, Scholastik und wir' certainly rubbed in *that* point. What one should be seeking is not, with Idealism, the non-finite 'transcendental' ego nor, with Romanticism, the depths of the soul, but rather, with the Gospel, the ever-greater God in his sovereign beauty. As a Flemish interpreter of Balthasar's project puts it: 'Only then can religious experience enjoyed on the basis of aesthetic find its way back to its original source. Otherwise the religiosity of the "presentiment of the infinite" deviates irremediably towards an anthropological aesthetic, where human beauty finally encounters nothing save its own image.'[3]

This might seem to imply that Balthasar would be best advised to leave these writers alone. But a number of the German Idealists had already recognized the need for a 'moment' of self-abandonment in the genesis of thought and action. Finite spirit must submit to infinite Spirit so as really to

2 Ibid., p. 4.
3 G. de Schrijver, *Le merveilleux accord de l'homme et de Dieu: Etude de l'analogie de l'être chez Hans Urs von Balthasar* (Leuven 1983), p. 76.

be spirit in the Infinite. It was widely recognized that the Absolute cannot be truly infinite if the Absolute and we are mutually 'heteronomous', each a law unto ourselves. In this fashion, Idealism recovered the religious sense of what was in many ways its parent philosophy, neo-Platonism.

But Balthasar parted company with Idealism whenever it espoused a doctrine of what he termed 'mystical potentiality': treating the human being as a potency that is self-creative in its mystic grandeur. This was the Idealists' version of the drive to pseudo-spiritual self-deification he had already identified as the chief symptom of original sin in 'Patristik, Scholastik und wir'. Here grace was completely misconstrued as self-elevation to the level of the Absolute. For such a misjudged philosophy, man, conquering his own limits, would grant himself the boon of true freedom, his victory placing him in contact with the Absolute itself. Neo-Platonism gets twisted out of true. No longer (as with the genuine article) are we brought to fulfilment by gracious favour of the One, which allows us to participate in its fullness. Rather, by a modern caricature, it is we ourselves in our own becoming who are the source of all that is sublime in the world.

Whatever Balthasar's criticisms of the Platonist tradition in other contexts, he considered that, once its ties with neo-Platonism are broken, Idealism slides into anthropocentrism of an inner-worldly kind. This may be in Promethean fashion, with an emphasis on self-mastery, self-emancipation. Or it may be in a Dionysian way, by ecstatic transport to the heights of consciousness. Thinking of Kant, Fichte, Schelling, Nietzsche, Balthasar finds their idea of beauty:

> too tragic, and also too artificial, to be the revelation of the moving beauty of the God who is Love who, under the deformed traits of his Suffering Servant, comes to share human misery. Neither the high and mighty status of Prometheus the ravisher nor the tragic personality of Dionysus broken by his rapture, bears comparison with the divine-human figure in whom the unnamed God speaks his name, by way of the radiance of his grace and glory of his kenosis.[4]

That splendid formulation by Georges de Schrijver can provide the reader with a helpful orientation in the ramifying enquiry that follows.

Balthasar's Introduction

How, then, does Balthasar proceed in this work? His introduction goes some way toward explaining his fundamental method. Though the language of eschatology may only be allusive, what it houses is 'the meaning and kernel of the whole'.[5] Its indirectness argues not at all against its objective truth and universal validity. Each sphere of knowledge has its own 'relative *eschaton*': what is most final and comprehensive in it. A decent methodology is concerned with protecting the jurisdiction of each such 'science' – as is well-known, the German word *Wissenschaft* extends well beyond the natural sciences – in its own special realm. It is plausible to say, Balthasar suggests, that as understanding is progressively unified we shall find such 'relative

4 Ibid., p. 79.
5 *Apokalypse I*, p. 3.

eschata' themselves pointing to an ultimate and unconditional *eschaton*, just as every eschatology – every account of what is ultimately valid – points to 'a *logos* [a true thought] about the eternal *eschaton'*.[6]

Is *philosophy* the appropriate discipline to provide this 'logos' or true thinking about ultimate reality? As the study of 'being qua being' and so an exploration which transcends all 'categorial' – the term is Aristotle's – distinctions between things in the world, metaphysical philosophy, at any rate, might seem an obvious candidate for this task. But philosophy requires detachment, something not necessarily in place here, while the 'apocalypse of the soul' always seeks that reality which is the most concrete of all – a demand that 'being' as (apparently) the lowest common denominator of things would seem ill-prepared to meet. Still, eschatology can certainly use philosophy as a means, *ein Mittel*.

At the same time, however, eschatology can also invoke both *theology* – an account of the unique God in his address to a humanity consisting of particular persons, and *art* – whose theme is 'showing what is most universal in an unrepeatable moment'.[7] The concrete nature of both revelation and the artwork can make good whatever is defective in conceptual abstraction. Philosophy, theology, art, then: these three witnesses agree. Or at least this is the hope. Balthasar intends to exploit their resources in the service of 'eschatology' in the sense he gives that word. This is, of course, just what we would expect from our scanning of his early essays.

Now the situation eschatology addresses is that of the individual, time-bound human being whose destiny is mysteric in its proportions. Hence the relevance to our topic not only of philosophical and theological enquiry but also of literature – for this drama of existence is the latter's chief stuff. (Here we catch a glimpse of the future author of *Theodramatik*, Balthasar's 'theological dramatics'.[8]) The soul discovers itself in encounter with other things: the environment, other persons, history, God. These, however, are not means to its own self-realization (shades of St Augustine's distinction between means and ends – realities it is appropriate to use, and realities it is appropriate to enjoy). Nonetheless, they are factors in its destiny. They are realities in whose path it is placed and which in one way or another it has to make its own. And yet the 'horizon' to which particular persons must be pointed is not, in this enquiry, that of individuals as such, but of humanity at large. Hence the need to incorporate in the discussion not only history – including the history of salvation, but also ideas – not least those that find their genesis in revealed truth.

Balthasar could, he says, have dealt with the topic of eschatology in a 'positive' fashion, mapping the sources with which religious studies presents us when we survey beliefs about ultimate destiny in different cultures or philosophical systems. Fascinating though such a 'scientific' study might be, its focus on the 'possible objective conditions of another world' merits Christ's warning to his disciples that it is not for them to know 'times and seasons' in the divine scenario.[9] The advantage of an 'existential' eschatology

6 Ibid., p. 4.
7 Ibid.
8 Balthasar, *Theodramatik* I–IV (Einnedeln 1973–1983).
9 Acts 1.7.

– counterposed here to its 'positive' rival – is that it seeks to explain only what will clarify the situation in which the soul encounters an ultimate dimension. Such an approach cannot dispense with the mythological language studied by comparative religion, but it differs from comparative religion in treating 'existentiality' as the 'measure of the livingness of eschatological myth'. It accepts myth to the degree that the latter is the necessary expression of lived existence, *lebendige Dasein*.[10] But the aim throughout is, very simply, to show the soul's relation to its last end.

Obviously, something needs to be said by way of comment here on how Balthasar uses in this work the slippery – and, in theological English, hopelessly compromised – term 'myth'. In a summary of *Apokalypse*, Balthasar elsewhere offered bemused readers definite help. A 'myth', he wrote, is

> the form of truth which gives expression to a world-interpreting or religious idea in equal distance from 'pure' concept and 'pure' percept [sensuous image]. The 'Christ-myth' is the eternal Truth become flesh, time, [biological] conception: it is not, therefore, in any sense unhistorical, but as a mythos can nevertheless enter into a conversation with the mystical sense of ultimacy in German Idealism and the 'philosophies of life' (Bergson, Nietzsche, etc.).[11]

In a simpler formulation by J.R.R. Tolkien which influenced C.S. Lewis: with Christianity, myth – in this case, the myth of a humanized, and dying and rising, God – became fact – in the Incarnation and the Atonement. But it did so without ceasing to be myth: a form of truth expressed as only eternal truth can be, in a way which is neither concept nor image but draws on both.

An 'existential' approach, as Balthasar understands it, does not mean one uninformed by the reflections of past writers. Indeed, as he now explains, he proposes to draw on a range of philosophers and poets, chiefly in the German-speaking realm, from the time of the Enlightenment to his own. Their philosophical and aesthetic understanding of the human condition will suggest ways towards a sense of what is final.

By itself, however, that can hardly be decisive. Without the 'religious pole' – and he adds, in its 'concrete appearance as Christianity' – a *simply* human eschatology will be incomplete. It calls for some answer coming from without – whether that answer be profound agreement or outright contradiction. Balthasar candidly admits there is an obvious sense that the book will not be 'real theology' – even if towards its conclusion it takes up a more confessionally Christian stance. It will offer no 'theoretical further development of the Word of God in human systematics, but only a bare portrayal of the standing, *Stehen*, of the soul in this Word'.[12] Literature and philosophy will not be sundered here, for they testify to certain symptoms of the inner soul. If literary images throw light on the *Bildung*, the formative culture, within which intellectual life is played out, philosophy can be said itself to explore the 'fullness of being' by means of 'essential images', *Wesensbilder*. Nor does Balthasar rule out a place in his investigation for the natural sciences, from

10 *Apokalypse I*, p. 7.
11 Balthasar, 'Apokalypse der deutschen Seele', *Schönere Zukunft* 14 (1938), pp. 57–59, and here at p. 58.
12 *Apokalypse I*, p. 9.

physics to pathology. They too can sometimes cross the limits of empirical observation and light up the wider situation of human life in time.

He is anxious to distinguish his project from that stigmatized by his mentor Erich Przywara as 'eschatologism': an outlook which is interested in events only as divine judgment bears on them, and so deprives the world, natural and human, of intrinsic value, out of enmity for 'earth and culture'.[13] There is such a thing as false apocalypticism, to be found not just in baseless calculations of the end of time but, more subtly, in a tendency to take catastrophe as the only alternative to salvation. Balthasar intends to avoid that, as well as its contrary – the attempt to eternalize time by finding beatitude in culture. Finding the right balancing point between polarities (the term was Pryzwara's favourite) is crucial to Balthasar's manner in *Apokalypse*.[14] Three more instances of it merit mention before concluding an introduction to this massive work.

Balthasar has already touched on the polarity of social and individual eschatology. In fact, this division can only be a distinction. Whether social or individual, it is all a matter of the same concrete spirit *either* in its relative uniqueness *or* in its relative bondedness in community. Existential apocalyptic must look at both aspects – and this means, then, that it considers neither a mere multiple of individual destinies nor some abstract ideal unity of them. (It is interested in the corporately concrete, as in people, state, culture or church.)

A second possible polarity is that of natural and personal eschatology. Balthasar's account centres on *Geist*, spirit. But, he insists, concrete spirit is not pure spirit. On the contrary, it has deep roots in nature, even if it must also be counter-distinguished to it. For spirit, nature is at once 'clothing and mirror, concealment and disclosure'.[15] So the natural must share in apocalypse along with the personal.

A third polarity is that between value and final purpose, or to use (as he does) the vocabulary current in the German Evangelical theology of Balthasar's day, 'axiological' and 'teleological' eschatology.[16] Does eternity intersect with time equally at all points, thus grounding values? That was the claim of the eschatological axiologists. Or is it meta-history, a goal for the historical process to be encountered only at the end of human time as presently experienced? This was the conviction of the eschatological teleologists. Balthasar is happy with neither pole taken alone. An eschatology of value soon becomes divorced from the subjects – human persons – who alone can strive for fulfilment in relation to the pertinent *eschata*. Such axiology sits lightly to history, where existential eschatology takes its stand. On the other hand, to characterize eschatology, with the teleological school, as wherever the historical process takes one – irrespective of the good, of intrinsic value – would hardly suffice. Evidently, then: 'concrete spirit is not ordered to its

---

13 E. Przywara, 'Eschatologismus', *Stimmen der Zeit* 117 (1929), p. 229.
14 It will recur in, for example, the theological anthropology of *Theodramatik*: see Balthasar, *Theo-Drama. Theological Dramatic Theory. Volume II, The Dramatis Personae: Man in God* (ET San Francisco 1990), pp. 335–429.
15 *Apokalypse I*, p. 12.
16 See G. Hoffmann, *Das Problem der letzten Dinge in der neueren evangelischen Theologie* (Frankfurt 1929).

eschaton purely axiologically or purely teleologically, but by the inseparable dialectic of the two together'.[17]

In the course of this discussion, Balthasar flags up an important point. The demarcation of 'historical' and 'meta-historical' as two separate spheres fails to do justice to humankind's eschatological situation. The contrast between the eternal as now and the eternal as future is entirely secondary and derivative. This is also a reminder that concepts alone cannot do justice to our topic. The human spirit needs the riches of image and myth, as well as the clarity of the concept, if it is to grasp its situation before what is finally final – God. Thus the introduction ends.

The 'Prehistory'

There remains, however, one important prolegomenon. Before launching into the world of the German philosophers and poets, Balthasar considers the dissolution of that unitary eschatological understanding which was still a reality in the Western Middle Ages. (Such understanding furnishes a benchmark for judgment throughout *Apokalypse*, albeit for the most part tacitly.) The claim to wholeness or completeness of the Western mediaeval Christian world-view in its Scholastic guise had no more decisive criterion than eschatology. That must be true of any world-view: here if anywhere it will be seen whether it has an overarching unity or no. But this particular world-view had to cope with massive tensions – natural/supernatural; human/divine; sinful/redeemed; sensuous/spiritual, so the challenge was especially strong. 'Forms from antiquity were drawn into the Christian reality, surrendered thereto their unique character, and were thrust into the movement of the new, essentially religious and supernatural, perspective.'[18]

The real formal principle of Christian eschatology – despite borrowings from Aristotelean, Platonist and Stoic ideas – was not cosmology but event, an event at once historical and meta-historical or supernatural. The determinative moments of its 'drama' (we note again here the early appearance of the later vocabulary of Balthasar's theological dramatics) were threefold: creation in grace; redemption; consummation. Like the graced creation and the free redemption, the consummation or fulfilment is also utterly original and unpredictable. No one but the Father knows its day or hour, remarks Jesus.[19] This 'absolute leap', says Balthasar, renders vain all attempts to assess the movement towards fulfilment *either* in terms of progress through the extension of the Kingdom *or* in terms of catastrophe. So much for ameliorist Liberal theology and early Barthian apocalyptic alike. And yet all roads converge on this indescribable point, including the ways of secular history.

The End, as orthodox Christianity presents it, is the centre of eschatology for the individual person. It will be the moment of the soul's (public) judgment and the restoration of the human being as a body-soul unity. It is also the centre of 'general' eschatology, the moment when humankind is judged as a unitary whole, the 'kingdom of this world' is cast down, and the glory of Christ's body and of his Bride, the Church, shown forth. Finally, the End is

17 *Apokalypse I*, p. 13.
18 Ibid., p. 21.
19 Cf. Mark 13.32.

the centre of eschatology for nature too, which up to now, in the words of the Paul of the Letter to the Romans, has been groaning in travail awaiting its full liberation.[20] Nor can these three sorts of eschatology – which, after all, simply name aspects of the total fulfilment – be separated one from another in the light of that supreme moment.

For Balthasar, the Christian hope is for a fulfilment which combines teleological eschatology – eternity as the future goal of time, with axiological eschatology – time as direct relation to eternity here and now, whether for *Heil* or *Unheil*, salvation or damnation. The location of this consummation in the divine counsel (and nowhere else) is vital. It means that no decisive meaning can be attached to either cultural development or such natural processes as evolution and entropy. What is important is, rather, the struggle, suffering and testing of the just in a world where good is mixed with evil – or, as Balthasar prefers to say, where suffering as punishment and reprobation is mixed with suffering as education, redemption, salvation.

This is the basic picture, the *Grundschema*. All the colourful legendary and poetic material in which the Christian Middle Ages invested its sense of eschatology is a matter of the individual forms, *Einzelgestalten*, in which this 'scheme' was rendered vivid and brought home.

Not that it went altogether unchallenged. A current of 'chiliastic dreaming of a kingdom of the End' was also flowing. Issuing at last in the theology of the twelfth-century abbot Joachim of Flora, its fundamental incompatibility with orthodox eschatology became plain. (Here Balthasar anticipates a late work of his mentor, Henri de Lubac.[21]) Though some of the Fathers and early mediaevals may think in terms of history concluding with an era of this-worldly fulfilment, for such Church doctors and approved divines – but not for Joachim – that millenarian era is always ordered to the meta-historical fulfilment lying beyond behind it. Balthasar notes likewise the survival into the Christian Middle Ages (notably, thinks Balthasar, at least at this stage in his writing, in John Scotus Eriugena), of an over-spiritualized neo-Platonic or Gnostic type of eschatology, for which esoteric knowing is the real ultimate. Balthasar dismisses this crisply. It is 'a gnostic naturalising of the supernatural and the contradiction-in-terms of an anthropocentric theology'.[22]

The Protestant reform might seem to leave the basic Christian scheme largely intact, but Balthasar detects serious shifts of emphasis. A low doctrine of the Church left the individual exposed on dying. And the loss of faith in the presence of Christ's natural yet risen body in the Eucharist also undermined confidence in the reality of his death-transcending ecclesial body, the Church. Luther's 'mystical existentiality' engendered new attitudes towards death, both in scorn and jubilation. Lutheran theologians went on frankly to deny any eschatological place to nature (except for the glorified human body).

In any case, the Lutheran fish were swimming against the stream. The more powerful cultural current flowing ever faster from the sixteenth century onwards was that of the developing natural sciences. The success of the exact sciences gave their methods potential hegemony over all knowledge. If

---

20 Cf. Romans 8.21–22.
21 H. de Lubac, *La postérité spirituelle de Joachim de Flore* (2 vols.; *Namur-Paris* 1979–1981).
22 *Apokalypse I*, p. 26.

mathesis universalis, mathematically expressed laws for the behaviour of things, be the criterion of the veridical, then the basic presuppositions of eschatology must be abandoned, and its truth-claims relegated from the realm of knowing to those of believing or hoping. At best, for thinkers who continued to work the vein of theistic metaphysics (Balthasar evidently has the seventeenth century rationalist metaphysician Leibniz in mind), it was by a *'mechanismus metaphysicus'* that God chose the best world, which itself unfolded inexorably in a 'gapless series of monads' from primitive matter right up to the highest consciousness.[23]

Actually, Balthasar thinks, the two attitudes – the Lutheran and the naturalistic – could co-exist. The Reformation could take an individualistic faith ('the free Christian man') for its own special religious preserve, while those who sought to establish the laws of human nature could concentrate on natural reason. Somewhat in the spirit of Maritain's *Three Reformers*, with its claim that the projects of Luther and Descartes are inter-related,[24] Balthasar considers that Luther's devaluation of 'works' as extrinsic to faith finds an echo in Descartes' dualism of body and soul. All in all, a profoundly unsatisfactory situation is developing. The hiatus between empirical reality and a human ideal grows wider: hence the popularity of utopian thinking and indeed the Great Revolution of the West, 1789–1815, with its massive toll in blood and tears. The person as a body–soul unity becomes a problem in Protestantism; the spirituality of the self, and its immortality, becomes a problem in science.

If anything identifiable emerges from the breakdown of the classical Catholic Christian presentation of the Last Things, it is a return of a sort to Stoic eschatology. The presence here and now of ultimate reality, despite the endless development of matter: what is this but a renewal of the teaching of the Stoic school? Learning to live with mortality as the natural boundary of life: what is this preferred inner attitude but an appeal to recover the Stoic virtues of fortitude and resignation? Classicism, and a host of men of ideas – among the later moderns, Balthasar names Oswald Spengler, pessimistic historian of civilization; Georg Simmel, sociologist; Rainer Maria Rilke, poet; Martin Heidegger, Existentialist philosopher – will take this way out. Meanwhile, the Baroque theatre would enact a contest, not between two doctrines – the fully Christian and the early modern alternative – but between each world-view's *Lebensgefühl*, its 'feeling for life'.

The eighteenth century saw the victory of immanence over transcendence. Yet moralists were unwilling to let go at any rate a *postulate* of immortality, if only to restrain humankind's evil deeds. Likewise, philosophers of history were unwilling to abandon an intrinsic orientation for history, if only to licence talk of 'progress', at any rate the progress of reason. But the questions of personal identity and destiny, and the goal of the world process, no longer had generally persuasive answers. Above all, with the marginalization of orthodox eschatology with its supernatural end-point, the various dimensions of personal and cosmic life it had held together fell apart. Balthasar lists the questions which had now become unanswerable: 'How is the perfected individual related to the still unperfected community? What general

23 Ibid., p. 29.
24 J. Maritain, *Trois Réformateurs* (Paris 1925, 2nd edn 1939).

meaning can be specified as the goal of social (historical) eschatology? What role does nature play in individual as well as social fulfilment? What is nature's own final end?'[25] Behind all these questions, an even more basic query raises its head. Does it make any sense to think of a striving which endlessly approaches or approximates to something (but has no guarantee it will ever get there)?

Where the force of such questionings was felt, it was hardly surprising that a neo-Chiliastic theology should revive at the hands of Pietists, the 'mystical radicals' of German Protestantism. Balthasar does not regard such a theology as merely an extreme if predictable response to Enlightenment Godlessness. If he did, he would not end the preamble to his main study on this note. On the contrary. This theology of a last age where evil self-destructs in world-judgment became the 'signpost for a new generation ...' 'Striving for a fuller world-picture than that of the Enlightenment, it was to build a new eschatology on the contradictions of the past, an eschatology which was truly the myth of its own ultimate attitude.'[26] This is the cue for Balthasar's account of Idealism and Romanticism, those twin progenitors of the thought and sensibility of the modern European age.

The reader should be warned that Balthasar's readings of the major philosophers (and other writers) he studies are highly personal. Presenting these thinkers in terms of the – compared and contrasted – figures of Dionysus and Prometheus to some extent forces them on to a Procrustean bed. Texts are re-constellated in new configurations which, to Balthasar's mind, give access to the – otherwise unobvious – overall orientation of this or that individual's thought. More specifically, it needs to be borne in mind that there can scarcely be a general philosophical movement termed 'German Idealism' when the authors concerned 'not only disagreed with each other but misunderstood each other'[27] – even though not all commentators subsequently recognized this fact. The consequent ruptures in sequential development of a body of reflection are elided by Balthasar in the interests of providing an instructive 'conversation' among his various early interlocutors. (For the use of readers who may wish to bear in mind the *chronological* relation between the various early modern and modern authors discussed, from now on until my presentation of *Apokalypse* is ended, their dates will be given in conjunction with their names and, wherever possible, in the context of their *principal* appearance in my text.)

---

25 *Apokalypse I*, p. 36.
26 Ibid., p. 41.
27 From a letter of 9 June 2004 to the present author from the historian of metaphysics, Edward Booth, OP.

5

❄️

From Lessing to Fichte

Lessing

First stop, Gotthold Ephraim Lessing (1729–1781), critic and dramatist, sometimes called the father of modern German literature.[1] Man of many masks, he stands for Balthasar at the centre of the struggle between the Enlightenment and Christendom. The basic problematic concerns the relation between, on the one hand, the non-historical 'apriorism' of reason in its Enlightenment mode (and this could also take a Christian form, *Vernunfts-christentum*, rational Christianity) and, on the other hand, the 'aposteriori-ism' of actual historical development (not least that of the Christian religion itself). The element of Lessing's thought most commonly met with in standard histories of ideas is the claim that no particular, contingent fact (such as make up the historical basis of Christianity) can serve to verify an allegedly universal and necessary truth.

Typically, Balthasar reinterprets this debate in his own chosen fashion – as a quarrel over the time/eternity relationship. In what sense, asks Balthasar, is the temporal the expression of the eternal? Is time, and therefore contingency, eternal truth's curtain, a veil that becomes more and more transparent as rational light ('necessity') pierces it through? That would be the classical Enlightenment view, and it amounts to a 'static' eschatology. Or is there a 'seed' of eternity carried by time (and thus 'contingency'), such that as time ripens, for good or ill, the eternal can increasingly be seen for what it is? That would be more dynamic, certainly. But neither of these is the authentically Christian solution which, rather, mediates between the two positions. The Resurrection of Christ, 'Christianity's most living point', is itself the mutual intersection of temporal and eternal. It is not so difficult to see what Balthasar means. The Resurrection happens within time, but it happens through bringing time proleptically – by way of anticipation – to its final goal. It is eternity breaking through now – but doing so as the manifestation of the ultimate End of all things when history as we know it will cease. Into this the disciples are invited both in the present, through faith and the sacraments of faith, and in the future, by vision and full participation.

For his own part, Lessing tries to combine two eschatologies, one for

---

1 As in the sub-title of a study of his work by H.B. Garland, *Lessing: The Father of Modern German Literature* (London 1937).

historic society whose true goal is the reign of reason, and one – very different, this – for the individual soul in the cosmic setting. Here the eighteenth-century thinker, unwilling to concede that even one human life can be ultimately in vain, posits the transmigration of incomplete personalities into new worlds. As Balthasar remarks, such diverse goals – higher culture and post-mortem rebirth – are not exactly easily united. This hardly seems to have bothered Lessing – perhaps, suggests Balthasar, because he regards the reign of reason, which has put to one side all mere 'factual' history, as an image of endless striving, and the transmigration of souls as, correlatively, an image of endless progress.

Lessing's objection to the eschatology of revealed religion is not so much to the content of its expectation as to the attitudes it would exact. This life ought no more to be dominated by a future one than today should be dominated by a future day. Fools lose this life in worrying so much about the next one. We must live for now. This is not, with Lessing, an Epicurean thought. Everything has its eternal consequences. Self-knowledge of an existential kind suggests to us how both eternal light and eternal darkness are possible. Lessing's opposition is thus rather to 'an objective treatment of eschatology as science at our disposal (*eine zuhandene Wissenschaft*)'.[2] Something like a foretaste of heaven and hell can certainly be *found* in inner experience, which in this way projects its shadow on the wall of eternity.

Hamann to Herder

Herder, the great philosopher of culture, is Balthasar's next main port-of-call, but he takes us there by way of some imaginative writers of Pietist background and, notably, Johann Georg Hamann (1730–1788), the 'Magus of the North' – later on, in Balthasar's oeuvre, a hero of the theological aesthetics.[3] In Hamann we have to do with a very different stream of sensibility from Lessing. 'Being as subjective-historical apocalypse' is Balthasar's epigrammatic summary of the philosophy of Hamann. Hamann's distance from his Enlightenment contemporaries is shown not only in the content of his doctrine but also in its form. The truth of human existence, were it to be rendered exclusively in concepts, would be for Hamann *Engelsprache*, the speech of angels, not human discourse. Humans need the image, the parable, the myth, for their self-understanding. Through these forms, Hamann seeks (in the words of a letter of 1773) a 'higher holiness' than anything the goddess reason can offer. Reason, seemingly so spiritual, is in fact limited by the senses, from which its analyses and constructions set forth. But the *totality* of our sensuous nature, actually, is found in existential, not rational, truth. Herein lies an affinity with religion. The ground of religion is *our existence as a whole*, which is why what Hamann terms *logos* – the 'revealed' language that is the speech of being – furnishes a wider-ranging and more penetrating discourse than does the concept, despite the 'impurity' of such 'logos-

---

2 *Apokalypse I*, p. 51.
3 *The Glory of the Lord: Studies in Theological Styles. III: Lay Styles* (ET Edinburgh and San Francisco 1986), pp. 239–78.

language' from a strictly rational standpoint.[4] 'Logos-speech' both unveils and veils – it clarifies yet takes us further into mystery.

What is the relation of this, though, to the language of the Christian sources? The answer for Hamann is that the salvation-historical revelation constitutes the concrete form of 'ontological revelation' (Balthasar's phrase here). The saving history of Scripture offers a '*Summa* of existence'. All purely literal interpretation of Scripture, so Hamann wrote in 1780 to Herder, misses the point; historical 'approximation' can only tell half the story. In his account of Hamann's thought, Balthasar anticipates, even at this stage of his writing, a good deal of the content of his own mature dogmatics. Veiledness and yet unveiledness reach their high point in Christ's death and Resurrection, which is 'God-transparency'. In Christ's Paschal mystery – and these are Hamann's words in the *Aesthetica in nuce* – 'most glorious majesty' and 'emptiest voiding' coincide.[5] For ourselves also, in Hamann's perception (and Balthasar treasures the insight as the key to his eschatology), only when self-knowledge descends into hell can it find a road through to divinization. How, according to Hamann, is this possible? Owing to the analogy-structure of human nature, made as this is in the image of God, everything divine is also in some way congruent with humanity and open to our reach. In an explicit comparison with Christology, there is a 'communication of idioms' between divine and human.[6] As in the case of the God-man, our *teleion*, or perfect goal, lies on the other side of death – but we develop a taste for it on earth in *signs*. The latter need not be exclusively biblical, though Scripture is full of them. They can be found, too, for Hamann, in fine art.

Johann Gottfried Herder (1744–1803), Lutheran pastor, philosopher of culture and history, and in his later years, opponent of Kantianism, represents for Balthasar an attempt to synthesize such an 'existential apocalyptic' with the serene deistic future hope of the Enlightenment mind. Anyone who attempted this feat had to be someone for whom the sense attached to personal existence and the meaning of human history at large were equally pressing concerns. If Hamann's interest was *existenziale Urgeschichtlichkeit*, 'existential primordial historicity' – basic temporality, our being in time at all, Herder's focus was *zeitliche Urgeschichte*, the concrete history of human beginnings and their aftermath. For Herder, the enthusiastic interpretation of myth has somehow to be married with cool objective research.

In his opposition to the French Enlightenment and especially the French Revolution, Herder rejected all abstract schemata of universal human development in favour of a plurality of schemes, each particular to its own national culture. There are many forms, *Gestalten*, of human completeness, each in Balthasar's words 'a spiritual-material whole, a myth, an organism'.[7] Still, Herder could also recognize a teleology dynamically present in the totality of these forms as they unfold in cultural history. In the end, 'everything is going to be integrated in the harmony of the concrete image of

4 *Apokalypse I*, p. 57.
5 Ibid., p. 60.
6 Ibid., p. 61, with reference to Hamann's 'Des Ritters von Rosenkreuz letzte Willensmeinung über der göttlichen und menschlichen Ursprung der Sprache' (1772), in *Sämtliche Werke, III. Schriften über Sprache, Mysterien, Vernunft 1772–1788* (Vienna 1951), pp. 25–33.
7 *Apokalypse I*, p. 63.

humanity', integrated into a cumulatively acquired human wholeness to which Herder gave the name *Humanität*. Balthasar describes Herder's view of the human eschaton by contrasting two Greek words for 'form' or 'image', *eidos* and *morphê*. Herderian humanity is: 'transcendent as the highest, as yet unrealised full form (*eidos*), immanent as the pervasive wholeness already present in the transient partial forms (*morphê*)'.[8]

Each age is immediate to God – as axiological eschatology would have it – but only insofar as it brings to actuality some lower potency of the ultimate whole, which is the typical demand of teleological eschatology.

What, then, might be the relation of the individual soul to this corporate *telos*? Each and every animal, so Herder admits in the *Ideen zur Philosophie der Geschichte der Menschheit*, attains what it should, given its organization. Is the individual human being alone not to succeed in this, because the aim of humanity is so high, so broad, so open-ended?[9] In point of fact, as we shall see, Herder by no means excludes such a comprehensive fulfilment.

So far Balthasar has only expounded his account of 'immanent humanity'. This is important – owing not least to Herder's influence on Balthasar's later *A Theology of History*. That influence is apparent when the Swiss theologian writes of such immanent development:

> In the philosophy and mysticism of the ancients, matter was regarded as a place of banishment and servitude from which the spirit had to liberate itself. But nowadays matter assumes another aspect. It becomes a hierarchy of successive and evolving forms of life (though by what means we still do not know) which are inwardly oriented towards the supreme form they attain in man, who ontogenetically recapitulates in himself, crowns and transcends, all the forms of nature. The lord of creation is no longer a stranger in his kingdom; he is ... one who has risen from beneath through the successive forms of his ancestors and is thus in his very being bound up with them, in communion with them.[10]

But this entire process of human development, incorporating as it does all the main stages in the emergence of life and directed as it is to the 'eschaton' of a plenitude of cultural forms, can also be regarded in another way, which Herder does not fail to do. It can be seen as immanent *precisely vis-à-vis a transcendent dimension*. As Balthasar reports on Herder's writing: 'The horizontal level of historical becoming is penetrated by countless lines of a vertical-ascending heavenly becoming.'[11] There is, for Herder, a 'realm of invisible powers', whose progress takes its departure point from the very human development already described. The words could be Hamann's. But the new context helps reintegrate the fate of the body with that of the soul. As Herder explains, all the impressions that shape spirit through the body leave their traces. These traces can help in the building up of a higher corporeality (which could also be thought of, however, as an inferior level of spirit). Herder speculates that after death, we shall come to appropriate eternal life 'by stages' – just as we have to come to be, through natural and cultural

8 Ibid., p. 64.
9 Ibid., pp. 65–66.
10 *A Theology of History* (ET New York and London 1963), p. 139.
11 *Apokalypse I*, p. 66.

formation, in stages likewise in this world. We would not cease to be creatures if we also proved to be, post-mortem, through our own ongoing
development, 'fashioners of great worlds'. Herder envisages the soul being
led by the Father's hand through such worlds, ever onwards, ever upwards.
Plainly, we are dealing here with a new mythology, indebted to the Christian
mythos but by no means identical with it.

Herder's account, comments Balthasar, leaves the soul somewhere
between form (*Gestalt*) and power (*Kraft*), between completion and unend-
ingness. Horizontally, or in terms of evolution, the soul is the receptacle for
all material, vegetable, animal development hitherto. Vertically, or in terms
of the experience of spirit, it is the memory of all the forms of historic
humanity. Its dynamic incorporation of all of these is what gives it a capacity
for eschatological wholeness – and yet surely wholeness on such a scale, at
once 'primordial creativity' and 'primordial form', can only be God rather
than any creature. Balthasar ranges widely through Herder's poetry to
indicate how this is so. The world-historical 'inner space' of the soul and,
inseparable from it, the space of the world itself, is projected into the space of
God, which the soul enters 'without either defence or conclusion' (*wehrlos
und ohne Abschluss*).[12] Balthasar emphasizes the ethical or quasi-ethical aspect.
Only by following the 'great, unique law of giving itself away into the world'
can the soul attain its own amplitude.

To try and make sense of the Herderian mythology, Balthasar reminds his
readers of the old Scholastic adage, 'the soul is in a certain sense all things'.
So by its ethical achievement – essentially, one of self-surrender, self-
abandonment, almost self-sacrifice (we might almost paraphrase the key
word, *Hingabe*, as *sacrifice*), the soul illuminates itself and the world as well.
As it does so, it shines out on the world a light that is not its own. 'So the soul
is, as it were, a shining between the light source of God and the lit up
world.'[13] The more knowledge and love souls have – of the all, for the all, the
more are they real participants in the divine. The greater the surrender,
paradoxically, the richer, the more creative – divinely co-creative – is the soul
in question. That, for Herder, *is* 'faith'. Balthasar finds in him the 'father of
the greatest German generation'.[14]

Alone of the major thinkers of late eighteenth and early nineteenth-
century Germany, Herder found biblical apocalyptic deeply interesting. He
approached the Johannine Apocalypse not chiliastically, like the Pietists, or
pedantically, as Lessing had done, but by combining a mystical with an
historical approach. Balthasar approves. The book's message is 'I come', and
Herder's sympathetic interpretation finds in this the eternal presence of
heaven pouring itself out into the temporal successiveness of earth, the 'self-
outpouring of the divine centre into the environing circles of creation'.[15] In
Balthasar's preferred terminology, God's advent – the true Eschaton –
expresses itself *axiologically* in a veiled presence of his coming now, *teleologically* in its unveiled presence in time to come. Simply to tie the book's
pertinence to the end of the world is a mistake, and in some wonderful

12 Ibid., p. 70.
13 Ibid., p. 74.
14 Ibid., p. 78.
15 Ibid., p. 81.

stanzas, Herder appeals to Christ to come and arouse now the soul whose eye is lidded by elaborately ramifying sensuous excursions into the world. ('The lamp [the soul's capacity] is there; where is the light?')

Balthasar does not claim – indeed, he expressly denies – that Herder's interpretation of the book of Revelation is a perfect match with that of the ancient Church. Given that Balthasar's own theology of Hell would be, in his latter years, a point of contention among orthodox Catholics, it is interesting to note his strictures on Herder's account of the same subject. For Herder, 'Hell' is the principle of 'inertia and wickedness' in human history. The 'lake of fire' of the Apocalypse is the residue of the outworkings of this principle.[16] What St John calls the 'second death',[17] Herder understands as the self-destruction of evil, death and suffering at that moment when the 'potencies' of humanity reach their ultimate (temporal) outcome. For Balthasar, the exclusion from this account of Hell (and its negation) of any reference to a personal spiritual decision of the soul is a big mistake. Herder's story, says Balthasar, is defective owing to its 'naturalism' – to be understood here, surely, as much over against personalism as by contrast with an invocation of supernatural good.

Moreover, as Balthasar points out, epistemologically speaking, Herder is in no strong position. What is Herderian faith? Granted that what Herder has put together is a new mythology, it is, in the last analysis, only hunches. Or, to put it slightly more flatteringly, postulates of the heart.

But neither of these are Balthasar's chief objection. That concerns, rather, the internal coherence of his scheme. Early Christian apocalyptic held together the supra-timely and the end-timely through the 'transfigured God-man', Jesus Christ. Its eschaton was the resurrection of the body as incorporation into Christ. Herder, for whom this approach is, owing to Enlightenment rationalism (and, to a degree, his Lutheranism) impossible, wished nonetheless to maintain both dimensions – supra-time and end-time. But he could find no way of envisaging their unity. In the final temporal condition of things – *Humanität*, sheer humanity – individuals will only share anonymously, via the trickle-down effect of their deeds through time. As personal souls, their only possible direction is the eternally upward one, in spiritual approximation to God.

For Balthasar, Herder's eschatology is at once close to the Christian, and worlds apart from it. It resembles it in its anti-Prometheanism. It is certainly not self-deification. It differs from it in regarding the human spirit and body as only facets of nature. In a give-away phrase, Herder once described the ethical as simply a 'higher physics', following this up (inevitably) with a rejection of any other judgment on this world than what the laws of nature bring upon the soul.

Kant

And so to Immanuel Kant (1724–1804), Herder's 'mighty opponent'.[18] Kant breaks with Herder's notion of a chaotic nature gradually undergoing

16 Apocalypse 19.20.
17 Apocalypse 20.6.
18 Ibid., p. 91.

metamorphosis into ever higher forms of which man is simply the summit. For Kant, the level of spirit cannot be attained in this naturalistic fashion. His covert analogy, in Balthasar's words, is not the caterpillar becoming moth or butterfly. It is the phoenix rising re-born. To Kant's mind (a powerful one, but Balthasar is not easily overawed, except by God): 'being-a-spirit has its essence (*Wesen*) from itself and so establishes its own "limit" as inner individuality, non-interchangeability, an interior world rounded off in itself ...'[19]

In other words, to be *Geist*, to live on the level of spirit, is to be a *subject*, that key term of the concluding section of Balthasar's 'Patristik, Scholastik und wir'. The idea of limit, *Grenze*, which figures in the Balthasarian summary of Kantian thought just cited, has here a distinctive new meaning. For Kant it is crucial that spirit can grasp itself in its interiorly limited character and appreciate this limitedness, indeed, as the condition of possibility for its own being the spirit it is. For him, remarks Balthasar ironically, the 'Last Things' – the most ultimate considerations in philosophy – are not so much God and the fate of the world as they are the *presuppositions* of spirit's own finite being.

That word 'presuppositions', *Voraussetzungen*, is all-important for understanding Kantianism. We are dealing here not primarily with an eschatological doctrine of the ultimate but with a 'transcendental' one. In Kant's work, 'transcendental' just means 'having to do with presuppositions', the presuppositions of spirit's – mind's – activity. In Kant's system, all other putative 'eschata' have to seek legitimation before this final court. They must pass the test of that 'self-apocalypse' which consists in ascertaining the conditions of possibility of human knowledge. So Herder's twilit world gives way to either light – transcendentally legitimated knowledge – or darkness – the shadow realm of metaphysics, the playground of intellectual charlatans of whom the spiritualist Emanuel Swedenborg (1688–1772) was, in Kant's eyes, the chief.

On Balthasar's interpretation of Kant's critique of 'pure' reason, the very 'to-and-fro' of the understanding (*Verstand*) in its dealings with nature, the to-and-fro', in which spirit comes to know itself as limited, points to a ground of unity which itself renders possible valid criticism (*Kritik*) and therefore genuine knowledge. For Kant, this most comprehensive feature of our existence is reason (*Vernunft*), in its non-finitude. The trouble is that this infinity has no 'mirror' in which to see itself. It cannot be known, then, as 'objective'. And yet it is here – according to Balthasar – that Kant's most passionate interest is focused. Reason is not only aware of understanding's limitations, it also sets them. This entails the vocation of spirit not just to master the realm of the finite but also to relativize itself through its ordering to a final value (*Wert*) which transcends it and which alone is true value.

This 'final point' – which in itself can never appear – Kant hails in a remarkable variety of titles: 'purpose in itself', 'the Holy', and 'solemn majesty'. Obscurely, one might be forgiven for thinking, Kant thus touches on the subject-matter of traditional Christian eschatological thought. Actually he comes a good deal nearer than that. Balthasar makes much of a tiny *opusculum* of 1794, bearing the title *Das Ende aller Dinge*, 'The End of All

19 Ibid., p. 93.

Things'.[20] This little treatise opens with the question, What does it mean to say of a dying man, he is 'leaving time for eternity'? For Kant the phrase indicates a form of existence that defies representation. The thought leads one to an abyss which at once attracts and terrifies – to *limit* in its most rigorous sense, *an Grenze schlechthin*, to 'limit strictly so called'. Kant distinguishes between two aspects of this frontier: first, the 'natural' end of one who was physically and morally finite, and secondly, the 'supernatural' or 'mystical' end of one who owns his own nature only in relation to a destiny 'beyond'. The first aspect Kant associates with pure reason's inability to locate an end to time. In this perspective, the biblical image of the 'Last Day' simply affirms that time *will* go beyond itself into eternity – 'somewhere'. But thanks to the 'imperative' of practical reason, the finite spirit of the human person knows of its finitude in another and more significant way as well. In this second perspective, the 'Last Day' becomes mythopoeic language for my relation to my final destiny. In this second context, the 'Last Day' is by no means an empty notion. Rather is it filled with the thought of the gracious or condemnatory judgment of the Judge of the world. And so what from the viewpoint of pure reason is rather a negligible idea – time going somewhere, none knows where – now acquires the extraordinary value of a mythopoeic expression for the axiological relation of the ethical to the Eternal. Human beings expect an end to the world. Kant would 'translate' that by saying: the continuance of the world 'only has value insofar as in that continuance rational beings are pursuing the final purpose of their existence'.[21] The option of Heaven or Hell puts in imagistic form the infinite abyss ethical consciousness finds when it considers the relation between good and evil. We cannot think otherwise than of an endless prolongation of the indefinite possibilities of ascent through dutiful action, descent through its contrary.

Now to synthesize spirit's unending (ethical) progress with a definitive arrival is clearly no easy matter. Kant is neither surprised nor dismayed that at this point people take refuge in mysticism, *die Mystik*. Reason cannot always be satisfied with its own practical uses. Not unreasonably, reason has its mysteries. Reason *wants* to draw into a synthesis eternity on the one hand, and the temporal task of being a person on the other. And here the mystical can help it. As Balthasar paraphrases Kant's thinking on this point:

> The apocalypse of the soul, as the soul's ultimate capacity for being whole, a capacity in which the meaning of the soul's tendency to transcendence (compare: our natural end) is clarified from the side of the meaning of the fulfilment of the transcendence attained (compare: our supernatural end): this apocalypse of the soul is *the* 'mystery of reason'.[22]

However, the treatise issues in a worrying – Balthasar actually calls it 'tragic' – dualism. The way Kant describes the human being as knower, spirit remains in darkness. Spirit can never be for itself an object in the world of

---

20 Published in the Hartenstein edition of Kant's writings used by Balthasar as *Werke*, VI, pp. 393–408. The most recent English translation is found in A.W. Wood and G. de Giovanni (eds.), *Immanuel Kant: Religion and Rational Theology* (Cambridge 1996; 2001), pp. 221–31.
21 *Apokalypse* I, p. 95.
22 Ibid., p. 98.

sense, where alone knowledge is possible. The human person's own centre, what is endlessly valuable and non-substitutable about him, the 'place' where he is free and indeed the lawgiver, ethically speaking, for the world, this is (literally!) eccentric, off-centre and off-limit, unavailable to him. Man is absolutely free to determine himself (Balthasar links to this Kant's notion of happiness) and yet altogether directed to a goal beyond his own existence (Balthasar links to this Kant's notion of holiness). Kant could find no way to reconcile holiness and happiness. In Kant's system, these two aspects of the eschaton can only be separately viewed. Can we rule out the possibility that a being for whom holiness is the highest good might be unable, in holiness, to possess that full mastery of nature which happiness demands? Kant can give no such assurance. Here, for Balthasar, philosophy breaks open from within to let theology enter. For we stand here on the threshold of a theology of grace. As Balthasar puts it:

> The 'objective' structure of spirit of itself demands only a striving after holiness and thereby striving after the 'highest good' – whether this can be synthesised [with the spirit] through unknown powers of nature or through divine grace or not. The task of the subject (as possessor of this 'objective' structure of spirit) is [simply] to choose.[23]

So the final meaning of transcendence is disclosed only in an 'existential' fashion. The proof of the pudding, as we shall find in the moment of death, is in the eating.

If the ultimate meaning of the act of transcendence, seen from the side of the human subject, is thus withdrawn from the speculative reason, how much more is this the case with the fully achieved synthesis of the state of blessedness. Taken together, the two 'moments' call for a 'meta-history' inaccessible to any 'meta-physic'. And, as it happens, this is where Kant's principal text in the philosophy of religion comes in, *Religion innerhalb der Grenzen der blossen Vernunft*, 'Religion within the Limits of Reason Alone'.

The starting-point of that treatise is 'radical evil', whose presence in human nature constitutes for Kant the opening to a religion of grace. Man emerges in the world as one whose noble species has decided, ethically speaking, against its own highest law: a state of affairs Kant can explain only by postulating something like the Judaeo-Christian primordial Adamic 'Fall'. Freedom was perverted close to source. But if in this way the fundamental human drive no longer expresses an orientation to the synthesis of the 'highest good', how can we hope ultimately to become whole? Granted radical evil, our capacity for relevant action no longer suffices. Human progress, history shows, is cultural. It is not moral progress at all.

We can only dispose ourselves, then, to *receive* a 'higher condition'. Radical evil has not destroyed the 'divine spark' in the ground of the soul. But we can now only look on that spark as a wonder, a gift to be bestowed. We must not allow ourselves to be deterred here by a seeming antinomy. Only on the ground of his (ethical) readiness, *Bereitschaft*, can man hope for grace. But surely ethical readiness presumes grace already given, for conversion of heart. It seems we already need the gift before we can even express

---

23 Ibid., p. 106.

a willingness to receive it. Speculatively, the conundrum is real. Practical reason, though, bids us not to speculate but to get on with our preparation.

What is the evidence for the reality of grace? The sign of grace is that throughout a life, despite falling away from the good, there persists the wish to be converted to the good. Such *Gesinnungsumkehr*, conversion of conscience, is the *only* sign of grace's existence. It more than suffices.

The topic of grace is *highly* relevant to Kant's eschatology. Speaking as Kant-interpreter, Balthasar goes so far as to say that the supreme 'synthesis' of the highest good is 'in its first aspect' grace: endless approach to the Holy through obedience to moral law. But in the second place that 'synthesis', for Kant, must be located in the *autonomy* which (he says) grace gives. (This second element has to be included if Kant is right in thinking that happiness is inseparable from self-determination.) As Balthasar points out, since by grace we are only approaching perfect conformity with the Holy whose law is not, then, our complete possession, this overall synthesis is only really thinkable from 'above', from an indeterminate transcendent point.

Kant cannot make the connexion which would enable him to say that the 'synthesis' he is seeking is God himself – holiness, happiness, totality in one – or that the divine Wisdom can itself become the light of the soul since grace comes to 'inhere' in the human nature on which it is bestowed. The divine Personality, indeed, never makes an appearance in Kant's corpus. And this is why in the last analysis the entire Kantian eschatology is threatened by conversion into immanence. It could all so easily be reduced through demythologization to a moralizing humanism. And yet Kant was far from starry-eyed. His hope for history, which issued in calls for a league of nations and a rejection of war as a means of policy, was tempered by the realization that, in his own metaphor, man is made from bent wood that is not readily straightened. Nothing much can be achieved lest Providence wills it so. History has the meaning the human spirit gives it in an exchange with the grace that alone can make perfect.

This sounds pious enough. But all the later Idealist philosophers in Germany had to do was identify Kant's view of Providence with his doctrine of the divine spark in the soul, and off they could go on their great aprioristic speculative endeavours. At the end of his life Kant himself placed less and less credence in the resources of practical reason alone – the experiential helpfulness of regulative ideas as such. Yet it was the notion of development (*Entwicklung*) as regulative idea for history that would inspire others, such as Fichte.

A First Glimpse of Schiller

So Kant left an ambiguous legacy to his successors. They were inclined to systematize the mystical metaphysics of the soul as divine spark – to make of Kant's eschatology precisely a doctrine of immanence. What is going on, Balthasar thinks, is the emergence with a *neue Endlehre*, a 'new doctrine of the End', of a *neuer Mensch*, a 'new human being' – to which, to be sure, Herder's eschatology is also pertinent. Kant's philosophy of spirit (highly analytic) plus Herder's philosophy of nature (highly enthusiastic) provided foundations for this 'new humanity'. The problem was how to bond them together.

This is where the dramatist-philosopher Johann Christoph Friedrich Schiller (1759–1805) enters Balthasar's picture gallery.

Beginning – philosophically speaking – as a pupil of the metaphysician Gottfried Wilhelm von Leibniz (1646–1716) and the moralist Anthony Ashley Cooper, earl of Shaftesbury (1670–1712/3), Schiller became a dissident Kantian in his middle period, developing his aesthetic theories *against* the new master, before in his mature writing dedicating himself to the task of synthesizing the work of Kant and Herder. The aim was to show the 'lived rhythm' which unites spirit and nature. This is what makes Schiller for Balthasar the 'real founder of the new generation'.[24] Schiller's idea of beauty as *erscheinende Freiheit*, 'freedom appearing', gives the key. In *The Critique of Judgment*, Kant interprets beauty as our response to the seeming design or purposiveness of the natural world. For Kant, the aesthetic is the tell-tale sign of a suitably teleological (and thus to a degree Herderian) view of nature. For Herder, if beauty is the 'last, most precious bloom on nature',[25] this is because beauty gives us a surmise of the realm of pure spirit beyond nature's purview (and thus makes way for Kant's most passionately felt concerns). To call beauty, as Schiller does, '*appearing*' freedom is, with Kant, to emphasize its natural reality. To call it appearing '*freedom*' is to say beauty goes beyond the natural – which also, as it happens, goes beyond Herder.

Schiller was a creative literary artist. But like his Romantic successors, he was, as Juliet Sychrava has written: 'primarily concerned with the structure of aesthetic experience and not with art-works as "objects". [The] form which underlies all art is identified with a "poetic" principle which is really just imagination.'[26] If so, then Schiller's aesthetic could well, as Balthasar claims, portend not only a new sensibility but a new eschatology – 'new', not least in the sense that, for the first time among the writers surveyed, classical Christian eschatology gains a competitor worthy of itself.

Like orthodox Catholicism in pre-modern times, Schiller was able to bind together individual eschatology, social eschatology, cosmic eschatology. What differed was the knot that bound them. In the case of the Church, the nodal point (*die Mitte*) was Jesus Christ. The God-man validated individual eschatology in the 'apocalypse' or unveiling in its final destiny of the soul's own innermost 'idea'. He guaranteed cosmic eschatology in the resurrection of the body. He made possible the identity of social eschatology with individual since it was the species and not just the person that the New Adam transformed. For people to strive after this 'eschaton' was both trusting faith and a rational act vis-à-vis a (theologically) knowable object. But once this 'principle' – itself not only transcendental but also existential – was removed by the denial, or at least neglect, of dogmatic confession, the various strands became disengaged one from another. It was Schiller's task to try and reconnect them in a different way – which meant, basically, regarding individual, social and cosmic eschatology as what Balthasar calls 'rays' streaming out from the new 'aesthetic' mid-point that is man-in-the-concrete, *der konkrete Mensch*.

And this is what Balthasar has in mind when now he speaks of the

24 Ibid., p. 125.
25 Ibid.
26 J. Sychrava, *From Schiller to Derrida: Idealism in Aesthetics* (Cambridge 1989), p. 128.

Dionysian soul. The Christian soul focuses eschatologically on a reality beyond it, namely Christ. It is faith that 'goes out from oneself to Christ', *von sich weg zu Christus hin.* The Dionysian soul focuses on its own inner existence. The comparison is with the figure of Dionysus in Greek mythology – a god of vegetation, of resuscitated life, a god of wine who loosens care and inspires to music. Dionysian faith is faith 'in oneself, addressed to one's own depths and divinity', *in sich hinein an die eigene Tiefe and Göttlichkeit.* Balthasar takes Christian faith to be 'Christ-objective', sober, 'en-spiriting' – in other words, in receipt of the Holy Spirit from the Father and the Son. Dionysian faith, by contrast, is subjective, intoxicated enthusiasm. It is in fact enthusiasm in its literal or etymological sense, for it seeks to awaken the god within, the *En-Theos.* As has been said of the (nearly contemporary) English Romantics: 'The poets' concern with "the human mind, its self-contained and constituent energies, its active transcendental powers" gained ground over their interest in "external nature and sensation and the language of the sense".'[27] The concrete human being is to send out 'revealing rays' that encompass with an aureole the great world and God himself, and all in relation to *this* man, Dionysian man, of whose 'faith', for Schiller, Christopher Columbus, not Peter the apostle, is the paradigm. (As in Schiller's poem, *Kolumbus.*)

Nonetheless, Christianity is for Schiller 'the only aesthetic religion' because it represents the humanization (incarnation) of the holy and thus *die schöne Sittlichkeit*, 'beautiful morality'. For Balthasar, German Idealism cannot be understood save as a response to Christianity. 'Its only theme is the incarnation of the holy as the concrete apocalypse of the soul.'[28] Unfortunately, at least as represented by Schiller, its 'life-rhythm' is a tragic one. Its lack of any transcendental object (like all modern eschatologies, it is 'formally subjective') condemns it to a perpetual oscillation between enthusiasm on the one hand, doubt and anxiety on the other. Schiller shows no final confidence that the truth that inhabits the 'summer riches' of 'appearance' in enthusiastic love, a feeling for the 'eternal' spirit in man, myth-filled Hellenic existence, is *more* true – a better guide to reality – than the 'winter landscape' of scientific physiology, the bewildering facticity of death, critical reason, or the cold asceticism of Christianity. For these contrasts no resolution is offered.

Balthasar will return to Schiller. Meanwhile, he wants to mention one last aspect of the new problematic. And that is the periodization of history Schiller had worked out by the time of the celebrated 'Letters on the Aesthetic Education of Man', the *Über die ästhetische Erziehung des Menschen*, of 1795. The fulfilment of humankind as 'beauty' happens by way of our confrontation with potentially tragic choices in ethics, since it is tragedy that discloses the higher beauty of which we are capable. In a nutshell: whereas Hellenism treated human beauty as natural, the Kantian Enlightenment introduced a dualism insuperable on its own level. But a higher synthesis lies in the human future. As found in plants and animals, organic nature – thus runs Schiller's thinking – already strives for the highest and greatest albeit

27 J.W. Beach, *The Concept of Nature in Nineteenth Century English Poetry* (New York 1936; 1966), pp. 25–26, citing S.F. Gingerich, *Essays in the Romantic Poets* (New York 1929).
28 *Apokalypse I*, p. 128.

without willing it, and this is a first inchoate sketch of freedom. (Human artworks show exteriorly what nature demonstrates interiorly in this respect, thereby making the artist an image of the Creator.) The human being shares 'architectonic' beauty with the beasts but as spirit he must make incarnate in full freedom a new form of the beautiful, what Shaftesbury had called 'moral grace', to be possessed not only in body but in mind. But as Schiller ruefully recognized, in dependence on Kant, human nature is delivered over to influences which disable this happy progression. And there's the rub. The Dionysian soul cannot guarantee the synthesis of nature and freedom. Despite Schiller's talk of the 'aesthetic play' of their relations, it confronts an alternative: salvation or, dare it be said, damnation. Schiller will recur in this story, but for the time being, Balthasar leaves him hanging.

The Prometheus Principle

'Prometheus' was the title Balthasar would give the second – but unaltered – edition of the opening volume of *Apokalypse der deutschen Seele*, when it was reprinted after the Second World War. This is an index of the importance he attached to the 'Prometheus principle' to which he now especially attends. Its flowering time was the only period fit to compare, eschatologically speaking, with the Christian Middle Ages. So which period was that? Balthasar is speaking of the era of Fichte, Schelling, Baader, Hegel, Schopenhauer; the age of (among others) Goethe, Schiller, Hölderlin, Novalis, Jean Paul, the Schlegels, Kleist. (We shall meet them in the course of this account so there is no need to give more detail now.) Though philosophers and poets have close affinities in the Germany of this period, the first set of names – the philosophers – testify to the intellectual powers of that age, even if the latter are, remarks Balthasar, 'not fully living'. The second set – the poets – attest the 'vital-emotional' capabilities that correspond to these intellectual capacities, even if these vital-emotional powers are themselves, in his words, 'not fully formed'.[29] These somewhat obscure criticisms at least show the influence on Balthasar of, respectively, late nineteenth- and early twentieth- century vitalism – *Lebensphilosophie*, and the ancient Hellenic – but also Goethean – philosophy of form.

The 'system' of the classical German philosophy of this period Balthasar characterizes as a collocation of all human 'part-realities' in a creative whole, which the concern for theoretical system reflected. *Totality* – and not system – is what is really important about it, which is why Goethe, who in the first scene of *Faust* rejects system, can still be included in the roll-call. Balthasar would remain, as theologian, favourable to totality-thinking, hostile to system.

The restlessness of the epoch, full of apocalyptic expectation, arose from the sense that life is beginning to reveal a 'comprehensive logic'. The attitude was: now or never must the day of truth dawn – as texts from Novalis, Friedrich von Schlegel, and above all Goethe bear witness. Far removed from the self-satisfaction of the rationalist Enlightenment, German Idealism's *Grundbewegung*, its 'basic movement', is inwards. World, nature, the 'not-I': all these objects are necessary to it as, in Balthasar's words: 'the mirror of

29 Ibid., p. 139.

what is within, the way to it, and so a part of it ... [I]n the kindling of the
outer light, the inner light flames up yet higher – in the image [is illuminated]
the archetype'.[30] Congruently, von Schlegel could take Kant's 'discovery' of
the transcendental subject as a sign that the self seeks through all its capabilities to find its own 'centre'. The presumption was that the self could only
find its centre 'ex-centrically', at its border or limit (*Grenze*).

So the 'movement' which underlies post-Kantian thought and sensibility
is a double one. There is not just movement to the centre *from* that circumference which is nature or the cosmic 'all'. There is also movement *to* the
circumference, as – so Balthasar puts it – 'to the wholeness of "God", of the I,
of spirit'.[31] (Balthasar places the word 'God' here within inverted commas
because the degree of overlap between the understanding of God in Idealism
and in Christian metaphysics is debatable.) And, says Balthasar, for all the
writers under discussion, the intersection of these two movements is man.
With the world, man is oriented in his total being to God; with God he is
oriented in his total being to the world. As Balthasar puts it, man is the *dia* in
dia-logos. He is the one through whom the divine Word to the world comes to
be. And this leads to the conclusion that God himself is 'absolute only in the
totality of the relative. [God] is the eternal through time, [God is] the non-
dependent through the dependent'.[32]

Of course, it would be false to say of God that he might not have been or
that he might have been temporal or relative. And yet, for this series of
philosophies joined by family-likeness, God can only be God if the
non-self-subsistent being, time and relativity of nature – God's mirror –
themselves exist. The *'dia'* that in twofold fashion 'goes through' the human
being, making him or her what he or she is, does not simply signal a dialogue
of love, though a Christian misunderstanding of the religious vocabulary of
Idealism might lead us to think so. A triangular love affair joining God, man,
the world, is not perhaps excluded. But there is a key prior stage. The really
primordial law is not dialogue but a *dialectic* in which *God's own being itself
comes to be for the first time*. That the selfsame *dia* is also *man's* first law as well
as God's makes this the 'law for a full apocalypse'. There is a new goal here –
a new mysticism going beyond what the usual ways of 'understanding,
reason, religion' attain,[33] which is as much as to say, going beyond Christianity. The 'pain' of dialectic (Hegel's term) is that each of the two movements this new goal calls for – a movement from nature through man to God,
and a movement from God through man to the world, can only fulfil itself
against the other. They cross. And hence they crucify. The first movement –
from nature through man to God – calls for entire self-giving, *Hingabe-
ganzheit*; the second movement – from God through man to the world – calls
for the exercise of unrestricted creativity, *schöpferische Ganzheit*. Each of these
plays traitor to the other. Whoever could bring off both together? This is the
primal tragedy of mystical dialectics, and in 1773 the young Goethe found
the perfect image for it in the myth of Prometheus.

---

30 Ibid., p. 141.
31 Ibid., p. 142. The ambiguity of the word 'God' here is also signalled by its juxtaposition
    with 'I' (and 'spirit').
32 Ibid., p. 143.
33 J.W. von Goethe, *Maximen und Reflexionen*, III, 'Aus Makariens Archiv', in *Sämtlicher
    Werke*, IV. (Stuttgart-Berlin 1903), pp 234–41.

The Prometheus symbol, not least in Goethe's appeal to it, had attracted nineteenth- and early twentieth-century scholars and Balthasar accepted Goethe's cue – even if the fact that Goethe's focus of interest shifted via Prometheus to Lucifer was not exactly encouraging.[34] (There is, presumably, some kind of imaginative and even conceptual link between the fire-bringing hero of the ancients and the light-bringing archangel of Judaeo-Christian tradition.) In the Promethean mythology Balthasar finds in operation what he terms a 'pre-personal dialectic' whereby not only guilt and redemption but also creation and 'Incarnation' originate from 'deep necessity' – precisely the view of the later Goethe. That is meant as a criticism. In Christianity, of course, creation, Incarnation, redemption (like, from the human side, guilt) are undertaken not out of necessity at all. They come sheerly from freedom.

Prometheus was a mediator between the gods and the world. He was so through defying the will of Zeus for the good of man – and the ultimate harmony of all things. In a nutshell, then, Prometheus represents 'creative negation as the dynamic cosmic centre between "the One" and "the All"'.[35] For this renewed mythology, the world is nothing other than 'fall from and return to the Original', and its cosmic rhythm, self-contradictory though it be, becomes conscious in humankind. Goethe was only twenty-four when he produced his incomplete poem cycle on Prometheus. But for Balthasar he had managed to put into language the basic attitude of the entire coming generation, constituting as its members did the golden age of German literary and philosophical culture. Others will echo it: Schelling, for example, when in *Bruno* he calls the Prometheus symbol the 'inclination to set the infinite in the finite – and vice versa',[36] the reciprocal dissolution of God into the world and the world into God, with man as mediating centre of this process. But it is Fichte, reckoned by the manuals to be the first fully-fledged Idealist in German philosophy, who gives the most comprehensive initial statement of a world-view for which the human task is to be the 'eye of God looking at the world, the eye of the world looking at God'.[37]

Fichte

Johann Gottlieb Fichte (1762–1814) invokes the Prometheus symbol in the context both of political ethics (the *Staatslehre*) and of religious interiority (his *Religionslehre*). The *scintilla animae* – the divine spark in the human soul – is so absolutely the law and centre of a world that God himself has no power to determine it. That could be Kantianism – the apotheosis of the sense of moral obligation – but Fichte's emphasis lies resolutely on *freedom*. Freedom renders spirit indifferent to not only world but also God *insofar as world and God are other than its own law*. Balthasar, as a young Jesuit, was aware how *Indifferenz* – *indiferencia* – was also a key term in St Ignatius's (1491–1556) vocabulary. But the context was utterly different. *Christian* indifference is exercised in

---

34 Balthasar mentions: E. von Lasaulx, *Prometheus: Der Mythos und seine Bedeutung* (Würzburg 1843); O. Walzel, *Das Prometheus Symbol von Shaftesbury bis Goethe* (Munich 1932, 2nd edition); F. Saran, *Goethes Mahomet und Prometheus* (Halle 1914).

35 *Apokalypse I*, p. 147.

36 Cited in ibid., p. 155.

37 Ibid., p. 156.

relation to 'value distinctions between worldly things from out of an ever greater, self-transcending love for God'.[38]

This does not prevent Balthasar from ascribing to Fichte an 'eschatological attitude to life': an attitude determined by, but also determining, Fichte's thought. With such German Idealists, *Kritik* does not, so Balthasar explains, enjoy its normal sense. It is not to be translated 'criticism', much less 'opposition'. Rather, *Kritik* is *the representation of metaphysics from the standpoint of life*. This is controversial. For Balthasar, Fichte is (despite appearances) a thinker supremely concerned with 'existence', someone who distinguishes formal knowledge from 'real philosophy' and treats systematic thought as simply the crystallization of living experience. Dogmatism, not realism, is the antonym of his Idealism, where 'dogmatism' stands for concepts putatively generated by 'things in themselves' (Kant's *Ding an sich* – which to Fichte is a self-contradiction, for a mere 'thing' can never be *an sich*, a true 'in itself'). Fichte's aim was to go beyond Kant by connecting a range of epistemological, ontological and religious themes in a unifying philosophy that turns on the finite self in its relation to absolute reality. In saying as much, all historians of philosophy would agree. But that is the limit of the consensus. Balthasar's seemingly anachronistic attempt to present Fichte's thought in the light of the concerns of vitalism – *Lebensphilosophie* – is partly vindicated, however, by Fichte's last writings. For the purpose of those writings is to manifest the infusion into finite individuality of absolute reality in the form of the power of love.[39]

As almost any encyclopaedia entry will tell us, the root of Fichte's system of transcendental Idealism is the proposition A = A. For Balthasar, this is not because Fichte's thought is logic-dominated. It is not, in fact, on *logical* grounds that Fichte posits such a fundamental axiom. That basic proposition, A = A, gives, rather, the formula of spirit (*Geist*). And the formula reads, spirit alone is 'for itself' in its self-illumination and freedom. To Fichte, the only real positivity is freedom. 'Being' (*Sein*) is a purely negative concept, not only derivative but derived more specifically from counter-distinction to activity. The 'within' of *Geist* is more than just being (which is how presumably supporters of the 'analogy of being' would consider it). *Geist* occupies centre stage, then, or should do, whenever metaphysics asks after the 'ground' of being – which cannot itself be simply being or else it would not constitute being's ground. From this the key tenet of Idealism follows, to whit: only by way of *Geist* can we grasp *that* a thing is and *what* it is.

The proposition A = A holds good for *finite* spirit, however, only in a fashion that falls short of perfect identity. The identity of finite spirit is a synthesis between being and freedom, so the predicate – the second 'A' in the formula – can only be synthetically ascribed to the subject, the first 'A'. It does not, as would be the case for *perfect* identity, belong to it analytically, by the definition of terms. The perfect identity of A = A belongs only to the Absolute: that is, to unconditional freedom. Still, a synthesis is not a product, a mere effect. So finite spirit can be said at least to *participate* in the Absolute.

The task of metaphysics is to seize spirit's primal act of self-possession and render it in terms of knowing. Only act, *Tat*, is primordially real,

38 Ibid., p. 157.
39 Thus above all *Die Anweisung zum seligen Leben* of 1806.

primordially true. And act is only unimpaired in its freedom when it goes ahead of the 'what' of things. But ordered knowing, such as one expects to find in a *Wissenschaftslehre* of the sort Fichte purports to offer, deals precisely with the scheme of things, the 'what' of things in its internally differentiated yet harmonious unity.[40] Act, then, appears to be at one and the same time the supremely rational (because primally true) and yet the irrational (since in itself impervious to knowledge). The paradox can only be resolved by proposing a mutual priority of act and knowledge. But such a reciprocal priority requires explanation. Fichte finds its ground in an *Urakt*, an unconditionally foundational act of intellectual activity where something is known because it is done. This, the ground of all consciousness, all experience, is not itself conscious, not itself the act of an experiencing subject. It is the 'point-source' of the 'I' wherever being an 'I', *Ichheit*, be found. It is the *Ich an sich*, the 'I-in-itself', even the question of whose ground cannot be raised without falling into contradiction.

To say as much inevitably invites us to ask what is the place in Fichte's thought of the concept of God. For 'God' is what all men call the Source whence all else flows. From one point of view, *Ichheit* or the 'I-form' is the true transcendentally unifying power in reality, and, as we have seen, *Ichheit* is not itself conscious, not even 'super-conscious' – which is how Fichte characterizes God. From another point of view, however, God in his perfect self-identity (his light, says Fichte, is always simply light and not the composition of the illuminating and the illuminated) remains for finite consciousness the 'eternal idea' which should regulate its progress. These two versions (one of the *archê*, the principle, the other of the *telos*, the goal) remain side by side in Fichte's account just as they do, for Balthasar, in Fichte's fundamental experience. They are reflected in the notion of the reciprocal priority of act and knowledge, but the difficulty of handling their interrelation becomes ever more acute in Fichte's own intellectual development.

Was Fichte recognizably a theist at all? His contemporaries put this question heatedly. The *Atheismusstreit*, where he defended himself against the charge of atheism – not a bagatelle in a Lutheran monarchy at the time of the French Revolution – led to a certain internal realignment of the elements of his thought. Nevertheless, it remained the case that, for Fichte, divine freedom, as grounded in itself, is one with human freedom insofar as the latter is self-grounded likewise. This 'insofar as' is for Balthasar the Achilles' heel of Fichtean Idealism, separating it for ever from Christian metaphysics while at the same time determining it as a philosophical system.

> If this 'insofar as' necessarily implies the inseparability of the Absolute and the relative (as their mutual grounding being), the freedom of God (always understood as absolute, ungrounded!) is of necessity inextricably interwoven with the puzzle of mutuality and thus with the dual dialectic of the concepts of the necessary and the contingent.[41]

The basic problem lies with Fichte's construal of his fundamental experience

---

40 Fichte presents the *Wissenschaftslehre* as the transcendent form of all knowledge. It unifies the formally disparate and empirically conditioned branches of learning in an unbroken organic continuity.

41 *Apokalypse I*, p. 169.

of a 'within' in relation to which *being* is merely a derivative concept. For all
his dislike of textbook neo-Scholasticism, Balthasar will never abandon the
Thomist conviction that the key to all adequate philosophy is a recognition of
the primacy of being.

He will return to explore more consequences of Fichte's basic – and
problematic – philosophical option. Meanwhile, he needs to look more closely at how Fichte grounds the definitive – eschatological – inter-relation of
Absolute and non-Absolute in finite spirit.

The (clearly stated) presupposition of Fichte's account is that consciousness's highest result is clear and complete self-awareness – which is
authentic freedom. Yet 'result' can hardly be the right word. What emerges
from consciousness here is nothing less than the freedom of the 'for itself',
and such freedom is just what provides consciousness with its own ground,
its own possibility. The explanation is that the sheer act of intelligence is
indeed the first and highest reality, but this 'sheer act' must allow itself to be
clarified. Hence the Fichtean axiom, 'The I posits itself as determined through
the not-I.' It is meaningless, in Fichte's eyes, to ask what the 'not-I' was
'before' this (or indeed to ask what the 'I' was, for that matter). For Fichte,
knowing (*Wissen*) should be compared to a freedom which, though genuinely free, can only *be* under definite conditions.

In the upshot, consciousness clarifies gradually, as self-positing is matched by the positing of what is other than the self. Only step by step does it
become apparent – both in Fichte's *Wissenschaftslehre* and in the world
beyond the text – what we eternally are. In his preface(s) to the successive
versions of this work, Fichte maintains there are two ways in which to
approach the matter. *Either* one can begin with the fundamental laws of
mind, and derive from there the ways in which its activity must necessarily
take place, and the objective representations, *Vorstellungen*, that arise with
that activity. *Or* one can treat these laws in their direct application to objects,
which means to their own deepest level, *Stufe*. In both cases, what transpires
is the 'ideal' genesis of mind from its own form – which is also its 'real'
development as consciousness moves upward from level to level. In the 1794
edition of the *Wissenschaftslehre*, Fichte explains his preference for the first
method, which alone overcomes the temptations of determinism and materialism. The a posteriori 'real' developmental unfolding of mind has as its
model the a priori ideal 'self-construction' of the intellect.

In what sense, it may be asked, is the former rooted in experience? Fichte's
answer, conveyed by Balthasar, is twofold. It is linked to experience inasmuch as its starting-point is a free act of self-consciousness taking itself as
object. It concerns experience because it is a free construction of experience
and finds its verification there. Balthasar himself puts it like this. I am
someone whose consciousness has come to be for me in a passive fashion.
But I experience myself in that consciousness as 'un-become', *ungeworden*,
and active in the most straightforward sense. 'Real' genesis seems to be
chronologically primary. But that is no objection, for the conditioning power
(which only apparently is what has been conditioned) is outside time.

Fichte's philosophy tries to deduce the whole of experience from the
possibility of self-consciousness. Balthasar's response is: yes, but Fichte
presumes there *is* a self-consciousness. That is, he fails to raise the question of
creation. Fichte represents the 'I' as itself a source of representation. That for

him is philosophy's highest task. But he explicitly states that, in and of itself, what is highest about the human spirit could be some quite different determination. However, in Balthasar's eyes, this concession renders problematic Fichte's whole project, by calling into question the priority of the ideal genesis of mind vis-à-vis its 'real' development.

Contrastingly, Christian metaphysics is much more satisfactory. Helpfully, it presupposes the 'I-reality', *Ichwirklichkeit*, of God, precisely in order that there may be the real *Ichheit* or I-form of Fichte's analysis – precisely, that is, in order that there may be finite consciousness of a kind that can synthesize all the non-identical contents of awareness with its own identity. Thus: 'self-thinking finite thought can presuppose for itself its own real possibility (which is possible through the reality of God)'.[42] Fichte's concept of God limps because he wants to regard God at one and the same time as unconditionally absolute (God as freedom) and yet also as only relatively absolute (God as idea). For Fichte, God is God because he posits himself as *sein-sollend*, 'One who ought to be'. He is already absolute only because he 'ought to realise himself as the Absolute through the non-Absolute'. Rather after the fashion of mid twentieth-century 'process theology', being without becoming and being through becoming are here placed on the same level.

This is for Balthasar the 'single root of German Idealism as a whole'.[43] It all turns on a postulate of the reciprocal priority of what is absolute *simpliciter* and what is only relatively absolute. Balthasar calls its world-view the philosophy of 'mystical potentiality'. He considers it to be Plotinianism *redivivus*, for that neo-Platonist thinker constitutes, he holds, a half-way house between ancient Greek metaphysics and Christianity. The divine *dynamis* in Plotinus (205–270) is charged with the same ambiguity as God's possibility or capacity, *Möglichkeit, Vermögen*, in Fichte. It is at once both the free power of the divine and also the activity which realizes a world *and is itself only through that realization*. And the upshot is: God as God, in himself, yes; but also God as God *through the world*. At this point, 'mystical potentiality' and Prometheanism coincide. As Fichte put it in *Die Bestimmung der Gelehrten*, he had grasped what determined him, and it was abiding: 'it is everlasting, and I am everlasting, like it'.[44]

In effect Fichte treads a middle way between a Christian-theistic metaphysic and its Hegelian-pantheistic rival. Balthasar has proclaimed, at least, that his chief interest in *Apokalypse* will be the existential message of the thinkers he discusses. Seen as an evaluation of life, Fichte's system has two summits (Balthasar's metaphor). One is thinking itself, *Denken*, through which God comes to self-consciousness in man. The other is vision, *Anschauung*, and in this mood – if for so austere a philosopher the term be allowed – Fichte treats all thought as merely schematic, or imagistic, in comparison with the only really valuable activity, that of transparency to the other.

In the effort to answer his own question – what basic attitude to existence does Fichte have? – Balthasar comes up with the notion of *Schweben*, the swinging of a pendulum, suspended between two fixed points. For Fichte's

---

42 Ibid., p. 174.
43 Ibid., p. 176.
44 Cited in ibid., p. 177.

deductive method, the basic form of synthesizing thought is creative imagination overcoming all 'rigid' categories in its dynamic movement between
otherwise counterposed realities – precisely so as to mediate between them.
'The highest knowledge remains an oscillation, *ein Schweben*, between subject
and object.'[45] In knowing, objectivity is not destroyed. It is revealed as a
necessary mode of subjectivity. 'Thinking only exists as an oscillation
between appearance and the one to whom appearance appears. But precisely
as such is it necessarily transcendental Idealism.'[46]

However, the ethical demands of the world force me to live not speculatively but by the 'real I'. 'Doing is the truth of thinking.'[47] Theoretical
considerations urged Fichte towards a conclusion he already considered
existentially desirable. The very structure of 'mystical potentiality' grants
thinking its positive role only when our freedom of consciousness is turned
into performance, for this gives expression to our relation to the absolute,
itself unconditional freedom of deed. Existentially, to try and think out the
basis of moral imperative (the 'ought of life') rather than to enact it is to
divert attention from its meaning, which is what really counts about it. I must
'live in obedience', remarks Fichte in the *Bestand des Menschen*, if I am to have
the truth. Fichte recognizes in fact the priority of the practical, to which, in his
view, the theoretical is subordinated as an instrument. Balthasar points out
how by implication this destroys the absolute character Fichte ascribes to
knowing.

It also points Fichte's way to that existential posture finite spirit should, he
thinks, adopt. The highest, wisest knowing is 'penetration', *Durchschauen*, in
which the strangeness of the world we experience as counterposed to us
disappears and the knowing agent finds instead spiritual – indeed, divine –
life. This Fichte hails in *Bestand des Menschen* as 'the eternal stream of life and
power and deed, of primordial life, – of *your* life, O Infinite'.[48] Balthasar calls
it (on Fichte's behalf) the 'eschatological meaning of knowing', and ascribes
to it ever greater prominence in Fichte's world-view.[49] It is intersected,
however, by a second principle of equal importance for the eschatological
orientation in Fichte's philosophy, and this is the principle of 'practical
appropriation', *praktische Aneignung*. Thinking only provides the concept of
the divine life (so understood). It can only assist doing in an external, ped-
agogical fashion.

My hitherto blind will needs to be able to see, and grasp, its own idea in
freedom. This is the emphasis of the 1810 edition of the *Wissenschaftslehre*,
which Balthasar calls the 'most light-filled' of all its versions. The 'dream of
thinking' is true insofar as its brightness leads to the illumination of the will.
It is *will* that binds idea and deed together, the realm of the invisible with the
realm of the visible. Here alone the bare schema of divine life, as available to
knowing, is filled with reality. Through the voice of conscience the spiritual
world bends down to me and counts me as among its members. Through free

45 Ibid., p. 179.
46 Ibid.
47 Ibid., p. 181.
48 Cited in ibid., p. 182.
49 Ibid., p. 183.

ethical obedience I raise myself to the level of the spiritual world, grasp it and become effective in it. Will unending is the source of that world – and of me.

Balthasar provides a useful shorthand for these two 'principles'. The first is intellectual mysticism; the second is practical mysticism. The ultimate attitude Fichte wants us to adopt unites the two: it is at one and the same time *both* 'eternity-contemplating rapture', *Entrückung* – a key term of Balthasar's future theological aesthetics, *and* 'believing deed' – a phrase highly applicable, at any rate, to his theological dramatics.[50] As Balthasar explains, for Fichte: 'The beatific vision begins already here on earth and endures for all eternity. Contemplating, man has grasped his idea in God, and, grasped by this idea, everything in this world becomes for him transparent to God.'[51] Those who say, 'We have here no lasting city but seek one that is to come' (Fichte means, of course, orthodox Christians)[52] are correct in their fundamental assertion. Dying to this world, born anew, beginning to live here another life, Christians are 'practical transcendental Idealists' without knowing it.

Balthasar is not convinced. On the one hand, I am immortal, for Fichte, as soon as I grasp the decision to obey the law of [ethical] reason (and not before). And on the other hand, even in eternity to embody the perfect idea of humanity will be for me an 'unattainable limit-concept'. Man can never become divine, abandoning all individuality to be assumed completely into the Absolute, but through assimilating as much of the noumenal essence as his individuated form can contain he can nonetheless be involved in a process of self-perfection, self-divinization.

If the contrast with the orthodox Christian doctrine of divinization is plain, the difference from Kant's eschatology is also palpable. For Kant, the 'ought' is duty, simply, and can be synthesized with happiness only by divine action. For Fichte, the 'ought' is not only duty; it is the source of my eternal being, and thereby it is itself my bliss. In eternity I am not merely to look (as the language of the 'beatific vision' suggests). The notion of an eternity that is *only* vision struck Fichte as a residue of 'Orientalism' and 'Jewish chiliasm' in Christianity. More adequate was to conceive beatitude as 'the everlasting coinherence of transfigured looking and transfiguring doing'.[53] Balthasar treats Fichte's eschatology as the typical existential eschatology of Promethean man. But it was not without its influence on him. It seems to be by a debt to this eschatology (and its refraction in Hegel), as well as to certain sayings of the Catholic saints, that in the final volume of his theological dramatics, Balthasar expended energy on rethinking what we may be about in heaven. He did not find the language of beatific vision wholly adequate, any more than Fichte had. It needed complementing – here he agreed with Fichte – by something more active. In the pages of *Apokalypse* he certainly seems to exempt the 'reciprocity of vision and deed' from any negative animadversions he may want to make on 'mystical potentiality'.

Yet the discontinuities are as striking as the continuity. There is no place for *grace* in Fichte's account. His futurist social eschatology – which points to

50 Ibid., p. 185.
51 Ibid.
52 Cf. Hebrews 13.14.
53 *Apokalypse I*, p. 187.

humankind building itself up in reason 'with sure and infallible hand' as the *Grundzüge des gegenwärtigen Zeitalters* puts it, is but the corporate equivalent to how he sees the future of the individual human being. He or she will progress from a life of instinct through the freedom of 'oscillation' to the visionary self-understanding and 'realizing deed' that fill the Fichtean Paradise. The younger Fichte sees this naturalistically, as taking place in some kind of cosmic environment. The elder Fichte, remarks Balthasar laconically, spread over it 'the silence of the wise'.[54]

Of course, Fichte's belief about God (in relation to man) becomes here an unavoidable topic, just as after the *Atheismusstreit* his own thoughts turned more and more to religion. As he comes increasingly to stress the 'existentiality of finitude', so 'oscillation' becomes evermore the key to his thinking. There is oscillation between a divinized world and the God who lies beyond all finitude. The world swings out in the direction of the God beyond it, and in this movement (we recall Balthasar's earlier comments on the 'twofold *dia*' in Fichte's grounding intuition) God himself swings out over his own *Abgrund*, his 'abyss' – over, namely, what is outside himself.

Existence is now for Fichte 'ex-sistence': being outside God. The 'truth' of existence is when this 'ex' becomes self-aware, in which moment existence becomes 'being-outside-itself back to God'. (There is a clear resemblance here to the *egressus/regressus* scheme of neo-Platonism for which all things emerge from the One and can, through mind, *nous*, return to It – a scheme given Christian application by Thomas Aquinas in the shape of his *Summa Theologiae*.) Though Fichte has no doctrine of grace, he *does*, in this context, have a doctrine of love. This descending and ascending movement expresses the *Schwebe* of absolute knowledge which in its active achievement, '*tathafte Vollzug*', is love.

Balthasar inserts here a brilliant attempt at intellectual cross-referencing. For Fichte, individual persons only really differ *ratione materiae* – inasmuch as they are differently embodied. Fundamentally, there is only one all-divine personal reality which 'loves' in its living image. Terms like 'love', 'light', 'life' in Fichte hover uncertainly between two sets of connotations, one Christian (if not Johannine then at least Eckhartian), and the other pagan or neo-pagan, combining at will features of Plotinianism and the Dionysian visions of the later Nietzsche. There is a paradox here. The rise of Idealism was empowered by a personalist reaction against the reifying tendencies of not only empiricism but also rationalism. And yet Idealism issues – in the way just described – in the destruction of the person.[55]

Balthasar wants to avoid the term 'pantheism' in this connexion, sharing Goethe's view that it says both everything and nothing. The world of Fichte is not God, but rests on the divine freedom, which is God's being. It will be transfigured only by an eschatological movement back to God. It touches God directly only at a tangent, in love – in Fichte's peculiar sense of the word where what is at stake is the *form of knowing*, the complete 'for-itself' which as form is identical with the 'for-himself' of God: namely, his substantial essence. God is the perfection of all human faculties, moral and aesthetic as well as epistemological. His essence *is* absolute knowledge. Man's vocation is

54 Ibid., p. 189.
55 Ibid., p. 194.

gradually to bridge the gap between itself and infinity through harmonization with the divine.

This emphasis on love as the unifying centre of both intellectual and moral freedom (what Balthasar earlier called 'intellectual and pragmatic mysticism') is the new thing as Fichte's creative work draws to its close. This is to Balthasar's mind the 'unique beauty' of Fichte's achievement in the 'form-world of Idealist eschatology'. Amazingly, Fichte's last stab at an eschatology (in *Anweisung zum seligen Leben*) takes Mary's Assumption as a model, seeing it as the proper outworking of the words 'I am the handmaid of the Lord, be it done to me as he wills'.[56] What the glorified Mother shows is 'beauty in a determinate form'.[57] As Balthasar interprets him: 'The rapture of Mary into everlasting beauty takes unconscious form as beautiful appearing, and the artist who, contemplating this rapture, grasps it is himself beautiful inasmuch as he expresses this vision both as action and in form.'[58]

No wonder Balthasar could say that in Fichte the (neo-pagan) 'mystical potentiality' still struggled for mastery with a genuine impulse of *Christian* mysticism.[59]

56 Luke 1.38.
57 Cited in *Apokalypse I*, p. 201.
58 Ibid.
59 Ibid., p. 204.

6

From Schelling to Goethe

Schelling

Friedrich Wilhelm Joseph von Schelling (1775–1859) begins as an enthusiastic pupil of Fichte, but from the first a new breath blows. Soon separation will lead to hostility. Once again, a new eschatology, a new apocalyptic, makes itself known. Balthasar takes it as the key to what would otherwise be the bewildering variety of Schellingian thought patterns. These changes of mind, though fortunately less numerous than in Fichte's intellectual development, are more radical in their re-orientation. After Schelling's early period (pre-1800), he moved on from the 'system of identity' in the years 1800–1804 to the 'teaching on freedom' of 1804 to 1810. The Jesuit historian of philosophy, Frederick Copleston, admitted the diversity but also saw a connecting thread of unity, describing Schelling's work as: 'a restless process of reflection moving from the ego philosophy of Fichte through the philosophy of nature and art to the philosophy of the religious consciousness and a form of speculative theism, *the whole being linked together by the theme of the relation between the finite and the infinite'.*[1]

Balthasar regards Schelling, not Hegel, as the climax of German Idealism. Schelling transforms Fichte's 'backward-looking', quasi-Christian existentiality into a much more thoroughgoingly Promethean version of the same. And he puts in place the theoretical principles which Hegel will exploit for his own broader – indeed monumental – work. So Hegel will find the 'new ethos' already there. Here in Schelling 'mystical potentiality' really rules the roost. With Fichte, there was always – despite his Lutheran critics – a tacit or explicit presupposition of the Christian God as sheer act, *actus purus*, which, naturally enough, qualified mystical potentiality thinking. But with Schelling we encounter that thinking in all its radicality. The 'amphiboly', or deliberate ambiguousness, of potency and act, possibility and reality, as Schelling presents these pairings is fundamental to his world-view.

For Balthasar, Schelling is the 'theoretical eschatologist of time' *par excellence.*[2] In the last analysis, Fichte leaves open the future to an inscrutable Providence. Hegel gives the history of the spirit *as it has become*, having nothing to say about what it will be. By contrast, Schelling is only interested,

---

1 F.C. Copleston, SJ, *A History of Philosophy, VII. Fichte to Nietzsche* (London 1968), p. 99. Italics added.
2 *Apokalypse I*, p. 205.

really, in the final upshot of history – which is for him the apocalypse of the living God. Even the style of the man shows it. He writes in 'poetic-prophetic' mode, not ascetically like Fichte, or with outward coolness, after Hegel's fashion. Balthasar compares him with the St John of the book of Revelation. The sole difference between them – but what a difference! – is that the God of one is Christ, of the other Dionysus. For Balthasar considers that Schelling unites Prometheus and Dionysus. This mage of Idealism, accepting the new Promethean starting-point, reveals its true face as Dionysian. His philosophy of the 'ages of the world' does not only situate him before the unknown God but would unveil the God of the future – and God's traits are as the myth suggests.[3]

From the start of his career, Schelling wanted to produce a total world-view. It was to be – *above all* in matters of the eschatological resolution of the world-process – as 'total' as that of Christian Scholasticism. This was, indeed, the fundamental task he set himself. But just how was he to bring world and eternity together in a form (*Gestalt*) as organic as that furnished for orthodox Christianity by the resurrection of the body? Schelling was preoccupied by 'the end-time in its spiritual corporeality', and this, he hoped, in a version which would improve on the Church's eschatology through avoiding all sense of rupture between earth and heaven. Whether 'improvement', thus conceived, is itself reality-founded is of course a moot point.

Schelling could find serviceable elements to hand in the philosophies of Leibniz (which was certainly dynamic) and Baruch Spinoza (1632–1677) (whose theme of spirit and extension as two modes of the divine substance was congenial). But these writers had been read in the 'mathematical, profane atmosphere of the Enlightenment', poisonous as this was to Schelling's project.[4] The exalted religious tone of Plotinus's *Enneads* – and indeed the beginnings of Christian metaphysics in St John's Gospel – could make good the deficiency.

The genesis of Schelling's difference of opinion with Fichte is a subtle one. Fichte had worked with two senses of 'idea'. One was related to the Platonist tradition's 'ideal being'. It is exemplified in Fichte's account of the divine essence as the simple unity of being and freedom in God. The other sense, most at home in Fichte's account of the moral imperative, is much closer to Kant's notion of a regulative ideal. In Fichte's writing, the unity of these two senses of 'idea' is only (in Balthasar's term) 'tangential'. For Schelling, by contrast, they form a single whole. Where Fichte conceived of freedom as the sign of absolute self-possession in being, Schelling did not consider absolute reality in its sheer act-character as separable from that oscillation (*Schwebe*) about the real which entails the equal admission of a considerable dose of *un*reality. In Balthasar's summary affirmation, a different experience of the 'existentiality of oscillation' distinguishes Schelling from Fichte.[5]

---

3 See H. Fuhrmans, *Schellings Philosophie der Weltalter. Schellings Philosophie in den Jahren 1806–1821. Zum Problem des Schellingschen Theismus* (Düsseldorf 1954). See also, for a more theological evaluation, W. Kasper, *Das Absolute in der Geschichte. Philosophie und Theologie der Geschichte in der Spätphilosophie Schellings* (Mainz 1965).

4 *Apokalypse I*, p. 207.

5 Ibid., p. 209.

Schelling on God, Nature, Art

Balthasar considers Schelling's doctrine of God to be a Gnostic one. Schelling deals with the 'real genesis' of God. This is not to be understood in the crude form that God needs to 'await' an historical process before becoming divinely conscious. But nevertheless Schelling thinks in terms of an aeonic process whereby the God who is always act becomes also potency and thus at the same time the tension between potency and act. (Indeed, in *Bruno* the theory of the potencies is made to justify an Idealist interpretation of the Trinity.)[6] It is from this eternal aeonic process that the temporal aeonic process of the world-totality flows as a past, a present and a future. For Balthasar, this structure of thinking about divine genesis in relation to cosmogenesis, and specifically the priority of God as act in this picture as a whole, explains Schelling's emphasis on the philosophy of nature (over against the philosophy of mind or spirit). Why?

For Schelling, nature is the vital first stage of spirit, just as is divine act for what will be the achieved divine consciousness. Cosmic and mental development lay out stages or levels in the relation of subject to object. They do so in such a fashion that the 'potencies' of that relation, which in God are hidden one in another, now come to exist outside each other in time. Indeed, this non-identity of the divine potencies or ideas, as found in the world, is what constitutes temporality as such. Eternity is the realization of a crucial presupposition of the whole process – namely, divine act. Temporality is the realization of what this presupposition posits in the way of becoming. (One has to bear in mind here the punning, or at least ambiguous, quality of the word *Voraussetzung* in this sort of philosophical German. A 'presupposition' is not just a proposition tacitly assumed. It can also be something that is *put in position* first.)

As a subordinated 'moment' of eternity, temporality is both *Realgenesis* – and thus requires the philosophy of nature for its understanding, and also *Idealgenesis* – and so necessitates the deployment of a philosophy of mind. In the years 1797 to 1799 Schelling concentrated on the first of these – and notably on the 'potencies' found in (progressively) the mechanical, the chemical, the organic, all of which are stages in 'objective appearing'. From 1800 onwards, he turned to the second great topic, investigating the stages of subjective appearing found in sensation, perception, reflection and willing. The climax of Schelling's philosophy of nature is the emergence of consciousness – and the discovery that *consciousness was always presupposed to this entire process*. In moral, historical, religious development that idea which was prior to nature is increasingly embodied, in co-fulfilment of a 'putting in place' originally begun in God. As the Schelling scholar Robert Brown puts it:

> Schelling rejects the Kantian phenomenal-noumenal distinction, and affirms that the external objects of our experience are the real objects themselves. The mind does not simply project onto the natural world the structures of its organization. The order of nature is objectively real

6 Thus in this treatise the Son is likened to the finitization of absolute essence in individuated form, the Spirit to the infinite striving of form to regain substantial wholeness. The Father becomes the perfect unity which grasps infinite and finite in one and the same act of divine knowledge.

because unconscious spirit is operative in nature, parallelling the conscious spirit that is the knowing object.[7]

Schelling's philosophy of art, which for Balthasar crowns his transcendental idealism, shows how nature and spirit are not really hierarchized in Schellengian thought. Rather do they count equally. The artistic genius produces his creations unconsciously, after the fashion of nature, as well as freely, after the fashion of mind. In so doing, he reconciles 'real' and 'ideal' aspects of the world process. In the words of Charles Taylor:

> Schiller's notion of the aesthetic as the locus of recovered unity between freedom and necessity is now [in Schelling] given an ontological foundation. Art is the point where the conscious and unconscious meet ... And this meeting-point is ... foreordained in the ontological fact that nature and consciousness have ultimately the same source, subjectivity.[8]

Unconscious and conscious appear together in the artwork. Thus the exploration of aesthetic experience can become the principal organ of philosophy. For the artist, finite and infinite, nature and God are poles apart – and yet, uniquely, the artist brings them together. In the _Philosophie der Kunst_ (1802) Schelling declares art to be in fact 'the only and eternal revelation', since it discloses the mysteries of the Absolute in a way that satisfies both man's self-awareness and his need for union with noumenal reality. In this system, 'aesthetic enthusiasm' brings into mystical potentiality thinking a sort of secularized version of grace.[9] Everything Balthasar calls 'Dionysian' about Schelling circles round this point.

With so much stated, Balthasar has given us the kernel of his Schelling interpretation. The rest of his account fills out these comments by looking at, first, the 'system of mystical potentiality' in its full theoretical form; secondly, its latent existentiality, and thirdly the eschatology which this attitude to existence implies. Let us begin with the first.

Schelling on 'Mystical Potentiality'

Balthasar's account of the 'system of mystical potentiality' is based chiefly, but not exclusively, on three texts: the _Darstellung meines Systems_ of 1801; _Bruno, oder über das göttliche und natürliche Prinzip der Dinge_ of 1802, and, written – but not published – in 1804, the _System der gesamten Philosophie und Naturphilosophie insbesondere_. It is rather odd that Balthasar concentrates on works of this period, the period of the 'philosophy of identity' or 'objective idealism', rather than the 'positive philosophy' of Schelling's last writings – for 'positive' means, not least, incorporating where possible the findings of the historic religions and, above all, Christianity. In his concluding remarks about this philosopher, he will look ahead to his final works. But the concentration on the middle period gives Balthasar's account its particular cast.

Balthasar traces the origin of Schelling's early-mature system from an

---

7 R.F. Brown, _The Later Philosophy of Schelling_ (Lewisburg and London 1977), p. 24.
8 C. Taylor, _Hegel_ (Cambridge 1975), pp. 41–42.
9 It would be left to Kierkegaard to point out how not art but the resolutory narrative of creation, Fall and redemption is the 'true reconciliation' since reconciling me to 'the reality in which I live'. Thus _Samlede Verker_ (Copenhagen 1962), 8, p. 255.

analysis of knowledge as the inner identity between subject and object, knower and known. In the case of the 'highest knowledge', Schelling calls the subject-object identity an 'eternal identity' of which the human 'I' is merely the organ. In a reversal of conventional epistemological expectations: because identity *is*, subject and object are what they are. What is fundamental is not a synthesis, to which subject and object are subordinated. What is fundamental is a higher unity where they are held together by the 'absolute In-itself' of all things: namely, identity.

'Identity' here must be taken, evidently, not in a formal sense but in a real one. It *is* 'of itself the affirming [the "ideal" knowing subject] and the affirmed [the "real" that is known]'.[10] And this is *God as the idea of all things*. Schelling is no less convinced than St Anselm (whom, in due course, Balthasar will draw into this discussion) that it belongs to God's nature, as absolute identity, to be.

Schelling (in the writings of 1801 to 1804 at least) has no proper doctrine of creation.[11] For Balthasar, Schelling's most fundamental assertion is that, once the concept (*der Begriff*) is posited, reality is given. Everything finite has its 'in-itself' outside itself, in God. It literally 'ex-ists'. There is thus in relation to the Absolute a nothingness about things, a *non-esse* as Schelling terms it – and Balthasar will shortly connect this to the 'Plotinian' aspect of the existential attitude Schelling would have us espouse. At the same time, and equally, there is a sense in which things are, in relation to God, divine – and from this Schelling will draw 'Promethean' conclusions far removed from the ethos of the neo-Platonists. As Schelling put it in the – much later – *Stuttgarter Privatvorlesungen* (1810), the primordial being (*das Urwesen*) as absolute identity of real and ideal 'must not only be in itself, but also outside itself'. That is, it must disclose or actualize itself (Schelling treats these terms as synonymous) in the world. The identity of the divinely real-and-ideal active source or *natura naturans* must persist in the (also real-and-ideal) totality of *natura naturata*, the 'all' that appears as the world. Only in totality, for Schelling, can truth be found, just as in true science one proposition only has its place in relation to the other propositions as a whole.

Inevitably, Schelling must confront the issue of the kind of being the finite can be said to enjoy 'in' the Absolute. He was inspired by the words of the Johannine Prologue: 'in him [i.e., the Word] was life'.[12] Schelling takes this to mean that there was and is in God not only divine life but finite, mortal life too. Anselm's *Monologion* had in more orthodox mode anticipated him by its teaching that, according to their unchanging rationale (*ratio*), things exist in

---

10 Cited in *Apokalypse I*, p. 214.
11 The situation would look different from the perspective of, say, the *Über das Wesen der menschlichen Freiheit* of 1809 – which was partly written to rebut Friedrich von Schlegel's charge that Schelling was a pantheist. The notion of the world as an act of divine self-validation whereby God unfolds what is implicit in himself – '*explicatio Dei*' – may not be fully orthodox but it is recognizably some kind of version of the doctrine of creation, in line with the concerns of the late philosophy. In the 'positive philosophy', the final form of Schelling's '*Realidealismus*', God would seem to be the real source of a world rendered coherent by his omnipresence in it. Balthasar's question would no doubt be, however, Is this a Christianization of Idealist thought, or merely of Idealist vocabulary?
12 John 1.4.

their primary truth in God himself.[13] Schelling goes further by requiring philosophy to show just *how* things are in God. In practice, this means to show how in the Absolute the typically finite tension between ideality and reality becomes direct identity. This philosophy can only do if it can draw on the resources of aesthetics, for it is the *forte* of art to uncover universality in the individual and particular.

Schelling is against all dualism, not least that between God and the world, infinite and finite. Fichte had seen the way ahead, but had refused to follow it. What else is his continuing distinction between finite will and the unending divine life if not this great refusal? The ambitiousness of Schelling's anti-dualism becomes plain in *Philosophie und Religion* (1804) where Schelling calls the 'birth' of things 'eternal'. 'The All' *is* God, so long as we add, 'God seen in the infinite consequences of his idea'.[14] What in everyday life we term 'concrete realities' are only relative to being, and hence a mixture of reality and negation. The concrete individual thing, so Schelling wrote, is

> in the All only inasmuch as it is penetrated by the concept of the All, saturated by the infinite, dissolved into the all-being. This dissolution is the true identity of the infinite and the finite. The finite is only in the infinite – but then by that very state it ceases to be the finite.[15]

The term 'dissolution', *Auflösung*, must be carefully handled. It denotes both the end of the single, concrete, individual thing (person) *inasmuch as this is limited*, and the co-constitution of eternal being by the offering of what is not only irreplaceably unique but also infinitely valuable about it (him, or her). *Infinitely* valuable? The adverb tells us that only when a special reality becomes a universe for itself can it be in the universal without restricting the latter.

Schelling's 'Existentiality'

On Schelling's 'existentiality', what existential attitudes might be called congruent with such a picture of the world? Balthasar's inclination is to say that the peculiar combination of positive and negative charges with which Schelling describes both God and the world tend to cancel each other out, leaving this question with no obvious answer.

On the one hand, the Absolute posits the range of 'potencies' outside itself in order to 'appear' in them as in a living mirror. Insofar as the mirror is not the Mirrored, worldly realities are, if not quite nothing, then certainly shadows. To wish to resolve concrete particulars into the divine realm as locus of the true ideas of things is tacitly to recommend an 'other-worldly' stance towards existence. Here 'ex-istence' can only mean (after the manner of Plotinus) *ek-stasis*, to be rapt up to the highest vision by leaving the mirror behind.

On the other hand, the appearance as non-being in relation to God also has its supremely positive aspect. Insofar as things have no *An-sich-sein*, that is because they *are in God*. Active in them are the potencies of creativity itself.

13 Anselm, *Monologion* 33.
14 *Apokalypse I*, p. 218.
15 Cited at ibid., pp. 218–19.

That is why the world in its development enjoys an increasingly vital life. There is not only God as the presupposition of the world. There is also a genesis of God from the world. But to work for the constitution of eternal being by the graduated transformation of some earlier state of things points in the opposite direction to the Plotinian. It points towards a 'this-worldliness' more redolent of Ludwig Feuerbach (1804–1872) than the ancient mystics, whether Platonist or Christian.[16]

The overall upshot is this: for Schelling, 'being over against God waxes in proportion to being in God; they can and must coincide'.[17] More and more, appearance, as found outside God, and the centre of that appearance, which is within God, come to be 'in' each other, and with that convergence the identity of being and essence, life and totality, intensifies in God himself. Thus for human beings, the existential attitude that is 'ec-stasy' (which takes us out of ourselves) must be complemented by the very different attitude of 'en-stasy' (which stabilizes us in ourselves). In man as microcosm of the world, all the potencies of nature are integrated – which is why man can be, for Schelling, the 'appearing All'. Thus the 'idea' becomes soul, though Schelling distinguishes between, on the one hand, soul as 'one with the body' in which case, indeed, it 'is the body', and, on the other hand, soul as intrinsically unbounded understanding. Balthasar compares and contrasts Schelling's anthropology with Augustine's. Both thinkers agree that the dwelling in the soul of the Spirit of God is the soul's truth and perfection. But for Schelling the soul is itself a condition of the reality of the divine Spirit since human and divine consciousness are, in their development, mutually dependent.

And so, in his fundamental existential attitude, Schelling oscillates between 'worship' and 'masterfulness'. It was a stance which would influence many succeeding figures of the German literary tradition but, to Balthasar's mind, provides no coherent basis for human living. If God and world exist *through each other*, it is hard to know what tone to adopt with each. But this is the outcome of Schelling's thought. 'The reality of God is the world's being – not, admittedly, as temporal but as eternal temporality.'[18] God in his extra-worldly existence is compared by Schelling to a fire that can only be etiolated flame until it has some 'stuff' to work on. His account of the thinness and poverty of God's being when deprived of its worldly correlate could hardly be further removed from the scriptural utterances which provide Christian metaphysics with their inspiration.

---

16 And this is so even if in another sense Feuerbach can make common cause with Plotinus against the Churchmen. When Plotinus sees finitude as the sheer negation of the infinite, and Feuerbach treats it as the infinite's proper if covert affirmation, both are rejecting, if not consciously then logically, the 'analogy-thinking' beloved of the Fathers and doctors. Finally, in yet a third sense, Balthasar would range Feuerbach with Augustine, for the pair share a concern for the establishment of personhood – and this over against Plotinus for whom personality is just not a philosophical topic.

17 Ibid., p. 223.

18 Ibid., p. 227.

Schelling's Eschatology

The fundamental ambivalence which this world-view creates for an attitude to life carries over into Schelling's eschatology. How could that eschatology not be affected by the double-think which in one breath recommends flight from the relative non-being of bodily existence into the realm of the idea and in the next prizes above all else the creative realization of the powers of body and soul in organic action? This is oscillation (*Schwebe*) with a vengeance.

For the eschatology arising from the spiritualistic-ecstatic side of Schelling's thinking, the soul lasts only as long as the body does. Its relation to the Absolute is interior, not futuristic. All seeking, all acting, that takes temporality seriously by that very fact 'turns its back on eternity'.[19] The vision of the divine idea, invisible Father of all things, is the 'true and everlasting deed' which 'annihilates time by setting in its midst absolute eternity'.[20] In Balthasar's favoured terminology, the eschatological is here stripped of all its teleological character, and reduced to merely axiological dimensions. The End is a single 'vertical' moment, and it is now. Thus are dreams of the future and nostalgia for the past alike swept away. 'Intensive eternity' Friedrich von Schlegel (1772–1829) will call it, in Schelling's wake. Schelling links it to beauty which is 'the absolute identity of the infinite and the finite, seen in its objective counterpart'.[21]

But Schelling's version of this ecstatic gaze cannot be stated non-paradoxically, and this because of the co-existence with the spiritualistic-ecstatic of that other, organic-creative aspect integral to Schelling's thought. The 'vision' is at the same time an 'active grasping and realising of the Eternal in us'.[22] That might seem encouraging for what is commonly called, somewhat minimalistically, post-mortem 'survival'. But two factors must be borne in mind. First, for those who in their lives successfully pursue this path, the dissolution of existence, freedom and consciousness into the idea will hollow out personal individuality from within. 'Our highest striving', Schelling wrote to Hegel, 'is the destruction of our personality, transition into the absolute sphere of being.'[23] Secondly, two other categories of individual hardly fare better. The failure of 'sensuous men' to make the 'absolute choice' for the eternal means bondage to the wheel of the natural cycle. And as for those who hope to reach the eternal beyond the grave – philosophically orthodox Christians are doubtless in view – they can expect no more than a continuation of their present mode of existence, the 'immortality of the mortal'.

Not surprisingly, Balthasar finds Stoic resignation to be the overall mood of Schelling's account of the 'last things'. In the *Philosophie der Offenbarung* Schelling himself praises the 'sweet gift of melancholy' transmitted by the highest art. Naturally he would – since the highest selfhood must coincide

---

19 Ibid., p. 231.
20 Cited in ibid.
21 Cited in ibid., p. 234. Balthasar considers 'charm', *Anmut*, the principal feature of Schellingian beauty: even sublimity, the key aesthetic motif for Kant and Schiller, is in its service. Charm is all that is left for art to achieve, indicates Balthasar, if the intensest selfhood is in fact one with dissolution into the unconscious generality of the idea. Appropriately, Raphael is Schelling's artistic *beau idéal*.
22 Ibid., p. 233.
23 Cited in ibid.

with the most total ruin of what is individual. That is what 'the twofold *dia* of the Prometheus-situation' would lead one to expect.[24]

Schelling's Philosophy of Freedom

Balthasar proceds to conclude his account of Schelling by an excursus on the philosophy of freedom in that author. In the 1804 treatise *Philosophie und Religion* Schelling for the first time expounds the Promethean standpoint as explicitly a 'dialectic of freedom'. Insofar as God's 'being-in-himself', his *In-sich-sein*, is not that of the ideal (but only of the real), a possibility of freedom arises in his eternal life. Freedom constitutes a 'fall' in the divine world inasmuch as such freedom is itself *not* God, *not* necessary. Human freedom mirrors the divine. Freedom is at once, writes Schelling, man's deepest alienation from God and the means of our return to the Absolute, our taking up (again) into the ideal. This confirms Balthasar in his view that Schellingian freedom is 'daimonic-oscillating indifference between good and evil'.[25] This 'inner-divine daimonry' points either forward, beyond Christianity, to Feuerbach, or backwards, towards a 'daimonic Gnosis' of the sort known from the syncretist mythologies of late antiquity.

Which it is would depend, presumably, on whether one saw Schelling's account as more essentially (Gnostic-type) *re*-mythologization or (Feuerbacherian) *de*-mythologization. Surely the former is alone plausible, as the 1809 *Untersuchungen über das Wesen der menschlichen Freiheit* makes clear.[26] Despite the concentration on *human* freedom announced in its title, Balthasar can declare of its author 'he gazes on the inner history of God with the lapidary and incontrovertible gaze of a Sibyl'.[27] Schelling believed one could *know* that, in Balthasar's paraphrase, 'in all production, considered as a consequence, *and therefore in God's self-production* there is, thanks to the independence of what is produced, something more than in the productive ground'.[28]

Schelling had also come to think that, in his own words, 'the concept of a derived absoluteness or divinity is so little contradictory that it is, rather, the central, instrumental concept (*der Mittelbegriff*) of the whole of philosophy'.[29] These notions form a basis for the vertiginous role Schelling will henceforth give to divine freedom, and the derivative divinity of human freedom as well.

But because man has arisen from out of an 'abyss' which is not himself, he oscillates between darkness and light. Such *Schweben* – the term is surely by now familiar to us – *is* his freedom considered as indifference. In God the 'dark principle' is not evil per se. It is that which lies beyond order and form in as yet unruled 'craving' (*Zehrende*). But in man the possibility of freely preferring such blind desire to the radiance of order, rule and form, gives rise

---

24 Ibid., p. 236.
25 Ibid., p. 238.
26 However, the literary critic August Wilhelm von Schlegel, in a letter to Schelling of 19 August 1809, hailed the treatise as signalling Schelling's adherence to the distinctively Christian notion of evil as the abuse of freedom in finitude.
27 *Apokalypse I*, p. 240.
28 Ibid., p. 240. Italics added.
29 Cited in ibid.

to evil. (In this way, Schelling attempts to solve metaphysically – not theologically – the problem of 'radical evil' recognized but left unsolved by Kant.) Thus Hell makes its appearance – for which there is divine permission, so that love may penetrate this daimonic ground and raise it into light.

The philosophy of history can show how, as God appears in nature, evil is gradually overcome by the victory of love. (Schelling, after all, is now in the phase of his biography where he seeks a reconciliation with what he considers orthodox Christianity in the style of a 'free' or 'non-Roman' Catholicism.) The birth of the Word on earth initiates a 'crisis', the beginning of the judgment of the world, and throughout the Christian centuries this will mount in intensity. Here Schelling announces the pattern which, more in connexion with the Atonement than the Incarnation, Balthasar himself will write into his theological dramatics. Though Balthasar will appeal in this connexion – and certainly not implausibly – to the evidence of the Johannine apocalypse, his Schelling study furnishes an uncanny anticipation, in strange metaphysical key, of the same idea. 'The more God's spirit triumphs, the more violent must the temptation of the ground become – for the power of this temptation is nothing other than the power of the divine ground itself.'[30]

So the stakes are raised ever higher – until ultimately, the good that has arisen from the 'ground' triumphs through a bonding, henceforth eternal, with the primordial good in God. Thus, in Schelling's version of St Paul's message in First Corinthians, the last enemy is annihilated and the Son lays the world at God's feet as his everlasting mirror, so that God may be all in all.[31]

The *Stuttgarter Vorlesungen* of 1810 confirm this eschatology and also attempt to highlight its implications for the individual. After death the blessed enter the world of spirits or 'the living ideas', but (physical) nature cannot be left to ruin, since God seeks his own objectification there. The 'long sickness of nature' must come, through a final crisis, to its end. Thus Schelling reaches the notion of *resurrection*. But the context is hardly a Christian one, for the definitive outcome is the incarnation of God in all humanity: what now only Christ is, we all shall be. At that point: 'the overall meaning of God becomes intelligible in man. It is the union of love between nature and spirit.'[32]

And – in conclusion, then – just this ultimacy of 'spirit-nature-love' is for Balthasar the 'sign of Dionysus' – and of Schelling. Despite the latter's appeal to the visions of John, notably in the late lecture courses *Philosophie der Mythologie* and *Philosophie der Offenbarung*, the gap between Dionysian and Christian apocalyptic remains too great to be bridged. In part, this difference is one of method or formal proceeding. John offers only images, respectful of the sovereign mystery of the God of the end, whereas on the basis of 'mystical potentiality', Schelling claims to provide science. But it is also an issue of substance or content. Not God but man the derived divinity, the 'Messiah of nature', is the Promethean centre of Schelling's system: the true centre of the world.

---

30 Ibid., p. 244.
31 Cf. 1 Corinthians 15.28.
32 Ibid., p. 246.

Novalis

'Novalis' was the pseudonym of the early Romantic poet Friedrich Leopold von Hardenberg (1772–1801). Twice a victim, through the death of his teenage fiancée and his own unsuccessful struggle with tuberculosis, Novalis's poetry is melancholic and itself death-oriented, as the *Hymnen an die Nacht*, in their very title, suggest. Though a Pietistic Protestant by upbringing, Novalis invented a personal symbolism and used it to express his mystical aspirations.

Contemporaries treated Fichtean and Schellingian philosophy as an invitation to live out an exalted destiny – live it out in both ethical and aesthetic terms. In all the main stages of life – childhood, youth, maturity – the real-ideal 'synthesis' of God and man, nature and spirit, was to be embodied. This aim deeply affected the high arts. Among the *Lebensdichter* or 'poets of life' who sought to articulate the imperatives and expectations of the new German thought in concrete terms, Novalis is the first Balthasar will deal with. Appropriately enough for the first in a series, Balthasar centres his account on Novalis's portrayal of the first of the ages of man. Novalis is a poet of mystical childhood.

For Novalis, the child is the paradigm of the human being caught between the finite and the last things. 'Is not the child the living idealist, when in play it builds and destroys its world, from out of an absolute, meaning-bestowing centre?'[33] Novalis compares the child to a magician who experiences his own magic as 'strange appearances that work by their own power'.[34] Everything appears to the child as spirit. Novalis had observed that, while children look on ordinary life as a fairy-tale, they never (or hardly ever) behave like separated islets, situated over against the mainland of reality as a whole.

Like the child, Novalis himself sees being as a permanent miracle. Balthasar evokes Novalis' characteristic attitude by reference to the paintings of the Northern Romantic artist Philipp Otto Runge, whose child figures look with wide, staring eyes at the natural things or human figures around them.[35] The 'miracle' or 'wonder' concerns 'the transparency of a mystery from within, a mystery that, shining through, remains the essentially hidden, precisely because it *is* wonderful ...',[36] a formulation which anticipates Balthasar's own account of the mystery of being in the opening volume of his theological logic. As Novalis looks within, into the 'depths of the spirit', he encounters the wonderful. The wonderful is not sweet. It is more terrible than jolly. This is the Schellingian descent into the divine ground. Here begins the dark staircase of German *Märchen* (a nobler genre than the English fairy-story). For this journey is not only inwards and downwards. It is also upwards and outwards, conformably with the way reality is itself an inner/outer exchange.

Every human being (Novalis thinks) hears at least once in life, 'You have seen the wonder of the world.'[37] Spiritual childhood means openness to this

---

33 Ibid., p. 257.
34 J. Minor (ed.), *Novalis' Schriften* (Jena 1907), II, p. 202.
35 See R. Rosenblum, *Modern Painting and the Northern Romantic Tradition. Friedrich to Rothko* (London 1975), pp. 50–53.
36 *Apokalypse I*, p. 258.
37 Cited in ibid., p. 260.

message. So far, the child of Novalis may seem – despite that menacing shadowy staircase – fundamentally Chestertonian, the wonder-struck theistic child of *Orthodoxy*. But Balthasar is sure that Novalis' child is really Promethean. In the poet's words, 'the highest principle must not be simply given but freely made'.[38] This child seeks to 'conquer the fiery centre' and thus to 'become himself'.[39] 'God', wrote Novalis, 'wants gods.' And he gets them through a process whereby, through the extension and formation (*Bildung*) of our activity, we 'transform ourselves into fate ... until in the end there will be no more negation but we shall be all in all'.[40]

In Novalis' eschatology, we await a magic world of 'pneumatic chemistry', where spirit will enjoy voluntary power over body, and be able to take as its organ whatever it likes. And as with Fichte and Schelling, there is that give-away 'oscillation', *Schwebe*, which in Novalis' case is an oscillation between becoming enchanted (*Bezaubertwerden*) and practising enchantment (*Zaubern*). In Novalis' writing, spirit understands its own becoming as a 'synthesis of lower powers and the emancipation to a higher sphere of the clamant natural essences'.[41]

It is Balthasar's judgment that none of the German Idealists lived so much in and for the future as Novalis. In Novalis, every teller of *Märchen* is a seer. For him, the playing of a child corresponds to what an adult dreams but does not yet dare, when wakeful and sober, to think. What is this audacious thought? It is the 'complete apriority of the world', on the basis of the 'I', the idea. Thus not the historical or empirical, but *that future whose development discloses the primordially eternal*, is the key to the real. As Novalis put it: 'Philosophy from its foundations up is anti-historical. It moves from things future and necessary towards the real, it is the science of the general divinatory sense. It explains the past from the future.'[42] To understand this passage, the reader needs to recognize how Novalis takes what is future for the lower potencies to be the eternal present for the higher powers (or for the powers in their totality).

Novalis ascribes to poets the privilege of living in the 'spiritual [or "fulfilled"] present', through anticipatory participation in the divine 'all-vision'. Indeed, inasmuch as the poet, with a wonderful concreteness of diction, can supplement workaday reality from this source, he is its only effective representative on the level of the inferior powers. The philosopher, who simply furnishes a schema of thought, is at a disadvantage when compared with the imaginative writer. To be sure, the artist should incorporate the philosophical element into his work, synthesizing the 'mathematical-schematic' with the 'living'. But only he has the capacity, through the creative act, to evoke the *wonder* which belongs to totality, the 'ever-more' (*Je-mehr*) of being.

Novalis' eschatology is 'sheer enthusiastic apocalyptic', concerning itself with the 'disclosure of wonder that by that very means remains wonder'.[43] He identifies the 'thousand year Reich' of German mediaeval legend with the

38 *Novalis' Schriften*, III, p. 130.
39 *Apokalypse I*, p. 261.
40 *Novalis' Schriften*, II, p. 198.
41 Ibid., p. 262.
42 *Novalis' Schriften*, II, p. 179.
43 *Apokalypse I*, p. 267.

scriptural 'last day', thereby fusing earthly expectation with heavenly: a 'synthesis of present life with life ... beyond death'. In this vision, comments Balthasar disapprovingly, the 'judgment of the world' of biblical eschatology lacks its properly judicial – and hence moral – force. Rather is it 'at best a more incisive phase of the transfiguration of the universe'. Unending time is *aufgehoben* – at once taken up into and yet, in its distinctiveness, abolished by – fulfilled eternity. To Novalis' mind, this can be anticipated here and now. Paradise latently co-exists with all temporality. For some – 'the best among us' – death is only in semblance. Novalis can think this because he considers outer nature to be a 'petrified city of magic', *eine versteinerte Zauberstadt,*[44] that conceals the flame of spirit within.

Moreover, Novalis regards human life as animated by a death-defying interior dialogue of the individual with an inner 'thou', an ' "I" of a higher sort'. Balthasar compares this 'thou' to the biblical 'Word' of God – not least because of the way Novalis proposes a love-relationship between the higher 'I' and the all too human ego. However, the status of this immortal dialogue is unclear. It seems to be a half-way house between a dialogue and a monologue. Balthasar proposes that what Novalis is trying to find is a middle way between the act-potency relation that characterizes God's rela- tionship to creatures, and the relation of pure act typical of the relationship between the Trinitarian Persons. Only if one denies the ultimate distinction between created and Uncreated could this be a possible undertaking. And Novalis *does* deny it. He takes God to be 'the supersensuous world in its pure form', ourselves to be 'parts of it, in impure form'.[45] Or as Balthasar glosses Novalis, the perfect – the idea, the transcendental point of freedom, God – is as such pure act. But, owing to the principle that the product changes the producer, it has as the basis of its own continuing – future-oriented – reality the impure potency of what is needy, yearning. Not only does potency come from act but, in a fashion bewildering to classical Helleno-Christian meta- physics, pure act arises from potency as well.

From the one God there will come – with the world's transformation – what Novalis terms the 'All-God'. Novalis looked forward to a convergence between, on the one hand, a 'romanticized' Godhead become personal and, on the other, a transfigured world due to become divine. For Christendom, the God who is pure act freely appropriated in the Incarnation a natural potency (human nature with all its agent powers). For Novalis, the Logos was double-natured from the beginning. It was pure act with an impure basis.

Influenced by ancient Gnosis and the mystical philosopher Jakob Böhme (1575–1624), Novalis calls the primordial, heavenly 'I' of ideal humanity 'Sophia'. (We are here close to the source of Russian 'sophiological' spec- ulation as well as German.) 'She' is not only one's own truest inner form but that in which God appears – and hence plays the same role in Novalis' thought that the Word incarnate holds in Christian.

> She is the locus of transition from human ideal to divine ideal, from the primordial image as thought to the same image as existing, from love of

44 Cited in ibid., p. 268.
45 *Novalis' Schriften*, II, p. 183.

self to love of God, and so the place of transfiguration and the great mediator. She is also thereby the heart of universal wonder, as is Christ as personal-cosmic principle in Christian apocalypse.[46]

But unlike Nietzsche with his 'Dionysus against the Crucified', Novalis' slogan was 'Christ *and* Sophia'. Whereas Schelling only came to some kind of Christianity when in his maturity, Novalis was marked for life by his Pietist upbringing. Somehow, then, Christ had to be bolted onto the 'Dionysian-Promethean dialectic'. Balthasar judges the operation unsuccessful. Novalis can merge natural, social and individual eschatology only because for him – in sharp contradiction to the Gospel – real eschatology is the process whereby the 'All-God' comes to be. Noteworthy to a Catholic philosopher in the tradition of the *philosophia perennis* is Novalis' contempt for the concept of *essence*, reduced by him to an outer shell. Buddhistically, he treats the world of discreet yet organized essences as a realm of *maya*, in which anything (including man) *could* become anything else – and *will* do when the (natural) drive to the full realization of freedom reaches the 'synthetic person' of the eschaton.

The following of Sophia, so Novalis believed, 'inoculates' death. As the poet of such a 'death', Novalis considered himself the 'artist of immortality'. The transfiguration of the material already meant – in Novalis' magical world of serious play – a mystical dying at the level of spirit. But seeking reality in its divine ground – true homecoming – entails more. The heart must shrink to its inmost flame, the outer light of the sensuous world become dusk. By sophianic death, the 'a priori of ungraspable freedom' can be regained through immersion in the stream of the 'theogonic' process where God in his ultimate condition comes to be. In his poetry, then, Novalis portrays life as a 'great pilgrimage to a holy grave', with resurrection the 'completion of burial in the abyss of the Godhead'.[47] 'Night' becomes for him the symbol of the 'abyssal endlessness of wonder' – if also of the weariness of the heart that does not yet know the answering abyss (*das Grundlose*) of sophianic love. There is, says Balthasar, a Christian 'going down' into the silence of God. But what Novalis describes, notably in the song of the dead in 'Zauber der Erinnerungen', is really a Dionysian whirling entry into the *Abgrund*, the ultimate foundationlessness of things.

And yet the golden age Novalis hoped for is still that of the child, albeit the Idealist child, which can only be, then, the child of Prometheus. The theme of spiritual childhood – in the Gospels, in St Thérèse of Lisieux (1873–1897) and in his own ponderings – will remain with Balthasar – but in radically Christianized form – from his perusal of Novalis on the 'kingdom of the child'.

Hölderlin

If, in Balthasar's eyes, Novalis stands for the 'realm of the child', Johann Christian Friedrich Hölderlin (1770–1843) represents the 'realm of youth'. Intended for the Lutheran pastorate, Hölderlin in fact made his living as a private tutor, at Frankfurt, Constance, Bordeaux, albeit in-between periods of

---

46 *Apokalypse I*, p. 273.
47 *Apokalypse I*, p. 285.

insanity. The great majority of his writings were published by friends, who took responsibility for them when his reason left him. Deeply read in the sources of ancient Greek literature, his poems convey an acute sense of the poignancy of human life. His own life embodied that poignancy. He spent its last phase in Tübingen, the city where he had been educated at the famous *Stift*. But now he had to be taken care of by a local carpenter.

For Balthasar, Hölderlin takes Novalis' fundamental approach, and gives it added existential potency – especially by his heightened sense of being's mysterious holiness, *das Heiligkeits-Geheimnis des Seins*, as well as of the 'brittleness', 'brokenness' and 'resistance' of the world through which alone, however, the way into the depths goes.[48] What this adds up to is not the astonishment of a child (that was Novalis' starting-point) but tragic surmising by a youth, *jünglinghafte Allesverschweigen*. The mystery of the night, already registered by Novalis, becomes more explicitly a grasp of the tragic character of existence such as adolescence tends to bring us.

In Hölderlin's expression of the tension between ideal and life – characteristically, the resigned attitude of the grown man to the dreams of youth, Balthasar locates what looks like a decisive encounter between Christian apocalyptic and its Promethean-Dionysian counterpart. Balthasar considers that *all* Hölderlin's literary work is apocalyptic, though he admits a great difference between the early writings and those of his last years. *Die Bücher der Zeiten*, a work of the early period, makes a connexion with the Revelation of St John, presenting evil in a remarkably un-Enlightenment manner. Evil is an unfathomable hostility to God and only an even greater and still more incomprehensible gracious deed can overcome it. Hölderlin's distance from orthodox Christianity is shown, however, when in 'Die Unsterblichkeit der Seele', he sets a question-mark against personal survival in the name of the fragility of spiritual being and all beauty.[49]

Unlike Novalis, Hölderlin cannot take the child as his exemplar, since its life *qua* child is lost as soon as it enters reflective consciousness. In his writing, the 'spirit of youth' is first and foremost the 'over against each other' of *Geist* and *Natur*. To be spirit is to be alone. Tragically, the lot of spirit in the world of nature is not a happy one. Hölderlin's way towards an ultimate integral union of spirit and nature will not be Novalis' path of magic play. Instead, he aims at a breach in that 'law' of human life whereby the personality becomes ever more particular as it matures.

Nor does Hölderlin emulate Novalis' attempt to hold Dionysus together with Christ. Not, at any rate, consistently. The optimistic assumption of their compatibility suited the poet of childhood, but is queried by the poet of youth. 'Hölderlin's youth is the Prometheus youth, and his heart is the midpoint of the world.'[50] Naturally enough, then, Hölderlin notes the strangeness to a Promethean heartbeat of a christological rhythm. This poet feels the need to decide where he stands. What shall it be: rejection of the Gospel or its appropriation? Actually, he continues to hesitate between the

48 Ibid., p. 294.
49 Hölderlin, 'Die Unsterblichkeit der Seele', in *Friedrich Hölderlin. Sämtliche Werke und Brefe*, I. (Frankfurt 1992), pp. 32–36.
50 Ibid., p. 296.

two – and in this (not least) shows himself to be the adolescent. But increasingly it is the Dionysian that wins out.

For Hölderlin, man is a god (and if a god, then beautiful) as soon as he is man. But in fact he is *not* man (as man should be). In one sense he is no longer man; in another, he is not yet man. He will become man (and thus god) when he is 'no longer the separation, but the whole, reality and idea', or, more precisely, 'the whole *and the half*' – since he has to 'synthesize' with himself the now tragic but to-be-reconciled world.[51] Longing and the 'interior death' of suffering are the channels through which perfect 'rest in the whole' is attained. The fulfilment of the world – and of man as its centre – will come about through the 'opening of the heart in boundless oblation (*Hingabe*) to the All'.[52]

In this 'inclusive revelation' (*Gesamtoffenbarung*) of the End, nature – predicts Hölderlin – will open herself to transfiguration. Here Schiller's pupil reaches before Schiller himself Schiller's key idea of 'freedom appearing', *erscheinende Freiheit*. Balthasar concludes that, in this eschatology, nature is to be 'an aureole around the self-offering spirit'. That vocabulary points at once to the ambivalence in Hölderlin's world-view. In point of fact, the spirit is the creative 'I' behind nature, so nature's transfiguration will in any case be the self-glorification of spirit. The poet's world is bathed in the gracious light which penetrates its 'spirit-atmosphere' as spirit draws from nature 'features of the divine face'.[53] Notice this is '*spirit*-atmosphere', a metaphysical challenge to empiricists. It is not just 'spiritual atmosphere' which even materialists finding themselves in a concert hall or art gallery, might, if grudgingly, agree to acknowledge. By the world's 'spirit-atmosphere' is meant, as Balthasar explains, something 'objective-natural'.

It has, however, a 'subjective-spiritual' counterpart. In Hölderlin's vocabulary, this is *enthusiasm*: utopian, world-changing, psychological power. That power is set to work to fuse the finite with the archetypal, so as to awaken the 'final kingdom': *das letzte Reich*. Balthasar remarks on the surprising fact that the 'kingdom' Hölderlin awaits is recognizably a version of Christian chiliasm. It is a 'new Church', purified from the spots and wrinkles of the old. All 'enthusiasm' that does *not* generate this end is, to that degree, illusory as well as proleptic.

Most human life will be lived by the resultant rhythm of creative enthusiasm and re-found sobriety. But there are also, so Hölderlin thinks, 'moments' when eternity breaks into time and, in his words, 'opens the door of the future in me'. Balthasar devotes considerable attention to what might constitute the 'fullness' of these privileged moments.

First, the plenary moment, when it occurs, is the 'flaring up of spirit in nature, the man of spirit in the natural man'.[54] Hölderlin employs for spirit the symbol 'sun' – in Latin, *sol*. Its rising is *con-solatio*, its going down *de-solatio* for man because, when the heart is 'nature and wood', it is powerless to en-spirit the world and conjure eternity from it. Then *secondly*, in such moments we escape from fetters into freedom – freedom from nature's laws

51 Ibid., p. 297. Italics added.
52 Ibid., p. 299.
53 Ibid., p. 301.
54 Ibid., p. 306.

and the fate they entail. I touch myself as sheer act, or as Hölderlin puts it, 'I feel in me a life no god has created and no mortal produced'. Feeling himself 'without a beginning', he concludes (there is an answer here to his own early doubts) that he is beyond destruction and so 'without end'. For Hölderlin, soul, when taken as totality, is the way out of nature into freedom. Balthasar illustrates this conviction of the poet's not only by the figure of Prometheus climbing out of Etna – a trope that stands for negative freedom or 'freedom *from*', but also by that of Ganymede, the beautiful boy who became the cupbearer of the gods – and thus can represent positive freedom or 'freedom *for*'.

Balthasar notes, however, that without an account of creaturely essence just *how* these liberties serve specifically human flourishing remains obscure. Yet 'mystical potentiality' – and this is the *third thing* Balthasar wants to say about the 'plenary moment' in Hölderlin – will remain right to the end. Indeed, it is Hölderlin's view that the alternation of *Besonnung*, irradiation by the sun – in German, *Sonne* – of spirit, and *Entsonnung*, its eclipse, amounts to a law of existence. This is a law with a purpose: it is how spirit draws more and more on nature's powers. The true symbol of the end is the thornbush of the book of Exodus, on fire yet never consumed.[55] In keeping with a 'mystical potentiality' metaphysic, the poet here tries to find an (impossible) midway point between the Uncreated – the God of biblical revelation, who is a 'devouring fire',[56] and the created order which God 'burns' so as to transform. 'The spark of the spirit is basically already self-transfiguring nature in the act of transcendence, lifting itself above itself in creative fashion till it reach the level of eternity.'[57]

Here Balthasar turns to Hölderlin's symbol-drama *Hyperion* – described by one Anglophone critic as 'the story of a modern Greek and the torment he endures because, as a modern man, he has lost contact with nature and has allowed himself to believe in the illusion of Critical Philosophy that man can "subjugate" nature to his own will'.[58] In the drama, final destiny is embodied by the figure of Diotima (the name is celebrated in ancient literature as the source of the 'myth of Love' in Plato's *Symposium*). She is the genius behind Hyperion's active struggle for the freedom of Greece (in the Russo-Turkish War), as well as the goal of his passive behaviour, his self-abandonment to nature's 'all'. Through a testing desolation he comes to an inner fulfilment since, in Balthasar's words 'the transcending immanence of Hyperion's soul is more deeply ordered to the immanent transcendence of Diotima'.[59] But the disappointing outcome of the war of liberation suggests to Balthasar an anti-Titanic side to Hölderlin's Prometheanism. It seems that 'the spirit is only pure when its basis is impotence, *Ohnmacht*; deed, *die Tat*, is fulfilled only in the slave-form of defeat'.[60] While aesthetically, this may simply mean withdrawal from the rough and tumble of reality into the sphere of dream and art, what it signifies religiously is something akin to the kenosis of Christ. And this is, in Balthasar's words, 'the tragic quality of the impotence of the

55 Exodus 3.2.
56 Isaiah 30.27.
57 *Apokalypse I*, pp. 310–11.
58 R.C. Shelton, *The Young Hölderlin* (Berne and Frankfurt 1973), p. 254.
59 *Apokalypse I*, p. 312.
60 Ibid., p. 314.

saint in the world'.[61] The tragedy is not itself, however, impotent. On the contrary, it is efficacious. As Diotima dies, she embodies the 'way of self-squandering, *Selbstverschwendung*, [as a gift] for the divine All', really becoming what in life she could only be 'ideally' and attaining the status for Hyperion of 'eschatological archetype' or *Urbild*.[62] In Balthasar's interpretation, it is here love's 'poor riches', love's 'rich poverty' that becomes the 'law of the world'.[63] All this is remarkably pertinent to Balthasar's soteriology, to what he most admired in Christ and the saints.

And this brings Balthasar to his *fourth* and final observation on the full meaning of the plenary moment. Not only is it the sunburst of spirit in nature, escape into freedom from nature's laws, and mystical potentiality expressed in self-squandering. It is also 'ever-growing incorporation of this potency, impotence, depth of suffering, into the very act that carries transfiguration – yes indeed, such that the deeper the suffering the deeper the transfiguration'.[64] Thus suffering and transfiguration develop hand in hand. This does but echo Hölderlin's words at Diotima's death: 'Does not holy nature suffer? O my Godhead! That thou couldst mourn, as thou art holy, that could I long not grasp. But the delight that does not suffer is but sleep, and without death there is no life ... Only death leads from one delight to the other.'[65]

The language is the language of mystical rapture, but what it denotes is not the beatific vision of the Christian hope. The ever-onward, self-transcending movement of freedom and longing – itself fruitful just because it is tragic – aims at transfiguration, but not the sharing in the Transfiguration through the uncreated energies of the Holy Trinity once shown the disciples on the mountain of the Gospels. *This* transfiguration means enclosure in the 'encompassing arms of the Dionysian natural All'.[66] Balthasar approves the pathos, and the ethos it commands, but not the goal, or the philosophy it presupposes. He cannot warrant Hölderlin's naturalism, nor sanction a movement of transcendence that, in effect, is simply a fresh entry into immanence: attachment in depth to the soul of the world.

So what, then, is Hölderlin's view of immortality and the world beyond? Hölderlin sees these as the expansion of the plenary moment, the 'glorification of the eternalizing moment' in which temporality is already integrated into the everlasting.[67] On one reading of *Hyperion*, and notably the elegiac 'Menons Klage', the conservation of love – the true fruit of that 'moment' – can survive the collapse of individual personhood. That of course implies a monism where the personal subject is swallowed up – though not without making a contribution to the all. On another reading, an attempt is made to reconcile the monistic and dualistic elements in Hölderlin's eschatology, and while those who have never understood how to live earthly life divinely become depersonalized, those who have learned to love find, as individuals, an unearthly cosmic niche.

61 Ibid.
62 Ibid., p. 315.
63 Ibid., p. 316.
64 Ibid., p. 316.
65 *Hyperion* cited in ibid.
66 Ibid., p. 317.
67 Ibid., p. 319.

Balthasar claims that this poetic metaphysic, which some might consider a Romantic curiosity, functions at the highest level of eschatological enquiry – as high as that of mediaeval Christianity itself. Its conviction that love is some kind of key to unlocking the puzzling box of human existence is married with a determination to do justice to all the relevant ultimate questions. For human beings are pervasively impelled not only towards heaven but also towards earth, not only towards God but also towards the world, not only in the spirit but also in the body. Still, however comparable Hölderlin's eschatology may be in quality to that of Christianity, the difference between them is also plain. In place of the grace of Christ as a 'grace of direct divine vision and the glory of bodily resurrection' we are offered the 'grace' of Dionysus: 'enthusiasm for the sublation of nature in mystical potentiality'.[68] Between Idealism and the *Gestalt Christi*, the 'form of Christ', no final peace is possible. Looking at Hölderlin's soteriological tragedy, *The Death of Empedocles*, will enable Balthasar to bring this home.[69]

This late work of Hölderlin's gives Balthasar the opportunity to offer a little theology of salvation, for *Tod des Empedokles* is, in his view, an attempt to translate 'the entire Johannine-Pauline, indeed New Testament world of thinking and feeling into Dionysian terms'. What is it, for these Christian texts, to have a Saviour? A Saviour is one who 'lifts the world out of guilt, inasmuch as he takes this guilt upon himself, becomes "sin" (Romans 8, 3), and in the extremest night of the heart, of self-emptying ("kenosis", Philippians 2, 7) wins again new access to that glory of transfiguration, for which the creature sighs (Romans 8, 22 ...)'.[70]

At first sight, Empedocles, the Sicilian philosopher of the fifth century BC who threw himself into the flames of Mount Etna so that by his sudden disappearance he might be reckoned a god, seems rather an odd counterpart to Jesus Christ. But Empedocles was certainly a teacher, and appears to have enjoyed some kind of gift of healing. Within the fiction of the poem, Hölderlin accepts the 'messianic' claims of Empedocles. Setting side by side texts from the poem and citations from the New Testament brings out some commonalities. Empedocles does not believe, he sees. He does not ask, he knows. His is the plenary life of the spirit, midway between the soul and God. To be the child of God is to be taken up into mystical unity with God's life, which means not only estrangement from the world but – more positively – overflowing existence as a 'sacrificial wine' where love passes into the Holy. Such is the space formed by the life of a redeemer, and notably his oblationary death. Personally, it brings on Empedocles a tragic fate, both within and without. He is persecuted by the official representatives of the sacred, and even his disciples do not understand him and attempt to deter him.

But then the differences from the case of Jesus Christ begin to show. In point of fact, Empedocles rejects the request of his disciples to have part in him. Unlike Christ's at the Last Supper, his farewell discourse is a conversation with himself, albeit on the edge of eternity. He proposes a

---

68 Ibid., p. 323.
69 A very different reading from R.C. Harrison's in *Hölderlin and Greek Literature* (Oxford 1975), pp. 121–59, who stresses the work's cosmological content.
70 *Apokalypse I*, p. 323.

purification in the 'natural abyss of fire', not through the Holy Spirit Christ willed to cast on to earth. And this leads Balthasar to make his decisive point. Empedocles is a human being, and thus (for Idealism) *essentially guilty*, since human consciousness awakes to the fate of individualization, *Vereinzelung*. Indeed, spirit as such, just because it implies consciousness, is deeply ambiguous, as Empedocles, on a note of bitterness, explains. His sacrifice is a

> toll-price paid to the wrath of the gods, which, more deeply seen, is, however, their favour … Empedocles, 'who has to die, because he lived too beautifully, because all the gods loved him too much', goes in such a death towards a higher life. With the dissolution of the isolating sun of the spirit, this death is the preservation at a higher level of the beautiful moment, its perfect eternalisation.[71]

His offering of himself (*Hingabe*) has, *qua* gesture, obvious affinities with the life and death of Christ. Yet in Empedocles' case it is an attempt to throw off the shackles of finitude, a protest against the temporality of existence and the way it limits our infinite capacity for love to what just 'happens to be to hand'. This protest against human finitude is, for Balthasar, the *really* guilty thing – Titanism – and it suffers from a profound metaphysical incoherence by conceiving the same attitude – and behaviour – as *both* sheer act (in the form of rapture) *and* sheer potentiality (in the form of longing).

Balthasar takes further his analysis of what he considers the contradictions of Prometheanism, as exemplified in Hölderlin's hero. Empedocles represents man as the true Logos, the centre of the world, the mediator between nature and the divine, and he does so in a fashion shaped by the Prometheanism of the Idealists. His attitude to what is 'above', *Hingabe* to the 'holy All', is impaired by the inevitable distance the Promethean stance of autonomous creativity entails. Outside the christological sphere, even something so admirable as sheer self-donation is 'already hidden guilt'. Likewise, his attitude to what is 'below', instrumental action on the world, is impaired by misuse of the holy – the 'theft of fire' on which Prometheanism rests. *Hingabe* can be spoiled, Balthasar explains, by the desire to enjoy or exploit it, to give it the goal of a 'social work of salvation', which is not in fact its end, since it has none beyond itself.[72] (We shall not go far wrong in finding in this criticism the seeds of Balthasar's later negative attitude to the 'liberation theology' of the 1970s and 80s. *Verzwecken*, the imposition of inappropriate purpose, is, in this section of *Apokalypse*, one of Balthasar's chief pejorative verbs.) Moreover, nature has its revenge on the would-be 'pure, law-giving spirit' by leaving it to its isolation: the Promethean creative fire soon becomes a hellish fire that eats away one's inner substance. To sum up, then: 'In these entanglements of metaphysical-tragic motifs, Empedocles is the most complete exhibition of existential Idealism.'[73] The hubris of Empedocles, which Balthasar defines as the 'absolutization of the essentially relative',[74] reflects the wider ' "ontological" situation'. It expresses the

---

71 Ibid., p. 332.
72 Ibid., p. 334.
73 Ibid.
74 Ibid., p. 335.

unavoidably tragic character of human existence (at any rate when lived without grace).

This prompts Balthasar to draw a further contrast between Romantic Idealism and the Gospel. In the former, a pervasive melancholy, *Schwermut*, is at once confirmed and abolished: that is, it is transfigured *as it stands*. 'Finally for Empedocles the Mount of Olives and Easter morning must coincide.' In Christianity, however, there is a *path* between hellish God-forsakeness on Good Friday and the Paschal alleluias – even if this path or way consists of 'only one step, a fall through the depths of Hell into the bosom of the Father'.[75] Balthasar finds something factitious about the later Hölderlin's claim that Christ is the 'last of the divine epiphanies' since, for the German writer, it is the (individual) human soul that really discloses the divine ground.[76] Empedocles is only a 'Socratic' mediator – one who functions simply as a signpost by his example. The real 'organizing principle of the mystical body' is, rather, the 'anonymous divine "all-life"'.[77] The unique synthesis of Christ – who can be both all and person just because he is the Word incarnate – is lost to Hölderlin's gaze.

The contrast (which by no means excludes all similarity) can also be expressed in terms of two accounts of *Liebestod*, death in love. Hölderlin's Empedocles, like Richard Wagner's Tristan and Nietzsche's Zarathustra, are the 'heroes of Dionysian *Liebestod* . . . the great simultaneity of love and death as final reality'.[78] 'Sinking into the groundless', for the Romantic Idealist, *is* the heavenly journey of the soul. Heaven and the Abyss celebrate their union. How different from the last journey of Christ, and thus the Christian *Liebestod* – even though, in his Passion, the Lord's sufferings could coincide with the unspeakable bliss at the 'apex' of his soul.[79]

Before taking leave of Hölderlin, Balthasar notes how, in his last hymns, Hölderlin's verbal resources are more and more under strain. As with the biblical oracles of Jeremiah, the dislocation introduced into this 'most sublime [expression] of German prophetic-apocalyptic poetry' testifies to a breakdown in the confidence of the speaker, who (in Hölderlin's case) feels called to express the depths of the world and the abyss of the Godhead – and thus to be himself the Logos-Son. Alas. In this project, so Balthasar opines, Hölderlin discovered through the poetic medium what Schelling had already affirmed in the philosophical: on Idealist presuppositions, the basis of *logos* – meaning – is alogical chaos and its 'hellish fire'.[80]

Balthasar has, then, laid out certain weaknesses of the subjacent metaphysic here, and the impossible strains to which the Idealist project is prone. But he also finds in one of Hölderlin's final effusions, *Patmos*, named for the author of the Johannine Apocalypse, lights that illumine Christianity itself. 'John who saw' – saw, leaning on the breast of his Master, the face of God, could tend the flame in the 'loving night', and the poet feels with the apostle

75 Ibid.
76 Ibid., p. 336.
77 Ibid.
78 Ibid., pp. 336–37.
79 At this stage of his writing, Balthasar clearly accepts St Thomas's teaching on the co-existence of perfect joy and spiritual anguish in the soul of Christ. Subsequently, he will consider this incompatible with a christological – and Trinitarian – kenoticism.
80 Ibid., p. 341.

and evangelist a secret unity. Balthasar can credit that Hölderlin preserved 'an interiorly hidden ... image of the Son of God', which shaped his more wholesome aspirations and discouraged the less wholesome from doing their worst. In England, Ulrich Simon would write of Hölderlin: 'Dionysus, who tamed the tigers, prevailed over the fury of the mob, and created the vineyard of spiritual inwardness, is his brother. But Christ cannot be brought into line with a common religious denominator. He stands alone.'[81] Balthasar finds in the last hymns a 'flower that blooms in the night', a noctural glimmering of the glory of the face of Christ. This shifts from its place the *Weltmitte*, Promethean man's would-be occupation of the centre of the real.

Schiller Revisited

In the opening volume of *Apokalypse*, Balthasar has already written of Schiller in connexion with the 'new eschatology' emerging in German philosophy at the turn of the eighteenth and nineteenth centuries. But now he returns to him, in order to compose a poetic trio of Novalis (the kingdom of the child), Hölderlin (the kingdom of the youth), and Schiller (the kingdom of the grown up). The aim is also to complete his account of the contrast between the 'Christian possibility' and the 'Idealist possibility' (throwing in for good measure the 'Antique possibility') – a subject broached in his studies of Hölderlin and, to a lesser extent, Novalis.

Growth to adult manhood (or, obviously, womanhood) is, says Balthasar, deeply influenced in this by his Germanist sources, growth 'from out of the idea into existence and a turning to the earth'.[82] But in the context of Prometheanism, this move entails the adoption of a 'grown-up "existentiality"' which reaches its 'eschatological synthesis' through *resignation*, as the limits of the adaptation of the idea to everyday reality become plain. 'Resignation' here betokens leaving space for the 'ungraspable, for destiny, for God'. As such it is a kind of sacrifice. Whether it be exalted *Hingabe* or merely the heightened concentration of our powers on some quite modest version of the human task, such sacrifice is always, in the setting of Idealism, a 'renunciation of the mastering of the "whole"'.[83] In the context of the Idealist project of coming to dominate the 'allness of nature from the absolute unitary standpoint of the "I"', *either* the totality of nature *or* the unitary standpoint of the spirit will have to be abandoned. *Either* there must go the project of rendering nature transparent by abolishing its alien quality – a project undertaken on the presupposition of the godlike freedom of the intellectual soul. *Or* there must be given up all claim to a 'complete unconditionedness of the inner sanctuary', and the totality of nature left to show its own organization and meaning, with – naturally – some contribution from human powers. Thus Kant retains the absoluteness of man but 'sacrifices' the conquerability of nature – and this comes to expression, in fact, in Schiller. But Goethe – whom Balthasar will treat, and highly sympathetically, when he is

81 U. Simon, 'Feast of the Spirit against a Clouded Sky' (= 'Religion and Literature', 32), *The Times* 26 June, 1976.

82 *Apokalypse I*, p. 347.

83 Ibid., p. 348.

finished with Schiller – retains the absoluteness of nature and treats the human spirit as (simply) the highest 'entelechy' or purposive form within the natural world.

Such is Balthasar's confidence in the spiritual power of sacrifice – even as thus defined, or exemplified – that he is inclined to see in such outcomes the entry into wisdom of the thinkers who reach 'resignation'. 'Everything sacrificed becomes spiritual possession' – and the attitude of the really dispossessed can transfigure their project of 'all-possession', once they have truly disengaged. Autumnal fullness comes to the idea when life so treats it. This leads him briefly to raise a corner of the curtain on the rest of his positive exposition in the opening volume of *Apokalypse*. In the novelistic writings of 'Jean Paul' (the alias of Johann Paul Friedrich Richter) who will follow Goethe in Balthasar's *galère*, life makes of the idea an 'all-feeling wisdom'; for Hegel, life properly grasped is the streaming vitality of the idea. With Hegel, in Balthasar's view, the variations the Idealists played on the Prometheus theme come to their close. What remains is disintegration.

So far as Schiller himself is concerned, Balthasar's chief attraction to him appears to lie in the way ideal and existential categories combine and coalesce in his thinking. Contrary to conventional evaluation, Balthasar finds him on this ground more many-faceted than Goethe, not less. His earlier – and rather general – presentation of Schiller's contribution to the 'new' (i.e. Promethean) eschatology of the turn of the eighteenth and nineteenth centuries has already drawn the reader's attention to Schiller's doctrine of beauty, the key (so Schiller considered) to the unity of the natural world with its intellectual-spiritual counterpart. As Balthasar points out, Schiller can see the relation between nature and spirit in the perspective of a non-eschatological optimism: nature rises through beauty to the truth that is also freedom. But there is another pathway leading up to the *sublime*, and here the last section of the journey is no simple harmony. Rather is it the tragic hero's 'beauty' in his seeming defeat. It is on this second line of advance that the eschatological really breaks through.

All in all, Schiller's dramas can express his sense of *the direction of human life* in one of three ways. He can present the true ultimate as freedom from the sensuous world in the self-emptying of the heart (this will be, in point of fact, the way of *Maria Stuart*). Alternatively, he can depict the abyss which opens between natural fate and freedom as somehow overarched by beauty – 'beautiful appearance', *Schein* – even though not truly penetrated and informed by it. (Such plays will be typified by a to-ing and fro'-ing between beauty and tragic truth.) Thirdly, the playwright can suggest a way of closing the gap, and thus envisage a true human totality – something which itself might be carried out in one of two fashions – both of which, it should be noted, are indebted to the *first* of these three ways. The playwright *might* succeed in showing forth the eschatological by working on an understanding of tragic freedom as itself so beautiful that it amounts to a manifestation of the divine in the suffering human being, and so can already count as such a totality. Or again, he might proceed on the basis of a conviction that the freedom involved here means freedom from the sensuous world and its fate and suggest how, precisely so, there is at any rate a *possibility* that the world of sense and its destiny could be incorporated in that freedom. In this manner he would indicate, albeit tangentially, the 'ideal of an absolute totality for human existence'.[84]

Balthasar resolves Schiller's somewhat complicated list into just three distinct possibilities and invents a terminology of his own for these *Grund-formen* or 'basic forms'. Each of the little formulas he comes up with joins the term 'beauty' in some fashion or other to the word 'abyss' – and the reader needs to understand that the abyss in question is that which separates the 'I' from nature. We get then: 'beauty above the abyss': this is intended as a formula for Idealist mystical potentiality in its existential form; 'beauty in the open abyss': here Balthasar has in mind the resignation to tragedy typical, he thinks, of the Greco-Roman world; and 'beauty in the self-closing abyss', by which words Balthasar signifies what he later calls the 'Christian totality-synthesis'.[85] That these *are* the permutations within which Schiller's drama moves proves him to be *the* tragedian *par excellence* of the 'Prometheus circle' – i.e. all those philosophers and poets, from Fichte to Hegel, who are Balthasar's subject in this opening volume of *Apokalypse*. For Schiller, nature, as man's *Gegenüber*, is sphinx-like, and there can be no assumption of an ultimate reconciliation between them. Hence destiny, *Schicksal*, is 'burdensome', and the situation of Promethean humanity truly dramatic.

Balthasar sets the scene. He describes the youthful Schiller's ambivalence towards the world, havering between enthusiasm for it and horror at it – between acceptance and rejection of Fichte's (and Schelling's) optimism that the 'all' can be mastered. The early dramatic masterpiece *Die Räuber* captures perfectly this original Schillerian *Weltgefühl*, its heroes 'daimonic, bright-dark flame'.[86] In the play, Franz proposes to root out everything around him of which he is not the lord. Likewise, Karl revolts against God and God's world in order to institute a more divine order. These are characters at a crossroads between ecstasy and despair. The unenviable choice is: be a higher human being, or be a devil. Karl's song of Caesar and Brutus, performed in the midnight forest, expresses more immediately his relation with his natural father but 'more deeply his tragic guilt relationship with God'.[87] Karl's nocturnal broodings about his future are the opening up of the 'abyssal space of his soul': as the character puts it, 'I am my heaven and my hell.' In other words, he carries his apocalypse within himself. Franz's dreams too are apocalyptic nightmares, as he oscillates between cynical materialism and cosmic despair, and finishes in a 'hellish-wormlike self-writhing before the immortal magnitude of his soul'. Karl, however, is purified by recognition of the inner impossibility of the cosmic Promethean attitude. That signifies, for Balthasar, Schiller's own abandonment of intellectual commitment to such pretensions. The playwright withdraws from 'a direct Prometheus-like possession of the beyond which one could turn directly into a space for drama' and concerns himself instead with 'the meaning of the human act of faith and hope as intentionally directed to the beyond' – which is something very different.[88]

---

84 Ibid., p. 352.
85 Ibid., p. 360.
86 Ibid., p. 353.
87 Ibid., p. 354.
88 Ibid., p. 356.

The only way 'existentiality' can really provide access to the Last Things, thinks Balthasar, is by such 'act-immanent relatedness'. As life-attitudes, faith and hope bear meaning in themselves. It is almost as if, Balthasar comments, Schiller were carrying out a Husserlian phenomenological analysis of these human acts. However, the ability of the attitude of hope to find happiness in modest means, or even privation, has to be balanced, for the realistic Schiller, by the ever-present human drive to seek enjoyment in 'sensuous time-eternity, *Zeitewigkeit*'. And this means, in the words of Schiller's famous *Letters on Aesthetic Education*, 'stretching oneself out into the non-finite'.[89] The trouble is, these two attitudes *are incapable of being united*. This is Schiller's fundamental problem and his casting about for a way to cope with it explains the variety of motive behind the composition of his plays. As Balthasar's Schiller chapter progresses, it becomes clear that what he admired in this author was not simply the combination of categories, ideal with existential. There is also a theological attraction to Schiller. Though Schiller felt the force of the 'Idealist' and 'Antique' (or classical) possibilities and never entirely left these behind, his drama increasingly gave expression to the 'Christian' possibility instead.

Idealist, Antique, or Christian?
How, then, does Schiller treat these three 'possibilities'? *First*, so far as the Idealist possibility is concerned, Balthasar turns chiefly to Schiller's philosophical writings to find the answer. In an intellectual atmosphere where the influence of Kant and Fichte predominated, it was hardly surprising that Schiller should have adopted some of their categories. Not, however, their overall views. It was the 'method of immanent analysis' he drew from them, adapting it to his own theme of what Balthasar calls the 'existential unsecuredness of *Dasein*, "being-there" '.[90] Whence arose one of Schiller's great discoveries. Sensuousness, *Sinnlichkeit*, being in and of the world of sense, not only furnishes us with a range of instruments for invasive action upon our environment, assisting our appropriation of the 'Non-I'. It is also a fifth column, the secret, traitorous presence of the 'Non-I' within the citadel of the self. There is a flux, moving in both directions, between the world and the self, something imaged in the situation of the island of Malta, defended by the Knights of St John but surrounded by hostile fleets, in Schiller's drama *Maltheser*. This is the chief reason why Schiller works in *existential*-ontological terms. At the same time, however, Schiller was convinced that the 'autonomy' of our intellectual being (*Wesen*) proves the immortality of the soul. So Balthasar can speak of the bipolarity of Schiller's anthropology which is tensed between two opposite infinites: the chaos of sensuousness and fate, and the inner orderliness, and order-giving power, of soul. For Schiller, trying to bring the anarchy of the world's sensuous appearances under the unitary rule of knowledge by allotting to them a coordinated goal is a hopeless undertaking. But it is also a valuable undertaking inasmuch as it provides us with an image of pure reason (*die reine Vernunft*) which precisely amid this jungle shows its own independence of natural conditions. In a way at once negative and positive, this raises the subject of death. As Balthasar

89 Cited in ibid., p. 357.
90 Ibid., p. 360.

concludes: 'Existence (*Dasein*) is, then, a battle for an unsecured land from a single secured point, and this entire [dialectic of] secured-unsecured is both cancelled and transcended (*aufgehoben*) when the land is lost.'[91]

In death, the 'awake centre' – the soul – loses its grasp on all temporal being. Yet just because the soul knows itself to be more sublime than temporality this can serve as an excellent exegesis of the figure of Prometheus chained – as Schiller points out in his treatise *On the Sublime*.[92] Interpreting the figure of Prometheus chained to Mount Caucasus, Schiller distinguishes between the nature that renders our condition fateful as *power*; the relation of our capacity for resistance to that natural fate, which, not to put too fine a point on it, is *impotence*; and the same relation when considered from the side of the moral personality, which he describes as *Übermacht*, 'super-power'. His own preference (in this Idealist mood) is for an interpretation of human fate whereby the only real conquest we can undertake is *self*-conquest. To set that forth in a world of 'unsecured being', Schiller develops a formidable phenomenological vocabulary that Balthasar regards as a worthy forerunner of Martin Heidegger's analyses in his celebrated *Sein und Zeit*.

We seem to have gone a long way from the key concept of Schiller's philosophy, that of the *beautiful*. But, still under the heading of the Idealist approach, the interplay of reason and sensuousness finds its clearest expression in two modalities of beauty: the beauty of spirit 'in' nature, which Schiller calls 'charm', *Anmut*; and the beauty of spirit 'above' nature, which Schiller calls 'value', *Würde*. In themselves they cannot be united, but they can *in the existence of a human person* – in whom, if it happens, humanity comes to perfect expression. Thus Schiller's celebrated 'aesthetic synthesis'. Drama is the interplay between these poles, and tragedy, alas, the normal expression of their bifurcation. It is, however, in the collapse of *Dasein*, the foundering of human existence, that the sublimity of spirit can best show itself. Death is the proof-stone of spirit, the 'ex-centric centre' of life.[93] This might be thought to be the final abolition of the aesthetic. But in fact Schiller understands the growth, both happy and painful, in our awareness of our freedom as a phase in the maturing of the beautiful. The aesthetic act is located somewhere between – in an oscillation between – sensuous immersion in nature and ethical freedom. In its object, the beautiful is *preparation for the ethically sublime*. Not only does aesthetic distance enable us to discover that 'inner archetypal world which first let [us] be creative enjoyers'. More than this, we come gradually to a higher concept of the aesthetic: that, namely, of spirit-in-nature or indeed 'beautiful spirit above the abyss'. This is where spirit has become in a sense free in nature's regard and yet knows that the abyss beneath it will never be overarched. In this Idealist way of thinking, Schiller treats the synthesis of nature and spirit as the highest ideal of humanity – and yet must ruefully admit that betwixt natural necessity and the free, ethical spirit never will league and covenant be made. Here again tragedy puts in its appearance. Victorious defeat – for the tragic hero triumphs even as disaster overtakes him – is the best we can hope to do in

---

91 Ibid., p. 362.
92 *Vom Erhabenen*, XVII. For an English translation of 'On the Sublime', see F. von Schiller, *Essays Aesthetical and Philosophical* (London 1875), pp. 128–42.
93 Ibid., p. 364.

appropriating destiny. It is for Schiller, remarks Balthasar, the 'limit concept of the beautiful'.[94]

In the *Letters on the Aesthetic Education of Man*, Schiller's existential anthropology presents the human being as abiding kernel, the *person*, together with changing husk, his or her *condition*. Only in the 'absolute person' (God) do all the determinations of personhood flow from the person, since everything the Godhead is, it is because it is. (This is reminiscent of the Thomist doctrine of the identity of *esse* and *essentia*, the 'act of being' and essence, in God.) Schiller expects something like this to become true of human persons too. The person, as he puts it, must become its own ground. Schiller takes the person to be, as such, supra-temporal and without origin. Man is a god in becoming, *werdende Gottheit* – even though Schiller also calls this 'really impossible', since as existentially minded philosopher (as distinct from full-blooded Idealist speculator) he has in fact abandoned the project of thinking through the becoming of God in relation to anthropological analysis. Nevertheless, the Idealist principle of the latent divinity of man remains (in this mood) the guide in his search for an existential fulfilment for human individuals and the human race, their eschatological condition. In this condition, man experiences the two drives – the material, to 'all-reality', and the spiritual, to 'all-ideality' – in such a way that he knows them to be one in him. He is neither matter nor form, neither sensuousness nor reason, but the ground of both.

Balthasar finds highly problematic the way Schiller, in Idealist mode, presents man as the 'womb and source-point' of both drives, and their synthetic result. Even though what Schiller is carrying out is a transcendental analysis (an analysis, that is, of the conditions of possibility of human existence as it strikes us), he tends to forget his own marching orders and treats these factors empirically, leading to the – erroneous – conclusion that the synthesis in question can in fact be concretely realized by this or that person in the midst of time. In Letter 21, however, Schiller seems to recognize his own false move – but then concludes with something approximating to Schelling's eschatology: an oscillation between infinity on the one hand, nullity on the other. A person who is, in their own foundation, sheer activity, stands over against the contrary pole of their passive, nature-bound condition. Letter 24 offers a final attempt to redeem the position. In that Letter, when spirit discovers what can only appear, in the perspective of concern with human destiny, the chaotic character of the world of matter, it also discovers its own deeper striving for 'inner spiritual allness, whence alone the outer abyss is to be banned'.[95] But as Balthasar points out, in raising this possibility of a definitive overcoming of fate, Schiller cannot be thinking of the human *Diesseits*, life on our side of the grave. He can only be thinking of what is, in his world-view, the 'semi-darkened background of the *Jenseits*', the life beyond. Here the existential has been once again built into the speculative.

Letter 26, finally, shows what is at stake. Schiller has two 'existential totalities', which *together* make up the 'authentic last longing of man'. And these are the 'wholeness of an infinite securing of his sensuous existence,

94 Ibid., p. 366.
95 Ibid., p. 374.

Dasein' and the 'wholeness of an infinite unfolding of his spiritual being, *Geistsein'.*[96] In contrast to Kant, it does not seem to occur to the Schiller of this treatise that these two totalities can only be attained – and converge – through grace. But Schiller shows no real confidence that the cleft in the human situation can *de facto* be bridged.

We turn now to the 'Antique' possibility, the *second* in Schiller's trio. Balthasar despatches it much more summarily, mainly through a reading of Schiller's *Wallenstein*, for this play he takes to be its embodiment. In *Wallenstein*, the whole question of the essence of *Dasein* is once again thrown open. This time, however, it is asked not in philosophical distance but out of daily, active life. The human being is confronted with fate as a 'counter-power' to his own, and if he *does* give himself distance (man, comments Balthasar, 'plays himself and sees himself playing, his essential name is "self-playing" '[97]) this will be as a way of dealing with worldly fate – either by mastering it or by *not* mastering it, as the case may be. To play against power: this is dealing with fate in (so Balthasar believes) a distinctly classical, or Hellenic-Hellenistic, or 'Antique' mode.

Wallenstein (the character, based on the imperial general and statesman of the Thirty Years War, 1618–1648) is presented as a 'realist' in that he knows, highly concretely, how his existence is situated and that his fate is to be mastered by decision-making activity. Not that he is a sheer activist. His 'deed', *Tat*, is an act of inner consciousness before it is political action. Will he treat his destiny in immanent fashion, which is the Greek way, seeing it as either 'blind, hostile power, demonic matter' (such a formulation evidently owes more to Manichaenism than to any authentic Hellenic source) or as the 'fearful necessity of the stars'? Or will he find his destiny in a transcendent form (also possible), as a service to that 'world-ordering and providence' whose personal, visible exponent is the Holy Roman Emperor in Vienna? This is the choice Wallenstein has to make. On his appointment, he insisted on unconditional power as the condition of accepting office, and this at once indicates to Balthasar that we have here a Promethean situation. In relation to what is above him, Wallenstein, like Prometheus, is a dependent totality. In relation to what is below him, again like Prometheus, he is a form-giving, 'creative', principle. He mediates God (read, the emperor) to the world (read, society), and society/the world to the emperor/God. As Schiller depicts him, Wallenstein has considered overthrowing the emperor. He has played with this thought 'as with his own, beautiful, idea', even though it strikes him inconsistently as both null and the infinite. But by the practice of astrological magic he has in fact paved the way for the deed. In his tower, a symbol of the soul's fortress, he computes the moment when he may set footfall on the flood of fate, justifying himself by the 'golden age' that revolution, through him, will usher in. In that moment – which is Wallenstein's *eschaton* – he gives himself to power (magic is essentially power), rather than giving himself in true *Hingabe*, to his rightful duty. In one sense whether the moment ever comes is beside the point. Waiting for it is already submission to its yoke. By submitting his existence to the 'synthesis' of fate (Schiller makes him say, 'Happen then what must. Fate always holds the right'),

96 Ibid., p. 375.
97 Ibid., p. 379.

Wallenstein is already guilty, before the Rubicon of public action is crossed. Wallenstein's end is apocalyptic because he turned the blindness of natural fate into his own blindness, suppressing the proper responsibility of his own spirit. His magic is the misuse of *Hingabe* to the world around him, and isolates him from that world in pure subjectivity. Promethean existentiality cuts him off from the nature beneath him, and breeds mistrust in his relation with his fellows. Thus the tragic uncertainty of existence becomes even more a gaping abyss than before.

The grasping at totality (*Ganzheit*) through magical power is obviously an extreme act. But likewise extreme was the aesthetic attempt to master it in the Idealist possibility. The *third* remaining possibility is also, in its own way, extreme. It is the Christian *eschaton*. Schiller's 'Christian possibility' is best exemplified, Balthasar believes, in the three womanly dramas: *Maria Stuart*, where it first appears in positive guise; *Die Jungfrau von Orleans*, which deploys its metaphysical background (there is also a touch of that in *Maltheser*), and *Die Braut von Messina*, in which Schiller shows a world-view becoming a practical formula for existence.

In *Maria Stuart* Elizabeth Tudor renews the 'method' of Wallenstein by putting a distance between herself and 'existential guilt' through rationalization. For Mary Queen of Scots, however, the play's 'heroine', guilt is a freely admitted fact which pains her heart but does not spoil it, and she is ready to make atonement in death. She taxes the English queen not with guilt, *Schuld*, but with *Unrecht*, wrong. In the famous (though unhistorical) scene of the meeting of the queens she holds out her hand to Elizabeth, in a gesture called by Balthasar 'neither titanic nor magical' but the gesture of a guilt-conscious heart. So doing, she re-shapes her destiny. As will become clearer in the case of Joan of Arc, a 'hearing heart' – such as Mary Stuart has come to possess – means purification. The death of the Queen of Scots is the transfiguration of her heart in her very dying, and Schiller portrays this as an event of grace. The Eucharistic sacrament she receives before her execution is the 'outer representation of the inner "sacrament" of humility worked by the apocalypse of the heart'.[98]

The 'fully transfigured existence' Mary Stuart wins in her death figures in *Die Jungfrau von Orleans* as a state of life, made possible by abiding grace. This is 'existence in destiny', and can be known to be gracious through the 'complete transparency and remainderless obedience' of Joan of Arc's soul. '*Dasein* thoroughly illumined by love has as its meaning the transparency of the instrument for a work of Providence ...'[99]

Such an existence is child-like. But Balthasar points out how Schiller takes pains to divert any Novalis-like suggestion that this is an infant spiritual genius who arrives on the human scene trailing clouds of glory. 'Her life is in no way childish pre-existence, but real eschatological existentiality.'[100] That is shown in Joan's moment-by-moment dependence on grace, her 'triumphant restlessness' in moving from one action to the next, and her continual

---

98 Ibid., p. 392. The sacrament is a pledge of a perfection not granted to man in this life where the disparity between ideal potential and real achievement cannot be overcome. The equivalent symbol of the fusion of real and ideal in *Die Jungfrau von Orleans* is Joan's reception into the arms of the Virgin.

99 Ibid.

100 Ibid., pp. 392–93.

listening for possible divine demands. She is neither *Anmut* nor *Würde*, in the key terms of Schiller's philosophically Idealist eschatology. Rather is she existential wholeness, thanks to 'securing' her existence through 'de-securing' it, by its *Entsicherung*, something she does in her complete reliance on divine grace. Paradoxically, 'blind' obedience to God's will opens her eyes. The essence of her life has become 'transcendental defencelessness', a concept Balthasar will put to good use later on in his theology of the Passion of Christ – and indeed, beyond that, his theology of the Holy Trinity.

The contribution of *Die Braut von Messina*, a play set at the foot of that very Etna whose summit figured so prominently in Hölderlin's *Empedokles*, is more modest but, in Balthasar's opinion, approximates best to Schiller's own 'line'. The characters are little individuated. More striking is a collectivity caught between guilt and a redemption only fully thinkable in a life to come. The drama clarifies purity of decision, in a context open to the 'other side'.

Goethe

Balthasar has put on record his love for the work of Johann Wolfgang von Goethe (1749–1832),[101] and certainly there is detectable in the writing of the opening metaphysical and epistemological sections of this hundred-page essay a quite definite warmth. We only have to look at its initial sentence to see that. 'If Schiller is pure, towering flame, Goethe is a broad immensity of fruitfulness, a tree bearing fruit of every kind.'[102]

Balthasar's early constellation of interests would surely have intrigued Goethe. But given the latter's largely negative attitude towards the Church, Christianity and its Founder, whether he could have found the patience to enter the world of Balthasar's dogmatic writings may be doubted. Anyway, it is not Goethe's theological views (or lack of them) that interests Balthasar but his ontology. The sheer flow of Goethe's literary production, which touches every important aspect of life and reality, was a 'streaming along with the all-streaming of nature', testifying to the 'decision of [Goethe's] spirit in favour of nature' and his abandonment to her 'streaming-reposing wholeness'. In a somewhat simplistic military image, Balthasar speaks of Goethe's opening up a twofold 'front' against both Kant and Schiller on the one hand, and, on the other, Schelling – with his hubristic claim to have mastered nature by thought. Still, Balthasar warns his readers against imagining Goethe has walked out of the circle of Promethean thinkers. Rather is his another variant on the 'Prometheus possibility' or, in another formulation, the 'existentially "awake" Prometheus-idea'.

Goethe's Cosmology

Balthasar considers Goethe's project to have been, at one level, making an 'existential-ontological analysis' of the human situation – of the generic kind he ascribes not only to Heidegger, who coined the term, but by way of anticipation of Heidegger, Schiller. Goethe's version, however, is entirely his

---

101 See the 'postwords' he wrote for the three anthologies he produced: *Goethe. Nänie. Auswahl aus seinen Trauengesängen* (Basle 1942); *Goethe. Bilder der Landschaft. Auswahl aus seinen Landschaftsgedichten* (Basle 1942); *Goethe. Ein Füllhorn von Blüten* (Basle 1951).
102 *Apokalypse I*, p. 407.

own. For Balthasar, Goethe's primary emphasis falls on man's condition as continuous with nature or indeed, nature-embedded. We are 'already in nature' before we begin to think about it: ours is a *je-schon-in-Natur-sein*. Accordingly, Goethe treats philosophy as a 'mode of existing' and the 'spreading out into nature' which is a feature of human existing as itself a 'mode of philosophizing'. Now the single most important philosophical influence on Germans of Goethe's generation had been Leibniz with his picture of reality as a divinely pre-arranged (ultimate) harmony of 'monads' – forces that, like the human soul, are, in the useful English coining, 'selved'. Balthasar alludes to this when he writes that (in both continuity and discontinuity with Leibniz) Goethe's fundamental 'feel for existence' is for the 'cosmic (*welthaft*) quality of existence, the insertedness of the monad into an unendingly relational, unendingly interwoven objectivity, which subsists on the basis of mutually engaging individual worlds and through which alone these worlds are what they are'.[103]

Here Balthasar differentiates Goethe from what he considers the originating mind-set of Idealism. Goethe never surrendered the 'inward primordial essence' of individualized realities to the play of the powers of nature. But just because such realities are 'life', they are, by their essence, *Ausbreitung*: a 'broadening out' into the world around them. Whereas for Fichte the 'world' is necessarily the mirror of spirit, and so in an important sense 'secondary' to spirit, Goethe would ascribe to world and spirit a fuller simultaneity. And the world he envisages is a world composed of the 'in-and-through-each-other' character of beings. In a way, Goethe establishes the model for all those later Romantics who sought both to articulate an adequate relation to the real world (compare 'nature') and also, at the same time, to find in experience a ground for affirming a transcendent dimension within and beyond daily life (compare 'spirit').

In Goethe's 'morphology', his most original contribution to a philosophical cosmology, the determinate form of something is at the same time its inner kernel – but a kernel that expresses itself in ever-differentiated images thanks to the determination of *outer* elements. The 'dynamic space' of Goethe's world, at once objective and subjective, both environment and the formation of atmosphere, is the locus, so Balthasar asserts, of the 'becoming as spirit of the organic-natural monad'.[104] Thus the 'philosophical experiencing' of this reality is more 'metahistory' than it is 'metaphysics'. What fascinates Goethe is not a 'systematic deduction of the genesis of ideas from the primordial divine being' (that, presumably, is intended as a summation of what was common to 'Idealists', ancient and modern). Instead, it is the 'experience of the ideal becoming of an entelechy [a purposive organism] in its real becoming'.[105] For the entelechy, by its self-formation, turns into reality its own idea. And Balthasar considers this orientation to 'experience and the real' connects Goethe with Herder. (To the annoyance of the historically minded, Balthasar gives almost no historical or biographical information to contextualize the figures discussed in *Apokalpyse*. Otherwise he might have mentioned at this point how Herder and Goethe were for most of their adult

---

103 Ibid., p. 409.
104 Ibid., p. 410.
105 Ibid., p. 411.

lives colleagues in the service of the same small Imperial principality, Saxe-Weimar-Eisenach.) And yet this orientation to things and events – which is what the term 'real' connotes here – must not be misunderstood in any brutally empiricist sense. What becomes perceptible through real becoming is precisely the genesis of the idea. And this conviction, then, links Goethe to Schelling, the great 'real-idealist' among the classical German philosophers.

In Goethe's name, Balthasar lays emphasis on the *activity* of the organisms whose 'ideas', in their shape-changing development, morphology studies. It is in the deed, *die Tat*, that whatever we can – 'objective-ideally' – know of ourselves enters into the co-constitution of the world, as indeed of our own persons, our own truth. The grand Schellingian panorama is only 'a piece of theatre' inasmuch as it leaves out of account the pain we suffer in turning the truth to our use. In fact: 'In the realm of ideal-real becoming the way to the fulness of existence is itself without outcome (*unvollendbar*). The circle cannot be rounded. The existential truth is – only idea.'[106] Our whole truth is that we are limited to a part of the truth: for Balthasar, as we shall see, this is the basic problematic of Goethe's *Faust*.

The absolute beginning and final end are, then, unattainable. Thus 'entry into the infinite' can only mean: go into the finite, but *on all sides*. The amplitude of this 'on all sides' is generous. So much so that, while ignorant of mediaeval ontology, Goethe does justice to the transcendentals – the true, the good, the beautiful – on which Balthasar himself will later construct his theological trilogy.[107] Of course, this cannot mean doing justice to the transcendentals in their divine source. *Welthaftigkeit*, 'worldliness' (not in a pejoratively amoral sense) is crucial to Goethe's outlook. If, for Schiller, a human being becomes heroic through confronting a difficult and even hostile fate, for Goethe, contrastingly, 'heroism' means 'adventuring in the primeval forest of creation'.[108] The apocalypse of the soul is now a moment within the apocalypse of being in its entirety. The realization of meaning comes from just this analysis of the character of the world as a world that becomes, a world that strives. But in this there *is* soul-making. On Goethe's behalf, Balthasar describes a process whereby 'sheer objective noesis', a thin creature, however indispensable a servant, becomes 'the comprehensive, plenary truth-attitude of thinking-doing-feeling'.[109] Not speculation (or 'theoretical vision') alone; not labour (or 'practical realization') alone; not eros (or 'aesthetic sympathy') alone, for the integration of all three is necessary to the mature striving of the monad, the self.

Balthasar holds that Goethe's attempt to find a via media between Herder's *primarily* realist and Schiller's *primarily* idealist starting-point uncovered an important concealed truth in all the main philosophies of the day. Whether the key category be existence or idea, all these writers tacitly ascribe to everything in process of becoming that it *seeks to be more than itself*. Everything finite is, in a word, 'ecstatic'. In a rather untranslatable construction, this is the '*Empor*' of finite being, its 'upwards- and onwards-ness'.

106 Ibid., p. 413.
107 Ibid., p. 415.
108 Ibid., p. 414.
109 Ibid., p. 415.

It is in ecstasy before the wonder of being that being attains transparency to eyes that themselves have become the media of spirit – of the person – in the fullest sense.[110] Paradoxically, self-possession ('enstasy', being most fully 'in' oneself) comes about through ecstasy (stepping 'out' of the self).

Balthasar has more or less denied Goethe has a metaphysic. But he pretty well eats his words in the section of his presentation of Goethe entitled 'knowing and things'. Goethe's theory of knowledge locates the limits on knowing in the selfsame spots where it finds openness to mystery: in the (aesthetic) attitude of abandonment (*die Hingabehaltung*), which teaches epistemic humility, and the (ethical) attitude of propensity to act (*die Tathandlung*), which schools us in a necessary epistemic asceticism. In relevant writings and aphorisms Goethe lays great stress on the moral preconditions of knowledge. 'Objectification' requires the humility to look away from oneself. 'Subjectification' requires the ascetic effort of appropriating the known. Just as the first cannot be entirely passive, therefore, so the second cannot be altogether active. (These thoughts have greatly influenced the presentation of a – fundamentally Thomistic – epistemology in the opening volume of Balthasar's *Theologik*, entitled 'Truth. Truth of the World'.) The consequent attitude is, Goethe holds, not irrational but, to the contrary, the only one deserving the name 'intellectual'. Neither pure *theoria* nor simple *empireia*, it incorporates aspects of both.

It shows the flexibility of Balthasar's use of apocalypse language that he regards Goethe as entertaining an apocalyptic – but one that is non-eschatological in character. 'Unveiling' here will not be of the future condition of things, as, most evidently, it was with Novalis and Hölderlin. Hoped for as it is from chastened exploration of things in their *Gewordensein* or 'having become-ness', it can only be in its basic orientation *protological*. In other words, it will be from start to finish concerned with *origins*. This opens a large perspective when we hear that, at any rate in principle, the primary object of knowledge must be the 'subjective-objective world-totality' and not the individual thing within it. (Balthasar assumes Goethe presupposed as much on the basis of the legacy of Leibniz and Herder.) But it is chiefly in regard to the individual thing before the mind's eye that one can make (some) sense of the claim that through *Hingabe* – meaning here a self-disciplining, respectful looking, the primordial phenomenon (*das Urphänomen*) – the point of genesis of all the forms a thing takes – becomes after a fashion visible.[111] It can become visible because it is signified in a thing's 'objective *Empor*', its 'upwards and onwards' dimension. As Balthasar admits, in practice Goethe shrank from any attempt to transfer the project of proto-logical apocalypse to the world order as a whole. 'Only within a little circle of forms did he venture the Promethean co-achievement of the creation –

---

110 Ibid., p. 416.
111 L.A. Willoughby wrote of Goethe's *Urphänomene*, 'they are the distilled essence of reality, but very definitely a sensuous essence. They could be thought of as types, such as the type plant that he imagined the *Urpflanze* to be. Potentially they might be thought of as existing in the phenomenal world, and Goethe had a momentary vision of such a type plant in the botanical gardens at Palermo.' Thus idem, 'Goethe the Natural Philosopher', in C. Hammer, Jr. (ed.), *Goethe after Two Centuries* (Port Washington, NY 1969), pp. 1–20, and here at p. 13.

something that, to be sure, he considered should be extended at the level of idea to a total scheme of all living things.'[112]

Looking back on his Cabbalistically inspired theogony in *Dichtung und Wahrheit*, where he *did* attempt to apply this approach to the totality, Goethe allowed himself a smile. However, the impossibility of a total apocalypse of the world's being does not prevent the wonder of 'primordial phenomena' from generating in the experiencing subject an *'Empor'* – an upwards and outwards movement – that can affect the whole person. In one of his aphorisms Goethe remarks that we know of no world except in relation to man. But then, surely, in relation to man we *do* know a (the) world.

Balthasar finds striking, and welcome, a significant shift in linguistic usage as between Kant and Schiller on the one hand, Goethe on the other. It concerns the little word *rein* – 'sheer' or 'pure'. With Kant and Schiller what is pure is either spontaneity or receptivity. And this leads by necessary entailments to that (erroneous) way of conceiving man's place in the world which *Apokalypse* calls 'mystical potentiality'. But Goethe speaks typically of a 'pure meeting together of subject and object' just as 'in a clear eye the objects of the visible world are mirrored'.[113] Balthasar also notes with seeming approval the way Goethe strove to extend the usefulness of certain metaphysical categories from ancient thought, especially Aristotle. Thus in Goethe's analysis of the *Empor* of things, he pressed into service the celebrated Aristotelean matter/form distinction, re-working it, however, so that there is neither pure matter nor pure form, but only 'self-forming matter, and self-materializing form'.

Despite his unspeculative bent (well, comparatively speaking, for a German of the period!), Goethe also turned to Plato. Specifically, he appealed to Plato's concept of participation in an effort to do more justice to the unified character of organisms than (he felt) Aristotelean hylomorphic analysis was able to manage. Balthasar points out that in his *Studie nach Spinoza* Goethe had managed to get hold of the idea of God as the complete coincidence of existence and perfection. And yet Goethe insists that we 'can only think things'.[114] But with the concept of participation under our belt, adds Balthasar, we can surely think things *as sharing in the divine infinity according to their own limited modes* – and hence in fact we could think, if we wished, more than things! Goethe's conviction that things are 'open to mystery', *offen ins Geheimnis*, points, after all, in this direction.

Goethe's dynamic interpretation of Platonic participation as the 'striving beyond themselves' of things (highly pertinent as this is not only to objective *Empor* but to its subjective, personal correlate in human experience), suggests an aspect of Goethean metaphysics which was really rather original, playing no part in the ontology of either ancients or moderns. This is expressed in the couplet *Polarität* and *Steigerung*. 'Polarity' denotes the way a thing in its becoming lacks complete identity, but is not for all that *divided* between two poles. Rather does it rest in a unity all its own, at the centre of an ellipse defined by poles. *Steigerung*, literally 'raising', might be translated 'increasing enhancement': it is this same unity, but seen as given in the 'upwards and

---

112 *Apokalypse I*, p. 424.
113 Cited in ibid., p. 428.
114 Ibid., p. 417.

onwards' movement. With such conceptual instruments in his tool-box it is hardly surprising that Goethe disliked the reduction of the qualitative to the quantitative then gaining ground in the contemporary natural sciences.

Nowhere is this clearer than in Goethe's exalted concept of *form* – as exalted, and ubiquitous in these contexts, as it will be both in Balthasar's own ontology and in his theological aesthetics. Not only is form (the same word here in German as in English) that which grants qualitative unity; it is also what makes possible the 'living *"Empor"* of being' in the 'ecstasy' of the wondering observer and the luminous intelligibility of the being she or he observes. Form creates *Gestalt*, a term Balthasar is using, then, not as a synonym for form but as a name for the configuration(s) form sets up in immediate perception. It is at form that Goethe's morphological method ultimately aims, and a hard task it is, given the Protean shape-shifting of nature.

But whatever the difficulties of Goethe's philosophical cosmology (the difficulties in grasping it, but also in applying it), its virtues render it worthwhile. Balthasar is particularly taken by the way the pairing of polarity and intensifying enhancement enables Goethe to dispose of that 'mystical potentiality' thinking with which the Prometheanism of classical German thought was so bound up. In living, developing things, 'intensifying enhancement' is the 'vertical' aspect of polarity, and so can never be sundered from polarity's complementary 'horizontal' aspect, itself so humdrum that quantitative scientific analysis is quite suited to it. For beings which exist by way of dynamic participation in the infinite, an 'upper' pole is always synthesized with a 'lower'. If that is one's fundamental picture of the living universe, then mystical potentiality's attempt to situate spirit-in-nature at a midpoint between the sheer actuality of godhead on the one hand and creaturely potentiality on the other is – thankfully – out of place.

> For Goethe, the totality of this world is called nature, not God. Just insofar as nature has its mighty stream of powers from God and its intensifying, upwards and outwards flow finds its meaning, its goal, only in the God who is near to, and interior to, this whole gigantic thing as a mother to her suckling child – only so far is this nature to be called 'God-nature', *Gott-natur*.[115]

Before leaving 'knowing and things' and moving on to whatever might be gleaned from Goethe about the *'last* things', Balthasar draws his readers' attention to two final points. First, in this 'rich vision of existence', Balthasar locates the idea of *symbol* – or *bedeutende Gestalt*, 'significant form' – as the operative controlling concept in the realm of Goethean objectivity. Meaning shines through form, awakening the longing of eros – a crucial theme in the opening volume of the theological aesthetics where Balthasar will set forth his account of beauty. Balthasar draws the conclusion that 'Everything really significant is symbol. This includes not only the phenomena and *Urphenomena* of nature, not only the forms of art, but also – and precisely – the highest philosophical concepts if it be the case that these co-fulfil the *Empor* in its becoming.'[116] Note that the functioning of such symbols is not ascribed

115 Ibid., p. 435.
116 Ibid., p. 439.

chiefly (if at all) to the structure of the human psyche. It depends on their service of the upwards and onwards orientation to the 'wonderful-terrible, in short, the Holy, the goal point of the existential dimension'.[117]

The corresponding controlling concept in the realm of subjectivity Balthasar finds to be *Ehrfurcht*, reverential respect. When the drive to action, the 'eros of creating', is integrated with the complementary attitudes of aesthetic 'abandonment' and contemplative (theorizing) distance, it takes on the milder form of the 'eros of reverential respect'. As Balthasar sees it, the idea of *love* in the Christian Hellenism of the Middle Ages is here both preserved and taken further – in the direction of a 'total concept of love'. (That is found fully-fledged for the first time, Balthasar suggests, in the early twentieth-century phenomenologist Max Scheler on whom he will have much to say in *Apokalypse* III.) It is in the context of such an attitude that Goethe expects the 'holy, open mystery' to declare itself, in a simultaneous illumination of the 'depths' of both subject and object.

Goethe's Eschatology

What, then, of 'Goethe's eschatology'? Does the phrase have any ascertainable sense? For Balthasar has already established that 'In the objective aspect [of his thought] Goethe's proper formal object is expressly the world of becoming in that very becoming. It is the ideal and real genesis of being.'[118]

But though Goethe situates himself at a midpoint between nothing and being, the question is scarcely avoidable, What is the provenance of becoming, and what is its *telos*, or end? To suppress these questions altogether is to content oneself with a 'half-reality' – to be compared perhaps to the existence-quotient of the artistic creation in which Goethe excelled. And Balthasar invokes as confirmatory evidence for Goethe's love-affair with half-reality his obsession with putting on plays, his attraction to court life, with its masked balls (and paper money), and various features of Goethe's *Faust* (the *homunculus*, the dream of Walpurgis Night, the magical conjuration of Helen of Troy). Then there is his biological concentration on plants (in preference to the fuller reality of animals and human beings) and the endless tinkering with colour theory – and even the fact that twilight was his favourite time of day. Yet, when we turn to the subjective pre-conditions of knowing which Goethe recommended, we realize this cannot be the whole story.

Balthasar describes Goethe as caught between two basic attitudes: an 'aesthetic' resting in the sheer transparency of the contemplative view (and this would imply, says Balthasar, that the genesis and goal of becoming is 'pure idea'), and a 'moral-active' attitude of *un*rest on the part of an eros which seeks rather the 'holy and beloved mysteries of the eternal' (and this in turn would imply, Balthasar explains, that the genesis of becoming is 'factual

---

117 Ibid. This citation suggests how the Balthasarian interpretation of Goethe's concept of the symbol condenses – and confirms – a whole process of intellectual development which has been described in these terms: 'From Kant's identification of the symbolic as a *presentational* kind of congition, where we are given an illustration or example to clarify a concept – a kind of cognition distinct from discursive cognition – through Goethe and Schiller to the Schlegels and Coleridge, the notion of the "symbol" as a unit of meaning which is in some way pictorial or plastic develops', J. Sychrava, *From Schiller to Derrida. Idealism in Aesthetics*, op. cit., p. 127.
118 *Apokalypse I*, p. 445.

existence' and its goal 'fulfilled existence'). Balthasar finds the first attitude embodied in Goethe's 'aesthetic' attitude towards his own past in *Dichtung und Wahrheit*, and the self-referential antiquarianism of his old age. He finds the second expressed in Goethe's repeated flights from the *Künstlichkeit* (artistry, or even 'art-nonsense') of subjective culture into the 'all-hallowing reality of nature'.[119] Either way, Goethe's apocalypse of the soul is *Bildung*, 'formation', which is not 'naked subjectivity' but takes in both and so comes about through a feeling commerce with the world.

That commerce is the index of Goethe's 'existentiality', and his existentiality discloses whatever elements of an eschatological attitude he may be said to show. Granted Goethe's lack of belief or interest in final beatitude, it is unsurprising that this eschatology should prove to be, basically, of the axiological, rather than the teleological, kind. In the 'dimension of ideal becoming and real having-become-ness, *Gewordensein*' the 'holy, open mystery' arouses a delicate reverential respect.[120] This is not anticipation of a definitive future but some kind of communion with the eternal now. And yet in Goethe's corpus there are also traces of teleological, futurist eschatology as well. Hints are dropped in expressions of longing, *Sehnsucht*, when the phenomenon stimulates the spirit's own *Empor*. However obliquely, there opens up here a 'contemplative direction towards the world's goal and the world's end'.[121] Typically, Goethe will allude to this humoristically – but humour, as Kierkegaard could tell us, is often the appropriate tool for expressing truths by indirection. Thus in 1828, some four years before his death, Goethe's conversation included a reference to a 'rejuvenated creation', though he added his opinion that much pleasure was still to be had from the old one for a few millennia yet. And as to individual, as distinct from cosmic, future eschatology there are touches, in similar vein, of the idea, found in Herder, that certain souls who have remained faithful to the person-making task earn an immortality denied to the insensitive masses.

Balthasar takes the reader on an illustrative tour of some of Goethe's better known writings. He begins with a few of the most personal sources in recorded conversation, written aphorism and poetry. The effect is to heighten the level of Goethe's quasi-eschatology. Balthasar refers to remarks where Goethe spoke of glimpsing divinity behind the *Urphänomenon*, and records his mixed feelings of amazement, *Erstaunen*, and anxiety, *Angst*, in the presence of certain powers of nature like the Rhine Falls at Schaffhausen in Switzerland. And to the role of *anxiety* here Balthasar connects a proposal about what may lie behind the *Urphänomenon*, this time based on some grim words of Mephistopheles in *Faust*. The phrase 'eternal empty distance' suggests that the answer to the question of what lies beyond the world may well be 'nothing'. But when a sense of the 'empty distance' overwhelms our active-striving self is not that how our eros comes positively to seek out the ungraspably divine? Balthasar concludes a subtle examination of this proposal by writing: 'Therewith the dynamic of "upwards and outwards" is no longer directed to the contradictory nature-God but to the God-Spirit existentially encountered in the mystery. And because it is the active-longing

119 Ibid., p. 449.
120 Ibid., p. 451.
121 Ibid., p. 452.

eros that empowers this dynamic, this is a God who is no "pure idea" but most highly fulfilled existence.'[122] Aesthetic vision finds its place in this context. The 'appearance' of the beautiful is situated on the path of ascent from bare existence to its ideally fulfilled counterpart. *Schein* is the shining through of that highest existence in the realm of becoming. In terms whose denotation is left open, Goethe says as much in book eleven of *Dichtung und Wahrheit*. The supreme office of art is by way of the shining appearance to let a higher reality through.

Raids on such major works in Goethe's corpus as *Werther*, *Iphegenia* and *Tasso* demonstrate the transformation of natural into spiritual (supernatural?) *Empor*. They prepare Balthasar for his lengthy exegesis of *Faust* in the light of the 'fundamental categories of Goethe's world picture'.[123] As is well-known, *Faust* is Goethe's reworking of the sixteenth-century story of an eerie Dr John Faust (the character has an historical basis), magician and necromancer.[124] This is a dramatic poem with a great variety of incident, mood and internal literary structure, which explores the destiny of one who places himself beyond the distinction of good and evil in a restless self-aggrandisement leading inevitably (unless supernatural redemption be possible) to self-destruction. Goethe – so Balthasar reports – always smiled at people who interpreted *Faust* in a rigorous philosophical framework. And yet, as a modern English critic has noted: 'More than all his other works it was the expression of his lifelong and strenuous engagement with the thought and literature of his time.'[125]

Against the background of his own interpretation of the philosophical elements in Goethe's writing, Balthasar regards the play as an evocation of a journey from 'idea' to 'existence' with an emphasis on the basic Goethean theme of *Empor*. Faust enters a phase of life where his eros, freed from the mere enjoyment of sentiment, leads him to believe he can by mastery become the whole. Under this rubric he tries out for size every conceivable kind of ecstasy including the 'maximum of *Hingabe*' and the 'maximum of creative negation'.[126] There is a basic philosophical flaw in all this. When the diabolic Mephistopheles confronts 'Mr Microcosm', Faust sees only the urge to intensifying enhancement of the horizontal pole in humanity, whereas in God's eyes that pole is, rather, the 'basis and occasion' for the *Empor* towards the higher pole that is God himself.[127]

Not surprisingly, Faust's striving becomes erroneous, confused. Hence the irrationality of the 'pacts' he makes. The earth spirit (the demon) furnishes the real 'truth' of Faust's condition, 'the "metaphysics" of subjectivity'. And this truth or metaphysics is the very substance of a 'polar-contradicting, essentially irredeemable attitude'.[128] Faust's subsequent collapse points to the 'impossibility' of such an attitude. Faust gives expression to longing, *Sehnsucht*, but his *Empor* is vitiated from within. When for the first time he speaks of the love of God, he also names the 'longing for life's source'. But in reality

122 Ibid., p. 465.
123 Ibid., p. 483.
124 N. Boyle, *Goethe. Faust, Part One* (Cambridge 1987), pp. 1–24.
125 Ibid., p. 18.
126 *Apokalypse I*, p. 484.
127 Ibid., p. 485.
128 Ibid., p. 487.

he is determined to adopt a new 'existentiality' which is based not at all on orientation to the supreme Good. Instead, Faust will make himself the subjective correlate of the 'objective eschaton' he divines. And what this means is: 'totality as deed', *Ganzheit als Tat*.[129] As Nicholas Boyle has written, 'The world will be alive for him only in so far as it will share in *his* life.'[130]

For Balthasar, that moment is when all the powers of the negative, the unclean, come together to begin this new existence. For there is not only transcendence as contrasted with immanence. There is also the contrast of pure and impure transcendence, and the 'impure in Faust's flame [his *Empor*] ... is what takes form in Mephistopheles', Faust's tutelary demon.[131] The telltale sign that whatever transcendence Faust recognizes is essentially impure may be found in his taking nature for spirit – and mistaking striving for love. 'Faust's *Hingabe*', comments Balthasar, 'is here the true prostitution of his higher essence.'[132] There was a purity glimpsed in the drama's opening scene where, on Easter Sunday, Faust walks out with a friend to enjoy the spring landscape, and is greeted by villagers who acclaim him as a benefactor for once helping to save lives during a plague. Later, on the Brocken, the mountain where witches and wizards gather for the worship of Satan in all manner of obscenity, Faust behaves more lewdly than Mephistopheles precisely because he embodies 'perversion of the "pure", the highest'.[133]

The contrast with Margarete ('Gretchen', the girl Faust lures into crime but whose love for him retains its integrity) is marked. Her 'pure *Empor* shines bright even in delirium' – the partial madness into which she falls before her death.[134] Whereas, at her execution, a heavenly voice declares 'She is judged. She is saved', the man who ruined her life must continue his pointless wandering. Thus ends *Faust Part One*, which is not simply the first act of a drama, but a complete play in itself.

Faust Part Two will paint the same picture but not so much on the canvas of individual biographies as on that of world events. Balthasar points out the semi-real (and therefore semi-illusory) character of the settings and incidents: the show of the imperial court, the 're-materialization' of Helen of Troy, linking this to Goethe's conviction that 'appearance', the world as given in immediate experience, is only *Halbwirklichkeit*, 'half-reality'. As such, however, its 'existential index' registers higher than the 'mere subjectivity' explored in *Faust Part One* – and yet lower than the 'eternal fulfilled existence of God to which in a "beyond" it points and strives'.[135] As Faust discovers, that insufficiency also governs the case of beauty: the 'aesthetic dynamic toward the mystery' is not the 'highest existentiality' either.[136] The scene with Medusa's head confirms in advance Rilke's assertion in the *Duino Elegies* that the beautiful may simply be the beginning of the terrible, set to destroy us. Yet the 'dynamically beautiful', mediated by Faust's memory of the lost paradise of first love, gives him a glimpse of the 'summit' that is pure

---

129 Ibid., p. 491.
130 N. Boyle, *Goethe. Faust, Part One*, op. cit., p. 27.
131 *Apokalypse I*, p. 492.
132 Ibid., p. 496.
133 Ibid., p. 501.
134 Ibid.
135 Ibid., p. 502.
136 Ibid., p. 505.

transcendence, or at least of the *Empor* that leads to it. In Balthasar's interpretation, this is a moment of grace which brings home to Faust the difference between the 'objective eschaton', which cannot be seized directly (it is
not to be found in this world at all), and the subjective, self-regarding 'be all
and end all' at which his ruinous project is aiming.

As to Faust's 'final situation', Balthasar ascribes to it a 'wide-ranging
significance'. It signals, first of all, the unreality of any thought that the
earthly and the eternal grow together – that the 'sphere of the earthly' can
simply 'broaden out' to become the 'sphere of the eternal'.[137] Here a classical
mind-set rejects one distinctive feature of the Romantic (including the Promethean) picture of the world. Magic, which plays so large a part in *Faust*, is
a good metaphor for that unreality. Secondly, it brings home to us that the
'totality' Faust has actually achieved is the 'closing of earth-life's circle',
expressed in spiritual ageing, in remorseless 'subjectivization' (to the point of
blindness), and becoming not child-*like* (childlikeness will be the supreme
virtue of Balthasar's mature spirituality) but child-*ish*.[138] What will become of
such a one, Goethe leaves open to the reader's own judgment – because it is
not possible to exclude redemptive grace whose purpose is precisely to meet
the need of the undeserving. Balthasar's own proposal for Faust's (and
Goethe's) 'final formula' is 'death in the fire of longing'. That explains how
Balthasar can regard the Blessed Virgin's prayer of intercession in the
'mystical epilogue' of *Faust Part Two* as the true high point of the work:

> From Gretchen and Helen via Sophia, who brings the best of our
> interior [effort] in her train, there is higher *Empor* ('up and beyond') to
> Mary. It is she, as the highest human mid-point who through her own
> looking to what is above and farther, draws us into the wonder of the
> mystery.[139]

These words anticipate what will be, as a theologian, Balthasar's characteristically 'high' yet far from 'separated' Mariology.

---

137 Ibid., p. 509.
138 Ibid.
139 Ibid., p. 514.

7

❧❦❧

From Jean Paul to Nietzsche

Jean Paul

Balthasar selects two 'autumnal fruits' of Idealism to round off his account of Prometheanism. They are a somewhat ill-assorted pair, Hegel and Jean Paul. Anyone even slightly acquainted with the history of European thought will have heard of Hegel. But who was Jean Paul? 'Jean Paul' was the literary sobriquet of Johann Paul Friedrich Richter (1763–1825), imaginative writer of novels often compared – for the benefit of English readers – to those of Laurence Sterne (1713–1768), and author of once celebrated treatises on aesthetics and pedagogy. The son of a poor country schoolmaster, he was fortunate to have a number of woman patrons, one of whom brought him to Weimar where he egregiously failed to secure the favour of Goethe. In 1808, the archbishop of Mainz, the erstwhile 'prince-primate' of Germany, gave him a pension which, in the years after the Napoleonic restructuring of the German States, the king of Bavaria continued to pay. Balthasar evidently considered the Bavarian government's money well-spent. He treats Jean Paul under the rubric *Das Reich des Alters*, 'the realm of [mature] age': thus making him the last in a quartet of which – to remind the reader – the previous three were Novalis (for childhood), Hölderlin (for youth), and Schiller (for grown manhood).

Balthasar appreciates Jean Paul not only for his humour but also for what he terms his 'ability to confer world-creating form' on diverse areas of human living.[1] Indeed, the Promethean-Idealist 'idea' is, in his writing, 'dissolved into life'. (Just so, by a convergent movement – Balthasar thinks – Hegel brought to a completion the integration of 'life' into the 'idea'.) It also helps that no other author of the period has so much to say about death, immortality and the end of the world – perfect material, then, for a study of the 'apocalypse of the soul'. Jean Paul took up a thoroughgoingly 'existential' attitude to the Last Things. They are for him, so Balthasar approvingly sums up, the medium of the soul's life ('that wherein and wherefore the soul lives') as well as its fulfilment. How much of Christian eschatology was mirrored in Jean Paul's version of Prometheanism – if such it is – will shortly be seen.

Baldly, Balthasar terms Jean Paul an 'opponent of Idealist subjectivity', a judgment based on Richter's sharp criticism of Fichte. That Fichte could find

---

1 *Apokalypse I*, p. 515.

a place for a 'thou' beside the 'I' only insofar as moral action entailed its postulation seemed scandalous to Richter. Indeed, Jean Paul felt strongly the incongruity of constructing a world-view on the basis of the subject, the human 'I', at all. He explained in a letter of 1800: 'The older one gets, the more humbly one believes in the almightiness of objectivity. *God* is the truest and the only subject.'[2] And in the preamble to *Clavis* he described reason or the 'I' as but a break in the clouds through which the 'distant, expansive fire of heaven' sends fitful light to earth. The personal 'I' is no 'temple, altar, or even representative of celestial truth'.[3] In a Goethe-like attempt to portray the truth of existence as the 'ongoing reciprocal incorporation of all the transcendental attitudes of man', he lists the 'primary things' as beauty (art), truth, morality, blessedness. A synthesis of these 'four evangelists' is not only necessary but *already given* in inseparable organic-spiritual unity.[4] Statements of partial truths must reflect this. A few 'truth-probes' into the individual's life are hardly a basis for coming to know the infinite in its eternity and incommensurability. This, along with an over-estimate of one of the foursome, namely art, is the burden of Jean Paul's criticisms of Goethe and Schiller.

For Jean Paul, just as only an infinite hand could have made man so only an infinite eye could see him justly. In *Etwas über dem Menschen* he wrote that the human creature is 'in a position to become everything, but not anything wholly or for long'.[5] Neither 'night' nor 'day' have the mastery in man; hence the twilight in which he moves. Two powers of the soul help us to see him aright: humour, which Jean Paul learned not only from Sterne but from Jonathan Swift (1667–1745), and, a far commoner feature of the contemporary literature, feeling (*Gefühl*). Somewhat vatically, Balthasar opines that, in Jean Paul: 'Feeling uncovers wonder, the positive, tender transparency of ... the more-than-earthly ... realm [while] humour covers it protectingly with the negative of nothingness and thus shows it off indirectly.'[6]

One main reason Balthasar chose Jean Paul to represent the 'realm of maturity' is his predilection for humour, the 'roguish wisdom of age'. Allusively, humour can point to ultimate truths. Jean Paul liked allegory, and Balthasar is inclined to think allegory bears a relation to humour. Allegory is based on the idea that between the mind and its expressions we have to take into account some distance, some disproportion. Behind humour, likewise, there lies a sense of incongruous lack of fit. More profoundly, Jean Paul's 'symbolics' (or 'allegorics') have not just an epistemological or anthropological meaning. They also tell of the ontological and the cosmic, or what Balthasar calls a 'tender harmony of the inner and outer world'. 'All is vesture, all is expression. The poet only selects from the infinite play of relationships the simplest figures.'[7] But 'simplest' here could sometimes mean seemingly crazy allegorically figurations. Whether by symbol or allegory, what Jean Paul wanted to get across to his readers was that soul-culture is not just self-referential. The eternal divine light shines through all objective

2 To Friedrich Heinrich Jacobi, 1 April 1800, cited in ibid., p. 516.
3 To the same, 6 March 1806, cited in ibid., p. 517.
4 Ibid.
5 Cited in *Apokalypse I*, p. 518.
6 Ibid., p. 519.
7 Ibid., p. 520.

realities (this is a difference from Goethe) even though (and here Jean Paul agrees with Goethe) what we seek in soul-making should not be 'cosmic consciousness' so much as the liberation, purification and strengthening of the love-capacity, for everlasting life. *Bildung* for this writer means, in essence, *interior apocalypse*.

Balthasar considers his 'existential eschatology' under three headings: first, that key concept of *Bildung* itself; secondly, Jean Paul's eschatology as the expression of his distinctive attitude to existence; and thirdly, the implications of his breakthrough – for this is how Balthasar tends to regard it – for the entire Prometheus problem.

For Jean Paul, the culture that is soul-forming is shot through with longing for (in his parable) a blessed island whose reflection we catch sight of in the deep sea of life. Above all in *music*. Such longing is not nostalgia for a land of the past but a quickening of desire for a land of the future. But the heavenly vision we glimpse 'below' and 'ahead' is, as the parable suggests, a mirror for what is really *above*. Jean Paul satirizes the evolutionary mythology which by an endless progression from the 'soul of an oyster to that of frog' and beyond, expects to see humankind cross the barrier of finitude through the impetus of natural development. As he put it in *Kampanertal* (1797), 'I believe in no created culmination.' It is not that the human essence will gradually approximate to the divine (as in different ways Herder, Fichte and Schelling thought would happen). Rather, the relation to God of our present and abiding humanity must intensify, through the formation (or culture) of love. The emphasis on love, an enduring programme for life, helped Jean Paul to avoid the Romantic cultus of privileged moments. For Jean Paul, the point of such moments is simply to exhibit the fullness of the flow of time. Balthasar thinks this is the reason why music accompanies all Jean Paul's 'high scenes', for music is beautiful only in and as the flow of time. Experience is not ultimate. It is just a given, the 'direction' of whose 'meaning' we must discern.[8] Jean Paul finds there are here only two possibilities. Either, longing is its own object: it is simply a datum of the human animal and there is nothing beyond that to say. Or else the solution to the contradiction of human longing and the human situation lies in a realm beyond the world – *in such a fashion, however, that that realm reaches into this world precisely as a condition of possibility for the occurrence of the contradiction in question.* In the short story *Das Leben nach dem Tode* (1794), Jean Paul points out that thirst is hardly conceivable if potable liquids do not exist. But in the case of the thirst for transcendence, what man strives for is what would cancel out his being as he knows it. Our highest freedom lies in seeking that which transcends our freedom as a whole, while at the same time we cannot find contentment unless we are rooted in this earth. Thus our essence tears apart. This affirmation leads Balthasar on to consider Jean Paul's 'existential eschatology'.

Jean Paul did not set much store by the philosophical proofs of the soul's immortality – the arguments from simplicity, non-corruptibility, and the like. Or rather, he was interested in them only insofar as their terminology could be translated into the language of love. The sort of 'proof' he went in for was an existential analysis of a kind Balthasar does not hesitate to compare with that of Heidegger – the Heidegger, presumably, of *Sein und Zeit*. The

8 Ibid., p. 528.

conviction of the soul's deathlessness, wrote Jean Paul in his posthumous
Selina, 'grows with a thousand invisible fibres from the wide ground of
feeling'.[9] As Balthasar comments, the climate of Idealism guaranteed a
hearing for Jean Paul's general approach, which has affinities with the early
Schiller's portrayal of the 'dialectic' between the 'day-side' and 'night-side' of
existence. But unlike later writers such as Kleist and Schopenhauer who tried
to integrate the negative aspects of existence into a unified view of *this* world,
Jean Paul maintains the necessity of an either/or. If death is the end and the
soul's flame turns at last to dust and ashes, then no one can say 'I loved', but
only 'I wanted to love'.

The most powerful of Jean Paul's eschatological writings is surely his
'Speech of the dead Christ from the edifice of the world that there is no God'
where the dying Jesus, buffeted by the storms of chaos and looking into the
eye of the Father, finds there only an empty socket and breaks out – or down
– in unceasing lament. The point of this disturbing vision is not to commend
atheism. On the contrary, its point is to picture what for atheists eternity
would be. And the answer is, it would be unsupportable because, quite
simply: 'God is the condition of possibility of human life the meaning of
which is love.'[10] And Jean Paul's dramatic stories, such as *Siebenkäs*, seek to
show how the attempt to affirm an unconditional love within the limits of an
absolute, atheistic finitude are illusion. Balthasar's finds his 'tragic-heroic'
(but also humoristic) portrayals among the sublimest products of German
Idealism: a 'summit' soaring above their neighbours.[11] They are a reply to
Nietzsche given in advance.

But there is not only the *whether* of eternal life; there is also – if eternal life
there be – the *how*. Jean Paul considered two possibilities. The notion of the
transmigration of souls who, embodied in ever 'higher' bodies, would come
to inhabit a form of time that approximated to that of eternity, had found a
supporter in Herder. But after Kant and Fichte, to consider time and eternity
on a single spectrum seemed hopelessly naïve. The alternative was the
concept of an immediate post-mortem return of the human spirit to God. The
trouble was that disincarnate existence did not seem to be distinctively
human existence at all. As Balthasar remarks, Jean Paul had unconsciously
stumbled on the necessity of the Christian doctrine of resurrection which
furnishes the missing link in the chain. Only divine transfiguration of man's
two-in-one nature can fit the bill.[12] Unfortunately, his 'grossly sensuous'
misunderstanding of what the Resurrection entails turned him against the
solution that was so close to hand. Yet, from a departure-point in Idealism he
had in effect rediscovered the essentials of Christian eschatology. He saw
how, on the one hand, 'the only thing that can still our longing is the breakthrough of the vision of God spilling its graciousness over all nature', and on
the other, 'like Christian theology he hesitates on the border-line between
natural and supernatural transfiguration'.[13]

Whether a 'natural' resurrection might have been possible; whether a

9 Cited in ibid., p. 533. Balthasar compares Jean Paul's use of *Gefühl* with Heidegger's
   favoured term *Gestimmtheit*.
10 Ibid., p. 535.
11 Ibid., p. 541.
12 Ibid., p. 545.
13 Ibid., p. 547.

'natural' transfiguration could be a preamble to a truly gracious version of the same: these are questions to which he has no answer. But then they are also, so one would have thought, questions a sane Christian theology (as distinct from a theology working with not just a distinction but a *separation* between nature and grace) has no particular reason to ask.

So far as the further implications of this eschatology, its wider purview, are concerned, Balthasar considers Jean Paul's thought a splendid statement of the paradox that makes men great and is the measure of their greatness. The paradox runs like this: when our highest earthly wishes are best fulfilled, then is our longing for a different reality most acute. Balthasar calls this state of affairs 'transcendental suffering'. At first sight it seems indistinguishable from mystical potentiality. No claim could be less true. Something new is in process of appearing: an apocalypse of the soul which expects an ever deeper love of earth coincidentally with an ever intenser longing for the eternal home. It is an apocalypse where the naked heart confesses its final defencelessness, its incapacity to fulfil its own desire. Neatly inverting a Kierkergaardian phrase, Balthasar calls its malaise not 'sickness until death' but 'sickness unto life'. For woe betide the person who is healthy vis-à-vis this sickness, who by coldness and closedness of heart, by formalism, lets his soul turn to stone. That is one common way into the realm of evil, and, rather naughtily, Jean Paul, who had been rejected by the master of Weimar, associated it with Goethe and his classicizing bent. The second route into evil is self-referentiality. Making longing a matter of enjoyment, aspiring to transcendence just for the sake of it, playing histrionics with the holy: these are the games of the self-absorbed. In keeping with his exalted view of Jean Paul's significance, Balthasar calls this the first appearance in German literature of the 'curse of modern schizophrenia and the immanent misuse of transcendence which is its secret ground'.[14]

Is there, then, nothing at all Promethean about Jean Paul's world-view? Balthasar will not say so. For Richter, every soul can be called 'Promethean' not only in its refusal to sanction finitude but also, and more strikingly, in the 'vehemence of its will to eternity'.[15] And once again there crops up that word *Schweben*. This is an anthropology where man oscillates or hovers between fulfilment and longing, world and God, time and the eternal, something memorably imaged in the love of one of Jean Paul's characters for high places – church towers, mountain tops, the upper branches of cypress trees from where Albano glimpses that perfect island in the Lago di Maggiore, Isola Bella. This is, as Balthasar remarks, a 'higher mid-point' from which to look out towards both realms.[16] And although Jean Paul certainly believed in an infinite personal God in the Christian sense, he could not envisage any way in which that God could touch the soul 'substantially' except in the experience of love between human beings themselves. In thus privileging the 'act' above the 'object', God's indwelling of human activity rather than God in himself, there is a sense in which this author so praised by Balthasar remained an Idealist to the end.

14 Ibid., p. 552.
15 Ibid., p. 557.
16 Ibid., p. 558.

Hegel

With the best-known of the classical German philosophers, Georg Friedrich Wilhelm Hegel (1770–1831), a Swabian and product of the Tübingen *Stift*, and from 1818 on an immensely influential professor in the University of Berlin, we arrive at a remarkably similar conclusion by what could hardly be a more different route. But Balthasar's language in introducing Hegel is itself apocalyptic. In language more normally applied by Scripture to divine being and action, he calls Hegel a consuming fire. He is a sacrificial fire, and a fire of judgment, and in both respects an eschatological fire, with which Balthasar does not hesitate to juxtapose a passage in First Corinthians often treated in Catholic theology as a 'proof-text' for the doctrine of Purgatory.[17] This is yet another 'Hegel image' to add to the gallery of such and, set forth in these high biblical terms, it is nothing if not distinctive.[18]

For Balthasar, Hegel's 'enthusiasm' is comparable with the Gospel leaven in the dough: it gets inside things and elevates them by patient intellectual labour. Eschewing Romantic feeling as all too contentless intensity, and classicizing all-roundness as all too empty breadth, the preamble to the *Phenomenology of Spirit* strikes out on a path of its own. His predecessors wanted the goal – the ripe fruit of totality – without putting in the necessary spade-work. Only by tracing the entire odyssey of spirit through human history, with all its ramifications in culture, will the philosopher be ready to offer a world-view: or rather, not 'a' world-view but the self-interpretation of spirit at last become transparent through the philosopher's faithful work.

For Hegel, process is the truth, the truth that is the whole. And conversely the whole is that being which through its own development has come to its fulfilment. Hegel's concern was with how spirit (or mind) comes to understand itself in that process of its becoming. This could be the key to a total picture of the real since Hegel treated as axiomatic the Fichtean conviction that spirit *is* the truth of nature. But Fichte had never been able to relate satisfactorily the two poles of 'thinking' and 'life', while, for his part, Schelling remained content with a purely contemplative (*schauend*) view of their interrelation – dubbed by Hegel, in an uncomplimentary phrase, the 'vanity of subjectivity'. The greater sense of concrete existence in such authors as Hölderlin, Novalis, Goethe, Schiller, allowed Hegel to fill out the bare Schellingian schema with the rich stuff of life-experience.

Though Hegel was a systematic thinker, Balthasar inclines to the view that the system in Hegel's writing is relatively unimportant. In all essentials the schema came from Schelling to whom it was far more significant. What really counts in Hegel is not system but synthesis, the synthesis of a wondrous process whereby the phoenix of spirit-borne reality rises again and again from what had seemed the ashes of its own contradictions. Over against Fichte and Schelling, Hegel always defined his philosophy, after all, as *concrete thinking* (however much in an empiricist climate, such as that of modern England, he may be regarded as an abstract speculator *in excelsis*). His most fundamental aim was to reconcile realism with Idealism. Schelling also had that in mind but far too tentatively. The 'I' is the 'I', it is its own object and

17 1 Corinthians 3.12–15
18 W.R. Beyer, *Hegel-Bilder. Kritik der Hegel Deutungen* (Berlin 1970).

essence: true (Idealism). But *only* true insofar as the 'I' realizes it is such, thanks to its relation with the 'other' (realism). Hegel's 'openness to the world' and in particular his desire to do justice to 'all the forms of humanity', equals Herder's, surpasses Goethe's. His appetite for appropriating the real in its diversity was 'insatiable'.[19]

Exploring the content of Hegelian apocalypse in the *Phenomenology of Spirit*, getting to grips with the ideas about death, judgment, transfiguration and eternity that belong with this utterly immanentist eschatology, and – on the basis not only of the *Phenomenology* but also of Hegel's lectures on the philosophy of religion and the philosophy of history – interpreting the last of the *Weltgestalten* to come from the circle of Prometheus-thinkers: this is Balthasar's programme.

Balthasar begins by showing how the 'apocalypse of the soul' simply *must* be a major preoccupation of Hegel's philosophy. For Hegel, a proof of God's existence is valid insofar as it is identical with the elevation of mind to God. Cosmological proofs of God's existence merely describe that elevation. The attraction to Hegel of his – idiosyncratic – version of the ontological proof was that, 'I myself [he means any "I"] as thinking am this going over [to God], this spiritual movement.'[20] The ontological argument, in Hegel's eyes, stands for just that. It is at once apparent, declares Balthasar, that 'the apocalypse of the soul' is going to be – under whatever description – a vital theme in Hegel's work.

But now Balthasar feels the need to indicate how, on his view, Hegel's corpus should be approached. Hegel's 'method' consists on the one hand in relishing the resistance offered to thought by objective reality in all its forms – a resistance that only little by little gives way to the thinker's onslaught. On the other hand, that method crucially includes what Balthasar terms the 'ascetic abstemiousness' (*Enthaltsamkeit*) Hegel brought to the furnishing of a conceptual scheme. There is for Hegel no objective measure for thinking, since spirit is the measure of truth and spirit grasps itself as true only in its movement – and thus from its last known measure. Yet this is no flight from objectivity, for spirit must constantly be testing its own adequacy to the object, in the tension between 'as I know it' and 'as it is in itself'. This takes courage, not Cartesian doubt – which, as Hegel points out in the *Phenomenology*, can itself quite properly be doubted. The fear of erring may itself be error. Even though Hegel's aim is to take what has been analysed, or distinguished, and unify it at a higher level, in the concept (*der Begriff*), Balthasar agrees that, from the standpoint of Cartesian rationality – its 'thought-ideal' and 'primal image of reason' – the Hegelian approach could only be deemed irrational.

But, he insists, that approach is *not* irrational if we see it as the mirror image of the 'oscillating, flowing character of thought itself'.[21] Hegel considered his philosophy to be inseparably ecstasy and repose, Dionysian and Apollonian. Balthasar regards it as the 'exact middle' between Leibniz and Nietzsche, between logic and the 'philosophy of life'. These are, on the whole, commendations. And the ground of this favour is not far to seek.

---

19 *Apokalypse I*, p. 575.
20 From the *Lectures on the Philosophy of Religion*, I, 166, cited in ibid., p. 569.
21 *Apokalyse I* p. 573.

Hegel rejects both pure Idealism and empiricism. He regards sheer subjectivity and mere objectivity as hopeless abstractions, 'dead immediacies'.
The 'yeast' of the infinite – but, by itself, vacuous – subject must be united
with the 'dough' of the finite object if epistemic nourishment is to ensue. If
anything, it was philosophies based on the empty infinite which excited
Hegel's strongest contempt. Balthasar explains why. 'It is when the generality of subjectivity makes itself the servant and underling of the generality
of objectivity ... that it becomes a concrete, in-formed generality, whereas
before it was only fanciful.'[22] The high point of subjectivity lies in recognizing
the authentic universality of the objective. (For Balthasar there is a link here
between Hegel and Goethe.)

What, then, in this Hegelian philosophy, *is* the content of the apocalypse
of the soul? It is an ever-deepening communion between the infinite-
subjective and the finite-objective, at all possible levels of consciousness. As
the *Phenomenology* has it, 'pure self-knowing in the absolute otherness of the
other being' is the 'foundation and ground of knowledge or knowing in
general'.[23] The being that is 'in itself reflection' – this is for Hegel the spiritual-intellectual dimension in which mind attains its own truth. And Balthasar does not hesitate to write that *love* is the real fulfilment of this spiritual
'dimension'. Where mind (or spirit) puts in its appearance as 'the other', a
new identity spans the abyss-like alienation which kept the two parties apart.
To leave the other its freedom and autonomy is not only humility. It is power
of the highest magnitude, because by its means nature becomes not only *an-
sich*, an 'in itself', but *für-mich*: 'for me', for spirit. And this is the power of
love, showing itself in such interaction as what spirit 'substantially' is.[24]

Since spirit comes to a judgment about itself only by way of its activities –
which must mean its appearance in *what is other* than itself – there can for
Hegel be no such thing as a direct apocalypse (in the sense of disclosure) of
the soul. No serious content can be read off from introspective findings, not
even from the aesthetic 'self-sympathy' of Schelling. How then is the soul
disclosed? By ascent to the 'metaphysic of love' through what Balthasar
terms, paraphrasing Hegel, the 'higher forms of self-emptying' or, in the
Swiss critic's own preferred vocabulary, *Hingabe*, surrender.[25] For Hegel the
law of love is the 'real structure of the world in its ascending potencies' – a
sign, for Balthasar, that mystical potentiality is back again. For in the intensifying love-enabled *Für-sich-sein* of objective reality (in, that is, the world's
developing subjectivity) these 'stages' show themselves as 'existential
potencies of God'. From below, from the world's side, this seems like the
'becoming' of God himself. From above, however, from God's side, the same
reality appears, rather, as the 'ever more inward participation of the world in
the eternal presupposition of the substantial divine love'.[26]

This is a 'structure' that finds its initial fulfilment in religion, considered as
relation to the 'plenary presupposition of love' – the absolute spirit itself. On
Balthasar's reading of the *Lectures on the Philosophy of Religion*, love is not just

---

22 Ibid., p. 574. The contrast of informed and fanciful is made by a German pun: 'gebildet'
    and 'eingebildet'.
23 G.F.W. Hegel, *The Phenomenology of Spirit*, 17, cited in ibid., p. 579.
24 Ibid., p. 580.
25 Ibid., p. 582.
26 Ibid., p. 583.

the bridge of identity between myself and another consciousness. It is also the bridge of identity God throws over to me. Just as I know myself in another, so God knows himself in me. This licenses Balthasar in saying that, for Hegel, religion *is* the self-consciousness of God (i.e., in us). Not only an analogy of being but an analogy of consciousness unites God and man – the affirmation of which is to Hegel the advantage of 'modern' theology over its classic (patristic and mediaeval) predecessor. Clearly, Balthasar rejects that reading of Hegel's work which would treat its theological – or 'ontotheological' – elements as mere surface, or useful code.[27]

But here Balthasar interjects a comment based on his rapidly developing acquaintance with those earlier sources. Treating man as graciously united with God not only as object but as 'inner act-principle' was not unknown to Gregory of Nyssa and Augustine (two of the patristic figures on whom he would either write or had already written),[28] not to mention Thomas Aquinas (on whose treatise on contemplation he would produce a commentary),[29] and a variety of mediaeval mystics (many of whom he would cite in, for example, the theological aesthetics and dramatics). It remains true that the idea of the activity of absolute spirit in the human spirit was taken further by Hegel – in ways not always compatible with the Gospel of grace – than in these pre-modern figures.

Not that Hegel lacks a doctrine of grace, as Balthasar's remarks on his account of revelation suffice to show. For Hegel, tutored here by Lutheran Christianity, revelation is the appearing of the divine consciousness in finite, sensuous form which is simultaneously the unmediated divine nature. It is not, however, a revelation of 'something', *Etwas*. Rather is it, in a seeming tautology, a revelation of God's own self-revealing. (This insistence that revelation can only be *self*-revelation was in the twentieth century to have a profound, and not entirely salubrious, influence on theology right across confessional boundaries. For where now is specific truth-content?) In the movement of revelation God becomes in his self-communication to us 'for himself' and not only 'in himself'. And this same self-disclosure, happening by grace in the activity of human subjects, in turn frees their subjectivity for God. From all of which Balthasar draws the large conclusions that, for Hegel 'love is therefore, simply speaking, the apocalyptic', and – further – 'person and love are reciprocally defining'.[30]

The absolute independence of the One – or a one, for that matter – was always a non-starter, as in different ways Hegel's *Logik* and his

---

27 Recent Anglophone examples would be R. Solomon, *In the Spirit of Hegel: A Study of G.W.F. Hegel's 'Phenomenology of Spirit'* (Oxford 1983); A. White, *Absolute Knowledge: Hegel and the Problem of Metaphysics* (Athens, OH 1983).

28 His earliest contribution to Augustine studies, a translation of some of the *Enarrationes in Psalmos* with an introduction, appeared the year before *Apokalypse I* as *Aurelius Augustinus. Über die Psalmen* (Leipzig 1936); in the year that *Apokalypse II/III* appeared he published a sketch of what would be his Gregory of Nyssa monograph as 'Présence et pensée. La philosophie religieuse de Grégoire de Nysse', *Recherches de Science Religieuse* 29 (1939), pp. 513–39.

29 For his chief contribution to the literature on Thomas Aquinas, see *Thomas von Aquin. Besondere Gnadengaben und die zwei Wege menschlichen Lebens. Kommentar zur Summa Theologica II-II, 171–182* (= Deutsche Thomas-Ausgabe, Bd. 23, Heidelberg Graz [1954], pp. 252–464).

30 *Apokalypse I*, p. 586.

Naturphilosophie claimed to show. And the ultimate upshot of this discussion is that triadicity or 'Trinitarianness' is the true idea of all being, whether in God or outside him. This proposal, expressed in the Hegel section of *Apokalypse I* in a fashion somewhat hasty and curtailed, is an issue to which Balthasar will return at some length in the final volume of his theological dramatics. Rightly, Balthasar remarks on how the Trinitarianism of the *Lectures on the Philosophy of Religion* explains Hegel's hostility to pantheism, and indeed to any form of 'all is one' thinking. His love metaphysic, in whose light Hegel, like Fichte before him, rejected the notion that vision is the ultimate in human activity, may also have influenced Balthasar's own eschatology, where the theme of the beatific vision is largely replaced by alternative accounts of the ultimate divine–human communion.

Which leads one to ask, what specific ideas of death and transfiguration *does* Balthasar find worthy of mention in Hegel's eschatology? Let it be said straightaway that, in comparison with the gallery of predecessors so far discussed, Hegel approached these topics with one enormous advantage. Whereas none of them had been able to resolve the inner contradiction between the divine and the worldly, Hegel had identified the means to do so. And this was *die Möglichkeit der Liebe*, 'the possibility of love'.[31] And yet things can hardly be as simple as that! In fact, Hegel brought the difficulties encountered by other thinkers under the concept, at his hands a comprehensive one, of 'creative negation'. What does Hegel mean by that? He means self-losing, self-giving, self-sacrificing, by the 'consuming' of everything that is particular about spirit, so as to allow spirit to step forth in 'naked generality'. He was referring to the kind of death for the sake of wider life that is not only biological, when the individual perishes in the survival of the species, but is to be found in analogous ways at other stages of the world process, in other orders of reality – and indeed of thought: 'abstraction' is actually the model for his concept of 'negation'. Such negation can be called 'creative' because it is, he considered, superlatively positive in its effects. Spirit finds its real magnitude in such seeming diminution. It is here, in this disruption, that it discovers its power, which is a power to give up its life and take it back again. 'True substance' is: 'being or immediacy which does not have mediation [expression in, and in favour of, what is other than itself] outside it, but *is* such mediation'.[32]

Just as generality is found dispersed in particularity, thus achieving the *An-sich*, so the particular dissolves itself into the general, but in a new fashion as the *Für-sich*. Spirit, self-conscious reality, is – in a metaphor already used for Hölderlin's attempt at a poetic eschatology – the thornbush of sacred Scripture, burning but never consumed, at once 'the *An-und-für-sich-sein* of the whole'.[33] (Why Balthasar likes that metaphor is fairly obvious: it stands for transformation in continuing identity.) In this perspective, transience looks remarkably different.

And now Balthasar introduces the Trinitarian comparison which, in Hegel's philosophy overall, was never far from the German philosopher's mind. If the Father is the moment of sheer essence in its immobility or at least

31 Ibid., p. 590.
32 Ibid., p. 593.
33 Ibid., p. 595.

unmovedness, then the Son is the moment of the painful yet blessed sacrifice of *Für-sich-sein*, at once joining himself to and separating himself from the Father. Yet only in that dialectic does the Spirit proceed from Father and Son. *Only in that dialectic are the two 'moments' living spirit.* And because the human being is divine, the total truth of human spirit can only take place, then, by way of all three moments, and so of the life-in-death they convey.

The *Lectures on the Philosophy of Religion* develop this bald claim – at once about the concept of death and the concept of thinking – by telling a story in Trinitarian terms. Considered as a philosophical model for such, 'the Father', once removed from the triune life, can stand for the sheer negativity that rests content in the general, excluding sacrifice, imprisoning all transcendence in the 'arid "I"'. But precisely at the zenith of this attitude it strikes awareness that being is left just 'lying there' by such absolute *In-sich-sein*. 'The heaven of subjectivity then becomes its hell.'[34] Creative negation now takes over as consciousness confronts total anxiety – an anxiety that concerns everything about its own existence. It abandons fixity and gives itself to flow instead.

Thus thinking enters the 'world of the Son'. It is the specifying mark of God's *An-sich* – his essence – to be *Für-sich*. The contradiction announces that existential dimension whereby the self suffers alienation within its own identity. *Negation is in God*, and this sets a great question mark against the reliability not only of eternity but also of truth itself. Now God's 'other', considered *as* other, is precisely the world, is ourselves. (Without the world, for Hegel, God is not God. Here, remarks Balthasar, the 'whole tradition of mystical potentiality, from Plotinus through Böhme to Schelling, is awake again'.)[35] This is both bad news and good news. On the one hand, negativity is the 'foundation of the world'. On the other hand, this same negativity is a *divine* moment – though in the content of the world it only is so as purified, sublimated, exalted, not just through the ascending stages of natural evolution with their ever greater possibilities of self-transcendence but above all in the predestined mystical head of the world, Jesus Christ. Unfortunately, for man, who is not only spirit (in which respect he shares in the divine existence) but *finite* spirit, the dialectic of bad news and good here may well consist in discreet phases in his life and consciousness. And this for Hegel is the meaning of sin and the Fall.

Man (rightly) sallies forth from his existence as simply part of nature, but in doing so, in entering the world of the conscious other, does he not experience an alienation from himself, and with this the possibility of the lie as well as truth, and hence of sin and spiritual death? With the Fall, man starts to experience himself over against God, and at the same time as a 'naked monad' that has lost the spontaneous comfort of the world. The Atonement for Hegel is when in Christ God takes on the infinite contradiction between himself and the world and appears immediately in the human environment as the conqueror of sin from the inside. The death of Christ is thus the epiphany of extremest love – which Hegel calls – and in the context of European events at the turn of the eighteenth and nineteenth

---

34 Ibid., p. 596.
35 Ibid., p. 597.

centuries the phrase was no empty one – the 'revolutionary element' that brings into the world 'another power'.

The outpouring of the Holy Spirit shows the redemption is fulfilled. The moments of 'anxiety unto death' and 'endless pain' are in different senses cancelled out and yet taken up into a higher synthesis, as is the death of negativity in God himself. The seriousness, pain, patience and labour of the negative must be incorporated into the idea of God's life as a 'play of love' if that phrase is not to trivialize its divine subject. 'Rest in unrest', *Ruhe in Unruhe*, is Hegel's formula for reality, and it links him more to Schiller, Goethe and Jean Paul than to the early Idealists. But ultimately, Balthasar would place Hegel in a series stretching from Luther through Schelling and Kierkegaard to Karl Barth, in whom, indeed, *Apokalypse III* will end, for all of these thinkers cannot imagine divine love without simultaneously invoking fearfulness, grief, worry and death. Of the five it is Hegel Balthasar praises. He is the 'brightest' of these figures, since 'his mystical flame does not let more darkness be sucked out of death than is necessary for letting darkness glow'.[36]

And so, through death, to Hegel on *Verklärung*, transfiguration. Balthasar points out that, despite Hegel's emphasis on the evolution of nature and history, a process of development whose stages he considered to be logically and not just empirically interconnected, his concept of eschatology is not at all teleological. He does not see things and events as in movement towards a 'fifth act'. Rather is his idea of eternity one of vertical relationship. It is world history itself, at each moment of its happening, which is the judgment of the world. World history is the 'interpretation of spirit in time'. For Hegel, teleology is dissolved into axiology, the eternal as *now*. As Balthasar points out, the reason for this must surely be the way in the *Phenomenology of Spirit* he regards the concept of the beyond, the world or age to come, *das Jenseits*, as basically a preliminary sketch of the true idea of ultimacy, which is that of a dialectical interpenetration of this world or age and the other – *Diesseits und Jenseits*.

This does not prevent Hegel from speaking respectfully from time to time of the scenario entertained by the Church. In the *Lectures on the Philosophy of Religion* Hegel in no way dismisses the Christian doctrine of an immortality that opens out onto conscious enjoyment of the truth of God, thereby allowing for an eternal relationship which is rightly described in future terms. But as a 'determination' and a 'life' that is no part of time or temporality such a belief cannot enter systematic philosophy where it could only be an esoteric element. Hegel, however, can still consider its odyssey under the rubric of the history of religion.

Here he considers not only eternal life for the soul but the life of the risen body likewise. Comparing and contrasting the Church's eschatology with a variety of competitors, chiefly from the Mediterranean basin and South Asia, Hegel regards the christological component in Last Things issues as key. Thanks to the Paschal mystery, Christian eschatology means not the final deconstruction of human nature but, on the contrary, 'its highest

36 Ibid., p. 602.

preservation even in death, and in the highest love'.[37] The mysteries of the Resurrection and Ascension bear this witness.

An unavoidable ambiguity, however, clouds Hegel's presentation. 'Immortality' for Hegel is being lifted above the power of (degenerative) change. But does he not make it clear how that is for him not so much a gift from God's reconciling action in Jesus Christ as it is an aboriginal possession of spirit? 'Eternity' is given with humanity itself. The self-consciousness of spirit is already a 'moment' in eternal life. The true measure of eternity for Hegel is participation in *Für-sich-sein*. The interesting thing about Hegel's account of the latter is its yielding up the axiom, 'The more ec-static a being is – the more it is for others, the more en-static it is – the more it is itself.' Which means that, in matters of the time/eternity relationship (and not only there) Hegel's ontology is – and all merit to him – an ontology of love.

Contrary, says Balthasar, to 'many interpretations' (he names, though, no actual critics of Hegel's corpus), Hegel tries to serve the truth of eschatology as a 'dynamic interpenetration of the general and the particular' – as, on Balthasar's account, he has done throughout his conceptual work.[38] The individual is incorporated into historically developing society and culture, and this grants the 'spirit of world history' a certain claim to use him or her as means to a general end. But just because the individual, thus incorporated, is a 'member' of a wider whole, does not give that whole the right to treat the individual as though he or she were *only* a member. To do so would be to misconceive the individual as the general – precisely what he or she is not! In the biblically suggested language of Christian discourse, the redeemed person is not simply a building-block in the New Jerusalem.

In his concluding summary, Balthasar will present Hegel's view of civil society, a dialectic of the abstract *Für-sich* of the individual and the abstract *An-sich* of the people, as to a degree the translation into secular terms of the Christian doctrine of the Church. (He will continue the compliment by repatriating a good number of Hegel's reflections on this topic, turning them to use in his own ecclesiology in the third volume of the theological logic.)

What in the last analysis Balthasar retains from Hegel's metaphysics and eschatology is its character as the 'glorification of sacrifice'. This follows, really, from Hegel's fundamental anthropology, whereby the substance of the 'I' is its self-emptying. The sacrifices we all make, in some form or other, on the altar of society 'show outwardly what spirit inwardly is'.[39] Such sacrifice is 'what is fruitful *simpliciter*', and it suggests, as the *Lectures on the Philosophy of Religion* do not hesitate to point out, how such 'lower' forms as marriage and friendship are taken up into, not rejected by, theandric – divine-human – love.

Balthasar's account of Hegel has been pretty favourable, and so it may come as a shock to read in his coda a demonstration of how Hegel was a rationalist to the core. The goal of Hegel's system is not in fact religious love, love considered as a mystical, grace-borne relationship. Its goal is love all right, but love only as absolute knowing, love as 'idea'. For Hegel love is only the *form* of that truly unconditional knowing which thus stands over above it.

---

37 Cited from the *Lectures on the Philosophy of Religion* at ibid., p. 605.
38 Ibid., p. 608.
39 Ibid., p. 610.

This is why he can be called a Promethean thinker *par excellence*. It *is* Promethean, Titanic, to *want power over what is highest*.

In effect, in Hegelianism, love is the rationality proper to a spirited animal of a (self-)sacrificing sort. Hegel may call religion the content of philosophy and philosophy itself worship. But that is another way of saying that only philosophy can grasp the concept to which religion points, can draw the truth out of that concept and come to understand its necessity. The faith that would understand (here Balthasar refers to Anselm of Canterbury's celebrated formula, *credo ut intelligam*) terminates in a knowing that, digesting revelation's objective content, is concretely one with God's own thinking of himself. Really, revelation for Hegel is memory, *anamnêsis*. It is what we ought to have known all along anyway. Ultimately, there will be no mystery undergirding us, only the complete clarity which knows how things had to be in the way God himself knows it.

For Christianity, by contrast, the overarching reality is always the 'non-coercible freedom of bestowing, participating, self-opening'. No 'cunning' can overmaster the mystery of gracious bestowal, for nothing can be more ultimate than the Holy Trinity whose mystery this is. The logic of love can never be reduced to a mathematical-style rationality for the simple reason that the freedom of love cannot be subordinated to any abstract necessity. (This is a theme that will concern the mature Balthasar in the second volume of his theological logic.) In the end, and for just the same reason, Hegel's philosophy is far more 'objectivistic' than Thomas's. Thomas's is 'in higher measure a philosophy of the free spirit than is absolute Idealism'.[40] Hegel is not, when all is said and done, a truly Trinitarian thinker. In his theology Father and Son are basically 'moments' of the being of the Holy Spirit, sublated into his reality. They are necessary preconditions of his subjectivity and nothing more. This is a strange neo-Sabellianism where it is the Spirit, not the Father, who is in effect the one God.[41] Hegel's rationalism explains how his nuanced attitude to the eternal could so easily collapse into 'Left Hegelianism' with its apotheosis of 'immanent unending progress'. Hegel's system suffers from the 'curse of misused love'.[42]

The Outworkings

Balthasar closes the first volume of *Apokalypse* by remarking on responses, Christian and – more influentially – non-Christian to the Promethean revolution in German thought and letters he describes. Idealism always had a shadow dogging it, the 'night side of nature'. One way to sum up the aftermath is to say that, after Hegel, commentators were the more aware of this, and whether on Christian presuppositions or atheistically existentialist

---

40 Ibid., p. 616.
41 Cyril O'Regan speaks of Hegel's 'narrative modalism': thus his *The Heterodox Hegel* (Albany, NY 1994), p. 21. O'Regan explains that 'The Hegelian rendition does not correspond to the Nicean view, or any facsimile thereof, and could not be expected so to correspond, given Hegel's fundamental critique of the language of person and his strange evocation of heterodox Christian thinkers such as Valentinus and Jacob Boehme', ibid., pp. 21–22.
42 *Apokalypse I*, p. 618. For more, see S. Zucal, 'L'interpretazione teologica di Hegel nel primo Balthasar', *Filosofia oggi* 3 (1985), pp. 523–48; 4 (1986), pp. 267–304.

ones, came to terms with it. Now the epithet 'irrational' is normally pejorative. But Balthasar uses the word neutrally when he says that both the 'Right wing' and the 'Left wing' succession to Hegel is, compared with the master, a victory for *Irrationalismus*.[43]

The Hegelian 'Right' (essentially, the Christian interpretation of Hegel's achievement) espoused a 'personal irrationalism' inasmuch as it adhered to a *supra-logical* philosophical master-idea. The Logos, the foundation of logic, is ultimately a *Person*, self-opening and not to be captured by thought. Here reason is, in the last analysis, hearing (*Vernunft* comes from *Vernehmen*).

By contrast, the Hegelian 'Left' is an impersonal irrationalism, since *its* basic thought is *infra-logical*, a naturalism. Here reason embodies the tragic non-ultimacy of love. Consonant with his plan of devoting the lion's share of these volumes to the spiritual situation of modernity, Balthasar gives less time to the Christian critique (and continuation) of Hegel than to the tragic existentialism which increasingly dominated the mid to later nineteenth century.

Franz von Baader (1765–1841) can stand for the Christian response. One of the 'Fathers' of Catholic Romanticism, the Catholic 'restoration' or revival, Balthasar has considerable respect for his judgment on Hegel's thought. Baader brought against Hegel the objection that, while *Aufhebung*, the notion of simultaneous annulment and transfiguration, is the key-idea of his philosophy, nowhere does Hegel consider the highest move possible in its practice. And this is the free *Aufhebung* of the person towards and for God. Hegel's thought is a (Luciferian) *non serviam*. Any claim that Hegelianism is interchangeable with Christianity can only be gross misunderstanding. Hegel's philosophy, on Baader's view, does not succeed in its aims for two reasons. First, it never attains a satisfactory account of personhood, and secondly it suffers from the defects of a severely truncated Christology. The 'concrete universal' sought by Hegel – i.e. a way of showing how the objective and general on the one hand, the subjective and the particular on the other, need not be contraries or even sundered – can only be Christ-and-the-Church as a single mystical body given from above by the Incarnation. Thus Baader's *Fermenta cognitionis*.

In criticism of Hegel, Baader insisted that philosophy never leaves behind its origin in wonder. Its primary organ is the creaturely 'ear', for it reasons on the basis of listening, not least to God. Its noblest task is to conceive the vocation of the person. It understands not only the personal but all reality in Trinitarian terms, as 'circumincession', mutual inhabitation – in various senses, to varying degrees. All of this is grist to Balthasar's mill, notably in the opening volume of the theological logic and the final volume of the theological dramatics.

Specifically on the issue of eschatology, Balthasar arranges Baader's ideas around the metaphor of *night*. The eschatological circumincession of God and the creature through love is not an exchange in which, *pace* Hegel, the creature comes to comprehend God. If it could, it would be a creature no more. Rather is it by self-abandonment, *Sich-lassen*, to God's mystery that it lives, and accordingly its most vital function is prayer. Its love will always

---

43 *Apokalypse I*, p. 623. On this, see J.E. Toews, *Hegelianism: The Path toward Dialectical Humanism* (Cambridge 1980).

have been tried and tested. Testing is necessary, it is not sin. Testing is not, against Hegel once again, the Fall. All this is for the human being a *salutary night*. That does not exhaust, however, Baader's exploitation of the night motif. As a creature, man is not perfectly unitary. There is in his being a real distinction between ground and form. Ours is a *natural* being. Its rootedness in nature means it inhabits a twilight world. Hence our neediness. 'The created spirit must be nourished by the divine Spirit',[44] and for this no danger is more mortal than the illusion which confuses the God speaking in our spirit with our own 'I'. Lastly, the vocabulary of night serves Baader's account of evil as the perversion of love. The malice of the Fall lies in the breakdown of fidelity to God. The delivering over of spirit to mere nature *is* Hell.

Countering the assertions or implications of those texts from Hegel on which 'Left' Hegelians would place such reliance, Baader denied that 'endless progress' could count as authentic eschatology at all. Endlessly to defer eschatological satisfaction is to treat the soul as the wandering Jew, to condemn it to the torture of Tantalus. The only 'concrete eschatology' (Baader's watchword) is, as mediaeval thinkers realized, a strictly transcendental fulfilment: the plenitude of the vision of God. Moreover, it is in the person of the divine-human Mediator, whose life is at once totally bodily and utterly spiritual, that the synthesis we need as the medium for sharing this vision can be found. Such concrete eschatology is Parousia and judgment for the world.

Balthasar cannot report that the Christian continuation by critique of Idealism made much mark on the intellectual environment. But Baader was not entirely without disciples. In particular, there was a most significant Russian-language appropriation of his thought in Solovyev and Berdyaev – not without, at least in the latter, some element of gnosticizing influence as well. There *were* Kabbalistic elements in Baader's work to which ancient Gnosis was perhaps akin. But his more fundamental project, so Balthasar holds, was to unite the best of Hegel with the best of Thomas Aquinas. In Balthasar's eyes this is a far from unworthy goal.

But what, then, of the *non*-Christian outworkings of Prometheanism? Perhaps because he has just been writing about Hegel, Balthasar can see more clearly, he thinks, the 'dialectic' of light and darkness, optimism and desolation, even in the original Enlightenment. In Fichte, this dialectic of the 'day-side' and 'night-side' of life had an especially striking character. Man is so determined as to strive endlessly for an unattainable divine imagehood, caught between conflicting demands from a 'mysticism of contemplative God-inebriation' and an 'heroic religion of the deed'.[45] Schelling attempts to put spirit and nature together again. But in his Objective Idealism the ideal or spirit is remorselessly bound into the evolution of the real world of nature, to a cosmos without a face. Retrospectively, Balthasar regards Schelling's late philosophy as mysticism perpetually threatened by materialism. The early Romantic poets in Germany, Novalis and Hölderlin, express this situation to perfection. Even Goethe, whom Balthasar so admires, can manage little more than silent resignation at the thought of the co-existence of the 'bright and

44 Ibid., p. 630.
45 Ibid., p. 637.

dark spheres'. In two more minor figures of German Romanticism, Ludwig Tieck (1773–1863) and Wilhelm Heinrich Wackenroder (1773–1798) who, however, collaborated with each other and the Schlegels in forming much of its idiom, there is at times a frightening experience of all this as deliverance to the fearfully sinister (*das Unheimliche*). With Ernst Theodor Wilhelm Hoffmann (1776–1822), fascination with the hideous and grotesque becomes a preoccupation of music as well. Hoffmann influenced Robert Alexander Schumann (1810–1856) in his *Kreisleriana*, and Balthasar implies that the madness of 'Kreisler' played its role in Schumann's own descent into lunacy. He places in the same context Franz von Sonnenberg's (1779–1805) *Donotoa or the End of the World* (1806–1807) – the 'greatest eschatological poem of German literature'.[46] Here *Weltangst* reigns. At the last judgment, in this 20,000 verse epic, creation returns to the 'sleep' of chaos. True, a divine reawakening of nature means that the final message can be positive. Love and death are one, every creature must die if it is to be transfigured. But Balthasar finds the dominant sensibility of the poem negative and fearful, reflecting the poet's own doubts about personal freedom and immortality. It points the way to the two last great figures of German Idealism, the dramatist and short-story writer Heinrich von Kleist (1777–1811) and the philosopher Arthur Schopenhauer (1788–1860) for whom amoral will is the mainspring of the universe.

Balthasar says that for Kleist death is 'all-dominating' and he calls Schopenhauer 'the metaphysician of death'.[47] Having lost his (Herderian) faith, the only unity Kleist could find in life was death. He is the poet of *Dasein zum Tode*, existence against the horizon of death. Behind him stands Schopenhauer, for whom the Hegelian dialectic issues not in the personal and dialogical but, contrary-wise, in the impersonal. Over against Baader's Christian interpretation of the 'Prometheus situation', for Schopenhauer the sacred is by no means the light unfading of personal reality. Instead, it is the 'negative enchantment of pre-personal, nocturnal unity'.[48] Balthasar does not linger long over Schopenhauer, though he admits the extent of his influence. Schopenhauer's philosophy combines an almost solipsistic individualism with the extreme anti-individualism entailed in the denial that persons have a distinctive ontology at all. Though we know nothing of what the 'world-will' portends, in becoming self-transparent in man it effectively achieves its eschatological 'deed' in him. By asceticism and self-negation, man can bring the world's sorry phenomenal history to an end. Without a subject, there would be no object. This is sometimes described as Schopenhauer's 'Buddhism'. The cosmic, anti-individualist aspect of Schopenhauer suggests to Balthasar's mind, rather, a family-resemblance with Hindu pantheism, which Hegel had treated as quite the most rudimentary stage in a doctrine of spirit. Contrastingly, the individualist side points ahead to the materialist, anarchist and radical atheist Max Stirner (the pseudonym of Johann Kaspar Schmidt 1806–1852), and in a different way to figures who will detain Balthasar much longer: Kierkegaard and Nietzsche.

---

46 Ibid., p. 638. Donotoa is Sonnenberg's name for the angel of death.
47 Ibid., p. 640.
48 Ibid., p. 641.

The 'Post-Idealist Time'

The middle decades of the nineteenth century in Germany were dominated, philosophically speaking, by the collapse of Idealism, regarded after Schopenhauer as a 'lost beautiful dream'.[49] But precisely this made it possible to see again the shape of the eschatological problem as posed in the Age of Enlightenment, whence the classical German philosophies arose. The basic paradox, the attempt to combine 'the pure eternity of spirit' – and so a sheerly axiological or static eschatology – with 'the endless forward movement of life' – and so a sheerly teleological, dynamic eschatology, now represented its credentials. In the 'post-Idealist epoch' this took the form of an unlikely amalgam of 'naïve' evolutionism with an everyday pragmatism spiced with nostalgia for utopia. Meanwhile, whereas in individual eschatology with its hopes for personal destiny 'poetic realism' was the watchword (death is the final horizon of life, giving life its seriousness), in social eschatology scientific evolutionism ruled the roost. Men might eschew notions of infinite progress for the individual. They nonetheless retained ideas of (evolutionary) perfection for the race. The incongruity between tragic realism for the individual and optimistic faith in progress for the race was hardly noticed as immanentist monism became more and more taken for granted. Nothing could be more different from Christianity (or from Idealism, for that matter). But after Schopenhauer, 'disillusion' sinks secret roots. There is something very strange about a world in which individualism sits side by side with an evolutionary collectivism where persons count for nothing. Somehow – where the 'how' is never explained – 'getting real' about things covers both. 'Here the "objectivity", *Sachlichkeit*, of Liberalism, Realism and Naturalism as well as of Socialism, have their source.'[50]

The 'pure teleology' element in mid nineteenth-century eschatological thinking is bound up, as Balthasar has indicated, with evolutionism of various kinds. One of them derives from the influential Protestant theologian Friedrich Daniel Ernst Schleiermacher (1768–1834). In Schleiermacher's *Christliche Glaubenslehre* evil is the 'not yet' of good, Christianity a phenomenon of excellence in historical development, Christ a powerful 'impulse' impacting on that development through the centuries as Tradition or the Church, but hardly the personal presence of the true centre of the world as lauded by Baader. Theology is reduced to the phenomenology of religious consciousness, as the Trinity dissolves into three ways of experiencing God and human individuality – in Schleiermacher's words, into an 'empty name'.[51]

Hebbel and Wagner

Balthasar will now take us on to Kierkegaard and Nietzsche, but via the dramatist, critic and literary theorist Christian Friedrich Hebbel (1813–1863) and the composer and theorist of the 'music-drama', alias symphonic opera, Richard Wagner (1813–1883).

Hebbel's dramas, still considered among the greatest in the German

49 Ibid., p. 645.
50 Ibid., p. 647.
51 Cited in ibid., p. 648.

language, pullulate with psychologically complex figures. His is a tragic world-view for which any strong or remarkable individual is bound to come into conflict with the general 'Idea' and be crushed. In Balthasar's terms he represents the crossing-point of two quite different eschatologies: the social-teleological eschatology typical of evolutionism's great age, and the individual-axiological eschatology reflected in what he calls the 'lyricism of the time'.[52] Unlike Hegel, Hebbel does not try to synthesize them: integrating the individual's sacrifice into the great oblation of the world. Instead, he allows the doubt to stand that any resolution of their tension is possible at all. How can the radically finite individual be identified with the *Weltgeist* (which for Hebbel havers somewhere between the God of Christianity and anonymous fate)? Of course, he can not: so Hebbel is a dramatist of pan-tragic pain. As he asks, rhetorically, unless life were unbearable, how could death be borne? Pain and consciousness, pain and life, are one. Hebbel writes of a God who is 'buried in the world'. Is this the Christian God of the paschal mystery? Or is it the Hegelian God who transposes himself from eternity to time? Or is it – with Feuerbachian irony – a 'God' who shall be in time to come?

Hebbel struggled with the idea of immortality. For Kant, Fichte, Goethe, Hölderlin, immortality is 'necessary' if thought and action are to reach their comprehensive term. Hebbel had no faith in such 'necessity'. Only humanity does not succumb to an error it does not need. If men knew now that immortalism were false they would render it true by building utopias. One of Hebbel's short stories turns on a future discovery of the elixir of life – but this is the final proof that those already dead are dead for ever. Balthasar describes Hebbel's 'neighbourliness' with the End-situation. An especially glorious German summer filled him with apocalyptic dreams. An End must come eventually, so why not now? Naturally, only a 'materialistic' end of the world is in question. Yet Hebbel seeks the dead *within* the world in a psychological, even spiritualistic, fashion that points forward to (among other things) Rainer Maria Rilke's *Sonnets for Orpheus*.

The hopelessness of the cosmological background somehow renders Hebbel's human beings more intensely valuable – as the religious poetry in which he gave expression to the meaning of his plays bears witness. Hebbel's dramas raise metaphysical questions of moment: *Judith* the Promethean *topos* of 'necessary guilt', suggesting a 'demonic' ground for the world; *Genoveva* the co-existence of self-giving and Satanic elements in love, implying an ultimate Manichaenism; *Herodes und Mariamne* the possibility that *death* is the true 'Absolute'. In *Gyges*, Hebbel's equivalent to Wagner's *Der Ring der Nibelungen*, contradictory pagan and Christian 'existentialities' are deliberately left side by side: testimony to Hebbel's doubt whether finitude has definitive – or even definite – meaning. Here his 'analytic drama' will be mirrored in the theatre of Henrik Johan Ibsen (1828–1906), where, from *Brand* to *Peer Gynt*, metaphysical confidence gradually drains away. Hebbel's unfinished play *Moloch* affirms both the impossible ghastliness of religion and the legitimacy of its cultural and moral fruits. His *Komödie der Zukunft* proclaims his pessimism, portraying an eschatological human being – the final generation of man – who turns out to be 'the president of the animals,

---

52 Ibid., p. 661.

nothing more'.[53] Balthasar finds Hebbel's 'helplessness', *Ratlosigkeit*, in the face of the 'last question' instructive: it shows the peculiar difficulties of the synthesis such later nineteenth-century writers attempted: an evolutionism leading to materialist disillusion, an axiologism veering between 'the eternalizing of a moment and anxiety about the grave'.[54]

Balthasar introduces the topic of Wagner's works by resuming the history of 'Ahasuerus', the eternally 'wandering Jew', cursed for his attempt to persuade Jesus to deny his prophetic charism, but a source of fascination to the nineteenth-century librettist. From modest beginnings in German literature, Ahasuerus achieved the status of a major symbolic figure of the age when Idealism was coming to its end. As it turned out, the two *eschata* – the teleological-social and the axiological-individual – could come together in his person. Seen as the universal human being he is unending progressive continuation in time. Seen as individual, he is *Dasein zum Tode*, 'existence towards death'. The combination of the two suggests real malediction: 'bad immortality', the 'tantalising withholding of the necessary boundary of existence'. This Jew is 'Prometheus's dark brother'.[55] Balthasar speaks of an 'Ahasuerus curse' hanging over all Wagner's work, what he calls a *Zeugungsunfähigkeit* or 'incapacity to bear life'. The twilight of the gods was meant to lead effortlessly to a new beginning for humanity. But the mythical *Urwelt* of a now inaccessible 'naïve-heroic' era is replaced by a godless yet essentially unenchanted, *entzaubert*, race. Ahasuerus-figures recur not only in *The Flying Dutchman*, which is based on the legend, but also, thinks Balthasar, in the 'Tantalus-suffering' of Tannhäuser, in Lohengrin's curse-bringing divinity, Tristan's curse of undying craving, the everlastingly burning wound of the Grail king in *Parsifal* and, in the Ring cycle, the entire symbolism of the 'unblessed god', the king of the Nibelungen, Wotan. In *The Flying Dutchman*, we notice, Wagner is not interested in the origin of the sailor's guilt. In effect, to be is to be guilty here, and the Dutchman looks forward to the Last Day as his long-awaited annihilation. True, he can be saved by a woman's love (Balthasar compares this to Schelling's metaphysic of the demonic 'ground' whose venom love draws), but the music of the opera gives the same weight both to the 'nocturnal, abyssal, demonic' rhythms and to the 'saving, brightening' ones.[56]

Balthasar also brings a Schellingian interpretation to the Ring cycle itself. Wotan is 'spirit, not life'. Beneath him and over against him is 'eternal non-spirit', represented by Wala, the Rhine gold and the world of the Nibelungen. It is Wagner's way of affirming the 'essentially tragic character of being'.[57] Wotan tries to close the abyss through a 'free and total hero', Siegfried, just as Schelling's God comes to active consciousness in man. But, alas, between Schelling and Wagner there come Schopenhauer and Feuerbach: the 'cold foreignness of the underworld is too primordial'.[58] 'Ground' becomes the altogether anonymous fate of spirit – signalled by the way Wotan becomes ever more passive as he grows in knowledge. The 'psychological' side of the

53 Cited in ibid., p. 676.
54 Ibid., p. 678.
55 Ibid., p. 681.
56 Ibid., p. 684.
57 Ibid., p. 685.
58 Ibid., p. 686.

divine is revealed as 'ideality' – which means that Wotan is in effect impotent in nature's regard. On Balthasar's interpretation, Wotan himself, the high god, ends up as an Ahasuerus-figure. This is world spirit longing for the end, a 'Prometheus with lacerated liver who no longer believes in his own unshackling'.[59] Wotan dissolves into nature: behind the Romantic apparatus, Positivism raises its head again. Will the decline of the gods draw humanity with it?

Balthasar thinks the astute Wagner deliberately left open three interpretations. Possibly, it is the ideal world that is extinguished, leaving us with only the Feuerbachian world of sheer Positivism. Or perhaps spirit too is mere *Schein* and even the 'realistic' world we imagine we live in has no proper consistency. Or maybe the message is Dionysian: the ground of the world is flame, burning up all that is formed. That would make Wagner a half-way house between Schelling and Nietzsche – but the ambiguity which makes of this only *one possible interpretation* of the Ring shows Wagner was no Nietzsche himself.

Kierkegaard and Nietzsche

We end the first – and by far the longest – volume of *Apokalypse* with two more portraits: Søren Aabye Kierkegaard (1813–1855) and Friedrich Wilhelm Nietzsche (1844–1900), under whose 'sign' Balthasar will place the second, central, book of this literary-philosophical trilogy.

Naturally enough, these are conflictual figures: indeed, Balthasar entitles his closing chapter 'The Duel of the Idea'. But they also have strange affinities. Balthasar begins from the famous speech of the madman in Nietzsche's *Die fröhliche Wissenschaft*, 'The Gay Science'. God is dead. We have killed him. God is dead in man; the glowing centre of the soul is left cold. Consequently, human beings have become puppets: for Friedrich Engels (1820–1895), 'paltry individuals'; for Schopenhauer 'nature's industrial production'. Balthasar calls Kierkegaard and Nietzsche 'two flames'. And in a daring comparison with the two eschatological witnesses of the Johannine Apocalypse, he hails them as 'judges of time', two witnesses of the Last Day. Each felt the ground giving way beneath them. Kierkegaard mocks the comedy of busy voyagers on a sinking ship (compare the English idiom of 'arranging the deck-chairs on the *Titanic*'); Nietzsche declares the ice that bears us up has become too thin: we feel the wind's warm breath that will destroy us. Neither man created a school or had disciples. The work of each is a 'cry', to waken sleepers in the last hour. According to Balthasar, both Kierkegaard and Nietzsche 'knew' their message about the present epoch to have the 'value of an everlasting apocalypse'. Though their (implicit) combat could not unreasonably be billed as The Last Christian v. The Antichrist, much in their backgrounds, development, life-stories, attitudes is alike. They shared a dislike of much in their period: its historicism; confidence in the 'systematic observation of everything'; dissolution of quality in quantity (Socialism being a prime example). They believed society was undergoing entropy. Like Kierkegaard, Nietzsche was hostile to Hegel and dialectic; like Nietzsche, Kierkegaard opposed 'culture-philistines'. Both thought

---

59 Ibid., p. 689.

Christendom had betrayed Christ. Both considered life will never be included within thinking. I live, therefore I think – not the other way around.

As Balthasar points out, such classical German philosophers as Fichte and Hegel himself were well aware that the tree of knowledge is not the tree of life. From the individual's standpoint, they stressed, time, freedom, decision, the unknown future rightly loom large. But for these thinkers, all this is, from the divine standpoint, sheer necessity. While they would have insisted that the theocentric viewpoint should not be taken as nullifying its anthropocentric opposite number, Kierkegaard was unpersuaded. What is such thinking but Promethean desiring to be God, the 'sickness unto death' of his time. Hence his rehabilitation of existence, the concrete moment, freedom of decision. Nietzsche seconded these themes. Both men applauded a life lived as a contest, in highest tension. Objectivity must be retrenched to make space for passion, for subjectivity is truth. Life discloses itself in risk and daring. Kierkegaard and Nietzsche were enemies of Progress. They did not, like the Idealists, seek mediating instances; rather, they sought out 'the magic of extremes',[60] the sharpening of oppositions, an 'either/or'. Nietzsche held that Nihilism was coming; Kierkegaard concluded Europe was heading for the spiritual bankruptcy court.

And yet these brothers are deepest enemies. For Balthasar the opposedness of their positions can usefully be stated in terms of their attitude to Socrates. For Nietzsche, Socrates is a dead end; for Kierkegaard he is a live beginning. To Nietzsche's mind, the irony of Socrates was the telltale sign of his deplorable alienation from the immediacy of life, unreflective aesthetic life. In Kierkegaard's eyes, the same irony sustains an in-depth unfolding of existence. Nietzsche takes life to be endless immediate power. Our true 'transcendence' is our unlimited capacity indefinitely to create something higher than ourselves. His *Übermensch* is not a fixed goal for human development but the expression of the fact that no such goal is needed. It is precisely by winning through to something ever higher that life has its own value. This is not Hegelianism; from the world as cosmos Nietzsche has made a 'monster of power'.[61] But it has links with Idealism. For Nietzscheanism: 'Dionysus, the bacchantic ecstasy, and Apollo, the lucid and simple rest – flame and light, then, form the single glow of existence.'[62]

Kierkegaard, too, is not without his links to that earlier movement. Balthasar singles out affinities with Kant, Schopenhauer and Baader for all of whom, in different fashions, the self combines finitude and lack of limit. The celebration of 'immediacy', so prized by Nietzsche, is no more than the illusion that existence can be tension-free synthesis – the lie Socrates shows up for what it is. Where Kierkegaard and Nietzsche are at one, for Balthasar, is in their conviction that *life has something before it which it not yet is*. Will man realize 'superman'? Will the self really exist? The shared starting-point is also, however, the beginning of their separation. Kierkegaard's Socrates reveals that thanks to the inevitable tension between finite and infinite, inwardness is suffering. Such suffering points to the fact that the self – which is really in the image of God and thus a finite-infinite relation – has not truly

---

60 F. Nietzsche, *Die Wille zur Macht*, I, 10, cited in ibid., p. 703.
61 *Apokalypse I*, p. 707.
62 Ibid.

posited itself, has not related itself, holding nothing back, to the utterly complete Reality which alone can fulfil it. Here public life distracts. Insofar as history is the stream in which the existent flows, it is meaningless – though for Kierkegaard (unlike Nietzsche) at one moment in public time the Eternal became historical, the Infinite finite, thus grounding the possibility of the cancellation of guilt for each and every human being. Only self-oblation leads to rebirth, rebirth into super-nature.

Nietzsche also values self-offering. It is how we can be the bridge between two life-forms: our own and that of the man of the future. Insofar as the individual loves the infinite in himself he loves the *Übermensch*. Nietzsche's commendation of *Fernstenliebe*, the 'love of the most distant', as quite the highest love follows from this. It is flight from the finite to the (non-theistic) infinite. The Incarnation gives Kierkegaard, with the apostle John, a different perspective. Without love of the brother we can see there is no love of God.[63] Nietzsche, by contrast, 'kills' God as 'a sacrifice to the ceaseless transcendence which should be faithful only to itself'.[64] Kierkegaard asks that man negate himself before the God of the Incarnation so as, through that God, to rise again as a new creature – and yet still the same man.

In such philosophies of existence, twins struggling together in the womb, the 'proof of truth' *is the manner of human existing*. Kierkegaard and Nietzsche took the way of 'active inwardness', *die tätige Innerlichkeit*. (Hence their praise – doubtless, in Nietzsche's case, somewhat ironic – of monasticism.) Knowing the soul cannot bear its own truth, they ventured into heaven and hell. Kierkegaard uncovers the 'dark district of the soul', the region of the 'virtuosity of masks', where melancholy – the 'hysteria of the spirit' – is wreathed in smiles. The knowing of endless unknowing is the condition from which alone worthwhile knowing can be expected. Socrates' negative analyses are openness to grace. Of course, for Nietzsche they are nothing of the sort. Rather are they a warning-signal of fall into the anti-instinctual state. To Nietzsche, appearance is truer than disillusion. The truth of subjectivity shows itself in the environing cultural world we ourselves make. Hardly surprisingly, Balthasar's sympathies are with the Dane. In Nietzsche, the dialectic of truth, flitting between illusion and disillusion, is only the play of lights and shadows on a deeper 'truth' – the single, monistic movement of life. For Kierkegaard, too, truth is dialectical. But the dialectic becomes *dialogic* – a favoured term in Balthasar's own thought. To come to know one's own boundaries is to be addressed from beyond those boundaries. One's word – *Wort* – turns out to be really an answering, *Antwort*. The whole is only visible from above. From below its meaning is only fragmentarily perceptible – like one side of a telephone conversation. The self-interpretation of *Dasein*, existence, is only one of a number of *Daseinsweisen*, existence's 'modes of being'. Only the *whole* of existence can be the whole truth.

These are also two wisdoms of the heart – of which only one can really be wise. For Nietzsche the bifurcation of the heart between love and power reveals a self-empoweredness, *Selbst-Mächtigkeit*, that proves power to be the truly comprehensive category. For Kierkegaard the heart reels between the true and the untrue and, aware of impotence and defencelessness, opens up

63 1 John 4.20.
64 Ibid., p. 717.

to God. To Balthasar's eyes, this is the higher *Hingabe* and it displays the falsity of power. Nietzsche's self-oblation, 'clarified' by an idea of higher power, allows *him* to claim, antithetically, the falsity of *Hingabe*. So the combat is indeed between 'Dionysus and the Crucified'.

Kierkegaard once spoke of St John Chrysostom (c. 349–407) as 'gesturing by his whole existence'. Balthasar thinks the same could be said of Kierkegaard himself – and of Nietzsche. Of all the figures he has painted onto his canvas so far, these best show what 'apocalypse of the soul' means. It means: 'Rushing into the centre where ice and fire rule together and out of this centre – Hell – the attestation of Heaven.'[65]

Someone might think that Nietzsche's terminal madness invalidated his 'gesture'. But Balthasar points out, with Dostoevsky's assistance, that madness can be, paradoxically, the symptom of healing for a sickness of the soul. With both men, European culture acquires an intenser sense of the existential. Balthasar proposes to follow up how the 'rhythms' established by Nietzsche and Kierkegaard were repeated, with variations, in what follows.

65 Ibid., p. 732.

8

✤

From Bergson to Dostoevsky

Under the Sign of Nietzsche

Balthasar opens the second volume of *Apokalypse* 'under the sign of Nietzsche'. In the later nineteenth century, Prometheanism gives way to a Dionysian approach to existence following – in some sense – Nietzsche's example.[1] In the early German classical philosophers, Fichte and Schelling, Prometheanism had been chiefly a 'view of the world'. But then people tried to live it out. As it became more 'existential', it took on the predominant mood of melancholy, resignation to the 'eternally unfulfilled'. For Balthasar, Hegel's attempt to interpret this idealistically, on the basis of a fundamentally congruent – and hence, Promethean – principle, revealed how questionable the project was. In Hegel's wake – and above all with Nietzsche – we hear a 'No' to Idealism and a corresponding 'Yes' to the heroic situation of life lived in conscious contradiction. Ultimacy is now located on, or at any rate through, the battlefield of contraries. To a degree, the same might be said for the thinking of Goethe and Hegel, but Goethe's 'conciliating nature' and Hegel's 'artistry of *Aufhebung*', at once cancelling yet preserving, took away much of its force. By contrast, Nietzsche rubbed the contradictions in. The key will now be the to and fro' movement of life between opposed poles: essence and existence, idea and facticity, synthesis and thesis.

This soon begins to affect, in the first place, general ontology. *Life* (and not, as previously 'Idea') becomes the real 'binding middle' between matter and spirit. This was a special concern of the French philosopher Henri Bergson (1859–1941), at whose hands it involved a new privileging of the investigation of *time*, the inner form of the movement of life. Bergson treats of a twofold becoming – from the life-ground to the heights of spirit, and from the 'abstractness' of spirit to the 'plenitude' of life. In these different ways, he proposed to trace the movement of finite, temporal existence to its own limits.

As we shall see, there is, on the trajectory that starts from Nietzsche, quite a development of a philosophy of existence as finite and temporal, that moves from Bergson through Simmel and Rilke to Scheler and Heidegger – figures who will capture Balthasar's attention in the closing volume of

---

1 See J. Gesthuisen, *Das Nietzsche-Bild Hans Urs von Balthasars. Ein Zugang zur 'Apokalypse der deutschen Seele'* (Rome 1986).

Apokalypse. The concern now is not with presuppositions, whether ontological or merely temporal, as in Idealism, but with sketching horizons projected in and through time. In this perspective there is a link between Bergson's empirical (indeed, almost biological) metaphysics and Edmund Husserl's austere phenomenology of finite *Weltsein*.

Not only ontology at large was affected, however. 'Under the sign of Nietzsche', shifts came about in anthropology and the philosophy of culture as well. The assumption now is that man and earth belong together. The 'space' where meaning – 'salvation' – may be expected can only be the temporally future. For Nietzsche's prophetic mode, the future is the basis of the present: he hails what is to be as the ground of what is. But, unlike for Israelite prophecy when taken in its fullest span, the 'future' here is that of this finite earth whose meaning can only be achieved by its own immanent means. History appears as progress, but not in the fashion of Enlightenment optimism. Technology – the chief manner envisaged whereby culture develops – is as ambiguous as life itself. Yet only such 'real' powers of this world enter into the making of final significance. The thought of the *Übermensch* is crossed by that of death and the finitude of the human species as a whole. But precisely this contradiction is where meaning is sought.

There is also a change in religious problematic. Balthasar puts this in terms of the meaning of 'limit', *Grenze*, an issue naturally raised by thinking of a 'finite horizon' to life. The *Zweikampf* of Kierkegaard and Nietzsche could be called a struggle over the meaning of finitude. Here the byword 'Dionysus against the Crucified' comes into its own. In the Greek myth, Dionysus is himself torn apart. So how does the contrast with the Christ of Christianity appear? Easily. Dionysus is the ruler of a world where life develops despite its tearing open by contradictions. (In his cult drama Dionysus is both tearer and the one torn apart by Maenads.) Rendered into little pieces, he is a promise for life: it shall be reborn eternally. This is how Dionysus is God: by being – like life itself – ever destructive and destroyed yet reborn continually. The God on the Cross, contrarywise, is for Nietzsche a 'curse' on life.

Balthasar considers that 'the sign of Nietzsche' dominated Continental philosophy in the period from the closing decades of the nineteenth century until the First World War. The key term is 'life', *Leben*, as in Bergson, in the philosopher and psychologist Ludwig Klages, now best known for his recommendation of the study of handwriting as a psychodiagnostic tool, and in all the writers whose work falls under the rubric of *Lebensdichtung*, 'the poetry of life'. But the *Lebensphilosophie* would eventually be transcended by concern for the relation between life and spirit, *Geist*. Thus the greatest Germanophone poets of the time: the Rhinelander Stefan George who shared Nietzsche's love-hate relation with Christianity and view of the poet as prophet; Balthasar's fellow-Swiss Carl Spitteler, a Nietzschean rebel; the incomparable German-Bohemian Rainer Maria Rilke, and the Austrian poet and playwright Hugo von Hoffmansthal, Richard Strauss's librettist and, like all those just mentioned, a fertile originator of new symbolisms.

Understandably, then, to the period dominated by *Leben* succeeds an epoch where what is predominant is *Geist*. Balthasar will mark the change in all three of: formal ontology (the advent of the phenomenological school of Husserl and Scheler), anthropology (Heidegger's pre-Second World War

Daseinsphilosophie), and theology (the amazing supernaturalist revolution of Karl Barth).

And, since these names take us absolutely up to date – to the date when Balthasar was writing – what will be the issue of this entire process? Why: 'Laden with the riches of the Promethean and Dionysian worlds [he means the sum total of the philosophers, playwrights, poets he is studying], we shall have to try and find again that eschatological unity from whose demolition we initially set forth.'[2] So Balthasar's *aim* is to reconstitute the wholeness of the Christian eschatology of the high mediaeval period. But in the service of that aim his *strategy* was not that of many of the Catholic intelligentsia of the 1930s – looking back with a view to founding a 'New Middle Ages'. Rather, he intended to learn new lessons which could help in realizing the overall aim – and these lessons would be especially useful, he thought, in the case of *Lebensphilosophie* precisely because the latter seeks to express the 'movement of life', *Lebensbewegung*, of the modern age.

Balthasar gives us some notion of the spirit in which he will approach these authors. Each 'circle' (*Kreis*, a Nietzschean term) has its own boundary, *Grenze*. For the subjectivity that gave it birth this boundary is a death, and thus an 'eschaton', a 'last thing'. A world 'rounds itself', therefore, in each circle. As enclosures, the form of these circles is 'Apollonian'. But in the sphere of *Lebensphilosophie* their content is Dionysian. Accordingly, their basic law can only be the necessity of rupture for each self-closing 'figure', *Gestalt*. The relative eschaton proper to each circle can in principle, then, be broken open, and a way out of tragic limit suggested which *might* point, ultimately, to salvation. Here is a pointer to the final solution of 'Apocalypse of the German Soul'.

The Mysticism of Life

Lebensmystik: that means for Balthasar, first and foremost, the philosophy of Bergson: agnostic Jew converted, on his death-bed, to Catholicism. Just as Fichte had answered Kant by saying, There *is* an intuition that can ground metaphysics, the intuition of the 'I', so Bergson starts from the same point. Philosophy is a simple act of intuition, itself of more value than any system, for systems are, at best, symbols of intuitions. Bergson emphasizes the role of images, and notably *convergent* images, in the expression of intuition. Such images lead to concepts which are themselves mediations between intuitions and (subsequent) systems. Conceptual schemes – and, therefore, schools of philosophy – can rarely be expected, so Bergson thought, to possess the whole. Art plays an important role in Bergsonianism. In *La Pensée et le mouvement* Bergson describes art as 'imagistic metaphysics'.[3] With art is bound up the possibility of primordial intuition, the intuition of what comes from the source. Bergsonian philosophy is a research that seeks in the same direction as art but takes life in general as its object. Bergsonian intuition is at once aesthetic and intellectual. Comparing it to Plotinus's 'conversion', *epistrophê*, Balthasar describes it as a swimming upstream towards the source

---

2 *Apokalypse der deutschen Seele. Studien zu einer Lehre von letzten Haltungen. Band II. Im Zeichen Nietzsches* (Salzburg and Leipzig 1939), p. 13. Cited below as '*Apokalypse II.*'
3 H. Bergson, *La Pensée et le mouvement* (Paris 3rd edn, 1934), p. 275.

of life in which counterposition one grasps life itself as object. Bergson thought it a mistake to place space and time on the same level. Time is far more significant for the understanding of existence. The sheer creativity of human life is found in *la durée, Dauer*, which 'preserves the past as memory and yet recreates itself ever anew as a whole'.[4] Our inner flow of intuitions comes over as a stream of consciousness that is 'pure qualitative ever-otherness', and this for Bergson brings us close to the reality of time which is simultaneously identical and changing. So in place of the favoured fire metaphor of the Idealists he substitutes a water metaphor for the 'absolute temporality of being'.

To Bergson's mind, metaphysics is at once sheer experience and true empiricism. Historic empiricism replaced true experience, which issues from direct contact with both spirit and object, by a contextless substitute.[5] The term 'empiricism' was not invoked lightly. Bergson sought assistance on the issue of spirit's boundary with matter from brain physiology; on the ontology of the social from parapsychology; and on the possibility of otherwise unsuspected deepenings of philosophical intuition from studies of mysticism. Mysticism, he considered, was not only, like philosophy, direct re-entry into the primordial stream of consciousness. It was also an intensification of that search, which went right down to the 'roots of our being and thus to the principle of life at large'.[6] Through repeated *Hin- und Hergehen* between such observatory materials and analysis of inner experience, what is given in intuition should receive more philosophically exact form. (Perhaps surprisingly, Bergson accepted René Descartes' [1596–1650] methodological demand for clarity and precision in philosophical writing.)

So, in Balthasar's summary, Bergson changed the Kantian-Fichtean transcendental-deductive method into a 'transcendental-empirical' one. Balthasar recognizes the audacity of Bergson's claims. From a grasp of the 'ground of life' he intended to reach results beyond all previous metaphysicians. What science constructs from outside Bergsonian intuition will reconstruct from within. After all: 'The matter and life which fill the world are also in us; the powers that work through everything we feel are in us too.'[7] In a remarkable judgment, Balthasar declares Bergson to be closest, among his philosophical predecessors, to Goethe. For both, as Balthasar puts it, imagistically, the white light is at the *source*. The colours of the spectrum – differentiated experience – are already its depotentialization. Bergson and Goethe have the same stress on the developing stages of finite being, and the same confidence, too, in the place of symbol in metaphysics. Balthasar finds a relationship to Husserl as well. In each case the foundational philosophical act is sheer perception by abstraction from what is constructed so as to concentrate instead on that which is just 'lived'.

Like the neo-Thomist Jacques Maritain (1882–1973), who owed his rescue from Positivism (and possibly suicide) to Bergson, Balthasar admires him warmly and yet expresses a serious reserve. Bergson continues the Dionysian *Urdualismus* in the form of a radical disjuncture between 'worldliness' (in the

---

4 *Apokalypse II*, p. 23.
5 H. Bergson, *Matière et mémoire* (Paris 20th edn, 1925), p. 202.
6 H. Bergson, *Les deux Sources de la morale et la religion* (Paris 17th edn, 1934), p. 207.
7 H. Bergson, *La Pensée et le mouvement*, op. cit., p. 156.

ontic, not the ascetic, sense of course) and temporality. Space is the exten-sivity of matter. But time is the *in*tensivity of space, and so the far more fascinating subject. For Bergson *la durée* is the essence of pure spirit. In the intensity of time lies the true concept of eternity. Time, as Bergson under-stands it, has nothing to do with number, the countable plurality of positions in space. Its manifold concerns, rather, reciprocal penetration and richness of quality. Because being is doing, there can be analogy between God and the creature. Indeed, the creature can participate in the creative act, the 'source'. In it, wrote Bergson, deliberately misquoting St Paul, we live and move and have our being. Breakthrough into the realm of sheer creative *durée* brings with it the joy of being, the blessedness of spirit, and this in turn allows one to experience reality as overflowing exuberance and yet the most substantial thing in the world.

In Bergson's anthropology, understanding has the basic task of securing calculative dominance, appropriate in the homogeneous space where quan-tity rules. It is natural for spirit to be turned towards matter. But if in matter there is an element of indeterminacy, spirit itself is essentially free. At the base of a pyramid-like model of reality is pure matter, a 'limit-concept' in Bergson's thought. At the apex is pure spirit *qua* the God who is transcendent vis-à-vis the world. Different levels of life mediate between base and apex, each stratum building on the one below. As movement, matter shares in the real at a level higher than itself, enjoying a certain analogy with our con-sciousness. Science follows the downward path of matter as 'falling spirit'. Philosophy must travel in the opposite direction, up towards the source. In its scientific capacity metaphysics seeks to deepen its grasp of matter through the exercise of understanding. But it reserves spirit entirely for itself. Philo-sophy, says Bergson in 'The Two Sources of Morality and Religion', is introduction to the spiritual life.[8] (One can see how Maritain was struck.)

As Balthasar points out: on Bergson's scheme, *la durée* carries the positive charge eternity had for the pre-moderns. 'Time', in his special use of the word, is the absolutely open. Its essence is the future, the possibility of progress without end. The *Lebensdrang*, the 'impulse of life', knows nothing of death. (Thus does Bergson transfer to time what Plotinus had affirmed of eternity.) For Bergson, age is the ripeness of past in present, 'time's self-inscription', and mortality a mere chance intervention in the life of spirit, sheer memory and pure creation. In *L'Evolution créatrice* Bergson hazards the opinion that when life makes an ever more conscious return to the source it may be able to overcome death through an 'absolute breakthrough'.

Balthasar finds Bergson's views unpardonably contradictory. On the one hand, Bergson proposes a pyramid with extended matter as its base, and as its apex the intensity of spirit as creative duration. Yet he presents the spiritual as the broad foundation, spirit forming what is below it by an ever sharper narrowing of the scope of memory until in sheer 'attention to life' it coincides with an actual moment of acting – itself made possible by the material structure of the brain. On Balthasar's analysis, Bergson is oscillating between two value systems and so two sets of ultimate attitudes. He treats as the paradigm of 'real existential deed' *both* the negative reaction of intuition to pragmatic materialism *and* the pragmatic itself. On his own principles he

---

8 H. Bergson, *Les deux Sources de la morale et la religion*, op. cit., p. 291.

cannot prevent a disintegration of present time into, on the one hand, the colourless background of spirit as entertained in 'memory' (Balthasar calls Bergsonian spirit 'concentrated emptiness') and, on the other, the warm, vital perception of the sheer material 'now'. Between the occasionally glimpsed humanity-as-it-must-be-as-a-whole and *de facto* instinctual humanity the discontinuity is simply too great. In Balthasar's view, this leads to 'aesthetic ethos-lessness', preparing the way for the all-absorbing Narcissus-motif of French and German *Lebendichtung*. One thinks of Gerhart Ladner's comments on Bergson in his classic study of 'The Idea of Reform'.

> It is characteristic of these anti-materialistic forms of vitalistic renewal ideas that they pass somewhat abruptly from instinctive and uncon-scious development to mystical transfiguration, so that rational finality recedes into the background. In Bergson's philosophy the intermediate sphere between the infrarational (the biological and social-collective) and the suprarational (the mystical) is thus to some extent lost sight of; the realm of ethics, of human morality, freely oriented towards ends, 'vanishes into thin air'.[9]

To this uncertainty about values corresponds a confusion about ultimate attitudes. Bergson cannot decide whether progress means waxing reconci-liation with the primordial life through mysticism or increasing opposition to it through technology. In his biologistic frame of mind, Bergson pronounces the world to be the creative development of matter, and truth radically historical. In his mystical manner, by contrast, he deems spirit to be self-transcendence: free self-invention in a world not ordered to pre-determined goals since it is 'open creation into the infinite'.[10] Perhaps parapsychology and mysticism will gradually effect a *rapprochement* between the beyond and the here-and-now and 'change humanity'.[11]

Despite the improbability of such musings, Balthasar cannot help being impressed by Bergson's account of the mystics – whose lives and *dicta* were the old Jew's way to the Church. For Bergson the highest philosopher is the mystic who, as supernatural hero, calls humankind to a love quite different from social love, for it is a love of others *in God*. True mystics open them-selves to a flood that pours through them to win others for its course. Vision explodes into deed, since their 'removal' from earth is a gathering of power to burst upon earth.[12] So it was with the apostle Paul, with Teresa of Avila and Catherine of Siena, with Francis of Assisi and Joan of Arc. For Bergson, whereas natural religion is conservative, seeking to preserve the essence of a people and their life-way, supernatural religion is divinely restless. It wants more than man, or at any rate it wants with divine help to complete man's creation. Between the 'closed' morality of the first and the 'open' morality of the second Bergson posits an 'absolute leap'. Here Balthasar enters a caveat. Bergson sometimes speaks like a Marcionite, for whom the God of nature is a

---

9 G. Ladner, *The Idea of Reform: Its Impact on Christian Thought and Action in the Age of the Fathers* (Cambridge MA 1959), p. 24, with an internal citation of J. Maritain, 'The Bergsonian Philosophy of Morality and Religion', in idem, *Ransoming the Time* (New York 1941), p. 92.
10 *Apokalypse II*, p. 50.
11 Ibid., p. 51.
12 H. Bergson, *Les deux Sources de la morale et de la religion*, op. cit., p. 241.

different God from the God of love. Surely there is more convergence between natural and supernatural progress than Bergson allows? Man the maker is also religious man who, if he wishes, can conjoin himself more fully to the ever-original divine will than to the 'compulsive power' of mere living.[13] Balthasar notes Bergson's unease with the social. Profound religious experience, it seems, is always on one's own. Parapsychology shows souls do not belong wholly with their bodies. Religious community – *Gemeinschaft* – is almost for Bergson a contradiction in terms.

The Mysticism of Life in the Germanic Realm

The outlines of a world-view are appearing. Its basic problematic is the relation of the God within to finitude, temporality, development. In specifically Germanophone *Lebensphilosophie* are found many figures. Balthasar begins by looking at the poets among them. In the new post-Idealist generation, Bergson's profile rose across the Rhine as philosopher of intuition and spiritual father of young poets. The concept, *Begriff*, treated rather sniffily by the master, was no longer the fulfilment of the symbol but its evacuation.[14] Anaysing the resultant images shows the firm spiritual world of the Idealists melting like snow before the hot wind blowing from the Dionysian direction, and the precipitation was absorbed into the river of life, the infinite *Gebärgrund*, 'bearing ground', of all. Balthasar notes that on certain Greek islands men celebrated Dionysus' birth *from the sea*.[15] In Hugo von Hoffmansthal's (1874–1929) *Oedipus und die Sphinx*, the ecstasy of the infinite life-stream flowing through me is felt on the pulse of the heart. Rainer Maria von Rilke described this river-god as daimonic. Arnold Böcklin (1827–1901) painted it. Sigmund Freud (1856–1939) tried to formulate it. For Balthasar we have here a 'duo-monism'. Unlike Idealism, whose 'two-in-one' is *Geist* (not just empirical subject but transcendental subject too), the two-in-one here is life itself (not just my individual life but the all-life). The relation of *Geist* to *Natur* is no longer one of superiority or even parity. Rather, spirit is *Scheinnatur*, a likeness of the natural; nature itself is always *Grundnatur*, the foundational thing. Form and ground are no longer dialectically related. Greater than all *Gestalt* is the *Weltgrund*, the ground of the world.

In effect we are dealing here with an accelerating monism. Nietzsche had denied the difference between the body and the 'I'. Freud had derived spirit from passional drive. Stefan George will treat body and spirit as equivalents. Balthasar finds Heidegger's *Dasein* to be indebted to the 'Dionysian world' as well, since spiritual goal-directedness is replaced by 'vital activity'. Embracing *Geist* through life: that could be called the hallmark of Wilhelm Dilthey's (1833–1911) *Weltanschauungslehre*, Georg Simmel's (1858–1915) *Lebensmetaphysik*; Ernst Troeltsch's (1865–1923) *Lebensethik*; Nicolai Hartmann's (1882–1950) *Erkenntnislehre*. In all of these: 'the forms of spirit and culture are crystallisations of flowing life, dams it raises so as to flow over'.[16]

Balthasar finds this concentration on sheer life-energy highly ambiguous.

---

13 *Apokalypse II*, p. 58.
14 Ibid., p. 62.
15 Here Balthasar is indebted to W. Otto, *Dionysus* (Frankfurt 1933).
16 *Apokalypse II*, p. 71.

The problem shows itself in the question of knowledge. For Nietzsche, George, Simmel, knowledge is scarcely a human good at all. Rather than take it – as Balthasar would wish – for the 'creative co-fulfilment of the trans-cendence of the life-ground', they treat it as in opposition to the 'sheer, animal-life streaming forth of life', the creative production of forms in which for the first time life can become fully aware. There can also be some dire results for ethics. Is appropriate action merely the deed in which life comes to itself? Worse, is it the 'creative' negation of constraints and hence conscience-less? Or should we reserve the term 'good' for the active subjectivity that hears and follows conscientiously its 'law' in its deeds? And then behind these issues of ethics and knowledge lies the deeper question of the value and significance of individual personality at large. Nietzsche found Scho-penhauer's *Allwillen* and Socialism's collectivity obnoxious. He aimed to introduce a new 'subjectification' of man. But, for Balthasar, he simply dreamed of a cosmic 'I', a prolongation of the primordial life-force. Against this vitalistic background the 'sun' of the human person looks feeble indeed. The climax of all these question-marks set against the 'mysticism of life' comes with the topic of death. In death, the opposition of the human person and this universal anonymity becomes unmanageable. Balthasar takes Carl Spitteler as emblematic. Born at Liestal in the Catholic 'half-canton' Basel-Land – the 1920 *Guide Bleu* to Switzerland describes this as a halt on the Paris-to-Lucerne railway – Balthasar might be expected to feel sympathy with this poet who was to die in his own home city, Lucerne itself. But Spitteler's portrayal of the 'feast of death' as a 'feast of love' shows man rising to superhuman greatness before sinking into chaos.

The emergence of such attitudes necessarily affected the way people inhabit culture, notably in regard to their sense of progress. *Lebensphilosophie* hails the triumph of life in its fullness over all conceivable catastrophes. In the English context, H.G. Wells exemplifies the refusal of biological optimism to be daunted by any tragedy. But the other side of the coin is this philo-sophy's disparagement of consciousness as alienation, and its deep suspicion of technology as a threat to 'life'. Culture tears apart, in fact, along the faultline of life and spirit. For Balthasar, a cult of life, simply as such, would be trivial. Only the element of internal contradiction makes this truly 'Dio-nysian space'.[17] It certainly has a maniacal shadow side. Nietzsche's man, despite the 'all is one' motif, is 'alone to the point of madness'. In *Der Mensch und die Technik* Oswald Spengler (1880–1936) stresses the isolation of the first human soul – which alone knows its own fate.[18]

Ludwig Klages

Despite his comparative obscurity (he figures in modern German studies chiefly as one of the 'cosmic' writers in the early circle of Stefan George[19]), Balthasar singles out Ludwig Klages (1872–1956) in order to exemplify what the radicalization of Bergsonianism looks like. For Klages, life and mind (spirit) are reciprocally situated as the 'unmediated other'. The living cosmos

17 Ibid., p. 77.
18 Ibid., citing O. Spengler, *Der Mensch und die Technik* (Munich 1931), p. 33.
19 M. Winkler, *George-Kreis* (Stuttgart 1972), pp. 35–36.

is the positive Absolute insofar as it expels the negative Absolute of *Geist*. Like Bergson, Klages finds in Plato the great falsifier, owing to his perpetuation of the Eleatic tendency to drain phenomena of substance in relation to noumena. The most positive reality is 'the happening'. Klages speaks of the 'event character of reality'.[20] The temporality of being is shown in motion, which Klages takes to be the visible aspect of the 'metaphysical movement of reality as such'. Positive eternity (shades of Bergson) lies in time when time's events are taken at a proper level of depth. In Klages' words, 'Reality is eternal and real time the pulsating of eternity.'[21] Balthasar would locate Klages roughly halfway between Bergson and Heidegger. Klages rejects Bergson's notion of infinite duration as contradictory, but unlike Heidegger he holds the concept of *la durée* to be the crossing-point of two infinitudes: life in its streaming and emptily identical *Geist*. But with mind bracketed out, time loses its actively creative aspect, the snowball effect of accumulated memory by which Bergson set store. Klages' description of the realm of the sensuous – it is *substantielle Scheinhaftigkeit*, 'substantial appearance' – is actually true, writes Balthasar, of his account of reality as a whole. His complex theory of 'mirroring' make him the theoretician of the Narcissus-problem in Spitteler, George, Hoffmansthal.

Klages is also known as one of the fathers of graphology, the inference of personality from handwriting. The way in which Klages states the presuppositions of graphology seems to anticipate the opening volume of Balthasar's own theological aesthetics. Graphology, so Balthasar tells us on Klages' behalf, is a 'cosmic language of signs'.[22] As Klages explained: 'The body is the appearing of the soul, the soul the meaning of the living body.'[23] The physiognomy of the cosmos yields the final ground of the world. Presumably only minds can register such, so what was the basis of Klages' hostility to *Geist*? For Klages, mind *qua* mind means objectification, rationalism, world-fleeing metaphysics. Klages declared war in no uncertain terms on the doctrine of eros of his great enemy, the shade of Plato. In loving another, do we love universal Beauty and Goodness through that other? On the contrary, inasmuch as that other is the beloved, we love him or her as distinguished from all thinkable essence. Rilke's poetry, and notably the eighth of the *Duino Elegies*, is for Balthasar a variation on Klages' conviction that consciousness is a millstone round our necks by making the self an intellectually external relator to things. Our eyes, as though 'reversed, encircle [the "creature-world"] on every side, like traps set round its unobstructed path to freedom'.[24] Salvation for Klages (hardly for Rilke) is

---

20 *Apokalypse I*, p. 81, citing L. Klages, *Mensch und Erde* (Jena 3rd edn, 1929), p. 36.

21 L. Klages, *Vom kosmogonischen Eros* (Munich 2nd edn, 1926), p. 140.

22 *Apokalypse II*, p. 86. Compare the title of the work one of whose theses these words summarize: L. Klages, *Ausdrucksbewegung und Gestaltungskraft. Grundlegung der Wissenschaft vom Ausdruck* (Leipzig 2nd edn, 1921).

23 L. Klages, *Ausdrucksbewegung und Gestaltungskraft*, p. 16, cited in *Apokalypse II*, p. 86.

24 R.M. Rilke, *Duino Elegies* (ET New York 1939; 1963), p. 68. Rilke's English translator J.B. Leishman wrote: 'In his letters we constantly find Rilke regarding external phenomena ... as externality to be internalised and thereby re-created into something existing both within us and without. Nature (including all the visible works of man) thus becomes a kind of externalised and visible consciousness, and consciousness a kind of internalised and invisible nature': 'Introduction', in ibid., pp. 15–16.

essentially salvation from *Geist*. In Klages' case, suspects Balthasar, what animates the discontent is 'rebellious Titanism', 'Titanic wilfulness'.

This is, however, mystical Titanism, not the usual self-interested sort. The soul unites itself ecstatically with that cosmic eros which the world both carries and is carried by: 'plunging back into the brimming source of the world'.[25] Klages recommends attitudes which will play a large part in Balthasar's own spiritual scheme: receptivity, self-oblation, sympathetic suffering. True passivity is not inactivity but self-forgetfulness. In such moments, says Balthasar, there is a death and resurrection. The way to life passes through the death of the 'I', as the heart rises up to what is ultimate in a movement of desire in comparison with which sexual desire is but a shadow. Klages' doctrine of eros probably confirmed Balthasar's suspicion that the eros-language of patristic mysticism has an important contribution to make in expressing the God-man relation. While expounding Klages' thought Balthasar comes up with the phrase 'marital distance'.[26] Distance is essential to eros. Only something 'eternally distant' can bestow itself with 'enchanting felicity'. Eros, then, may be a 'marriage', but along with vision of what is nearby it also combines distance. In this way, eros is the fulfilment of the 'rhythmically polar basic experience of time'. A grasping conceptualism foreshortens this crucial distance, turning metaphysics into something quantifiable and killing revelation stone-dead. Klages calls eros – in the title of one of his books – 'cosmogonic' because it is a state of outpouring fullness that creates moment by moment the order of a world. For Klages, the fulfilment of inter-personal love comes when the 'common revelation of a world' shines through two souls who see in each other 'the sensible image of eros'.[27] 'Immortality' consists in the horizontal perpetuation of the vertical dimension of depth found in such moments in time.

And if this thought is reminiscent of some of the Romantic and Idealist (or 'Real-Idealist') writers of the nineteenth century, Klages' account of mind as a spectre impotent until it drinks the blood of the passsional instincts reminds Balthasar – rather cruelly – of the early Karl Barth. One step more, says Balthasar, and Klages' *Geist* would be strangely like the God of Karl Barth. Barth's God is a deity who, considered in himself, is sheer actuality, but in the world is traceable only – to borrow Klages' language about mind – through the 'suppression of the well of life'. The *Geist* of Klages is the pursuing God of the Reformation who, with a glowing sword, slays and recasts everything that is 'merely [sic] alive'.

For Balthasar, the whole of Klages' picture of the world is contained embryonically in the opening paragraph of Hegel's *Phenomenology*. That work opens with the counter-pointing of the seemingly richest experiential awareness and the seemingly emptiest possible *Geist*. This contrast for Hegel *is* the consciousness of the emptiness of what seems to be the richest and hence the beginning of philosophy. For his part, Balthasar aims to show how all this is better understood by reference to a *positive* concept of mind (not unlike what Klages associates with the word 'soul'). He surely has in mind the Aristotelean-Thomist account of the intellect which is 'potential' in

25 *Apokalypse II*, p. 93.
26 'Vermählende Ferne': ibid., p. 94.
27 Ibid., p. 95.

relation to all forms: as Aquinas remarks, 'the soul is in a certain sense all things'.

Klages, thinks Balthasar, is haunted by nostalgia for the world's lost youth. So-called progress is the victory of mind over life. Technology means destroying the last vestiges of the earthly Paradise. Directing our gaze to the future is only possible for spirit – which necessarily deprives things of magic and hence is nihilistic. Klages longs for an epoch when nature and man enjoyed mutual immediacy. At his hands philosophy becomes 'the service of holy presentiments'.[28] This is a world-view even more 'aesthetic' than Bergson's for Klages has little to say about *deed*. Balthasar underscores his *Weltbild*'s dreamlike character. The person has no enduring substance. He or she is only a 'point through which things pass'. Reality may be *Geschehen*, 'happening', but it is not 'history', *Geschichte*. Mind, freedom, deed, responsibility are, in effect, eliminated from the sphere of vital expression. Klages was right to identify a certain tension between life and mind. But this tension is not a tragic animosity, it is a sign of man's metaphysical 'intimacy' and 'value'.[29]

What we have in Klages, by and large (Balthasar excepts from his negative critique Klages' congenial doctrine of becoming creative through being receptive), is a mysticism of life sinking down into an 'existentiality' of dream and death.

Dream and Death

The poets will make this clear. A gallery of poets of the period manifest a dual attitude. They aspire to 'become one in love with the life-ground'. They also treat mind as a 'lucid but cold standing over against things'.[30] In Hugo von Hofmannsthal's *Kleine Welttheater* the great stream of life beneath and beyond its changing forms is the 'real actor', while in the rest of his lyric drama the characters are 'masks of Bacchus', mouths through which a 'deeper, more comprehensive life' can speak. Balthasar describes them as dream figures who understand themselves out of a single 'dream-centre'. Of the poet, standing midway between the 'figures that are formed' and the 'formative ground', it can be said in Hofmannsthal's own words 'Holy is his sleep. He sees into the innards of the world.'[31] Dream here, insists Balthasar, means immanence. The poet's art is magic because he claims to master transcendence from within the dimension of immanence. Or as Balthasar remarks of the poets who worked 'under the sign of Nietzsche': 'Because the "ground" is beyond all form, no longer Hegelian Logos but an Unnameable, myth now can only consist in the way the form yields as window into this ground.'[32]

The Dionysian myth 'lives from subjectivity'. It cannot survive the depredations of literary artists who seek to 'express this cosmic nimbus in the

28 Ibid., p. 103.
29 Ibid., p. 106. Here Balthasar is agreeing with Max Bense's *Anti-Klages* (Berlin 1937), pp. 14–15.
30 *Apokalypse II*, p. 108.
31 Cited in ibid., p. 111.
32 Ibid., p. 112.

historical realm'.[33] That judgment is passed collectively on the *See-lenwanderungsromanen* of the 1900s, and the various works that took as their theme the Nietzschean motif of 'eternal return', in the years immediately preceding and following the First World War. For Balthasar Freudianism – originated and diffused in the years in question – is simply the conceptual articulation of the Dionysian picture of the world. There is salvation from neurotic loneliness through return to the depths of pre-existence. Beauty and intellect can be interpreted on the basis of blood and sex. Destiny is the breaking of drive on the rock of consciousness. Ethos – moral character – is the result of a deep, amoral, primordial happening. The *Geist* Klages found so problematic is 'nothing other than' *Triebmechanismus*, the clockwork of drive. We should note, however, that Freud's 'deeper strata' are indebted to the Dionysian circle where the passionate was not only biology but mysticism as well.[34]

The blood has a magic rhythm. So thought Rilke in the third of his *Duino Elegies*, Stefan George (1868–1933) in *Der Stern des Bundes*, Richard Beer-Hofmann (1866–1945) in the *Schlaflied an Mirjam*. Given the well-known role of appeal to the blood in National Socialist ideology, it seems curious that Balthasar finds *Blutzauber* – 'blood-magic' – a predictable inheritance from a *Jewish* thinker: the Bergson whom he regards as the intellectual parent of the German-language 'philosophy of life'.

More sympathetically, however, these poets, as others, are concerned with that key quality of Balthasarian spirituality, *Hingabe*, oblationary self-abandonment. As Balthasar explains, between *Grund* and *Gestalt* there is in Dionysian sensibility an alienation that cannot be overcome without the help of a more marked attitude of this kind than Idealism knows of. For George, for instance, behind the humanized, formed earth lies an uninhabitable demonic nature. Reality divides into the 'bright world of forms' and 'the dreadful night of "the other"'.[35] And this is so even if, more feebly, George hints at a higher spiritual reality, sheltering and almost gracious, symbolized as stars and light, at work in that dark 'abyss', *Abgrund*, which is the fundamental apocalyptic space of these writers. When George states his eschatology positively, it is all a matter of the depth-dimension of the moment ('the moment is eternal'), but there are also discreet references to a possible teleology of reconciliation ('the light to which we travel').

Carl Spitteler (1845–1924) too has a radical dualism to cope with – in his case between on the one hand, the 'I' or *Geist* and, on the other, the *Weltgrund* or matter. For Spitteler, the 'ground of the world', necessity, is an 'automaton, raging and stamping in its meaningless circlings, ever and again crushing down the blossoming, living thing'.[36] His plays work with different mythical schemes but the shaping spirit is Dionysian. For Balthasar, Spitteler is a frightening figure, mired in a materialistic mechanism its victim hates. 'God' is Spitteler's image for power: the crude power of matter considered as the enemy of life. Indeed, the Dionysian world, as transmitted by these poets, is essentially perishing. Even when they give glory to form, the forms they

33 Ibid., p. 114.
34 Ibid., p. 117.
35 Ibid., p. 119.
36 Ibid., p. 122.

praise have about them something at once unfinished and fading. Rilke uses the image of a North Sea island continually threatened by the invasion of the sea, and also the figure of 'Egypt', a narrow land between the ever-flowing river and endless stone. 'The plenary moment is thus ambiguous. As enjoyment of the unique and unrepeatable there is intermixed with it a sweet (and also enjoyed) mourning, mourning for a perfect beauty that in the next moment becomes meaningless – the incomprehensibly seductive melancholy of the immediate.'[37]

The myth of Hades recurs. Signalled in, for instance, Stefan George's *Jahr der Seele*, it provides an image for a world that is 'meaningless and groundless, in an empty but perhaps in some way sweet state of mourning' – a world 'sunk in mourning in the midst of cheerful existence'.[38] One need only think of the Freudian 'death wish', which the Viennese psychologist understood as an egoistic drive, bound up with the eros principle, but seeking the restoration of the primal condition. The source-point of life is lifeless, so the 'I-drive' is near neighbour to the 'death drive'. For Balthasar, this comes close to saying that life is a sickness of being. Hermann Keyserling's (1880–1946) *Südamerikanischen Meditationen* would make one think so, with their affirmation that 'In the beginning was the murder'.[39] For Keyserling, *Angst* is not – as it was for Kierkegaard – a condition of the human spirit, simply. Things are a good deal worse than that. *Angst* is the 'primordial phenomenon of the ground'.[40] Josef Winckler's (1881–1976) 'The Maze of God or the Comedy of Chaos' seeks to show that no version of *Lebensphilosophie* can succeed. Why? Because form is for a brief moment the house of life and then becomes a dead shell.

There is one thing in all this Balthasar can underwrite. Both Bergson and Klages had seen something true. There *is* a mysticism of the moment – what the New Testament would call the *kairos*. Klages knew that the moment gives shelter to distance; life's depth dimension is simultaneously the irrecoverable, inviolable past. Bergson emphasized that in the 'now' all pastness remains near yet changed – changed by creative rejuvenation. In memory – in German, *Erinnerung* (literally, 'taking something within') – the space of the present broadens so as to take within the treasure of what has been through becoming. But, adds Balthasar: 'To the extent that the *kairos* expands in this way, it spiritualises itself as distance in its own regard, thus for the first time winning with this accepted weight of a life-history the aesthetic "ripeness" which makes it desirable as a sweet fruit. A pure impressionism is impossible. It is always and already a remembering, form-giving, expressive spirit that opens itself to the new.'[41]

So Freudianism was right to see that the past held creativity but wrong to read those resources in the manner of Positivism. Memory is an appropriation of life through which the experienced is integrated on a higher level. There is a 'magic' here indeed, and it is deeper than that of the Dionysian moment. Relying on Hofmannsthal's *Gestern*, Balthasar identifies the proper

---

37 Ibid., p. 131.
38 Ibid., pp. 132, 136.
39 H. Keyserling, *Südamerikanischen Meditationen* (Stuttgart and Berlin 1932), p. 59, cited in ibid., p. 137.
40 Ibid.
41 Ibid., p. 143.

attitude to the mystical content of the moment. It is when an ' "enthusiasm" of memory' makes possibly the 'continually arriving time'.[42] The problem is explored in Hofmannsthal's lyric drama 'The Gate and Death'. As the dead appear before Claudio they give him 'the catchword of their art'. It turns out to be *Treue*, fidelity. Fidelity entails a binding together of moments into something greater – which presupposes, then, spiritual reality. As Balthasar remarks: 'Fidelity means death to the moment – but also the moment's ability to give itself more deeply.'[43] In recognizing the truth of this statement, so Balthasar believes, the immediate circle of Nietzsche's followers is left behind.

The Journey to 'Meta-cosmos'

Fidelity oversteps the limits of any mere environing 'world'. Human life is more than a flowing stream. There is a love in it whose horizons stretch beyond the factual, and for whose sake alone life is worth living. One might almost say, in the title of one of Balthasar's later theological studies, *Glaubhaft ist nur Liebe*: 'Only love is credible.'[44] The human awareness that this is so creates a tension between essence and existence, posits an 'essence-ideal' as a goal-post, an 'end' for the world. This is not, admits Balthasar, an easy journey to negotiate. The 'I' must become world and the world 'I'. But only too often the consequence is that the soul seems to split, and to stand both *diesseits* and *jenseits*: being of the world as well as beyond it. Balthasar mentions in this connexion Paul Claudel's contrast of *animus*, the labouring manservant in us, and *anima*, the lady at rest, as well as Maurice Blondel's distinction between *la volonté voulue*, will as we actually exercise it on finite goods, and *la volonté voulante*, will in its – in principle – quasi-infinite scope.

Nietzsche and the poets whom he influenced have themselves mythologems that point in this direction. Nietzsche speaks of *die Göttin Seele*, the 'goddess soul', 'my terrible lady'. The soul's betrothal means the enchantment of existence which is – in a way both like and unlike Idealism – more than itself. The meaning of the world is spirit's search for itself. In Idealism, which appealed to the presuppositions of spirit on its scheme of things, the happy outcome of this process was not in doubt. But in Nietzsche, George, Spitteler, this changes: all that remains is the uncertain and possibly tragic outcome of the individual's destiny. 'The higher world-spirit of Idealism no longer moves through individuals. The human being and his soul are here the lover and the loved.'[45] Even so, the soul figures as a kind of gracious power working from above in the manner of an ideal attracting: the 'pure illumination of the sun'. (There may be a comparison here with the non-realist 'metaphysics' of the English novelist and philosopher Iris Murdoch who in her last years rallied to a religiously minded atheism of a paradoxical kind. Plato's metaphor of the sun for the 'sovereignty of the good' appealed to her.)

Max Scheler – leaving his Catholic interlude aside – has a similar

---

42 Ibid., p. 144.
43 Ibid., p. 145.
44 *Glaubhaft ist nur Liebe* (Einsiedeln 1963); ET *Love Alone. The Way of Revelation* (London 1968).
45 Ibid., p. 150.

approach. In *Der Formalismus in der Ethik* he calls man a 'tendency to the divine', whose essential kernel is a spiritual act of self-transcendence. The question remains, however: self-transcendence towards what – or whom? Balthasar suspects that what the later Scheler really means is that man is 'the highest peak of nature's vegetation cone', casting its shadow as the 'ideal' onto nothingness.[46] Scheler's man is utterly alone. The world cannot help him; before him is 'the task and nothing'. The world religions seek to silence this heroic loneliness, but no assurance is possible, only risk and a journey into the unknown. Neither, as Scheler glacially remarks in *Die Stellung des Menschen im Kosmos*, is 'metaphysics an insurance company serving the feeble who are looking out for support'.[47] In his renunciation of a God-centred teleology Scheler appealed to Freud, but, as Scheler himself had written in his 1929 'Philosophische Weltanschauung', 'the psycho-analyst of history has not yet appeared who can make man free of the *Angst* of this earth'.[48] Here the spiritual goal may be loved but it is hardly known. Rather is it the 'ecstatic excursion of the heart' where one dares 'the goddess' in the 'adventure of nothingness'. This is no longer Schellingian mystical potentiality. At best it is Goethean resignation. Above all, it is only about man.

Balthasar draws a comparison with Paul Claudel (1868–1955) to the advantage of the latter. (This was the period when Balthasar was completing his principal Claudel translations.[49]) For Claudel too the relation of the 'treacherous, sly blackguard spirit' and the 'secret mystical soul' is difficult, an 'unhappy marriage', but even so it remains love. In Claudel's story of their fate, they are saved when the soul 'doubles herself into serving maid and divine Lord', and they find their flourishing in 'explicit religion'.[50] Where this resolution is unavailable – so Balthasar judges – the space between *Seele* and *Geist* expands into the abyss of the 'Nietzsche problematic'. The opposition of spirit (mind) and soul, it seems, *is* the human situation *de facto*. In the 'mystery of self-encounter' there is not much firm ground to occupy between pride and service.

Balthasar notes the popularity in the post-Nietzschean writers of the imagery of *mirrors*. The Idealists knew of mirrors – in the 'eye to eye' of the *Weltgeist* and *Allnatur*. They expected to see the spirit reflected in the 'land of the senses'. But in these Dionysians writing under Nietzsche's sign the 'innermost two-in-one, dialogical essence of being' has a sharp, self-contradictory profile. Poles that cannot be unified must be made into a single spirit. This for Balthasar is the point of Oscar Wilde's (1854–1900) *The Portrait of Dorian Gray* whose mirror image in the attic is at once Gray's (ghastly) ideal and his creation. Narcissus looking at his reflection is a favoured motif not only of André Gide (1869–1951) and Paul Valéry (1871–1945) but also of George, Hofmannsthal, Rilke. What does it mean? Vanity as frustration – or

---

46 Ibid., p. 151.
47 M. Scheler, *Die Stellung des Menschen im Kosmos* (Darmstadt 1928), p. 112, cited in ibid., p. 152.
48 Cited in ibid.
49 Notably of *Cinq Grandes Odes* (thus *Paul Claudel. Fünf grosse Oden* [Freiburg 1939]), and *Le Soulier de Satin* (thus *Paul Claudel. Der seidene Schuh* [Salzburg 1939]). Balthasar revised the latter for its ninth edition in 1959.
50 *Apokalypse II*, p. 158, with reference to P. Claudel, *Positions et Propositions* I (Paris 6th edn, 1928), pp. 55–57.

as generative self-duplication? In choosing a frame of reference we can oscillate between the merely aesthetic and the religious. In Hofmannsthal's *Stadien* a boy tries on masks before a mirror until he finds the mask of a madman. In *Der Rosenkavalier* the Marschallin reads her whole destiny from the strange face that appears in the mirror. The message here is existential ambiguity. In George's 'Three Poems from the Vicinity', subtitled 'Mirror-ings', a mirror gathers up the streaming phenomena of our sheer transience into an eternity-reflecting bowl out of which we can be recreated. Here the mirror has something of the force of the (divine) 'ideas' according to Plato, Augustine and Thomas. Rilke's angels, surely, are mirrors that take the beauty that has streamed forth from them to recreate it anew in their own faces. But the ambiguity persists. In his *Narziss-Gedichte* Rilke portrays a mirror-existence that in its existential unreality expresses the distance from the world of pure spirit. In his French-language 'Rose Poems' mirror-existence is aesthetically beautiful but unreal. 'It is your within that ceaselessly caresses itself ... by its own illuminated reflection'.[51]

For Balthasar, the myth of *die Göttin Seele* is the myth of man as a 'tragic Narcissus who hourly must want what is denied him'.[52] The backcloth is provided by the tension Nietzsche identified between 'ground' and 'form'. The ideal stands over against man as a mask. Existence is role and dissimulation. Its genuineness is falsity, its truth a lie, and only in this lie is it creative. For Keyserling, *Schauspiel*, play-acting, is the only life that determines spirit. Everything *geistig* is *spielerisch*, unserious. All happening is theatre. But, asks Balthasar, does our *Geist* want finally to play with itself in a 'kiddies's paradise'? Or does it want to recognize itself in a 'truly existential dialogue'?[53] Does it not in fact want to win through, from the existential lies in which it finds itself caught up, to its own existential truth? For Keyserling, this is out of the question. A final and decisive meaning can be neither represented nor thought. Each realized 'meaning' simply opens more horizons (the parallel with the neo-Nominalism of later twentieth-century post-modernism emerges here). The world is a divine dance (compare post-modernism's 'play of signifiers'). It is the everlasting creation of the *Abgrund*, the abyss. Balthasar comments that really, objectivity should be taken up into subjectivity, but here spirit can no longer serve things by exhibiting some inner logic. Instead, spirit goes under in the 'labyrinth of demonic objectivity' where everything is 'unintelligible and hostile'.[54] Thus, for instance, Hofmannsthal's 'Tales of the 672 Nights', or Max Herrmann's (1886–1941) poem *Weltuntergang*: 'Strange was the same, weird a brother to the other./ Annihilation began: the rift went right through the world.'[55] The world becomes alien as if – Balthasar writes – in a mirror an unknown face were looking at us. And in this process the 'I' becomes likewise alien to itself. 'For the I, which should have become world, detaches itself from the centre of the person like petals from the rose; roles and characters fall from their bearers

---

51 R.M. Rilke, *Poèmes français* (Paris 1935), p. 85, cited in ibid., p. 165. Balthasar's earliest comments on Rilke's poetry, for which he retained a lifelong admiration, appeared as 'Rilke und die religiöse Dichtung', in *Stimmen der Zeit* 63 (1932), pp. 183–92.
52 *Apokalypse II*, p. 168.
53 Ibid., p. 169.
54 Ibid., p. 170.
55 Cited in ibid., p. 171.

like so many scales.'⁵⁶ Anxiety about being-in-the-world becomes anxiety about the person. In Hoffmansthal's *Turm*, Sigismund asks: 'Me? Who is that? Where is its goal? Who first called me so?'⁵⁷

This is the anthropological crisis of identity to which Balthasar's theo-dramatics will be, ultimately, his response. He will maintain there that roles are providential ways in which one becomes a person through mission, the 'I' coming to itself by taking responsibility for the world. The 'I' should be the 'mirror and the robe' (*Gewand*) of the world of objects, but instead a 'strange and lawless' world surrounds the 'defenceless self'.⁵⁸ The 'grace of the goddess soul' abandons her servant, and Promethean-Dionysian man finds himself without goal, ideal or meaning, alone with his guilt. To Balthasar's mind, Franz Werfel (1890–1945), in his *Der Gerichtstag*, gives this classic expression as the rapturous celebration of nature, the ideal, co-humanity, turns to 'icy smooth, impenetrable prison walls'. In the 'mirror', the poet recognizes 'curse and hell/ thine "I" and everything, this complete fullness of nothing', and identifies himself as 'the body of emptiness', more null even than nothingness, since he is only nothing's appearance.⁵⁹

Lost in the Hall of Mirrors

From this bleak prospect, Balthasar now turns to *der erhörhte Narziss*, Narcissus heard–over-heard and his boon granted. The question here was, How can the existential lie that is the 'truth' of our being be resolved into a higher truth? How can the mirror character of being still be acknowledged and yet be – as is surely desirable – transformed? In other words, poetic intelligence after Nietzsche sought a way out of the Nietzschean impasse.

Balthasar finds that the attempt follows four possible routes. In the first, people try to overcome the magic of the *Seinspiegel* – the mirror that is being – specifically as *evil* magic. Maybe the shadowy mirror partner, the perceived self, has to be tolerated for a while. But if it can be brought to nought the soul's free flow will start again. Balthasar calls that a 'Buddhist-Schopenhauerian' solution and it is summed up in Werfel's *Spiegelmensch*. The 'Mirror-man' of the title is 'the truth as disclosure of false ideality'. In the poem, when the person whose reflex 'Mirror-man' is matures into his own pure truth then the Mirror-man sinks back into the mirror. The mirror shatters, and in its place arises the great window of a Buddhist monastery, looking upon the 'consciousness-less blessedness of Nirvana'.⁶⁰ But, as Balthasar points out, this means the sacrifice of *Geist* in its most elevated form – self-possession. It means a return instead to the awareness of the animals. That cannot be right. Keyserling was correct to say there can be no going back on man as actor, for the mind or spirit of man and his reflective activity are one and the same. But in that case, since all man has of himself are images, must it not be true that the tragic tension between 'longing and fulfilment' cannot ultimately be overcome?

56 Ibid., p. 172.
57 Cited in ibid.
58 Ibid., p. 173.
59 Cited in ibid., pp. 173, 175.
60 Ibid., p. 175.

Here we come to a second way, and George and Spitteler are notable for
following it. Why not consider the 'goddess soul' to be: 'not something alien,
but the furthest flung horizon of our own spirit: the very content of its
longing in its radiance but that content now become discourse (*Rede*)'.[61]
Spitteler's Prometheus may found a 'messianic *Reich*', but in his pride and
loneliness the world is without resonance for him and God himself an
enemy. 'The mirror in which he sees himself is, until the end, himself.'[62]
Promethean world redemption is but a *pareschaton*, something penultimate,
merely. All we know is the 'meta-cosmic mirror process'. And indeed for
Spitteler, though the hard granite of the world's ground can show paradisal
flowers from time to time these always turn out phantasmagoric. For him just
because the cosmos is *not* meta-cosmos it is in the final analysis unredeem-
able. One could speak here, once again, of a Gnostic-type dualism. But Balthasar thinks it more penetrating to say that, for Spitteler, the world is
'everlastingly ill'.[63] Prometheus's love for his soul can be no solution of the
mirror-problem, because between the two no world arises that can embody
the ideal. By contrast, George does not have this seeming *Leibhass*, hatred of
embodiment. On the contrary, the need for embodiment is effectively the
poet's starting-point. For George, metacosmic flight – as with Spitteler, his
'daimon' is the endless horizon to which the soul flies – should surely be met
by divine condescension, a grace bestowed for the full humanizing of the
self. So the person is: 'the child of the "I" and the *daimon*, fruit of the
movement of longing and its reflection from out of the divine mirror'.[64]

But then something like the predicament of Spitteler's Prometheus recurs.
The hero transcends society, bestowing upon it the divine. He alone
undertakes the dread adventure, to plunge down to the depths of the world-
ground thence to bring home the 'other' as its philanthropic magician. But,
asks Balthasar, 'is not the Dionysian abyss in every soul?' 'Can it be sub-
stitutionally surmounted?' The problem of the mirror can have no solution,
surely, that does not do justice to the *social dimension*. In effect, thinks Balthasar, George presumes a solution that is breathtaking in its hubris. The new
man, born from the deed and longing of the hero, while remaining for the
hero himself in the 'immanence' of his mirror-situation, enters the social
world as a transforming existential, a fresh constitutive dimension of human
existence. And this is for the others, the hero's disciples, a *thoroughgoingly
transcendent reality*.[65]

George's philosophy suffers from another drawback as well. George has a
passionate desire for response from reality as well as a powerful will to
personal becoming. These can only be satisfied simultaneously by creating a
'thou'. But since – comments Balthasar, the theist – there *is* an actual Thou,
God, who needs to be taken account of in this equation, George teeters on the
brink of solipsism: he is immured with a self-created other.

61 Ibid., p. 176.
62 Ibid., p. 176.
63 Ibid., p. 177.
64 Ibid., p. 178.
65 For George, 'God reveals himself directly to men through human beings who sym-
    bolize or "re-present" (*darstellen*) His spiritual ideality to such an extent that they seem
    to be "begot by the stars"', M.M. Metzger and E.A. Metzger, *Stefan George* (New York
    1972), p. 162.

Ironically, Balhasar compares George's religiosity with that of Pascal. With reference to the seventeenth-century Frenchman's 'memorial' of his night of fire when he discovered not the 'God of the philosophers', but the God of Abraham and Moses who is also the God of Jesus Christ, Balthasar writes of George and Pascal (1623–1662): 'God had to obey their love. It was a conjuring kiss planted on the infinite mirror ... Pascal's magic had its answer in the *Mémorial*. George's had none.'[66] It is a terrible thing to be imprisoned in an anti-universe of one's own making.

So, then, after the way of the mirror as the 'I' and the mirror as the 'thou', what third way can be sought? A possibility suggests itself. Might one not find the 'I'-mirror in the 'thou'-mirror? This solution has two possible valencies. Taken together, they will give us all the 'four routes' Balthasar mentioned at the outset. For there is one rift between the 'I' and the world of things, and another between the 'I' and the (human) 'thou'. Rainer Maria Rilke (1875–1926) will take the first – the self and nature – as his special province, Hofmannsthal the second – the self and other selves.

Balthasar places Rilke only partially in the world of *Lebensphilosophie*: the 'Dionysian myth' of the 'goddess soul' is absent from his work. Rilke has before him no 'mirror of the "I"'. For him, this mirror is already shattered and its shards are found among things. Orpheus, the God of nature in its wholeness, has been torn apart. Hence his apostrophe: 'O thou lost God! Thou unending trail' (*Spur*). Rilke sees his poetic task as the following of this trail, the seeking out of this lost divinity in all things, through service of 'the existing'.[67] For Balthasar, it is because Rilke seeks in everything not himself but the lost God that he becomes 'a mirror in which things recognise themselves, indeed reach their own idea, their own truth'.[68] In the opening volume of the theological logic, *Truth. The Truth of the World*, Balthasar will make plain his conviction that this is how it ought to be.[69] Things should come more fully to themselves in the generously knowing self. Balthasar applauds Rilke's notion that, when things come home to the soul that has, as it were, open arms with which to greet them, they cease to 'weep' for their aloneness. In the mirror of the soul, there looks toward them the only redeemer that can save them: save them from the bewitched character of their 'transiently lower' existence, save them by a different kind of enchantment. The soul, after all, can creatively draw from them their 'idea' and read it. Here Balthasar, like Rilke himself, tries to tread a precarious tightrope between Realism and Idealism.

But the soul was to seek the lost God in things. Here things find themselves in the soul. Do they not, then, find their God – the lost wholeness of Orpheus – in the soul too? The soul wanted to go beyond. Can it be the beyond itself? The answer is clearly, No. By its 'creative' power, the soul has shown things their faces. Rilke does not say that this gift is also a creative, apocalyptic gaze for the soul itself. Balthasar compares Rilke's soul of man to a nun, a Sister of Charity, comforting and tending the sick in a loving that

66 Ibid., p. 180.
67 Ibid., p. 181.
68 Ibid., p. 182.
69 *Wahrheit Wahrheit der Welt* (Einsiedeln 1947); republished with a new introduction as *Theologik I. Wahrheit der Welt* (Einsiedeln 1985).

(generally speaking) goes without response from them, a loving that somehow, indeed, goes beyond them, being as it is at another's bidding. Yet the
soul too is a thing, albeit a unique one, and its idea needs to be 'read'. But
how? The fourth of Rilke's *Duino Elegies* draws attention to the soul's
occlusion.

> Then, for the sudden sketchwork of a moment,
> a ground of contrast's painfully prepared,
> to make us see it. For they're very clear
> with us, we that don't know our feeling's shape,
> but only that which forms it from outside.
> Who's not sat tense before his own heart's curtain?[70]

The soul's authentic reality does not appear on the stage of this world. Rilke
consoles himself with the thought that 'one can always watch', and Balthasar
interprets this to mean there is a powerful watching that, as with Werfel's
Spiegelmensch, is not into a mirror but out through a window, onto the play of
things and indeed the interplay of their ideas. This is the changing of the
world into *Eigentlichkeit*, authentic reality. But it is enacted, comments Balthasar, like a grand opera staged in a cheap theatre in a provincial town. The
soul lacks the necessary resources. It cannot reconstitute an 'unbroken
theatre of the world'. The soul cannot make of things a mirror of the comprehensively real. That only Christian revelation can do this – and even then
not until its eschatological consummation – will be the message of Balthasar's
Theodramatik. Balthasar calls Rilke's *Elegies* his tragic interpretation of the
world, and they point towards an unsurmountable duality – the pure idea
and sheer existence. But Balthasar considers Rilke's approach to the 'mirror
problem' an advance on the two previous 'routes' he has examined,
remarking enigmatically that Rilke's contribution to the eventual solution
belongs not to the present context but to another *Lebensraum*.[71] (He will in fact
return to him in connexion with his discussion of Martin Heidegger's philosophy in *Apokalypse*'s closing volume.)

As has already been noted, Rilke's gaze, while illuminating things, dust-
particles caught in light, could not enlighten himself. Will Hofmannsthal do
better? This poet treats his deep soul (not the 'everyday I' which is but a role
and a husk of the spirit) as the centre of a sympathetic communion of figures
all of whom, however, return his own face as were he surrounded by many
mirrors, not just confronted by one. This does not sound encouraging but
there is something of a breakthrough. As always, however, Balthasar is on
the *qui vive* for signs that a true breakthrough to the self in communion with
others, and with nature, en route to final destiny *cannot be achieved at the level
of immanence alone*. In his essay *Ad me ipsum* Hofmannsthal recognized the
antinomy of aloneness and community, *Einsamkeit und Gemeinschaft*.[72] After a
false start which sought the solution in blood and race, Hofmannsthal came
to a deeper analysis. Each spiritual 'I' is a monad with its own cosmic law.
No two monads are alike. The 'law' of each permeates with a 'colour-tone'
the objectivity of the world. Thus 'the problem of the monadically

---

70 R.M. Rilke, *Duino Elegies*, op. cit., p. 41.
71 *Apokalypse II*, p. 186.
72 Cited in ibid., p. 188.

constructed world, seen as a problem for living, becomes the fundamental problem of Hofmannsthal's master-works'.[73] Human beings constitute an immense number of 'absolute' midpoints incapable of mutual incorporation and thus bound in mere relation. The monads can neither communicate properly nor be 'fully their own architects', shaping their personal appropriation of the world (Balthasar calls this, on Hofmannsthal's behalf, *ihre Welt-ver-Ichung*) in 'purity of style'.[74] In the prism of other monads the light of the soul breaks up, and alien lights strike through its own prism too. In this 'tangle', the space between people fills with an atmosphere of ethical confusion and impurity. 'The "same" world-material is formed throughout from different "I-centres" and so is divided into a multiplicity that admits neither exchange nor objectivity and yet is nothing other than the plurality of the centres and the unique colouring the objective order receives from them.'[75]

As Hofmannsthal recognizes, two movements of (relative) transcendence are required: first, for the 'I' to enter its own world, and secondly for the closed worlds of two monads to touch each other. The first presupposes a 'pre-established harmony' (shades of Leibniz's monadology) whether the source be God or an 'idealistic I-centre'. The second is impossible without a 'living interchange of worlds'. The first may conceive the second – the 'genuine and break-making transcendence' – in an 'aesthetic, dream-like way'. It can not, though, comprehend it. Yet all remains tragic inasmuch as each midpoint – each self – can only make itself known in 'mirrors, roles, and games'.[76] In *Andreas oder die Vereinigten* Hofmannsthal faces the difficulty of this 'second transcendence'. As his character Sacromozo asks: 'How can worthy substance come from unworthy, the eagle from the chameleon, from the dirt ivory?'[77] In the figure of the Countess, Hofmannsthal shows the pathology that can accompany the attempt at such second transcendence, when lived out within immanence, a plurality of 'world-rhythms' centring around the 'I'. The Countess's personality becomes doubled as saint and whore, and holds together only in the shape of the little dog that accompanies her in each – at once a symbol of the animal body and the meaninglessness of the metaphysical bearer of 'character'. Thus the movement of love is inverted, for love should join two bearers in one 'world'.

Hofmannsthal directs us to what he calls, in a coining of his own, the 'allomatic'. By this antonym of the *automatic* where the 'other' (*allos*) takes the place of the 'self' (*autos*) he means, Balthasar explains, a 'transcendent mutuality in the laws of living [of the monads], their salvation through each other'.[78] Yet even in the fullness of the love experience, earthly experience shows its 'paltriness', its impurity. This is Andreas' discovery in the play: 'In man, aloneness and mixing with other people are one.' Hofmannsthal's greatest dramatic masterpieces, *Ariadne auf Naxos* and *Die Frau ohne Schatten*, depict this 'polymonadic' existence and its insoluble difficulties – insoluble since no standpoint can be found outside the worlds that break upon each other there. But Hofmannsthal does not let matters so rest. In the loving

73 Ibid., p. 189.
74 Ibid., p. 190.
75 Ibid., p. 192.
76 Ibid., pp. 192–93.
77 Cited in ibid., p. 194.
78 Ibid., p. 197.

exchange of looks between Bacchus and Ariadne he shows the mystery of grace, symbolized in the golden canopy that descends on them from on high. From now on, a 'radiant festivity' pervades Hofmannsthal's writing since two 'worlds', however laden with 'self-being and aloneness', can sink into each other not as tragedy but as love. Perhaps it will be said, this is not much of an eschatology. It is only a rupture of the 'monadic world-sphere'. Yes, says Balthasar, yet it can be not unlawfully compared with the jar of nard that, in the holy Gospels, was broken so that the scent of the ointment filled the whole house.[79] The allomatic is always a marvel. In *Die Frau ohne Schatten* Hofmannsthal leaves us, finally, an image of love as 'the streaming law of life of full humanity'.[80] Taking the courageous patience of 'openness and reception', it is fruitful. This 'new, blessed transcendence' creates a 'new immanence', bringing forth its 'child'. As the playwright of the 'allomatic', Hofmannsthal opened a door onto inter-subjective communion in real history. He goes beyond Rilke, for in his work 'the mirror of the "I" and the mirror of the "thou" become one in gracious, if also tragically rupturing, events'.[81] But even he could not decipher the 'dark longing' in man to break all mirrors, rather than to see himself in them and be possessed by the ideal. Balthasar's confrontation of Nietzsche and Dostoevsky (who, in reality, though contemporaries, never met) will give him an opportunity to take this thought further, as he brings the second volume of *Apokalypse* to its close.

Nietzsche and Dostoevsky

Hofmannsthal leaves us in an unsatisfactory situation. He invites us to an ethical purity that is actually, so Balthasar writes, 'ontic impurity, as brokenness'.[82] Hofmannsthal represents the ethical as the power to declare odd things even but looking – and stepping – away from the disaccord in reality and in that fashion *changing falsehood into truth*. 'The tears of liberating understanding seem already the cancellation of guilt', but in point of fact he brings that guilt in all its facticity before our eyes.[83] The reconciliation scenes in Hofmannsthal's plots show up the guilt he uncovers in the very plea of claiming to surmount it. If the truth of existence is the unveiling of its brokenness, then truth can hardly be 'the unbroken, the whole'. Indeed, the more exalted the reconciliation (*Versöhntheit*) the deeper the lostness (*Verlorenheit*). The heights it reaches enables existence to measure its own abyss – the rift within it, and what was longed for turns out on reflection to be, contrary-wise, insupportable. Thus spirit, which has to be consciousness and not 'the animal's vacantly open look', condemns us to enclosure in endless finitude. The openness of spirit to the world is purchased, it seems, at some cost. Its price is the pain of spirit's simultaneous closedness (the world is always 'my' world, the world-for-me). Its truth is the non-identity of 'ground' and 'form': reality and its expression are not the same. How can such a being ever be in *the* truth? Indeed, how could it ever be really *good*? It

79 John 12.3.
80 Ibid., p. 199.
81 Ibid., pp. 200–201.
82 Ibid., p. 202.
83 Ibid., p. 203.

may attempt love and self-giving but these will be at the expense of its own proper power, and in any case, owing to that gulf between reality and appearance, never reach fulfilment. Such a being can live neither from its own centre (*zentrisch*) nor from the centre of another (*exzentrisch*), but only oscillate between the two in accumulating guilt for infidelities to both.

Nietzsche's *cris de coeur* on the point gained him the accolade 'pathological' from his German critics, but Balthasar defends him. Such 'pathology' points to a genuine contradiction in existence. Of course, Nietzsche himself treated religion (Christianity) as pathology – and indeed it makes its appearance in the midst of this contradiction without, however, claiming to resolve it at the immanent level. As Balthasar puts it:

> The final, redemptive image cannot as image be devised. It is withdrawn from view and can only be 'believed'. In such faith, the pathos of existence achieves its own representation. Existence in a state of doubt about man's ultimate possibility swings up onto the level of the superhuman. The contradiction between, on the one hand, the 'for itself' of spirit, which isolates him and dictates to him the law of power, and, on the other, the worldly quality of this 'for itself', which binds him and prescribes to him the law of love, cannot be resolved on the level of the human. If man is true as a mirror then he is false as a window. If he is 'good' as an ego, then as a lover he is 'evil'.[84]

In this sense, the essence of religion (as of Nietzsche's anti-religion) may be said to fall on the further side of truth and falsehood, as of good and evil.

The liberation from the guilt of contradiction into wholeness of life, just because it concerns 'an unviewable, credited whole', is the realization on the soul's part of an unconditional freedom to elect its destiny. This is altogether the soul's doing – and altogether the work of grace. So far as consciousness goes, we are dealing with the soul's creative self-interpretation in faith. But so far as action goes – the 'pure creating of the deed', we are dealing with the 'impossible' (to immanent thinking) breakthrough of grace. *Pace* suggestions of pathology, this is not schizophrenia. Grace is found immanently within freedom – which remains my freedom even though, owing to the 'contradiction' in existence, I am helpless to bestow it on myself. Freedom exists in transcendent guise as grace – which remains a gift, even though it is my very own (new-found) freedom. But all this implies a mystery – that of the 'frontier' between God and man. And here we must be clear-sighted. If the indwelling of grace in freedom means simply a rediscovery of the self, beyond every alienation, then all we should be dealing with is the 'God' of Dionysus – the full realization of the 'self-encounter of the "ground"'. Rather, on the Catholic Christian view, is that inwardness of grace to freedom so 'radical' that it becomes the 'inner transcendent abyss of freedom itself' – the God who is, in Augustine's famous saying, 'more interior to me than I am to myself'. God is the centre of freedom, he is 'comprehensive super-freedom'. In no way is he encircled by the freedom of the 'I'. Now the 'play of mirrors' between the ground and the form of the soul becomes 'in its entirety so permeable that it is a window for the self-encounter of God'.[85]

---

84 Ibid., p. 205.
85 Ibid., p. 207.

Antichrist or Christ?

This prepares the way for Balthasar's contrasting of Nietzsche and Dostoevsky. However abstractly stated the parables of the mirror may be, concretely the choice is stark: Antichrist or Christ. *Formally speaking*, Kierkegaard
may be a more obvious conversation-partner for this 'new eschatology'. But
in terms of the *content of the Nietzschean world-view* an interlocutor was
required who could enter more fully Nietzsche's problematic. In his correspondence Nietzsche recognized this partner with enthusiasm: Fyodor
Dostoevsky (1821–1881), the artist of unmasking, the author of 'notes from
the underground'. Nietzsche was not put off by the description of him sent
by the Danish literary critic Georg Brandes (1842–1927): a Christian sadist,
who perfectly fulfilled Nietzsche's caricature of Christianity 'slave psychology'. Nietzsche replied that, on the contrary, he knew of no more valuable
psychological material anywhere. For his part, Balthasar thinks Dostoevsky
could have made of Nietzsche, had he known him, one of the great 'atheist-
figures' of his own fiction.

In point of fact, the idea of comparing the two men was not new. Among
others, Leo Shestov had devoted an entire book to the topic, though Balthasar
considered it mistaken.[86] Romano Guardini, (1885–1968) the Berlin professor
and forerunner of *nouvelle théologie* Balthasar admired, had also touched on
the matter in his 1932 essay *Der Mensch und der Glaube*, but the treatment was
too short to be satisfactory.[87] Balthasar's two hundred pages were intended as
a definitive Catholic treatment.

Unmaskers of Illusion

Dostoevsky's mistrust of his own psychological mastery commended him to
Nietzsche, himself the master of suspicion. Psychological nature cannot be
the law of freedom, if freedom is free to set its own law. For Dostoevsky,
whereas the ant knows the formula for building its anthill, man knows none
for his life. Perhaps he was put on earth to see whether such a creature is
possible – or not. Man is, as Nietzsche wrote, the 'as yet unestablished animal'.[88] For Balthasar, faith, *qua* experience of the human–divine frontier,
necessarily has a passive aspect to it – only as *in receipt of grace* does it relate
to the frontier's 'other side'. So he is not non-plussed by the Dostoevskian
statement that the believer has 'seen the truth' not by finding it with the
understanding but because its 'living form everlastingly has filled the soul'.
The 'tiny' heart and the 'wayward' understanding could not in any case
come up with so great a revelation of truth. Nietzsche too regarded as 'fact'
some sort of 'revelation' that shakes the soul to its depths. There are disclosure situations where one does not ask, one simply takes. If we enquire
what could there be in common between what these two men *mean* by
'revelation', Balthasar points to the 'transcendentals' of Scholastic philosophy. It must be some version of the true, the good, and the beautiful in their
united refulgence of which they speak. The 'super-truth' of existence,

---

86 L. Shestov, *Dostoewskij i Nietshe, Filosofiya tragedii* (Berlin 1922). This work exists in
   English translation as *Dostoevsky and Nietzsche: The Philosophy of Tragedy* (Athens OH
   1969).
87 R. Guardini, *Der Mensch und der Glaube* (Leipzig 1932).
88 Cited in *Apokalypse II*, p. 210.

pointed to beyond its 'absolute contradiction', can only be available to the sum-total of attitudes openness to the transcendentals in their unity impels, or what Nietzsche called, ironically, his 'practical goal': to be a creative artist, a loving saint, and a knowing philosopher all rolled into one.[89] Where God and immortality are concerned, says Dostoevsky's *starets* Zosima to a doubting woman, it is in the measure that you make progress in love that conviction will come to you.

To academic philosophers, then, both Nietzsche and Dostoevsky are 'poor' thinkers. They treat the 'sharpness' of the concept as an objection to any claim made through it to 'total truth'. Nietzsche's mythical figurations, like Dostoevsky's fictional characters, are for Balthasar 'embodied feelings, instincts, evidences'. It is not so much thoughts that need to be integrated into such total truth – it is 'final, contradictory life-experiences, mutually exclusive ontological "instincts"'.[90] Compared with Kant or Hegel, the thought of both men is utterly chaotic. But Balthasar sympathizes with Nietzsche's statement that the thinkers for whom the stars move on cyclic courses are not necessarily the deepest. Following Nietzsche and Dostoevsky through the 'labyrinth' of existence nonetheless requires – so Balthasar warns – deep breathing.

Strange Affinities
Both set out to be unmaskers of illusion: for Nietzsche the illusion of the gods of humanity's childhood, now to be replaced by the knowledge that man, who is human, all too human, stands alone; for Dostoevsky, the illusion of naïve, sentimental realism, to be replaced by the naked confrontation with evil in the human underground. (Here Dostoevsky's Siberian exile was decisive.) In effect, both sought to study the roots of the superhuman in the caves of the subhuman. Both men knew some kind of 'descent into hell'. The 'shafts' of the Christian soul, which Nietzsche sought to undermine, were his own depths, while the 'hiding-places' of the atheistic spirit Dostoevsky traced were hidden in himself. Thus the atheism Dostoevsky combats seems sometimes more triumphant than Nietzsche's. Nietzsche can mount a defence of Christendom more vigorously than Dostoevsky. There is another similarity. The further Nietzsche steps out into a wider world the more he speaks of himself – until in *Ecce homo* his 'I' has 'devoured the world'. Likewise, Dostoevsky's wide-ranging sympathy does not prevent him from transforming in his fictions the main events of his own life (the death penalty, the pardon, exile, epilepsy, the struggle for faith, the bite of conscience, the love-hate relation with the West). And of course each of them is aware of the fact – which is why they can confront the problem of perspectivalism in a world of monads.

Balthasar proposes to show for each writer how they confront that problem in three realms – the theoretical, which raises the issue of 'the lie'; the vital, which raises the issue of 'sickness', and the ethical, which raises the issue of 'evil'. In each case, since they are seeking the whole of existence from a situation of absolute contradiction, we want to know in what way they propose to integrate the lie into the total truth, sickness into total health, evil

89 Ibid., p. 211.
90 Ibid., p. 212.

into total goodness. In a certain sense this is the Hegelian problematic for which the triad thesis, antithesis, synthesis furnished the means of integration. But for Hegel the end of this process, as the preface to the *Phänomenologie des Geistes* tells us, is the overcoming of 'common indeterminacy and the poverty of the common human understanding' in the 'authenticity of self-conscious reason'. By contrast, for these more existential thinkers, that could only be a deviation into impersonal generality. Dostoevsky and Nietzsche propose to transform the abstract knowledge of finitude and relativity into concrete experience, and to show that 'outside this relativity existence possesses no absolute'.[91]

First, then, the theoretical level: the issue of 'the lie': namely, the character of finitude as mirror or appearance – in which alone truth is brought forth. Nietzsche states the problem, indeed, more theoretically than does Dostoevsky. For Nietzsche there is no *Ding an sich* and therefore no absolute knowing. All is perspectival, deceiving. Life is the condition of knowing, error the condition of life. Vital error, then, is the ground of truth. 'In this sense', writes Balthasar: 'the fundamental movement of Nietzsche's metaphsyics is the ever more radical technique of dismantling all inflated spiritualities, moralities and "absolute" insights into the origin of instinct and life'.[92]

The lie that contradicts truth becomes in this unmasking of truth the truth of the lie. The 'co-achievement' of drive, now seen as the real manifestation of 'ground' or ultimate reality, becomes 'the formal locus of truth'. Truth is what is practical in life, including the way life goads itself to fresh efforts as spirit strips away the masks of 'higher' – more objective, less perspectival – truth-claims. Truth is 'absolute appearance'.[93] Nietzsche is bemused as to why people should think there is some essential contradiction between truth and falsehood. Why can't there just be levels of seemingness, 'brighter and darker shades and overall tones of appearance'?[94] Nietzsche admired the ancient Greeks for, as he thought, worshipping appearance. He describes them as 'superficial – from the depths!' For Balthasar, Nietzsche's use of the word 'superficial' here is telling. To call truth appearance is not a harmless verbal stipulation. It calls into question all ascription of meaning and value. Nietzsche's 'inexorable suspicion' is neither scepticism nor pessimism. It is the 'subjective expression of the ultimate character of appearance itself'.[95] The 'hollowness' that inhabits as its presupposition all the fullness of the world awakens in Nietzsche two equally fundamental attitudes: reverence before the mysterious creativity of life, projecting its own horizon ever forward, and disdain that in this very creativity only appearance, lie, error emerge. In this sense, Nietzsche is indifferent between love and contempt. It is against this 'midpoint of indifference' that all Dostoevsky's attacks will be launched. For its true name is *Macht*, power. As Nietzsche remarks, our degree of feeling for life and power gives us the measure for being. Love is really the cunning

91 Ibid., p. 217.
92 Ibid., p. 219.
93 Ibid., p. 220.
94 Cited in ibid., p. 222.
95 Ibid., p. 224.

of power. When something is loved more than life itself, you can be sure, thinks Nietzsche, that what you are witnessing is the will to power.

Here we touch on the theoretical aspect of Nietzsche's ethics. Good and evil are anchored in our vital powers. For the evolutionist in Nietzsche, the *geistig* is founded on the *tierisch*, the spiritual on the animal. Struggle is the meaning of life, and the very concept of an earthly paradise a contradiction in terms. Having enemies is man's strongest need, resistance and opposition are his most favourable circumstances in life. Nietzsche compares mankind to a tree which grows higher into the light the deeper its roots lie in the dark depths – which he does not hesitate to identify here with *das Böse*, 'evil'. This is intimately bound up with his fundamental metaphysic: as between two contradictory appearances of finitude neither one can be the direct appearing of the absolute. The latter only shows itself in their contradiction. To reject the complementarity of good and evil is to negate life, which in its instincts always says both No and Yes. Death itself is not an argument against life. As with the relation between truth and falsehood, or good and evil, 'the life of life is life between life and death'.[96] So what can Dostoevsky offer us to offset – if that be the word – Nietzsche's position? Not a theory, and yet 'the philosophy of the lie runs as lived thinking through all Dostoevsky's works'.[97] Hence the strength of the 'will-to-be-true' shown there. The message of the *starets* is that whoever yields to the lie – perhaps through self-disgust – ceases to be able to discern truth, grows in contempt for him/herself and others, and finally becomes unable to love. What Nietzsche and Dostoevsky have in common is that both are *directed to the total truth of existence by the continual removal of masks*. This 'formula' tells us nothing about its own content, but it indicates a 'mission'. To be an angel of truth is why Alyosha leaves the monastery to return to the world. Indeed, Balthasar's summary statement gives us the entire thematic of *The Brothers Karamazov*.

'The world', however, is ambiguous thanks to the play of appearances. The man from the underground maintains that, where truths about the self are concerned, some one tells to one's close friends; some one tells only to oneself, under the seal of silence, and some one never tells, even to the self. Of course vanity is involved here, but for the man from the underground such vanity is unavoidable, owing to, in Balthasar's phrase, the 'evil of existence'. For Prince Myshkin in *The Idiot*, there is in every thought something one fails to communicate, not for want of trying but because transmission makes truth non-truth through its form. That would appear to be the primordial movement of human existence, which can affirm its truth only 'as the accompanying midpoint between two mutually destructive untruths'.[98]

Moreover, there is in Dostoevsky's writing a sense of helplessness and incomprehension at the way the ethical is sunk in the cruelty of brute nature – symbolized by Alyosha's shock at the stink arising from the coffin of the holy man Zosima. Not only interpretation is ambiguous. So is what is interpreted. A choice must be put in place. According to Balthasar, Dostoevsky's interpretation of the world is just such a choice, which is why his

---

96 Ibid., p. 228.
97 Ibid.
98 Ibid., p. 230: a paraphrase of Vasin's speech in *The Raw Youth*, a short and rather neglected novel of 1875.

work lies 'on the further side of descriptive realism'. Dostoevsky called himself a realist only 'in the higher sense', who aimed to make his characters forms 'more real than reality itself'.[99] Through the multiperspectivalism of his characters' points of view, Dostoevsky attempts to reach the truth as a whole, while recognizing that such truth can be known only 'in approximating brokenness'.[100] All Dostoevsky's characters learn painfully the element of un- truth in the truth of existence. Hence the role of experiences of the unreal in his fiction: hallucination, dream, indeterminate presentiments and forebod- ings. But – and this surely is the key point – appearance, seeming, does not have for Dostoevsky the ultimacy it carries for Nietzsche. Rather, it 'breaks into a ground of real being'. In the parable of the Grand Inquisitor, the 'eschatological kingdom of the all-lie', which the Inquisitor governs, is 'enveloped by the silent look of the imprisoned Christ'.[101] The good for Dostoevsky does not consist in the integration of 'power' and 'love', as for Nietzsche. It is found as the *direction* in which this entire contradiction breaks down and the Absolute shows through. To be 'drawn out' from the situation (here we return to the theme of grace) is the only way out of the contradiction of finitude, whereas not to be 'drawn out' is to be imprisoned in seeming, a perpetrator of abstractions and (religiously evaluated) evil – which is how, thinks Balthasar, Dostoevsky would consider Nietzsche. *Without* eternal life, Dostoevsky's world is quite as nihilistic as Nietzsche's own. But the differ- ence *with* it is immeasurable.

The True Sickness
And so we come to a second level of analysis where Balthasar names the issue for both Nietzsche and Dostoevsky as *Krankheit*, 'sickness'. Both men give an ontological charge to the phenomenon, rather in the manner of the Augustine of the *Enarrations on the Psalms* who spoke of temporality as decay. (What Balthasar has in mind is the physical aspects of the wider emphasis of the Fathers on *mortality* as the condition from which we are redeemed.) Not only were both men continually subject to physical illness, they also have something in common in the way they evaluate it. Dostoevsky exposes his heroes to it; Nietzsche actually wished it on people, since (he thought) illness alone shows their worth: that is, their steadfastness.

For Nietzsche, earth has a skin; the skin has sicknesses; one of them is man. As intellectuality and individuality develop, so do illness and the capacity for suffering. *As distance from life, mind is itself illness.* By compen- sation, however, mind is also what enables that essential 'suspicion' which uncovers the life-ground in its own healthiness. For Nietzsche, then, sickness belongs with the health of the life-force as its necessary resistance if we are to have eyes and ears for it. Clearly, the concept of illness here shares in the character of the more comprehensive concept of the lie. Nietzsche speaks of the 'transfiguration' of particular illnesses into the condition he called 'the great soundness', *die grosse Gesundheit*, a state more exalted than either sickness or health, as empirically understood. It is philosophy that achieves this transfiguration, a kind of limit-experience which Nietzsche's Zarathustra

99 Cited in ibid., p. 231.
100 Ibid.
101 Ibid., p. 235.

announced and Nietzsche himself claimed to have experienced – for example, when looking at the landscapes of the seventeenth-century French painter Claude Lorrain. (Balthasar thinks this is what prompted his belief in the 'eternal return', the affirmative justification of all time in a single moment.) But this reciprocal cancelling of illness and health in a new, ecstatic state of mind which Nietzsche calls a higher health would seem to some only another form of illness. Balthasar mentions how for Karl Jaspers (1883–1969) in his study of Nietzsche, it requires biological, if not psychiatric, explanation.[102] Is the fresh synthesis really only a new thesis? Or should we say that, whatever the rights of the life sciences in their own domain, they are out of their depth in philosophy? To Balthasar's eyes, the 'great soundness' is the (attempted) aesthetic justification of the world as seeming, the 'music of [Nietzsche's] proclamation – and contradictoriness'.[103]

Dostoevsky's idea of illness virtually attains the status of a general philosophical category likewise, and once again it belongs with the formal structure of 'ground' and 'form' as 'life' and 'spirit (mind)'. But in the Russian writer, influenced by Slavophilism, the focal point of sickness is intellectual haughtiness and isolation over against the 'life-ground' of the people. Such a mind-set breeds decay, fantasy, madness and neurosis. The Russian 'disease', so Dostoevsky judges in his celebrated address to the memory of Pushkin, need not be fatal. The death of the patient will be avoided if Russians re-attach themselves to the *narod* – the folk – and their religious wisdom. Reason is, no doubt, a good thing, but it contents only the reasoning faculty in man. This, however, is not the whole of the story. Dostoevsky's man from the underground prizes suffering (which, naturally, includes sickness as commonly understood): it creates distance vis-à-vis immediacy, and thus can be a value. Despite his plea for return to the people, Dostoevsky frequented the salons of the intellectuals, valuing the distance their reflections could lend. Only in that way could existence unveil its 'limits and roots, right down to its contradiction and sickness'. So reflecting, Dostoevsky could call suffering the 'only primary cause of knowledge'.[104]

Balthasar points out how, like Nietzsche, Dostoevsky reported experiences of ecstasy linked, in his case, to his epilepsy. He spoke, in the moments immediately prior to the seizures, of a sense of universal harmony, a real Dionysian *Gesamtverklärungsgefühl* or 'feeling of the transfiguration of all things together'. But these moments of extreme intensity, which he spoke of in terms of a beautiful and prayerful 'flowing together with the highest synthesis of life' (compare Nietzsche's language of 'falling into the running brook of eternity'), Dostoevsky was careful to insist were simply facts – symptoms – of illness. He resisted the temptation to give them a supra-ethical significance. On the contrary, he allotted them an infra-ethical significance. They do not constitute a dark joy beyond good and evil. They are, if you will, a token of eternity – and yet in itself the token is utterly indifferent. As Balthasar writes: 'The moment is this side of the frontier, it is the sickness of existence in its full, dangerous blossoming and ambiguity, and

---

102 K. Jaspers, *Nietzsche* (Munich 1936), p. 82.
103 Something of a pun in Balthasar's German: *sein Hin- und Wider-sprechen*. So *Apokalypse II* at p. 242.
104 Cited in ibid., p. 244.

precisely as this highest and yet in no way ethical moment, this Dostoevskian moment is an inexorable eye-to-eye with Nietzsche.'[105]

Dostoevsky is conscious, as Nietzsche is not, of the difference between the content of the experience and its form, which is illness. In no way is the moment a 'higher being'. For Dostoevsky the ethical demands the elimination of the indifferent from the ecstasy, and the calm integration of such chance experiential flashes into the daily continuity of a lasting 'transfiguration feeling'. That alone can bridge the gap between experiential form and content. By all means, put the clinical illness into the context of the wider 'sickness' of finitude – but with the aim of allowing the experience of transfiguration *as unmerited grace from beyond* to pour in.

As with Nietzsche, 'the transfigured world' means for Dostoevsky the opposite to the 'underworld'. Zarathustra's call to his brethren, 'Be true to the earth!' is mirrored in Zosima's parting counsel to Aloysha. But Balthasar interprets the *starets'* command to love the earth as a reference to the new earth of Christian eschatology which is the old earth – already in principle redeemed by Christ – transfigured. This transfiguration – and resurrection – is anticipated in the enthused soul where, comments Balthasar, 'in increasing degree ecstasy is one with descending grace'. It is in fact 'the mystery of the single present and transfiguring love of God'.[106] *Heiterkeit* – cheerful serenity, thought by Nietzsche to be the proper outcome of life's journey – seems to Balthasar a good term with which to characterize the death scene of Zosima in *The Brothers Karamazov*. It combines the Dionysian feeling of transfiguration with Christian mysticism, expansive longing with the supervening light of grace, in 'a unique redeemed happiness in the world', and in continuity with the divine salvific work the human heart seems to 'change creation'.[107] Each spirit, Dostoevsky seems to be saying, brings its own 'earth' with it, and for a Russian Christian with love for his neighbour filling his heart this is an earthly paradise if only we knew it. Here illness is drawn into soundness and guilt is pierced through by the divine light. The final transfiguration is thus an 'ecstasy of vital illness' purified and made necessary by the ethical – and in no other way.[108] Balthasar notes, however, the chiliastic tone of Zosima's words in the novel. He seeks an 'all-Church', incorporating the Russian *obshchina*, the peasant commune, and doing away with the need for the institutions of the civil law. The kingdom of God will not come about through earthly progress, the airship and telegraph, but from within the loving hearts of the saints. This is religious Slavophilism. But there is also something more (or is it less?). Balthasar is anxious that Dostoevsky preserved in the vision of the Russian ecstatic too much of the 'illness form'. Zosima's Utopia comes too close to the dreams of a final age by the intellectually lunatic Versilov in *A Raw Youth* and even the sheerly Dionysian cult of nature of Maria Lebedkina in *The Devils* to be theologically a comfort.

If Nietzsche strives for a higher soundness, incorporating both sickness and health, one that is supra-ethical – vitalist and aesthetic, Dostoevsky

---

105 Ibid., p. 246.
106 Ibid., p. 248.
107 Ibid., p. 249.
108 Ibid., p. 250.

proposes to transfigure religiously the 'illness' in this highest moment. Though Dostoevsky's vision of the end – the transformed earth – may seem too much aesthetic, too little religious in character, he clearly intends it to be the absolute truth, in which respect all counter-truth is diabolic. This brings Balthasar to the third and final level of analysis, where the topic is ethics – and more specifically the 'integration' of the evil in the good.

The Evil and the Good

Here the two thinkers could scarcely be further apart. To Nietzsche, ethics lies in the 'purity of indifference', above the restrictiveness of 'good' and 'evil'. To Dostoevsky, ethics lies in 'purity of choice', and the sensitivity whereby from out of absolute contradiction one can separate 'good' truth from 'evil'. Both men were conscious of the unsatisfactoriness of common-place ideas of good and evil. But Nietzsche chose to 'unmask' ethics by showing up its relativity and genealogy. He considered 'virtue' to be, as Balthasar puts it, 'a proliferating reckoning and measuring', petty and suf-focating.[109] Humility is anxiety about our security. Magnanimity is the sud-den abatement of rage through 'saturation and disgust' on the part of the victor. Balthasar's beloved *Hingabe* – loving self-offering – is a perversion of the drive to power: we enjoy an upside-down feeling of power by sub-ordinating ourselves to others. Saintly asceticism is high-grade vanity. The list of unmasked virtues continues. We need, says Nietzsche, to abandon the realm of that 'good' which defines itself over against 'evil'. 'The intrinsically good', like 'duty' and 'virtue', are Molochs of abstraction on whose altar we would be sacrificed. All the man of renunciation is left with is a name for it. What Nietzsche recommends instead is heroic striving for a goal we our-selves choose to will. The real mystery of the soul is its secret nourishing of the 'super-hero' of the future.[110] Actually, remarks Balthasar, there emerges from the fire of Nietzsche's criticism of morality two creatures: the 'invisible, transcendent *Übermensch*' and, far more patently in Western culture after Nietzsche, the 'positivist-immanent good European'. 'Positivism in regard to truth, historicism in regard to goodness, phenomenalism in regard to beauty: these are the consequences of exalting the vital above the transcendentals.'[111] It is no use complaining that Nietzsche's thought is riddled with contra-dictions. It is, quite deliberately, based on contradiction. Nietzsche the self-confessed 'Antichrist' writes more wonderfully of the kenotic heart of the God of Christianity than perhaps any other nineteenth-century thinker. He would reply, it is out of contradiction that the flame of life rises up.

Dostoevsky was equally conscious of cultural 'relativity', suspicious of the notion of a 'science' of ethics, convinced that much 'bourgeois' concern with the virtues was really concealed egoism, and as hostile to casuistry as Nietzsche himself. Dostoevsky too goes 'beyond good and evil', but *his* way begins from Jesus Christ. Thus the 'Meditations on the Bier' (of his first wife), entitled *On Christ*. The Word incarnate's two natures make Christ the 'mirror

---

109 Ibid., p. 258.
110 Cited in ibid., p. 262.
111 Ibid., p. 266.

image of God on earth'.[112] In his concrete personality he is thus the over-coming of the abstract-ideal synthesis of the Idealist philosophers. He is also the elevation of the 'allomatic' mirror-world of the realist-ethical world-image of their literary successors, which now enters the stage of the religious. As Balthasar puts it, the Christ of this early Dostoevskian essay is 'the transcendent unity of the unbroken (as ideal) and the redemptive (the real)'.[113] Only the transcendent God who by humanization comes down to our level, can achieve the ideal for which man strives, not any law of nature – including there the law of the development of personality. By no such law can we 'love everything as ourselves', Dostoevsky's re-working of the love-command in the Synoptic Gospels. By natural egoism it is always the 'I' that we really seek in claiming to love the other. Such is the contradictory char-acter of our situation. For there to be, accordingly, even a 'possibility of the wholeness of existence', the reality of Christ is the *conditio sine qua non*.[114] This contrast – the upward movement of natural self-redemption which is doomed to frustration, and the downward movement of the Redeemer which alone is successful – would of course govern Balthasar's own earliest state-ment of his theological programme in the essay 'Patristik, Scholastik und wir'. *Hingabe* towards Christ is the exit from our schizophrenia, and his 'existential wholeness' the truth of all wishful human aspiration in the same direction.

But at all costs none of this must be turned into an *idea*. Dostoevsky's Christian characters – from Makar to the two Sonjas – move out beyond ideas by *representing* the living truth. To the extent that, though mired in 'guilt and sickness', they participate in Christ they participate in the 'judicial' character of truth as a whole, which, to act as judge over good and evil, must indeed lie on their further side. Dostoevsky thinks in terms of a struggle between two forms of truth – one that listens humbly to a truth coming from beyond, another which is fixed in one's own, godlike 'idea'. What Balthasar finds odd in Dostoevsky's writing is its failure to come to terms with the question, How does one move from the second type to the first, from 'evil' truth to 'good' truth, from unbelief to faith? Dostoevsky often broaches the question, but his descriptions of such movement never get further than introducing this or that intermediary step. It is as if he were, in this matter, a victim of Zeno's paradox, for each unit of such motion can, it seems, be subdivided without end.

The confession of Stavrogin in *The Devils* is a case in point. Stavrogin's 'lukewarmness' – the reference is to the message to the Church in Laodicea in the Johannine Apocalypse, whose members were neither hot nor cold[115] – which may understand faith but not lovingly embrace it, is for Dostoevsky the 'basic problem of evil itself', for evil is precisely negative, impotent, self-enclosed.[116] And yet in the 'man from the underground' impotence *becomes* strength – draws on the abyss of evil which conventional people cover up with lies and cowardice. Balthasar has an explanation for that. Dostoevsky's

---

112 Cited in ibid., p. 270.
113 Ibid.
114 Ibid., p. 271.
115 Apocalypse 3.15–16.
116 *Apokalypse II*, p. 279.

darker figures undergo an experience of 'indifference' – wanting to be 'neither hero nor worm', 'neither Napoleon nor a louse', and this experience can be interpreted *either* as a neutrality neither truly good nor truly bad *or* as the overcoming of 'good' and 'evil' in an 'amoral magnitude'.[117] In both, lovelessness is key. Balthasar thinks Stavrogin's problem was Dostoevsky's own problem: the torment that he did not love with his whole soul, that he could not 'leave the final icy zero-point behind'.[118] This is intimately connected with the issue of how to describe – and make! – the leap of faith. Dostoevsky's writing is open to the interpretation that this 'torment' should be understood psychologically, as a neurosis, deriving from early conditioning and suchlike. (Dostoevsky himself, after all, makes use of 'Nietzschean' reasoning of this kind.) Alternatively, it could be besiegement by evil as *das Nichtseinsollende*, that which ought not to be.

What are we to make of this ambivalence? We might reply that two souls struggled in Dostoevsky's breast: the soul of a Nietzschean and the soul of a Russian Christian mystic. Another answer would concern rather the nature of Dostoevsky's literary project. In one sense, he seeks to lay out the objectivities of existence – including religious, even Christian ones – in a psychologically acute manner so as to show their inevitable upshot. In another sense, as ethicist he puts into his characters from the beginning the evidence for the conclusions he would draw from them at the end. (Compare his argument that atheists 'must' contemplate suicide: that is hardly an observational claim.) The same existence can be construed by the measure of either 'dark' truth or 'light'. This gives his characters their 'perspectivity'.[119]

If we are to give Dostoevsky's position a more unified cast we might do so, thinks Balthasar, by noting how the role of the neurotic impulse – whether in faith or in non-faith – can itself be seen from a religious standpoint. *Ex parte hominis*, it is a problem of willing, or rather of non-willing (not an intellectual problem). More profoundly: *ex parte Dei*, man's being 'pulverized' between the rocks of faith and non-faith is how he is rendered 'soft' for the supernatural, the supra-human. That is the implication of Ivan's dialogue with the Devil in *The Brothers Karamazov*.

What, then, can be gained from a comparison of Nietzsche and Dostoevsky in the ethical (or perhaps we should say 'meta-ethical') domain? Given Nietzsche's definition of conscience as the movement of surpassing the difference between good and evil, leaving behind all such oppositions in a 'wise forgetfulness', it is easy to forget that 'conscience' means in practice for him striving for the 'pure and the high'.[120] But this hardly informs us about the *content* of moral effort. It simply speaks of its *intensity of mode*. And in any case, despite the holy trinity of the Nietzschean imperatives – revere life, purely adhere to it, and go with its instinctual flow (*Ehrfurcht, Reinheit, Instinkt*), morals for Nietzsche are a distraction: with his Lutheran background he can point out with especial relish that salvation (justification) does not depend thereon. Nietzsche's version of Kant's deontological maxim runs, 'Act as you would wish to act for all eternity.' But this, so Balthasar remarks,

117 Ibid., p. 281.
118 Ibid., p. 283.
119 Ibid., p. 293.
120 Ibid., p. 297.

is an illusory norm if from it we are supposed to draw an ethical pro-gramme.[121] Nietzsche opposes religious asceticism, yet recommends poverty, humility and chastity *if* they set us free to follow the 'primordial movement of life' as instruments for *der oberste Herr*, the 'supreme lord' (definitely *not* capitalized according to English usage!) in us.[122] All the inner tensions which 'bad conscience' shows, and which point to the fact that man has yet to give himself due form, ought not to be regretted. On the contrary, they should be embraced as eloquent of this 'new, unheard of, riddling being, full of con-tradictions and full of the future' that has appeared on earth.[123] Nietzsche knows full well that all the 'genealogical' unmasking of culture, institutions, morality can in and of itself do nothing to deal with the cruelty in life. He can only hope that 'bad conscience' will prove the active preparation of the superman, that man will turn out to be a 'way' to something, a 'great promise'.[124]

Dostoevsky's concept of conscience has a dual character. That is pre-dictable, given the way he can look at things either simply *sub ratione boni*, with the vision of 'light truth', as Balthasar puts it, or, alternatively, in more complex fashion, in the perspective of a 'dark truth' which notes for instance the neurotic element in moral behaviour but itself is patient of a religious interpretation, and so of integration into 'light'. At its light pole, the Dos-toevskian conscience reaches 'instinctively' (Nietzsche's word) through guilt to grace. This is heart knowledge. The *starets* Zosima has a curious image for it: God has planted 'seeds of corn from other worlds' in us; when they come up, we become aware that we are in touch with 'other mysterious universes'. If this feeling fades and dies in us, so do the corn-shoots likewise.[125] Versilov, who lets the feeling die in him, Dostoevsky portrays as a 'hopeless abstract human being' despite Versilov's practice of a Romantic 'art of sympathy'. To Dostoevsky's mind, such abstractness bespeaks egoism and consequent spiritual unfruitfulness. Ivan Karamazov's 'abstract heroism' is comparable, as is Raskolnikov's 'abstract dialectic'. But in the way he depicts Raskolni-kov's 'superman ethic' Dostoevsky meets Nietzsche – and overcomes him. For Raskolnikov all great men are transgressors – moral criminals – in their breakthrough to new 'orders and values'. Over against Nietzsche's hubris, which is willing to experiment with man as others with animals, Dostoevsky points to the limits of spirit in the nature from which it arises – which means in the last resort in the God-relatedness of every human intelligence and will. However, Dostoevsky was perfectly capable of entering into the mind-sets of those who, like the Devil in converse with Ivan, spurned the goad of con-science as mere conditioning. He had met such ruthless men in Siberia, and was fascinated by them 'as by a temptation'.[126] For a moment, at any rate, the authorial voice in *Crime and Punishment* seems one with the murderer's lack of conscience – and raises the question whether behind such evil lies *merely* the 'lazy cruelty of neurosis' or something deeper: a 'cruelty according to

121 Ibid., p. 298.
122 Ibid., p. 299.
123 Ibid., p. 300.
124 Ibid., p. 303.
125 Cited in ibid., p. 305.
126 Ibid., p. 309.

essence of self-lacerating life'.[127] In which case, the Satanism of the man from the underground was correct: Dostoevsky himself boasted that no one had furnished in literature so powerful a statement of 'No' to God as he. Yet even this can be religiously interpreted. The Hebrew Bible, St Paul and St John know it well. Is it not the perfect expression of man's unrighteousness before God? To be on the further side of the struggle between good and evil is only possible through 'descending grace'.[128]

Prophetic Message?

How do these so different – yet not unrelated – world-views work out when applied to the historical process in all its concreteness? What is the 'message' of these 'prophets' for times and seasons? Balthasar proposes that, in the philosophy and theology of history, what corresponds to the pairing 'ground' and 'form' in general ontology would be, on the one hand, 'the people', *das Volk*, and, on the other, 'isolated, free spirit'. In this context, Nietzsche and Dostoevsky are poles apart. Nietzsche recognizes the *Volk* as the 'stuffy womb' of the free spirit but, seeing himself as a 'flying fish', cutting through the air high above the heads of the people, wanted nothing to do with their bovine complacencies. They are at the antipodes from the passionate, knowing spirit that lives in the 'thunderclouds of the highest problems and heaviest responsibilities'.[129] Dostoevsky thinks exactly the opposite. 'The return of the free-as-a-bird spirit to the bonds of the destined natural and supernatural community is for him co-identical with the "driving out of demons".'[130] Balthasar quotes approvingly on this subject from Nikolai Berdyaev, the twentieth-century Russian philosopher, living in post-Revolutionary Parisian exile: 'The great Russians lack the pathos of the dizzy ascent. They fear the loneliness, the abandonment, the cold. They strive for the warmth of the corporate life of the people.'[131]

Dostoevksy's longing for Russia when abroad was no ordinary home-sickness: 'the people' were for him the mystical body of the Redeemer – only through incorporation in their life did one have part in the all-redemption. Dostoevsky considered this identification of *Volkstum* and the order of redemption *the* national idea of Russia. Shortly before his death he remarked that whoever denies (Russian) nationalism denies his own (Russian Christian) faith. There is a 'Russian Christ' to be revealed to the world and, especially, to a Europe sick from atheism. Politics in the wide sense for Dostoevsky meant that each people should develop its own latent 'idea'. But as Shatov tells Stavrogin, since there is only one divine truth, only one people – the Russian – has God. This does not misrepresent the author's own view.

Nietzsche, by contrast, hated German nationalism only slightly less than he hated Wagner and Christendom. 'Nothing sharper, more malignant, on the subject of *Deutschtum*, Germanness, has ever been said.'[132] Nietzsche

---

127 Ibid., p. 310.
128 Ibid., p. 312.
129 Cited in ibid., p. 313.
130 Ibid.
131 N. Berdyaev, *Die Weltanschauung Dostojewskijs* (Berlin 1925), p. 149.
132 *Apokalypse II*, p. 314.

looked to the emergence of an essentially international, nomadic human being',[133] though that did not prevent him regarding a united Europe – in practice, in the form of a democratized European *Volksbund* – as due to inherit the earth. That was owing to the invincibility of the technology, above all in transport and communications, that Europe was pioneering.

If that sits curiously with Nietzsche's intellectual-spiritual disdain for the crowd, there is also a paradox in Dostovesky's national-religious patriotism. Nothing, it would seem, could be more unlike Western atheism, which takes flight into what he stigmatized as 'Europeanism, the abstract realm of a fantastic "all-humanity"'. Yet when Versilov selects as the 'highest thought of Russian culture ... the universal reconciliation of ideas' and 'love for the whole of mankind', this is not, to Dostoevsky's ears, an idiosyncratic voice. It fits perfectly with the sentiments Dostoevsky expressed in his famous Pushkin speech. On that occasion, he expressed the hope that Russia could bring to Europe a capacity to cancel the contradictions in the idea of pan-unification – in, more simply put, the love of one's neighbour. That is why he could regard the push towards Europe not as un-Russian but, on the con-trary, *narodnii*, essentially 'of the people'. Beautiful. But just as Dostoevsky's ethics are to a degree Janus-like so here too he knew this was not the whole story. The cry of the 'man from the basement' puts the Slavophile pro-gramme in question. Dostoevsky had seen a side of the common Russian people far less pleasant to behold. He knew that nihilism was not the pre-serve of an élite. Thus his sketch 'The Penitent' where two fellows enter a wager as to which of them can be the more disgusting and one spits on the consecrated Host. Like Nietzsche, Dostoevsky saw we have to reckon with the beast in man. This colours both of their approaches to apocalypse – the interpretation of time and futurity.

Both men had a premonition of imminent catastrophe in history. For both, nihilism stood waiting at the gate. Oddly enough, they largely agreed on the cause. In Dostoevsky's words, 'Without Church and Christendom, the anthill is already as good as undermined.'[134] For Nietzsche, 'passive nihilism' – the sort he disapproved of – will be the upshot when those who have been Christian for two thousand years cease so to be. This coincidence of analysis does not, however, alter one fact: Nietzsche's 'wish-image' was Dostoevsky's Satanic apocalypse.

Nietzsche's scenario was based on his conviction of two necessities which pointed in very different directions: cultural levelling in a mass society and evolution. With the breakdown of the old order in Europe, he expected an initial chaos, typified by 'the nearness of barbarism, awakening of the arts, greatheartedness on the part of the young, fantastic madness and real power of will' – together with a 'spiritual slavery ... such as never was before' and a massive inflation of State power. The masses will become 'machine men', but oustanding individuals will emerge to administer them as 'lords of the earth'. Wars will be ideological – between, notably, on the one hand, levelling democracy and, on the other, what Nietzsche termed 'my movement', which,

133 Cited in ibid.
134 Cited in ibid., p. 321. He added that 'Catholicism is no longer Christendom and gone over to the service of idols; Protestantism is drawing close to atheism with the steps of a giant.'

contrarywise, would 'sharpen all contradictions and rifts' and 'abolish homogeneity' so as to create the 'super-mighty ones' whose existence would justify all the preceding.[135] Dostoevsky had a not dissimilar prognosis. The coming time will be one of 'glorified mediocrity and insensibility'. The 'greatest uncertainty' will reign, a demonic liberty where anything is possible. An unrestricted freedom will end in equally unrestrained despotism. Dostoevsky envisaged a coming Socialism where, under the direction of one-tenth of the population, the remaining nine-tenths will surrender personality to become sheep safely grazing in the earthly paradise. In the 'parable', the Grand Inquisitor is comparable to the Nietzschean *Übermensch*, bearing all the strains of moral freedom to give security to moral slaves.[136]

Nietzsche says yes to all this, Dostoevsky, no. Clearly, the background and motivation of such conflicting replies must be very different. For Nietzsche, only sentimental enthusiasm could make people claim to foresee human progress towards the pre-set goal of eliminating elitism and struggle. No species that has learned to make war will unlearn these things; such optimism is merely an illicit extrapolation from the abandoned Christian belief in a divine plan. In any case, for humanity to abandon elitism and struggle would be disastrous. These things are preconditions of all earthly greatness. Balthasar stresses that, in these judgments, Nietzsche is not a social Darwinist. For Nietzsche, as for later Christian 'creationists', Darwinism is merely a hypothesis; its contrary is equally well-evidenced. Nietzsche merely wants to raise future necessity to its 'highest intensity', whatever that necessity be.[137]

What would Dostoevsky reply? Like Nietzsche, he thinks the State was created for the mediocre: the 'ideal State' of Roman Catholicism is the third Satanic temptation.[138] Yet does it not have an obvious 'Augustinian' justification: to restrain the wickedness in fallen nature? Men as we now know them, says Dostoevsky, were born to torment each other, which is why all hopes placed in 'development' are risible. What the Socialists fail to reckon with is the passionate love for destruction and chaos in human breasts. The instinct for self-preservation is matched by an instinct for self-destruction. In any case it is fortunate that precisely humanity's 'crazy dreamings' and 'fundamental stupidity' prevent them from making themselves into 'piano keys', to be played at will.[139] But this does not obscure the fact that an *Urbösheit*, a 'primordial evil', is at work in the world. Ruling out as he does the 'crystal palace' of Socialism and the superman's power-State of the Grand Inquisitor, Dostoevsky does not for all that want to leave the plate of eschatological hoping empty. Like Zosima, he hoped that Orthodoxy would,

---

135 Citations from Nietzsche's works in ibid., pp. 322–23.
136 Citations from Dostoevsky's works in ibid., pp. 323–25.
137 Ibid., p. 327.
138 Balthasar cannot help noting the divergent attitudes of Nietzsche and Dostoevsky to Catholicism. For Dostoevsky, Catholicism is not a faith but the continuation of the Western Roman empire. It is worse than atheism, and atheism, like Socialism, is its product. For Nietzsche, the Roman church rests on suspicion of nature, man and spirit, but at the end of the day the difference between Protestantism and Catholicism is simply Northern versus Southern taste. Nietzsche would have liked to see Cesare Borgia as Pope; this dream, comments Balthasar, might be considered fulfilled in Dostoevsky's Grand Inquisitor: ibid., pp. 325–26.
139 Cited in ibid., p. 329.

maybe after centuries, become a unifying, world-encompassing inspiration, such that on the Last Day, an upwards movement from the earth could meet a downwards movement from heaven. Balthasar notes the chiliasm in Dostoevsky. The dream of *some* kind of earthly paradise, if not that of his Socialist and Catholic opponents, keeps recurring in his work. What its *actual content* would be remains, however, unclear.

In both authors what we are observing, remarks Balthasar, is a retreat from content-filled eschatology to the 'formally apocalyptic'.[140] Nietzsche spoke about 'knowing silence', Dostoevsky of the human revulsion against the very idea of a 'final word'. Each shows a 'prophetic' compulsion to say something without, however, a knowledge of what that something should be. Their tropes are minatory yet vague, reminding Balthasar of 'animals trembling before something frightening that gets closer and closer'.[141] As in the eschatological discourses of the Gospels and the oracles of the Old Testament prophets: 'through the catastrophic categories of temporal history a far more radical end-of-history catastrophe is breaking through'.

But this 'event' is beyond their grasp, and all talk about it no more than the 'excited gesticulations of the dumb, which no one understands'. In an obvious sense for Nietzsche, as atheist, the Last Things emerge from the soul: heaven is its purity, hell the 'abyss in myself'. (From where else could they come?) But for Dostoevsky too the 'beyond is gained only from and through the abyss of the here-and-now – which is the decisive "proof" of Christianity'.[142] To this extent, Berdyaev was right to call Dostoevsky's way a 'way of immanence'.[143] But Balthasar adds a corrective: Dostoevskian immanence is the 'deciding locus of transcendence'.[144] The 'formally apocalyptic' here is at the same time something inner, existential. That, no doubt, explains the incapacity of both men to be more assertoric. It hardly helps that the two of them felt obliged simultaneously to affirm the world and to deny it or go beyond it. The world flashes into their mind's eye in its 'fullness and hollowness', and Balthasar proposes for this ambivalent radiance the name 'beauty'. If so, then beauty is ambivalent too. Balthasar links it to Nietzsche's description of life in its self-dissolving quality as an 'artistic game'. He recalls Dostoevsky's evocation of the beautiful as (in the words of Dmitri Karamazov) 'something frightful and mysterious ... God and the Devil are wrestling there'.[145] Riddling, mediating between 'light' truth and 'dark', it is, opines Balthasar vatically, 'the heart of apocalyptic' – meaning, one presumes, that only when beauty's character has been definitely declared, its ambivalence resolved, will ultimate reality actually be unveiled. The most Nietzsche and Dostoevsky can tell us is that human beings will correspond to the unveiled heart of the world only through 'formal greatness'. In just what qualities such 'greatness' should consist we have from them no consistent doctrine. Of course, Dostoevsky, in his own voice – and the voices of a number of his characters – praises love, but his assault on any version of

---

140 Ibid., p. 333.
141 Ibid., p. 335.
142 Ibid.
143 N. Berdyaev, *Die Weltanschauung Dostojewskijs*, op. cit., p. 35.
144 *Apokalypse II*, p. 335.
145 Cited in ibid., p. 337.

natural law eviscerates his ethic, leaving standing only the 'pure positivity of Christ's love-command'.[146]

There is a way out. In his essay 'Suicide and Immortality', Dostoevsky tells us of natural love's hopeless linkage to an absolute fulfilment. Awareness of its impotence to assuage the sufferings of man, such love easily turns to hate. Now we see the pertinence of revelation and its subjective correlate: faith in immortality and resurrection in Jesus Christ. In 'Guilt and Atonement', Dostoevsky interprets the parable of Dives and Lazarus along these lines. Throughout this lengthy – and still not completed – comparison of Nietzsche and Dostoevsky, Balthasar has been engaged in showing the startled reader similarities at least as striking as the differences between them. No more. Nietzsche ends with final contradiction and the reduction of the world's meaning to nature, Dostoevsky with the one, transcendent, self-revealing God. 'Christ and Anti-Christ?': the contrast is not overdrawn after all.

That is not to say Balthasar will simply underwrite Dostoevsky's vision of the real. Considered as a 'metaphysics of apocalypse', there are enough weaknesses to put on a comparative scale with Nietzsche's own. Since neither man will provide a comprehensively objective criterion for final truth, Balthasar proposes to measure each with the yardstick of the other – and then deal distinctly with any significant 'remainder'. First, then, Dostoevsky's dark picture of the atheist hardly touches Nietzsche's case: Nietzsche's atheism issues not in perverse crimes, like Stavrogin's, but in 'heroic asceticism, a glowing "and yet ..."'.[147] That shows Dostoevsky's apriorism: he is more consistent than is life. Comparison with Nietzsche points up Dostoevsky's pessimism, his mistrust of the truth-content of the world. That pessimism is perhaps the deep source of the 'apriorism' in question. Balthasar has the impression of a 'forced transcendence', divided between a 'melancholic-passionate embrace of the earth' and a 'Utopian-fantastic enthusiasm for the abstractly ideal'. In Dostoevsky's way of speaking of love for the world there is something alien to the New Testament, and in his 'disciples' (Balthasar has in mind, one supposes, the later Russian Sophiologists, including Berdyaev) this led to a 'demonic, Gnostic Wisdom ... of the tragic, necessary love for the world of God'.[148] Balthasar finds in Dostoevsky an oscillation between a love of pain or agony (*Qual*) and a desire to take flight to a sinless, unshadowed landscape of 'pure nature' which, for Catholic doctrine at any rate, has never existed. Surely the speeches of the *starets* in *The Brothers Karamazov* represent something much more fully evangelical? Even these Balthasar considers more Claud Lorrain than Fra Angelico. We hear of a 'mystical Christ' with certain Orphic and Dionysan traits rather than a personal one. 'The ecstatic expectation of the resurrection, of the transfiguration of this earth, comes to fulfilment more in the "idea" of Christ than in Christ as "medium", in a way suited to a personal primal cause. Christ becomes a means (*Mittel*) but not a midpoint (*Mitte*).'[149]

146 Ibid., p. 340.
147 Ibid., p. 343.
148 Ibid., p. 344.
149 Ibid., p. 346. Several Russian Orthodox commentators – notably Konstantin Leontyev, Dmitri Merezhkovsky and V.V. Rozanov – noted that even in Dostoevsky's mature 'conservative' period his doctrinal orthodoxy was not entirely secure: A. Boyce Gibson, *The Religion of Dostoevsky* (London 1973), pp. 6–7.

Harshly, one might think, Balthasar considers the loving streaming forth of the soul here as, first and foremost, a form of self-love, a 'resting in *Hingabe*' which prefers the state to the supposed object. Dostoevsky speaks of humanity, indeed the entire redeemed earth, as the mystical body of Christ, but Balthasar finds it suspicious that Dostoevsky nowhere hits on what he – Balthasar – regards as *the* metaphor for the union of Christ and his mystical body: the nuptial union, marriage. Nuptial symbolism will be a very noticeable characteristic of Balthasar's own theology and spirituality. When in *The Brothers Karamazov* Dostoevsky cites one of Balthasar's favourite Johannine texts, 'Unless a grain of wheat falls into the earth and dies, it remains alone, but if it dies it bears much fruit',[150] the meaning is 'ecstatic', not 'realistic'. All in all, Dostoevsky is too close to Hölderlin for comfort. Christ and Dionysus draw too intimately together. Here Balthasar supports Nietzsche: we cannot allow ourselves to be swept off our feet by the appeal of such ecstatic 'streaming forth'. Where is the truth in all this feeling? Balthasar fears Dostoevsky's religion could become a 'masked eroticism'. This would be Christian eschatology 'seen through a Dionysian curtain'.[151]

But it is time to use Dostoevsky against Nietzsche's vision in its turn. Is not the 'sickness' of the 'earthly-ecstatic' more healthy in the last analysis than Nietzsche's much-vaunted 'great soundness'? It is precisely the hopeless 'brokenness' of the soul's ethical situation in this world which presses it to seek transcendence. Without God, such transcendence is an unattainable goal, and 'every eschatological centre a deeper eccentricity'. Nietzsche would attempt to 'unmask' this reply psychologically and show it to be based on an 'eternally unproved a priori of all religion'.[152] He might also add that this whole search-for-transcendence phenomenon is really the discovery of a deeper immanence – the stream of life itself, in its entirety. Dostoevsky has a character who captures perfectly this twofold response of Nietzsche: Kirillov. And notice the choice over which Kirillov havers: either to 'cancel' time in an inner-worldly eternity or to commit suicide – which would be a proof of my freedom vis-à-vis my own limits and thereby liberation from the anxiety induced by my positioning before the 'other side' of that frontier. (Every frontier, after all, *has* two sides.) Advocate the suspension of time? Nietzsche knew better than this really, for he knew that his 'icy-lordly aloneness was death-dealing'.[153] Is not, then, the first option linked to the second, the option of suicide? Nietzsche tried to persuade himself death was banal, a 'stupid physiological fact', and nothing more.[154] Dostoevsky looks at these inter-related possibilities through his lens and finds utter inconsistence. Is one claiming to be God, or a gorilla? His diagnosis runs: they are placing *Angst* before *Hingabe*, *Angst* before God. Baleful consequences follow when the fine apex of the soul is truncated, and spirit pointed down again, back to nature. There it can never be fully at home, but discovers a 'new, driven homelessness' leading those who experience it to a constant search for some unheard-of novelty, or what Nietzsche's Zarathustra calls 'the angel above

---

150 John 12.24.
151 *Apokalypse II*, p. 349.
152 Ibid., p. 350.
153 Ibid., p. 354.
154 Cited in ibid., p. 355.

his head'.[155] Balthasar does not hesitate to say that on this search Nietzsche is in a situation which has to be called 'religious' – or even 'mystical'. The trouble was, Nietzsche believed the 'distinguished soul' rightly to exclude the 'art and gesture' of receiving gifts from on high. Knowing its own dignity, it rejects such philanthropy. 'Nietzsche pushed purity so far that all *Hingabe* seemed to him unclean.'[156] Or, as Balthasar puts words into Dostoevsky's mouth, he could not say 'Thou', he could not love.

Balthasar has been submitting both Nietzsche and Dostoevsky to a 'purifying fire' – largely at each other's hands. A nugget of gold emerges – and it is their willingness, in a situation which may broadly be termed 'mystical', to ask after the essence of love. But they interpret it antithetically. Dostoevsky recognizes the necessity of *Übergabe*, giving oneself over to the divine (here self-enclosure would be guilt), but a residue of anxiety delays the leap (Balthasar is thinking of his difficulties in analysing the passage from nonfaith to faith). Nietzsche thinks he 'sees through' *Hingabe* as 'aesthetic delusion', saving his inner 'purity' of strength for a final 'Yes' that only some utterly unconditional necessity could elicit. To Balthasar, both men suffered from a failure to grasp the coinherence of freedom and grace whereby the 'absolute self-choice of freedom' can only be thought as the transcendent gift lifting one out of contradiction – and so as the 'immanent choice of oneself'. As Thomists so frequently have to repeat: grace and freedom are not in competition! Dostoevsky's anxiety about the manner of grace's indwelling in freedom lies at the root of his (psycho-neurological) difficulties in giving himself to God. With Nietzsche, the difficulty is not just psychological, it is also theoretical, for, unlike Dostoevsky, Nietzsche misinterpreted love as power, as will to possess. Nietzsche *did* see a point to love as creativity. But he forgot what should have been the lesson of his father's Lutheran manse: namely, that the form of the 'slavish love' which subordinates itself and gives itself away, 'is already immanent in the form of the "divine" creative love, insofar as the latter is a making known, *Kundgabe*, and a parting with, *Entäusserung*'.[157] This response, incidentally, looks ahead to Balthasar's embrace of kenotic accounts of God in himself, and in Jesus Christ, in his mature dogmatics. We shall hear more of it in a moment. The point here is that, like Dostoevsky, Nietzsche offers to love both a Yes and a No. Nietzsche seeks a sort of immaculate 'super-love' by which, in a heroic sacrifice of communication, everything transitory and 'ontically unclean' is overcome: in such a state one would be blissfully 'beyond' even oneself. Balthasar is inclined to consider Dostoevsky's approach to the love question 'feminine' (his problem is a neurotic anxiety about its difficulties), Nietzsche's 'masculine' (his problem is creative egoism). But in their very different ways the reproach levelled is the same. It is *the failure of love as love*.

Does not the contrast of Nietzsche's unbelief with Dostoevsky's faith mean they are talking about different things? But can one speak in so unqualified a fashion of Nietzsche's 'unbelief'? Nietzsche registered a 'feeling above all feeling' when he considered the prodigal squandering of being that we call 'the world'. That the world is continually poured out 'like

155 Cited in ibid., p. 358.
156 Ibid., p. 359.
157 Ibid., p. 365.

precious wine and ointments into the ocean': this filled Nietzsche with a
sense of religious mystery.[158]

Biographically, though the aloneness of this 'squandered' man became
ever icier, Nietzsche gave vent to his thirst for friendship, active benevolence,
love in cries launched into the silence that are certainly religious in spirit
(thus his *Sanctus Januarius* and the *Klage der Ariadne*, the latter of which calls
on 'You unknown One – God' to 'break, break this heart'[159]). Balthasar
gathers citations to show Nietzsche's ambivalence: is the ultimate mystery of
life a mystery of cruelty – or one of desiring and loving power? Nietzsche
affirmed the first, but was this not en route to a second affirmation of the
'eternal Yes of being' for which – who knows? – the word 'God' may be a
synonym. 'Nietzsche's face is turned toward a mystery withdrawn from all
looking.'[160] Balthasar is tempted to say that in the 'mystical situation' vis-à-
vis the 'positive eschaton', 'Dostoevsky better understands than he accomplishes, Nietzsche better accomplishes than he understands' – and that is
maybe typical of 'feminine' and 'masculine' types of love.[161] In each case,
however, their difficulties with love as the true 'metaphysic of the apocalyptic' are rooted deep in themselves – Dostoevsky the everlasting doubter,
Nietzsche the 'self-executioner' (his own description). Both can say 'No', and
for both that is an expression of impotence. But it is *also* a 'No' of ethical
interpretation (thus, so Balthasar implies, no convenient appeal to the
defective psychological make-up of these two massive figures will suffice to
answer them). Yet their 'unmasking' of unpalatable truths about the world
has its defining limit in their discovery, nonetheless, of love. As Balthasar
writes, 'Love in general cannot be unmasked. Unmasking is only feasible for
the masks of power (and impotence).'[162] When Nietzsche strove to identify
philosophy with suspicion, he was unfaithful to his own practice. 'Truth as
criticism' is recalled to its own limits by 'truth as love'.[163]

A Theological Resolution

As if to exemplify such a view of truth, Balthasar turns to his final topic in the
second volume of *Apokalypse der deutschen Seele*. 'All is good': Nietzsche and
Dostoevsky's character Kirillov have used those words. What do they mean?
It is the issue of the contextualization of factual evil in a more comprehensive
good – the 'synthetic' good Balthasar will call it – and the related question of
a super-ordinate 'necessity'. Not many historians of ideas would have
thought of it, but Balthasar divines in Nietzsche and Dostoevsky an affinity
with Hegel – not Hegel's methods (hardly!) but his goal. Writing to his
brother shortly after the pardon he received from the tsar, Dostoevsky asked
for a copy of Hegel's *History of Philosophy* because (he said) his future hung
on it. In *The Brothers Karamazov* Ivan's dialogue with the Devil is, Balthasar

---

158 Ibid., p. 371.
159 Cited in ibid., p. 376.
160 Ibid., p. 380.
161 Ibid., p. 381.
162 Ibid., p. 384.
163 Ibid., p. 385.

believes, a 'satire on Hegel'.[164] (The Devil tells Ivan to learn negation, because without negation there is no criticism and 'What would a newspaper be without a critics' corner?') As for Nietzsche, he considered that Hegel had uncovered the meaning of all German philosophy: to think through a pantheism in which evil, error and suffering will not be objections against Deity. But Nietzsche's project, like Dostoevsky's, is to 'grasp the good in its new, non-Idealistic sense'.[165]

Nietzsche had always been interested in contradictions as providing an opportunity for unity (thesis-antithesis-synthesis). In his later writings he was increasingly preoccupied by the world-totality for which, alas, synthesis remained in contradiction to what as thesis – for example, the tragic deaths of innocent children (Ivan Karamazov's problem) – one had to take with full seriousness. In Nietzsche's own interpretation, synthesis is the deed of the strong, who alone can say yes to the 'highest star of being'. But this 'highest star' can hardly be thought of except as the Absolute of value – and this really is a contradiction if anything can be called such! Nietzsche tells us that the concept of a 'reprehensible action' is difficult for him. Nothing of what happens should be called 'reprehensible', for if something can be excluded then anything can. So, in the light of the synthetic good, is the antithetic evil to be refused the name 'good' too? Nietzsche denies it, but his practice implies otherwise. Here he enters a 'fruitless', 'empty' contradiction, and his thinking sinks into a 'desert' of sterility.[166] Hypostatizing this contradiction, we have the Dionysian world of everlasting self-creation and self-destruction, which Nietzsche himself called a 'monstrosity of power, without beginning, without end'.[167] Goethe, who started from the same viewpoint in his early fragmentary writings on nature at least progressed towards the realization that what seemed contradictory might rather be placed on a scale of ontic comparison where being intensifies as the finite approaches the infinite.

That, however, is not Balthasar's chief response to Nietzsche's mistake which will be to place his thought no longer in a religious context, merely, but in a strictly theological one. Nietzsche's refusal to see the 'condition' of man in the world as a 'situation' of being addressed by God represents a philosophy deprived of a theology. And this, in the *de facto* single concrete supernatural order (Balthasar had, evidently, taken this emphasis from his Jesuit studies in Lyons) can only be part of the truth. 'Grace is concretely the final form of nature which in that form fulfils itself.'[168] Philosophy, says Balthasar, can only now – he means with the coming of revelation – be theological or atheistic. Either it can consciously or unconsciously recognize the supernatural order of God as its goal, or it rejects the 'situation of address' with a 'no' which is not a mere description but a refusal. Balthasar added something which may be either a personal interpretation of Thomas Aquinas's thought, or a reflection drawn from his reading of Barth in the inter-War years. 'That' there is a God and 'what' God is cannot nicely be

---

164 Ibid., p. 388.
165 Ibid., p. 389.
166 Ibid., p. 392.
167 Cited in ibid.
168 Ibid., p. 393.

divided here. A refusing 'no' to the revelation of divine address calls into question the 'that' as well as the 'what' (Barth). In God essence and existence are the same thing (Thomas).

This might be expected to lead to a *non possumus* where further theological dialogue with Nietzsche's negations is concerned. But in fact Balthasar draws Nietzsche into the web of (Christian) negative theology. As Balthasar explains, at the hands of its patristic and later practitioners (he mentions explicitly Denys, Eckhart and Angelus Silesius), negative theology is purification of all worldly concepts applied to God, a catharsis 'through the fire of negation'.[169] The 'that' of God's existence is not excluded here: for negative theology God does not exist in the sense of worldly existence. But theology does not stop with that. After the *via negativa* comes the *via eminentiae* where God's being is lifted above both existence and non-existence. Nietzsche's atheism, in this perspective, does not consist in his original 'no' to the existence of God (which, put like that, Meister Eckhart might also share). It consists rather in his refusal of the integrative 'way of eminence'. Yet *eminentia* insinuates itself here and there for all that. A pathos appears in him deeper than his 'no', and Balthasar finds its theological evaluation to be: 'the inner, supernatural correspondence with the outer being addressed by God, the supernatural *archê* of nature answering to nature's supernatural *telos*'.[170]

Nor is this all. Negative theology houses another truth. Nietzsche's emphasis on the gratuitousness of things, their being 'for no reason', the way reality seems squandered, this is a view of things that bears a relation to the theology of the Cross. Negative theology does not only concern the act of creation, the fundamental God-world relationship. It also concerns the act of incarnate atonement, when that relation was for ever changed. 'The concrete address of God to the world happens uniquely in the mystery of the Incarnation as the emptying out of the fullness of God into the nothingness of the creature (inasmuch as the hypostatic union unites all-being and nothing in the closest way).'[171]

Balthasar goes on to claim that all nature is 'plunged' into this emptying of God into the gratuitous, sheer bestowal, extravagant squandering when Christ as head of the mystical body gives the world its final form. The God who so bestowed himself has gone 'as far as the concrete frontier-form of nothingness, right down to the refusing No'. The divine emptiness of atheism 'looks the divine emptiness of Golgotha eye-to-eye'. In this, Balthasar considers, Nietzsche's 'synthetic good' is established – but from the side of God, not of man. All man can do is grasp its necessity, which he will do when he so grasps it as God does: as the movement of God's own *Vergeblichung*, the divine giving itself away. The 'whole' then is what Nietzsche obscurely surmised: it is the 'mystery of Love's descent into Hell'.[172]

Can Dostoevsky's case be similarly 'resolved'? In his celebrated Pushkin centenary speech of 1880 Dostoevsky identified for his audience *the* question of theodicy: if it were a condition of general felicity that even one human

---

169 Ibid., p. 394.
170 Ibid., p. 395.
171 Ibid.
172 Ibid., p. 397: Balthasar gives the words 'descent into Hell' in Latin, *descensus ad inferos*, to make it plain he is referring to the relevant article in the Apostles' Creed.

being should be tortured to death would we give 'the architect of the building' our warrant to go ahead? In other words, 'in the necessity of the synthesis (itself given with the impossibility of the thesis) lies the necessity of the antithesis as means'.[173] It was at this that Ivan Karamazov launched his protest when, unwilling to reconcile himself to the suffering of innocents, specifically, he proposed to 'hand back his entry ticket'. Ivan asks Alyosha whether it is justified to love life more – by (Dionysian) natural instinct – than life has meaning. Here two 'absolutes' collide: the 'absolute' of life-affirmation (in each moment the eternal 'now') and the 'absolute' of unconditional seriousness in love for the earth (and its suffering inhabitants). Is this, though, a case against God – or only against the divinization of life after the Dionysian manner? In this clash, Ivan's condition is very much that of a young man. Balthasar thinks Dostoevsky inscribes into the composition of the novel something like what he himself attempted in setting out German Idealism according to the 'existential potencies' of child, youth, adult, old man. Dostoevsky's world is a 'poly-veridical world', where the truth of a living human being is a developing truth, caught in characteristic perspectives at each stage. Dostoevsky is justified in not reducing his figures to a single 'truth centre' but allowing each *Gestalt* its part of the truth as a whole.[174] That is not to say, however, that the whole truth cannot be gathered up into a single figure *if finite truth in its own movement suggests as much*. Balthasar does not propose to let Dostoevsky sink into a relativistic morass. At the back of Ivan's rectitude (against God and Hegelianism) lies a 'melancholy' issuing from his own sense of solidarity with transgressors. But is a true grasp of 'necessity' available to those in the condition of guilt? 'For out of consciousness of guilt arises existential knowledge of God as the goal of the renouncing No, and out of being-in-a-condition-of-guilt the impossibility of grasping directly after the necessity of the absolute synthesis.'[175]

As Balthasar reconstructs a Dostoevskian answer to the issue of synthetic good, the concept of guilt is key. Through 'existential communication' we know that all are guilty, and owing to the 'radical circumincession' of 'all consciousnesses and wills' in the same human nature, no one is uninvolved in the guilt of others (the latter statement represents the doctrine of the *starets* in *The Brothers Karamazov*). True, I must judge the guilt of others – but I can only do so if I 'co-judge' myself. I must make myself co-responsible for their guilt – and so must we all. There is real justice only when there is *express community in guilt*. And this is as much as to say there is real justice only in the Church. The Church can be a community in guilt (and its confession) only because 'the Church has already brought redemption from guilt from above in the Incarnation of Christ'.[176] The grace that has been poured into human nature enables the confession of guilt of one to be the petition for forgiveness for all. The fulfilled realization of this pardon is Paradise. And so the grasp of 'necessity' is not achieved in Hegelian fashion, but through a

---

173 Ibid., p. 399.
174 Ibid., p. 403. So Balthasar goes one better than the eminent Russian critic M.M. Bakhtin who first drew attention to the 'multi-vocal' character of Dostoevsky's novels. Thus Bakhtin's *Problemy tvorchestvo Dostoevskogo* of 1929, incorporated into his *Problemy poetiki Dostoevskogo* (Moscow 2nd edn, 1963).
175 Ibid., p. 405.
176 Ibid., pp. 408–409.

confession of guilt where the pious humble themselves before the impious, as Zosima does before the old libertine in the novel. So, writes Balthasar: 'In mystical annexation to such saints in whose hearts rests the "mystery of renewal for us all", Alyosha sees the way to the synthetic good: "And all will then be holy".'[177] This is love not as unmasking but as covering – quite the opposite.

So in the last analysis the 'people' about whom Dostoevsky wrote with such embarrassingly Slavophile unction is primarily a theological reality. It is Russia as gifted with knowledge of 'the mystical Christ, of suffering and all-redemption in the loving confession of guilt'.[178] Only secondly is it a sociological reality – and then simply because the Russian people had, so Dostoevsky believed, a mission in this regard to the universal Church. Balthasar relegates to a third place, in this more merciful judgment of Dostoevsky's intentions, his chiliasm and (typically Orthodox) 'blending' of Church and State. The ecclesial folk is where the decisive grasp of necessity is possible, just because it is the locus of communication in guilt, the locus of redemption. Here the Russian thinker can see further than the 'lonely Nietzsche', because he can see *ecclesially* which means *theologically*. No philosophy sundered from theology, thinks Balthasar, can get further than Idealism.

That takes us to the threshold of a 'Christian metaphysic of original sin', itself thinkable, so Balthasar concedes, only in the light of revelation.[179] This is the mystery of the origination of a will to solidarity in evil, resting on the necessary 'circumincession' of all freedoms in our single humanity. Sometimes Eastern Orthodox apologists consider it an Augustinian innovation by the West, yet the consciousness of it permeates *The Brothers*, Dostoevsky's greatest novel. It helps him to show how 'sin as such is the egoistic, it is the rupture of communication, the refusal of "going-over".'[180]

How then is redemption to be realized? By, says Balthasar, planting the will to community of holiness more deeply in human hearts than the will to community in guilt already there. And this is feasible, for 'deeper than Adam in the heart of human nature is Christ'.[181] For Dostoevsky, the crossing-point of the two communities is the will to co-suffer, which in its roots – a final Balthasarian touch – is *Hingabe*, oblative self-giving love. From there can necessity be surveyed. It is not a 'logical', Hegelian necessity but the need to turn to Love (Balthasar plays on the German words for 'need' and 'turn' that make up the compound abstraction *Not-wendigkeit*), as Peter, in his finitude and guilt reached out, when he was sinking, for the Saviour's hand.[182]

177 Ibid., p. 409.
178 Ibid., p. 411.
179 Ibid., p. 413, together with footnote 4.
180 Ibid., p. 415.
181 Ibid., p. 416.
182 Matthew 14.30–31.

9

From the War Poets to Scheler

The Soul and Science

The third volume of *Apokalypse der deutschen Seele* opens by setting the scene for what will be, on Balthasar's reckoning, the most significant currents to affect the flow of sensibility up to the outbreak of the Second World War. What is added thereby to the second volume is chiefly the new twist given by the 'Great War' of 1914–1918. He looks at the attitudes to the 'last things' in the epoch which, in retrospect, that War defines – the 'chaotic period' running from the turn of the century to the 1920s, and does so above all through the 'imagistic-mythical expression' its eschatology finds in poets.[1] The main *Leitmotiv* he identifies is the 'tragic judgment of the soul right down to its hell' – so this is the 'site' not of naturalism but of Expressionism. It is a time of 'tornness' for the German soul, and one when Jews are remarkably prominent in German literature – something Balthasar links to the 'agitatedness' (*Gehetztheit*) of the Jewish people situated as they are 'between blood and spirit, streaming forth and glacial reflection'.[2] There is, he is saying, a strange affinity between Jewishness and the German sensibility of the period. Franz Kafka's (1883–1924) *The Trial* and *The Castle* seem to Balthasar symbolic of the new situation. 'The Old Testament disputation with God reaches an extent hardly seen before.' The sense of human guiltiness, which Balthasar studied in Nietzsche and Dostoevsky under the general heading of *Lebensphilosophie*, endures, but the 'Judge' appears to disintegrate in an 'anonymous array of incalculable points of judicial reference (*Instanzen*) without a head, without a final judgment'.[3]

The sense of being in a maze, or labyrinth, is not of course the only defining feature of the period. It is a time of increasing reliance on technological rationality: developmental, humanly initiated. A sense of final fulfilment based on these things is at the antipodes from the roundedly theological eschatology of the mediaevals which remains Balthasar's principal point of reference. Behind technology there lies of course physics. By the turn of the nineteenth and twentieth centuries physics was beginning to generate an *endzeitlicher Optimismus* – and also *Pessimismus* – of its own.

---

1 *Apokalypse der deutschen Seele III. Zur Vergöttlichung des Todes* (Salzburg 1939), p. 5. Cited below as *Apokalypse III*.
2 Ibid., p. 6.
3 Ibid., p. 8.

Optimism, because physics lent itself to applications that opened the door to supreme mastery of matter by man. At the same time, the discovery of entropy produced a scientifically founded pessimism – rather than the speculative version earlier associated with Schopenhauer. The future 'cold-death' of the planet, galaxy, cosmos, argued Eduard von Hartmann (1842–1906), a philosopher who sought to synthesize the thought of Schelling, Hegel and Schopenhauer, exhibits a 'dysteleology' which disproves the optimism of evolutionists. The mood thus generated fitted well with prognostications of a 'culture-entropy', a progressive (if that is the word!) levelling-down of values. But the evidence for technical progress through scientific invention reassured others that Enlightenment optimism still remained a better guide. Biological (and sociological) theories of development might be regarded as giving this 'exact' form. Between these two viewpoints, each claiming scientific respectability, there was – needless to say – no chance of convergence. They did, however, share something. What they had in common was a willingness to draw *Werden und Geschichte*, 'becoming and history', whether depressingly or encouragingly, from out of matter itself. Thus Ernst Bloch (1885–1977), later the philosopher of 'the principle of hope', in his early *Geist der Utopie*, draws 'physicality' directly into the eschatological question, treating matter as the 'essential stuff of our active fulfilment'.[4] Physical fatalism could become the marriage partner of Dionysian pessimism as in Georg Strähler's (1864–1937) 1922 drama, the point of which is indicated by its title: 'The Last Human Beings'. On the other hand, optimistic exploitation of the coupling was also possible as in Friedrich Dessauer's *Philosophie der Technik*, published five years after Strähler's play, where Nietzsche's 'universal pathos is transposed into an enthusiasm for continued world-creation through humankind'.[5] It is not that man has to *think through* the world to the end. Rather, he must *actively build it* until the end – notably through technology where *homo sapiens* and *homo faber* come together as man the creator. Novalis's dream of the material universe re-created as the pliant instrument of humanity is 'fetched down from the heaven of ideas onto earth'.[6]

For the scientific pessimists, the question is how to deal with earth's terminal decline – migration to the planets of other stars? What Balthasar finds alarming is the way such scientifically envisaged possibilities as world destruction through atomic warfare are so quickly trivialized in commonplace novels. 'The tragedy of the world's decline becomes a bagatelle.'[7] That man's 'highest world-mastery' should bring with it 'a final metaphysical threat of doom' demands a seriousness of ethical treatment it rarely received. What are the implications if 'technique as realization' becomes the 'life-form' not just for one people (for example, the Germans – for whom as early as 1901 Max Scheler declared 'work' to be the ruling idea[8]) but for humanity as a whole? True, some Germanic essays in the philosophy of work stressed

4 Ibid., pp. 12–13; cf. E. Bloch, *Geist der Utopie* (Munich 1918).
5 *Apokalypse III*, p. 15.
6 Ibid., p. 16.
7 Ibid., p. 18.
8 M. Scheler, 'Arbeit und Ethik', republished in *idem, Christentum und Gesellschaft* (Cologne 1924). See idem., *Schriften zur Soziologie und Weltanschauungslehre. Gesammelte Werke* 6, (Berne-Munich 1963), pp. 221–324.

their own 'Classicism' (over against Romanticism). Work does not seek to express 'everlasting unfinished striving' but, to the contrary, a finished, measured, law-abiding construction. For Scheler, however, the contemporary privileging of 'work' as activity escapes the bounds of Classicism. It implies value for the action irrespective of any finished product. To Eugen Diesel, the union of technologically inspired labour and a presumption of optimism summed up the entire 'tragedy of modern culture': objective spirit is detached from its Creator and what results is the frenzied, unstoppable, pointless – indeed in any ultimately worthwhile sense counter-productive – activity of the sorcerer's apprentice.[9] The linkage between the service of technology and hubris quickly becomes a theme of the early twentieth-century novel. Balthasar thinks it is clear that in the 'machine age' modern technology has helped to sunder soul and world – even though, considered as a kind of 'art', its aim was in an obvious sense to bring them closer together. This contributes significantly to the neurosis of modern life. 'It seems that the more the world strives towards a *mathesis universalis*, the higher the misunderstandings mount up, and the story of the Tower of Babel repeats itself ...'.[10] The 'titanism' of physics and technology suffers the punishment of Prometheus. This helps to explain the predominance of artistic Expressionism (at any rate in northern Europe) in the period. The inner is parting company with the outer world, so naturally we get an art of 'the mere soul and its innards'.[11]

This brings Balthasar to another typical expression of modernity: psychology considered as science. Here the soul's 'standing before its own frontiers' becomes a putative object of exact research. This is a topic Balthasar will return to at more length when he considers Max Scheler's phenomenology as an assault on 'psychologism'. Here he wants simply to note its presence in novels of 'the End', where writers attempt an exploration of the psychological consequences when people realize that catastrophe is imminent. Balthasar thinks it not a coincidence that about the same time – the early decades of the twentieth century – would-be 'scientific' interest arises in the psychology of Jesus's End-expectation too (alongside novels about ancient chiliasm, modern Bolshevism, and announcements of the Second Coming). The names of Jewish authors crop up, partly owing to the revival of the issues brought about by Zionism. Which are we to support: 'suffering, loving waiting' or 'Zionist active construction'? He comments on the intriguing fact that a journey through the imaginative literature tends to take one from 'psychological objectivity' to 'existential subjectivity', which surely shows *some*thing.[12] He implies that only the second – 'existential subjectivity' – exemplifies what Nietzsche called interpretation on the basis of the 'highest strengths of the present'. (That was an imperative Balthasar already recalled in 'Patristik, Scholastik und wir'.) But at any rate, suchlike psychological exploring, in whatever mode, holds up a mirror to the soul in its 'standing before judgment' and 'uncertain awaiting'.[13]

9 E. Diesel, *Weg durch das Wirrsal* (Stuttgart and Berlin 1927).
10 *Apokalypse III*, p. 22.
11 Ibid., p. 23.
12 Ibid., p. 24.
13 Ibid., p. 30.

Antichrist and Christ Again

That confronts people with 'decision' of some kind – what sort of stance to take. And such decisions, writes Balthasar, have their 'myth'. Once again, it is Christ or Antichrist, to use the terminology which Nietzsche – with some help from the Romantics – rescued from the contempt into which it had fallen at the hands of rationalism and theological liberalism. Balthasar shows the interest the Antichrist aroused in novelists re-alerted to the 'fundamental problem' of evil, painting frescoes of apocalypse whether quasi-magical – as with the Austrian dramatist and lyric poet Friedrich Schreyvogl (1899–1976), the Swiss visionary E.F. Ramuz (1878–1947) – or more soberly social in character: here Balthasar mentions not only the Germans Ferdinand Brockes (1867–1927), Arnold Ulitz (1888–1971), Max Fischer (1893–1954), but also the English priest-novelist Robert Hugh Benson (1871–1914), the Swedish woman writer Selma Lagerlöf (1858–1940) and, most influentially, the Russian Vladimir Solovyev (1853–1900). In his 'Short Tale of the Antichrist', Solovyev presents the final human embodiment of evil in similar terms to Benson's. The Antichrist is a spiritualist, to whom Solovyev counter-poses the truth of Christ's Resurrection as the 'definitive synthesis of body and soul, idea and appearance, from above down'. There is a polemic here against the Nietzschean super-man, whose possibility Solovyev disputes, since 'all becoming is "hidden dissolution"'. Balthasar sees the Church, in Solovyev's writings, as in mystical correspondence to Christ's mortal body, to be fulfilled in an analogy with his risen body. Contrastingly, the 'organism idea' in all writers affected in some way by the German Idealists suggests a caricature of the mystical body, ever menaced by 'naturalistic magic'.[14]

The ironic theme of Churchmen as Antichrist to Christ, sounded by Nietzsche and Dostoevsky, raised the question, if Christ returned to earth would he be crucified again? That could be in the context of an axiological eschatology – 'on earth it is always the Last Judgment' wrote Richard Dehmel (1863–1920), and so there is always Christ, 'wandering with us'.[15] Alternatively, it could be in the perspective of an at any rate prospectively teleological eschatology as in Ricarda Huch's (1864–1947) *Der wiederkehrende Christus* where the Lord, returning to a society of cinema-going, spiritualism and finance, is imprisoned, released and disappears again, stepping across a darkened heath with two endangered fellows, speaking of love.[16]

War as Judgment

But the full 'eschatological form' only appears thanks to the experience of the First World War. Balthasar places this under the rubric 'world war as judgment of the world', recognizing that the theme of world-judgment is not only a biblical category but to be found in the most influential of the immediately pre-War poets in Germany, the Stefan George of *Der Stern des Bundes*. Balthasar calls the eschatological images of the work's first book 'prophetic traces of the ceaselessly approaching *Unheil*', the 'woe' as distinct

14 Ibid., p. 38.
15 Cited in ibid., p. 41.
16 R. Huch, *Der wiederkehrende Christus* (Leipzig 1926).

from 'weal' of the Hebrew prophets.[17] A collection of 'German Poetry of the Present', published in 1923, noted in its introduction how, under George's influence not least, so many of the poets represented 'felt beforehand the nearness of catastrophe'.[18] In his pre-War essays, Karl Kraus (1874–1936) spoke of spirit as undergoing annihilation and asked whether after that a world could stand. Writing just after the War ended the physician and philosopher of art Max Picard (1888–1965) considered man was dead, but the name survived and some relic could be examined in a chemical retort. What these authors have in mind is a judgment coming from within which is why its approach can be felt. The War, as war and the sort of war it was, nonetheless remains crucial. Balthasar cites some words of Barth: 'War expresses this: we have known man as he is in his impossibility, and we should like to be done with him – a falsified expression.'[19]

Such a false concept would be our mistake, but, comments Balthasar, this war struck people as going quite beyond the normal scale. In the War's horrors, 'mankind was placed under judgment'.[20] In Cuno Hofer's (1886–1931) *The Game of Hell*, a slight inclination of the great balancing-scales of good and evil grants Hell power over the earth.[21] In Karl Röttger's (1877–1942) *Weltuntergang*, set in the War's last freezing winter, the Christ-child descends to set a candle on the breast of each fallen soldier. When the thaw comes and military action resumes, the firing fails to target the enemy and is turned against the sky, wherepon the stars fall and burn up everything on earth. Balthasar sums up the message of the short story as 'Collapse of the world as a consequence of the freezing of love.'[22] In Kraus's *Die letzten Tage der Menschheit*, the War appears as 'the gruesome dance of death of a spirit already in terminal decline'. Kraus identified the true war-guilt as not so much the newspapers setting the machines of death into motion but the way 'our heart had been so hollowed out that we could no longer represent to ourselves what that might mean'.[23] Balthasar regarded the end of the fifth act of 'The Last Days of Humanity' as Kraus's greatest poetic achievement, Dantesque in its evocation of public personages as 'hyaenas of the field of battle', terrifying in its portrayal of the realm of the Antichrist – the press, the cinema, and technology gone mad dominating the Last Day in defiance of God. 'Voice from above: "The storm succeeded. The night was wild. God's image is destroyed." (Great silence.) The voice of God: "I have not willed it." '[24]

While admitting these are not hermetically sealed compartments, Balthasar distinguishes between those who experienced, those who suffered and those who judged. In one sense the War could be lived through as something comparable to an overwhelming experience of nature – a tornado, or

---

17 *Apokalypse III*, p. 47.
18 Cited in ibid., p. 48.
19 Cited in ibid., p. 53.
20 Ibid.
21 C. Hofer, *Der Spiel der Hölle* (Leipzig 1922).
22 *Apokalypse III*, p. 54, with reference to K. Röttger, *Das Jüngste Gericht. Sechs Spiele vom Leben mit einem Nachspiel, 'Im Jenseits'* (Leipzig 1922).
23 Cited in *Apokalypse III*, p. 54.
24 Cited in ibid., p. 56.

tsunami. But after the shocked silence comes an appeal to the soul from a world now made strange so as to attempt some explanation.

And so poets produce reflection – and choose. Owing to the 'sheer emptiness of its outer proceeding', the Expressionists among them bracketed out the content of the First World War to leave only its 'infinite formal rhythm', the 'apocalyptic rhythm of the heart'. In this gigantic orgy of chthonic powers was not the heartbeat expanded to cosmic dimensions, redeeming the soul from the 'numbness of the grave of the "I"'? What can go unnoticed here is that the soul, thus experiencing, 'co-consummates the judgment on itself'.[25] As in Johannes Becher's (1891–1958) war poetry, by closing his eyes to the War's meaningless brutality and hymning its redemptive quality which makes humanity the 'opened heart of things', the poet re-encloses the judgment situation, with its transcendent implications, in a new, regrettable immanence. By avoiding concern with the content of War, Expressionism also avoids judgment – that is, *meaning*. In such a mindset a chasm is fixed between intellectual spirit and life, and, writes Balthasar, more careless of anti-Semitic overtones than he ought to have been by the end of the 1930s, 'behind the glow of experience there stands a cold, spiritually Jewish, calculation'.[26] Balthasar prefers the attitude he calls 'suffering endurance in unconceptualized judgment' – 'unconceptualized' because the concepts available – duty, sacrifice, heroism – do not help in understanding the 'ghastly external material of this duty and its naked "that"'.[27]

One poet, however, rose fully to the occasion – if prophetically, since he died at Cracow in 1914. This was the hyper-sensitive Salzburger Georg Trakl (1887–1914) in whose poems, says Balthasar, no symptom of a world in collapse goes unremarked, nothing within the world provides illumination, and yet all things are 'set in an invisible order'. Everything 'dark' is still mighty, but somewhere God has atoned and all is right and well.

> The disintegration of the poetry, the seemingly contextless series of impressions and expressions, becomes itself the image of a disintegration of the world as a whole. The ruin of time in War and in Trakl's soul becomes an image of everlasting ruin. The eschaton of a [limited] circle opens itself to the supratemporal Eschaton; the terror, *Unheimlichkeit*, of a time reveals the homelessness, *Heimatlosigkeit*, of all earthly things.[28]

And yet 'this way is the soul's growing discovery of itself, and in its final self-loss it finds its own truth: the Judge above it'.[29]

The Image of the Ark

Balthasar passes on to the years following the First World War under the soteriologically pregnant heading of 'Flood and Ark'. With the War's

25 Ibid., p. 57.
26 Ibid., p. 59.
27 Ibid.
28 Ibid., p. 61.
29 Ibid., p. 63.

infliction of judgment in time the 'everlasting situation of judgment' stood revealed. This is why the period was also *gracious*. 'Nothing can show us more clearly world history as world judgment.'[30] But in point of fact world history is always world judgment. And that is why his own period – the 1920s and 30s – cannot withdraw itself from the immediacy of the Last Things which are not of course 'things' at all but God himself. There should be no apologies for the 'existentiality' of the post-War time, in which the soul bore defencelessly its own 'apocalyptic' nakedness before God. Balthasar compares such existentiality to the waters of the Great Flood which rose so high as to leave no steeple of 'saving "objectivity"' visible. 'There can be no more "flight out of time". Everything must undergo this baptism of death.'[31]

Was it surprising that older people were consumed by doubt and gave up the present as long lost? When in *Steppenwolf*, published in 1927, Hermann Hesse (1877–1962) escaped from the 'gigantic jumble-sale and culture mart of this time' into his 'inner enchanted theatre', the only solution he could offer was a smile more ghostly than Zarathustra's.[32] Gerhart Hauptmann's (1862–1946) *Till Eulenspiegel*, in circulation by the following year, rolls out to the accompaniment of a 'bewildered gallows humour' the carpet of the last days, showing first the kingdom of the dead, body lying upon body in 'meaningless funereality', and then the day when the sun fails to set and, as anxiety mounts, cities go up in flames. The hero journeys in search of the world's meaning but finds only an ever-deeper silence. If he moves towards anything it is 'toward galloping lunacy'.[33] However, Balthasar notes that on Till's last expedition Christ appears to him as shepherd thus opening the possibility of a 'still to be achieved inner ripening of humanity' – though against the background of the work as a whole this broadens the range of questions rather than answers them.[34]

But on the flood waters there lifts a profile, and its shape is an ark. An ark does not imply easy salvation. To be carried by it is to abandon oneself to an insecure mode of transport on a sea of submerged rocks where, quoting Karl Barth, 'the highest peaks of earth's mountain ranges remain, under our feet'.[35] Journey by the ark, amid the 'hurricanes of annihilation', is only undertaken by way of a 'higher obedience and service'. But that means it is also: 'a sailing in hope after surviving judgment, an expectation of Ararat and the new sin-expiated earth'.[36]

Paradoxically, when the image of the ark first appears in the modern German novel it is freighted with a quite antithetical charge of meaning. A supreme technical achievement intended to outlast the fire of judgment, the ark assures man against God.[37] Other novels where the ark is a controlling image are science-fictional without the (pseudo-) theology.[38] But then the theme begins to receive a handling at a deeper, symbolic, level. In Robert

---

30 Ibid.
31 Ibid., p. 64.
32 Ibid.
33 Cited in ibid.
34 Ibid., p. 65.
35 Cited in ibid., p. 66.
36 Ibid.
37 R. Falb and C. Blunt, *Der Weltuntergang* (Berlin 1899).
38 W. Scheff, *Die Arche* (Berlin 1917); Kopernikulus, *Weltuntergang* (Leipzig 1928).

Neumann's (1897–1975) *Sintflut* and Arnold Ulitz's *Ararat*, the flood is humanity's inner collapse, but seen beyond it on the horizon is a 'real historical beyond, on the further side of all the disasters of the present'.[39] The full religious import of the symbol appears in the Prague-born Jewish writer Max Brod's (1884–1968) *Die Arche Noachs* where the ark becomes the scene of a 'blind being delivered over to God, in the darkness of loneliness'.[40] The novel orchestrates the conflicting instincts and passions of those aboard the ark. When Shem, raging against God, finally breaks down the hatches to let the water flood into the ship, it is sunlight and the rainbow of reconciliation that he sees, and the ark stays fast. For Balthasar this is a tell-tale symptom of the 'new religious poetry' which is typified by an 'awareness that the way goes through the outer darkness, and faith that man's self-reliance breaks down there, but that this is God's warning, and grace follows testing'.[41] Man is at an 'end' he has not arranged for himself, or it would not yet be the end. The Jewish convert to Catholicism Leo Sternberg's (1876–1937) *Gaphna* is a flood drama that identifies the end as gracious but concealed love. What is 'formed', *gestaltet*, in love is itself the true ark, which no outer catastrophe can destroy.[42] Karl Jaspers, in the last volume of his *Philosophie*, called this in a cognate nautical metaphor 'landing in foundering' for really, concludes Balthasar, the great flood and the ark are in the last analysis one and the same.[43]

The interior landscape we are beginning to glimpse is the mystical night of the heart, when against the background of a truly hellish night, the 'bloodstained face of the suffering God' can begin to be discerned.[44] In the sculptor, graphic artist and dramatist Ernst Barlach's (1870–1938) *The Great Flood* God himself appears, albeit as a beggar limping along on crutches. Boys beat him up, a leper spits in his face. Only the angels can distinguish him and understand what is happening: God loves earth more than he does 'the kingdoms of the light-born giants', the world of pure spirits.[45] What Fichte and Schelling speculated about is in a sense true: 'God's way goes through the night to God'.[46] God is not only the unmoveable rock on which one both suffers shipwreck and lands. More than that, he is *in* this landing – and shipwreck. In one point only – but an absolutely fundamental one – did these Promethean thinkers go wrong. Their doctrine of mystical potentiality placed the blessed God at the disposal of human freedom. This is why the 'Prometheus world', unlike the Dionysus world, could never in a thousand years issue in Christianity. The 'divine primordial ocean' surges in a sovereign freedom utterly its own – which is how the journey on the ark is full of divine surprises.

Over against the impossibility of a Promethean Christian soul there is, thinks Balthasar, such a thing as a 'Dionysian Christian soul': it is one that

39 R. Neumann, *Sintflut* (Munich 1922); A. Ulitz, *Ararat* (Munich 1920).
40 *Apokalypse III*, p. 68, with reference to M. Brod, *Die Arche Noachs* (Leipzig 1918).
41 *Apokalypse III*, p. 68.
42 L. Sternberg, *Gaphna* (Wiesbaden 2nd edn, 1922).
43 *Apokalypse III*, p. 69, with reference to K. Jaspers, *Philosophie III. Metaphysik* (Berlin 1932), pp. 233–36.
44 *Apokalypse III*, p. 70.
45 E. Barlach, *Sündflut* (Berlin 1924), cited in ibid.
46 *Apokalypse III*, p. 71.

takes the waves on the stormy sea of this world to be 'the as yet unordered song of coming eternity'.[47] Balthasar treats this as the best tradition of the German soul: at once Classical and Romantic, but with the Romanticism surrounding and sheltering the Classical. When the German soul 'fully understands itself', there is no renunciation of Apollo (the Classical) nor is sheer 'Storm and Stress' (unadulterated Romanticism) its decisive form. Intellectual spirit can thrive in life – they need not be contradictories. Balthasar regards Ludwig Derleth (1870–1948) whose *Fränkische Koran* he much admired, as exemplifying such issuing of Dionysianism into a Christian sensibility. Derleth reaches what Nietzsche, Bergson, Klages, Spitteler and Hofmannsthal only intermittently aspired to: not the conquest of spirit by life but spiritual life. Here the features of Dionysus are only 'sketches for the mystery of Christ'.[48] When after all possible *débâcles* on earth the narrative of the 'Frankish Koran' breaks through to a new paradise in a hermits' wilderness, this is no flight out of time. One should think rather of Zarathustra's search for the 'greater health' of the soul beyond the world yet for the world. In his revolutionary proclamation of a new sacral order on an ecclesial basis, Derleth has in mind 'a re-enchantment of the world ... a new "transcendental childhood" of the soul'.[49]

Scheler

Can Balthasar relate Max Scheler (1874–1928), phenomenologist, personalist, and, for a time, convert to Catholicism, to this new start? Before attempting to answer that question, two caveats require insertion. First, though the First World War certainly shows some sort of death of a world, Balthasar is not so enamoured of novelty as to suppose that any brave new world would be an absolute beginning. 'Nothing true is ever lost, it lives in the *Gestalt* that follows, being saved and transformed.' The ark survives annihilating waters. Secondly, he warns against any expectation of a quick response. The 'world journey' of the 'Frankish Koran' showed in poetic fashion what he will now have to try and lay out philosophically in slow motion. Only by such reflection can one measure the scale of the catastrophe, the relation of what is saved and carried over to the new, and, not least, the 'essence of the German soul at the end of its Dionysian phase'.[50]

Scheler is special, not to say unique. He had his roots in the past of Bergson, Nietzsche, Dostoevsky. His war books showed how deeply he lived out the 'judgment' the Great War represented. And thanks partly to another thinker – Edmund Husserl – but not exclusively so, he put forth a 'decisive new principle' for a new epoch, even though this principle was, modestly yet confidently stated, simply a 'departure-point'.[51] No one tried as hard as he to put together into a meaningful unity all the disparate key processes of his time. From philosophy, science (or scholarship, *Wissenschaft*), culture, he aimed to compose what Balthasar terms on Scheler's behalf a 'total

---

47 Ibid., p. 80.
48 Ibid., p. 75, with reference to L. Derleth, *Der Fränkische Koran* (Weimar 1932).
49 Cited in *Apokalypse III*, p. 81.
50 Ibid., p. 84.
51 Ibid.

anthropology'. Of course it was all too much for one individual. His synthetic power approaches syncretism, his brilliance superfluity, his Titanism the fate of Icarus. And yet despite all the shadows he is a real mid-point – the only one around. Balthasar salutes the richness of his thought and the indebtedness of inter-war Catholicism to him who made himself 'quite self-consciously its intellectual head'. As Balthasar sees things, Scheler sought to bring together the elements of truth in *Lebensphilosophie* (*not*, then, its relegation of *Geist*, intellectual spirit) and the elements of truth in the continuing tradition of Idealism (*not*, then, its refusal to renew its concept of spirit in the light of the 'philosophy of life'). It is from out of this twofold effort that Scheler's root-concepts of the 'phenomenologically concrete "essence"' and the 'individual intellectual-spiritual person' emerge.[52] Scheler saw the attraction of looking at the real from the side of 'life' – with its temptation to pragmatism, and of looking at the real from the side of 'spirit' – with its temptation to treat truth as the enemy of life. *Pace* his predecessors, he had the enormous merit of seeing 'that man forms a paradoxical unity, only describable inasmuch as it is analysed into its two (abstract) components – "ground" (life, drive) and "form" (spirit, image), and that this tension constitutes the very sign of his creatureliness which sets him over against the unity of the Absolute'.[53]

Regrettably, this insight was obscured in the measure that Scheler exalted man (after the fashion of the Prometheans) to be 'the absolute midpoint of the world'. In his thought the abstract components come to take on the character of cosmic potencies. Man's dual shadow lengthens, affecting adversely Scheler's philosophy of God which starts to mirror what is worst in Schellingianism – a God who is tragically divided between 'primordial ground and essence, life and spirit, blind drive and clearsighted impotence' and can only achieve the wholeness proper to him through man.[54] But even if these diseased buds begin to sprout as early as Scheler's Catholic period, Balthasar still considers that, nonetheless, he succeeded in making two points very plain. Intellectual spirit cannot be reduced to life – but nor is it life's 'transcendently inbreaking foe'. And furthermore, in the course of his battle with Kantian formalism, Scheler honed a new concept of the person which raised the gains of *Lebensphilosophie* to a higher level – one that was less 'biologically and relativistically coloured'. Just as Scheler rescued from Bergsonian empiricism the vision of essence and the analysis of the 'world as such', so he likewise salvaged from 'sheer temporal exchange' the thought of the 'pure being-other-ness' of the person and the absolute *non-exchangeability* of each personal essence with any other. So on Balthasar's reading the triumphs won may be said to concern, first, general ontology, and secondly, the ontology of the person.[55] The names we give these breakthroughs are 'phenomenology' and 'personalism', and the two thinkers who, after Scheler, will dominate the final volume of *Apokalypse der deutschen Seele* – namely (the early) Heidegger and Barth – will not be unfaithful to them. Admittedly, such 'breakthroughs' bring problems of their own. For

52 Ibid., p. 85.
53 Ibid., p. 86.
54 Ibid., p. 87.
55 Ibid., p. 88.

example, with the enhanced emphasis on the personal, what becomes of the social, national and cultural realms in any account of 'the last things'? When (secularized) eschatology was governed by ideas of 'reason' or 'life' that question might be avoided – but hardly now, not with the new individualism. But Balthasar's prime anxiety is *unilateralism* – above all, in Scheler's account of the 'midpoint' by reference to which the unity of intellectual spirit and life can be bestowed. He lodges the same criticism in connexion with Heidegger (and Rilke) and Barth. Only the conclusion of this mighty work will show where and how correction is needed.

Balthasar is insistent that Scheler's innovatory attitude was born of the experience of the First World War as 'judgment on the world'.[56] True, some factors were already in place before August 1914: engagement with Husserl, the turn to a 'metaphysics of emotion', the fight against Kantianism. But Balthasar shows by a wealth of citation that Scheler considered the War itself to have been decisive. It was 'cognitively dispositional for absolute realities'.[57] The War itself was 'the great Existential philosopher', bringing spirit up short before nothingness – and thereby showing how extraordinary it is that there is something rather than nothing after all. Essentially, this was a 'contrast-experience': the 'daring' by which in time of war I gaze at the frontier of life itself, and the 'love' that – hiddenly, through grace – sustains this daring, disposes me as knowing agent to grasp the excellence (*Erhabenheit*) of existence and with that to grasp likewise the continuance of the person beyond the life of the body. Anyone can be a metaphysician, Scheler told his readers, insofar as anyone can be a hero. 'True speculation', over against 'positive science', is nothing more (or less) than 'the heroism of thought'. War brings insight into the 'grace-character of all deeper feelings of happiness', and the possibility of rejoicing, somewhere deep down in the heart of the person, even 'in the midst of watching the continuing devastation'. Life is not the highest good. It is a good inasmuch as it is the 'scene for the breaking through and appearing of the Kingdom of God'.[58] The discovery that this is indeed so should awaken the souls of individuals and nations to the 'super-living God'.

At the same time, Scheler also analyses war as a 'human-natural happening' placed between spirit and life. On this level, Scheler sees war not as a continuation of animality but something far different: a return to the creative origin whence the State arose, since – whether for good or ill – there are no natural frontiers to which the State must passively adapt nor is there a ready-made international order of justice that does not rest on the 'ever-flowing relations of power and amity of unitary States'. By raising human aspiration above the sphere of utility and comfort, war – Scheler optimistically observed – serves higher values. (Scheler interpreted a war he expected the Central Powers to win as a revolt by populist instincts in Russia, France and England against the aristocratic German heart of Europe.) This must be set against the destruction of cultural monuments it brings in its train. There is no event of world-history, however seemingly hellish, through which a 'new good' cannot be formed. Apocalyptically, the First World War disclosed evil, but

56 Ibid., p. 89.
57 Cited in ibid., p. 91.
58 Cited in ibid., p. 92.

eschatologically it re-established human beings in the truth.[59] Writing as a Swiss, Balthasar marvels at the paradoxical union of German militarism and universally human spiritual nobility in Scheler's account. But Scheler believed that Germany had a 'knightly' (*ritterlich*) ethos which the rest of humanity needed if it was ever to 'recognise the other as other in the distance of attention and respect'.[60] To his mind, the ethos of heroic war in no way challenged a renewal of the ethos of religious faith.

Love and the Real

If this is the right context for Scheler's phenomenology, his philosophy will hardly be footnotes to the rather technically epistemic 'logical investigations' of Husserl. What Scheler acquired from Husserl was a tool that allowed him to take up a fully cognitive attitude towards the real, the objective, the essential – thus eliminating all that belonged to the merely pragmatic. By borrowing from Husserl two vital presuppositions, namely the independent reality of *Geist* and the equally independent reality of the 'essential', objective object, Scheler proved able to re-create the idea *what has eyes for the real is love*. This is not love as drive but love as *Geist-Liebe* which cancels what is narrowing and subjectivizing in merely pragmatic human attitudes and makes possible the genuinely cognitive attitude in all the forms through which the 'foundational radiance of life' communicates itself to us.[61] For Balthasar, this changed everything on the philosophical scene (or should have). His sources helped him – not only Husserl but also Bergson (with Nietzsche) and Dostoevsky. Scheler appreciated in the 'philosophers of life' what Balthasar calls on his behalf their 'powerful deviation from the high road of modern thought as a whole'. In place of the mistrust of the phenomenon in Descartes and Kant, Scheler advocated a 'courageous taking leave of self in perception and in loving movement toward the world'.[62] Eschewing 'calculative will' and 'proud sovereignty' alike, the human being contemplates the world 'as the object of a potential nuptials (*Vermählung*) in perception and love', in 'an intensive concentration of mind in self-oblation (*Hingabe*) to the pure "what" and essence of the appearances'.[63] In his essay 'The Idol of Self-knowledge' Scheler took a decisive step beyond Bergson. For Bergson, once we leave the realm of 'man the maker', where intellect is ordered to the world as pragmatically re-worked by human beings,[64] intuition has no object left to it save only 'sheer non-identical becoming'. For Scheler, by contrast, intuition has as its object the 'pure world of forms of "essences", ordered to the supremely living spirit, the person'.[65]

Scheler appreciated Nietzsche's stress on the immediacy of experience while deploring his forgetfulness of *Geist* without which man is but a 'sick animal'. Nietzsche's fears are unfounded. *Geist* – intellectual spirit – is quite

59 Ibid., p. 96.
60 Ibid., p. 99.
61 Ibid., p. 101.
62 Cited in ibid., p. 102.
63 Cited in ibid., pp. 102–103.
64 Balthasar calls this in a memorable phrase Bergson's 'mystical-magical convergence of technology and religion', ibid., p. 109.
65 Ibid., p. 104.

other than a mere negation of life. Its use constitutes an 'ascetic act' in the 'development' of life. In a nutshell, man is the 'ascetic of life'. *Pace* Nietzsche's critique of the Christian love-ethic, Christian love fulfils this preexisting pattern. Nietzsche complained that Christianity reverses the *Aufstiegsbewegung*, the upwards movement of life, and makes life bow down in the service of the defective and the ignoble. But even at the natural level one can see how this could well be the expression of overflowing richness of soul. Seen at the supernatural level, this movement of descent is a becoming like God. (We have here the nucleus of Balthasar's dogmatic scheme in his first theological programme in 'Patristik, Scholastik und wir'.) What is involved is personal love of such a character that its 'act-value' is the most positive imaginable. The ascetical moment in the Christian ethos is – as even Nietzsche realized at times – the expression of a 'strong' life not a weak or pathetic one. As the status of the saints shows, Christianity's ethics is no less 'aristocratic' than Nietzsche's own.

Balthasar wholly approves Scheler's repudiation of everything that smacks of 'mystical potentiality' in the schemes of thought of German Idealism. Derisively rejecting this 'arrogant quasi-religion of the learned class', Scheler repudiated all attempts to flatten out the 'tension between the distance and nearness of man to God'. The resolution of this tension turns on the positivity of both loving centres (i.e. God and man), and is not to be had through a 'naturalistic fusion' of the two.[66] *Lebensphilosophie* had made of the metaphysical principle of Idealism an empirical one in the idea of evolutionary progress. Scheler usefully denies that the realm of inter-personal revelation in the encounter between God and man is ruled by the law of such progress. (Nor for that matter can the history of culture draw its meaning from the sort of end-goal that 'Socialism and Positivism' claim: here Herder was right: each epoch has non-interchangeable uniqueness.) However, love itself can 'make progress', and so persons can make progress in love's gradual emancipation for the sake of its own proper activity. In society at large, there is no accelerating intensification of values in the goods human beings attain – only an increase in the range and complexity of the 'apparatus' for producing 'pleasant and useful things'. True, Scheler sees man as called to work with God in bestowing meaning on the sub-human creation by (shades of Schelling) awakening the 'reason' that 'slumbers' there. But this must be done (here Scheler moves far from Schelling) on the model of God's action in Jesus Christ – i.e. through sacrificial service. The consequent achievements of culture may only be on the 'periphery' of the Kingdom of God – whose possession is 'the most central, and the highest, of all the expectations of the human soul', but they nevertheless 'offer themselves' as material to be taken into that Kingdom's 'eternal transcendent form'.[67]

Dostoevsky is perhaps a more minor interlocutor, but it was to him that Scheler owed his emerging emphasis on all-human solidarity. This he used not only to encourage Germans to open up their concerns to a wider world (his last works dream of a 'European–Asiatic synthesis'), but also, notes

66 Cited in ibid., pp. 106–107.
67 Ibid., p. 110.

Balthasar, in more strictly philosophical mode, as a pillar of a 'universal sociology of knowledge'.[68]

The Use of Husserl

These, then, are the seeds cast on to the soil of Husserlian phenomenology in Scheler's life-work. Edmund Husserl (1859–1938) too had an 'eschaton' – inasmuch as he considered the form of his philosophy to be the 'final form' at which all philosophical thinking from the Greeks onwards unwittingly aimed. By which he meant, not that philosophy ended with himself, but that it took its *definitive starting-point* from him, since now its basic task was clear. The Cartesian *cogito*, owing to its misconceived 'purity' and 'absoluteness', had created a schism in thought between the mathematical objectivism of abstract rationalism and the sceptical subjectivism of empiricism. Neither Immanuel Kant nor David Hume (1711–1776) nor the 'philosophers of life' could put Humpty Dumpty together again – though Husserl applauded the *Lebensphilosophie* for salvaging the notion of primary, reality-encountering intuition. What needed to be added, thought Husserl, were the notions of universality and necessity – without these no rigorous philosophizing can endure. If we are to consider any given 'whole' *sub ratione philosophiae* we must consider it not as an individual 'that' – which belongs to the realm of the contingent, but as an 'essential what' – for this pertains to the realm of the necessary. Within the individual whole, fact must be distinguished from form (Husserl writes for this: *eidos*) if we are to discern the fullness of its concretion for the 'eidetic consciousness' – something within our power if we practise the relevant suspension (Husserl's famous *epochê*) of all mere registering of simple facticity (which phenomenology retains, however, as the 'residue' of essence, so this is not the same as the Scholastic 'abstraction' from the material). The phenomenological 'look' (*Schau*), suggests Balthasar in a daring metaphor, is like the silence upon which breathing makes itself heard. Transcendental subjectivity in its very performance brings us to the 'givenness', the datum. 'In the moment that I "live into" the natural contingent environment it becomes plain to me how my "I" "brings about" that "living into", how it "worlds".'[69]

Balthasar stresses, however, that this is no full-blooded ontology. The world has, in Husserl's words, but 'presumptive existence'. Husserl's kind of analysis cannot pronounce on the delicate point when 'meaning-bestowal' implies actual objective 'being'.[70] The *noêma* – what is perceived in Husserlian intuition – can provide no 'absolute guarantee for natural being', as the master freely admits in his study of 'formal and transcendental' logic.[71] For Balthasar, such neutrality renders Husserl's positing of essence impotent. Balthasar speaks of a 'haze' enveloping objective being – and non-being for that matter, a 'deprivation of existing ground' reminiscent of the 'becoming strange' of the world in Bergson, Klages, Rilke, George. Husserl lets a sense of unreality affect even that positing of essence which brackets austerely all merely 'factual' considerations. The reason is anxiety about the 'I', its

---

68 Ibid., p. 111.
69 Ibid., p. 114.
70 Ibid., p. 117.
71 E. Husserl, *Formale und transzendentale Logik* (Heidelberg 1929), p. 250.

'conversions and aversions' (*Zuwendungen und Abwendungen*), and a lack of confidence in the transparency of the 'transcendental' operation he proposes. (Perhaps it is only entertaining images, after all.) Husserl is stuck in the old Nietzschean trap, the inability to move from 'ground' to 'form', from 'form' to 'ground'.

Balthasar divines in Husserl's texts a 'feeling for the world' that deems the object halfway between reality and unreality, and an 'existentiality' for which perception really contributes and yet is held at a distance. The problem comes to a head over inter-subjectivity, which Husserl would like to affirm, but the ghost of solipsism haunts him. To Balthasar's mind, Husserl never clarifies how contemplative, receptive looking differs from the creative, 'cosmogonic' gaze which brings before us a 'world'. Transcendental subjectivity emerges as the 'absolutely active centre of world-postulation', *Weltsetzung* – which explains how Husserl can call phenomenology (or rather his version thereof) 'universal Idealism'.[72] Balthasar objects. Husserl's elimination of all merely 'biologically pragmatic' attitudes in the *epochê* is animated, so it now turns out, by a 'transcendental pragmatism'. This hardly represents a significant advance in the direction of *veritas*. What is Husserl's transcendental subjectivity if not an eery doublet of God? Husserl 'eliminates' God – not atheistically but *de facto* – yet his 'phenomenological reduction' proceeds as if consciousness were absolutely, divinely spontaneous. What Balthasar misses is any sense of the element of appropriate *passivity* in human awareness. In this way, the removal of God from the picture confirms everything that is least admirable in Husserl's scheme. The manner in which the 'daring and cool' phenomenological judgment 'floats above the shambles of world-construction' reminds Balthasar – *ceteris imparibus* – of the problematics of Kraus and even Kafka. Here is human judgment that is highly elusive and yet claims sovereignty over all it surveys.

Husserl is certainly to be congratulated on the way he resurrected, after centuries of neglect, the real distinction between essence and existence which constitutes, to Balthasar's mind, the (Thomistic) highpoint of Western metaphysics – as the third volume of his own theological aesthetics will in due course explain. But the total separation Husserl tried to create between 'fact', *Tatsache*, and 'form', *eidos*, spoiled most of what he achieved. This is the mixed inheritance, then, into which Scheler comes.

What he takes from it is methodologically good – so Balthasar implies. In place of 'criticism, interpretation, deduction', Scheler privileges 'vision, description, analysis'.[73] Moreover, he supplements an egregious lack in Husserl by writing approvingly in this connexion of one's *Gefühl* – 'feeling' or 'affectivity' – in the sense for which these powers are not merely self-referential but encounter the real. 'Intentional feeling' is a key phrase in Scheler who, in due course, will be celebrated for his robust statement of the significance of *sympathy*. Like Goethe, Scheler presents our foundational attitude in the experience of being in terms of 'an aboriginal passivity in relation to the phenomenon, allowing itself to be determined thereby'.[74] The

---

72 Cited in *Apokalypse III*, p. 122.
73 Ibid., p. 126.
74 Ibid., p. 127.

parity which such a stance enjoys with the spontaneously go-getting in our cognitive make-up had been overlooked by Husserl. To Scheler it was self-evident. Scheler asked humility from knowing agents, and considered 'reverence before the phenomenon' a necessary condition of scientific pro-gress. Nor did he forget the analogous role of humility in the essential passivity of conscience vis-à-vis God. Nietzschean epistemological power-relations, which still influenced Husserl, are here utterly set aside. Balthasar finds it accordingly strange that Scheler continued to treat phenomenology as the total opposite of psychology, and, in particular, maintained the Husser-lian antithesis of essence and fact. However, the atmosphere of the phe-nomenological reduction was now changed. The spectral anxieties had gone, and with them the Descartes-like search for security in the transcendental subject. In their place is 'fearless *Hingabe* to nature, to the objectivity of things'.[75] It is only the biological environment, not the world itself, which is 'bracketed' now in the 'reduction'. Otherwise, the emphasis lies on what is given, not on any subjective a priori – though Balthasar warns against taking Scheler's protest *too* comprehensively. As we shall see, Scheler also has a teaching on love, *Liebe*, the 'streaming forth of energetic ground', as the 'presupposition of all thinking'. Scheler represents a 'liberation of true spiritual life from the chains of pre-judgments that cover up knowledge and narrow down life'.[76] At his hands, phenomenology is a strategy for elim-inating thought-systems of premature 'closure' and all possible 'deceptive direction' so as to direct our gaze to 'God, outer things and oneself'. Posi-tively Goethean – for Balthasar the epistemologist, this is the highest com-pliment one can pay.

Not that Scheler quite matches Goethe's high standard. Whereas Goethe was keen to integrate with a sheerly passive or receptive 'openness to the world' those three basic human activities that are knowing, doing and enjoying, Scheler prefers to locate these on two distinct levels. Passive, objective knowing of things occupies the upper storey. 'Pure, streaming religious love' belongs on the lower – but more foundational – storey which, in the total construction, carries the floor above it. Philosophical knowledge of essence is objective, but it has ethical preconditions, and these are furn-ished by a 'love-determined act of participation' by each person. And if we ask, 'Participation in what, pray?', Scheler's answer would be: in the world-ground, understood as a universal impetus of life and love.[77] To grasp this is no fit task for philosophical knowledge; rather, one makes a free sacrifice of philosophical identity so as to attain it. As Balthasar comments, this moves Scheler away from Goethe and brings him closer to Fichte. It follows from the separation of knowledge (passive) and love (active), and insinuates – with possibly baleful consequences – the shortcomings, nay impotence even, of intellectual-spiritual knowing.

75 Ibid.
76 Ibid., p. 128.
77 Ibid., p. 130.

Scheler's Phenomenology

Balthasar will lay out the 'tragedy' waiting in the wings when he describes Scheler's personalism. But first he must do more justice to Scheler's – in many ways admirable – phenomenology itself. In his metaphysics (Balthasar does not fight shy of the word in this connexion) Scheler begins from Bergson's account of images. In perception we are already in the outer world. In such outer perceiving, it is nature as a whole that is given to us. Reversing the thrust of empiricism: sensations are the 'ideal ... residue' that is left over when we analyse the total perceptual act.[78] Likewise, in inner perception the totality of the 'I' is given as well – only against this background does this or that aspect of the perceiving subject stand out. 'These two horizons – the nature-totality and the "I" – totality are *de iure* both fully given. They are in the consciousness.'[79]

The tendency of modern philosophy to treat the world of appearance as subjective synthesis Scheler deems an absurd exaggeration of human powers, and a sad testimony to man's estrangement from nature. Rather, the 'partial identity' of our life with that of the image world of nature – 'the life that underlies everything there is', makes comprehensible our 'possible part-share in the images [of things] through our "perception"'.[80] The 'vital, productive imagination' is responsible for 'formal, mechanical consideration of the world' as well as for 'vivid, sensuous images' – at any rate in what concerns *homo faber* with his practical everyday concerns.[81] By sober correction over time, man draws from the 'pre-form' of the images appropriate concepts (*Vorstellungen*) in which to present the content of the 'concrete wholeness' of external and internal perception. (Here Scheler both drew upon, and helped to make possible, modern 'Gestalt-psychology'). In his phenomenology, then, Scheler affirms the 'equal originality of the poles of intentionality': spirit and nature, spirit and life, spirit and drive. The outstanding problem will be: how to reconcile the productivity of drive with objective knowledge of essence. How are the objects of vital sensuous subjectivity also topics of spiritual-intellectual knowledge? What Scheler is attempting is to render bearable the considerable tension between the (presumed) intelligible content of natural essence and intentional (would-be) knowing – 'noema' and 'noesis' in Husserl's phenomenology – through a synthesis of pragmatism and the Aristotelian–Thomistic (Balthasar actually writes 'Aristotelian-Scholastic'[82]) theory of knowledge.

Unfortunately, as already noted, since Scheler links objectivity with passivity there is no real equivalent in his theory to the 'agent intellect' of such Scholasticism, with its power to complete what is lacking in the 'patient intellect' which, certainly, Scheler affirms. But Scheler made valiant attempts to solve the problem. Over against Husserl he insisted that the 'being and being-just-so of the world' was quite independent of its 'being-there' as an object for the act of some individual seeking to grasp it – even if the notion of a universally unknowable being is itself contradictory. Finite spirit and the

---

78 Ibid., p. 133.
79 Ibid.
80 M. Scheler, *Die Wissensformen und die Gesellschaft* (Leipzig 1926), p. 458.
81 *Apokalypse III*, pp. 134–35.
82 Ibid., p. 137.

world are relative to each other, 'noema' and 'noesis' co-conditioned, and this is no destructive relativity since man is 'cosmomorph' just as things are 'anthropomorph'. Now the 'fit' of things to the mind, and vice versa, can be registered without appeal to more ultimate considerations. And yet the final reason for that convenient 'fit' lies in the way absolute truth is 'raised above spirit and nature' – is *personal*. Personal perspective is, therefore, an advantage not a disadvantage: the 'act of loving taking of interest' is of 'metaphysical-ontic significance', and not merely psychological.[83] If truth is ultimately personal, then we can safely lay the opposition of objective and subjective to one side. As soon as I become aware of a call to strive for a moral good which is both a good in itself and a good for me (nothing logically contradictory in *that* combination), I can apprehend that call as simultaneously objective – a 'divinely sketched value-image of my person', and subjective – a personal appeal directed to me, suiting me, and not to be exchanged with any other. Such an experience entails an acknowledgement of creaturehood. It is, remarks Balthasar, the 'fissure' (*Riss*), the place of appearing of God.[84]

In this scheme there was room, so Scheler thought, for a great variety of types of human experience – such as, in particular, evolutionary thought and Spengler's morphology of human cultures might wish to house – without any danger of overthrowing the unitary 'object-relatedness' of knowledge.[85] Ethical absolutism – a total moral system recognizing all unconditional moral norms – would not necessarily be threatened by the assertion that various moralities might contribute to such recognition in partial fashion. By such *Funktionalisierung*, each could have hold of one leg of the elephant. Like Rilke, Scheler found something holy in human knowledge. For Rilke, things are redeemed through humanity when people bring them to their full truth. For Scheler, that means: bring things to the truth of their 'ontic participation in God through partial conquest of the idea God has of them'.[86] Reality becomes conscious of its meaning and value in and through man. Where, however, Scheler differs from Rilke is in leaving space for God – and indeed for the grace of God – to fulfil this work of coming-to-identity.

Despite the favour he bestows on these judgments, Balthasar deems Scheler by no means wholly free from the Bergsonian opposition of mind or spirit and nature or life (what Scheler sometimes 'drastically' calls 'belly'). That is reflected, Balthasar thinks, in his counter-posing of intellect and will. Pure spirit, for Scheler, neither wills nor acts (Balthasar calls this view, in frank terms, 'absurd'), and thus lacks contact with the reality of existence, as distinct from that of essence. In such 'emancipation' of praxis from the guidance of spirit, Scheler's Christian mindset, so apparent in much of his phenomenological thought, passes over into Titanism. This was not unprepared. Balthasar thinks of the way the phenomenological gaze is for Scheler a direct sharing in the divine Ideas, an a priori of all possible worlds, and even a 'co-creation of the world with God'. He remembers too how Scheler deduces phenomenal time from the supra-temporality of spirit, itself at the

83 Ibid., p. 138.
84 Ibid., p. 139.
85 Ibid., p. 140.
86 Ibid., p. 141.

summit of a Bergsonian 'pyramid of life', and how all reality, indeed, is drawn out by the productive imagination. Finally, he recalls the way Scheler approves of the *scintilla animae* concept of much mysticism, whether pagan or Christian, according to which there is a 'place' – the apex of the soul – where spirit sees God without mediation. All of this, warns Balthasar, is only too reminiscent of Kant and Hegel, those 'mortal enemies' of the Schelerian personalism he will shortly expound.[87]

Nor should we forget in this context the worrying antithesis of instinct and love which made Scheler a disciple of François de Salignac de La Mothe Fénelon (1651–1715) in the famous seventeenth-century controversy over 'disinterested love'. Misunderstanding the 'genuine Augustinian and Thomist doctrine', the archbishop of Cambrai refused to allow that self-love can be integrated into the highest love of God. Scheler's agreement (whether implicit or explicit Balthasar does not say) exemplifies how knowledge and love, philosophy and religion – like spirit and nature, intellect and will – would, in his philosophy, so easily fall apart. This was tragic, since so much is owed to Scheler for his two key insights: love makes one to see; essence gives itself to be seen. Balthasar is inclined to think it all goes back to a preliminary philosophical false move: the 'deliberate hushing-up, *Vertuschung*, of fact'.[88] This pre-announced what later became apparent as the 'hopeless indifference between drive and spirit' – and, in Scheler's post-Catholic thought, the moral equivalence (Balthasar does not hesitate to term it 'cynical') of sexuality and spiritual love. Seeking behind the personally active divine Word a 'presumably supra-logical Absolute', Scheler would find the very idea of a personal God seeping away.[89] Though the Catholic Scheler had at one point recognized a 'middle zone' where sensuous and spiritual love might be held together and their common limitations overcome, this was established by a curious and suspect anthropology which called for (these are Scheler's own words) 'heroification and stupidization in one', *Heroisierung und Verdummerung in einem*.[90] I am, for Scheler, less than a human being with 'reason and worth', yet more than an animal that exists 'in' its bodily states.

What saved Scheler from intellectual, spiritual, moral shipwreck for so long was, Balthasar implies, his devotion to St Francis of Assisi. In Francis, Scheler could find a figure who 'realized the midpoint' through mediating between extremes. As Scheler himself wrote in 'The Nature and Forms of Sympathy', Francis extended the 'Christian love emotion' for God and one's neighbour in God to the whole of sub-human nature while at the same time lifting up that nature into the 'light and radiance of the supernatural'.[91] He bound together the saving sacramental order centred in the 'supernatural sacrificial event' of Jesus Christ with the natural sacramental order of all creation, spiritualizing life and vitalizing spirit. This was the ideal that, says Balthasar, 'lit up' Scheler, but which, alas, he never reached.[92]

---

87 Ibid., p. 146.
88 Ibid., p. 147.
89 Ibid., p. 148.
90 M. Scheler, *Wesen und Formen der Sympathie* (Bonn 2nd edn, 1923), p. 150.
91 Ibid., p. 103.
92 *Apokalypse III*, p. 152.

Scheler's Personalism

So far, however, we ourselves have not reached the true 'sanctuary' of Scheler's thought, namely, his personalism which wrought for the German 'philosophy of life' a quite new *Gestalt* or total form. The classical German philosophers had little time for the person, subordinating it to a higher impersonal law. In theory, Nietzsche prized the individual as unique but in practice also subordinated it – in his case, to fate. Positivism with its mathematical-scientific ideal of truth ignored it. Neither saw the importance of an 'in itself' which is at the same time 'for me': indeed, they treated it as a contradiction in terms. Treating the personal as, in a pejorative sense, subjective, they failed to realize it is, in Scheler's words 'the maximally and supra-normally objective'.[93] Any philosophy looking for inspiration exclusively to the ancient Greeks would, thinks Balthasar – following Scheler – make the same mistake. To evaluate the personal properly, one needs to know that the Logos itself is person and love. That was not a real possibility until God in Christ had carried out his 'movement of descent', thereby inverting the 'entire ancient movement of ascent of eros to the supra-erotic, absolute Object'. (One begins to see why *Apokalypse der deutschen Seele* will take as its final master Karl Barth!) In a passage that is really key for his future development as a doctrinal theologian, Balthasar goes on: 'In this self-outpouring in freedom there was disclosed for the first time the intrinsic glory and highest sovereignty of this Love, bound as it was to nothing, duty bound to nothing. After its first achievement in Christ this "inverted movement" will henceforth be precisely the authentic access to the highest.'[94] And Balthasar shows by citation how Scheler at some point had grasped this: self-abandonment is the way to 'become like God'. Of course personality is not itself of the supernatural order. But thanks to the self-disclosure of just those qualities in the divine Personality it was Christianity that let us see it in its intimacy and freedom.

Scheler's philosophy of personhood begins from the observation that a person is not an object. Only a person, he noted, can keep silence, and only in this case (within the world) is unknowability a sign of perfection. For Scheler, indeed, a person has no objective being, existing only in act – or acts – through which alone it becomes knowable to another without for all that becoming object to them. Persons are radically, qualitatively different one from another. Such otherness has intrinsic value owing to the way it mirrors the divine Personality. Though the Trinitarian dimension to this proposal (crucial for the Balthasar of the dramatics) is not emphasized, Scheler saw that the closer a creature stands in relation to God the more unique it is, and the less any other can be substituted for it. Balthasar terms this a 'sacral metaphysic of spirit'.[95]

The impossibility of objectifying personhood withdraws it, so Scheler claims, from both the bodily and the psychic realms which are, rather, its fields of operation. Scheler exalts the person over the political – and for that matter over the 'I'–'thou' relation since an 'I' calls out for a 'thou' whereas personhood exists in itself. Scheler regards such 'Christian individualism' as

---

93 Cited in ibid., p. 153.
94 Ibid.
95 Ibid., p. 156.

the 'dearest inheritance of the European – and especially of the German spirit – over against the chaotic, collectivist East'.[96] But Balthasar soon takes back the word 'individualism'. Scheler treats the person as 'supra-political' but nonetheless intrinsically social, a co-responsible member of a community. Scheler grasped the genius of Christianity in uniting the two – individuality, sociality – by the complementary doctrines of creation for the first and, for the second, the mystical body of Christ.

Some False Moves

Unfortunately, the outworkings of Scheler's wider metaphysical and anthropological principles threaten to furnish for this ('Augustinian-mystical') teaching a frankly atheistic outcome. *Prima facie*, nothing could seem less plausible. Like Newman, Scheler singles out the phenomenon of conscience, the experience of guilt and remorse as our primary pointer to a God surmised as 'Holy Judge'. He sees in the 'process' of personal remorse an intuition, moreover, of pardon and grace – a 'fresh power from out of the centre of things'. Seen positively, the person, thus limited negatively vis-à-vis God, can also be described as God's 'natural revelation', a living mirror of the divine – which is why Scheler argues religiosity is not a chance development but constitutive of the human essence. In fact, he calls finite spirit in its createdness a 'prayer' 'simply because it is a finite consciousness',[97] even though, strictly speaking, a religious act needs for its verification the 'diag-nostic notes' of a world-transcending intention of a kind that only the divine can fulfil. In his own way, Scheler was a virtue ethicist, but for him the really decisive virtues are those which issue from the 'ontological depths of [the human] essence where the foundational religious act has its roots'.[98] That is why he places humility first on the list, and, over against Nietzsche, con-siders it the typical virtue not of slaves but of lords. The highest meaning of human existence is identical with the idea of man in God.

Just here is where the trouble comes. Where such a premise is put in place, one false move and what should be man's *gracious* divinization as he reaches his identity in God can become merely a matter of natural ontology. And in point of fact, assisted by flaws already noted in Scheler's thinking, a 'pri-mitively Platonist, primitively Gnostic' rupture opens up in his portrait of the human being: man emerges as two-natured: an 'earthly-natural' and a 'heavenly-divine' being. 'Grace' for Scheler transmogrifies into the 'peak', *Spitze*, of nature and becomes quasi-indistinguishable from spirit, while the divine being itself undergoes 'anthropologization'. In the essay, crucial for his later development, 'Zur Idee des Menschen', Scheler declares that the natural man is no more than a beast – he was and is an animal and will eternally remain so. As person, however, he is essentially a God-seeker, removed from nature, a 'theomorphic' being that cannot be defined except to say it is an 'inbetween', a 'boundary', an appearing of the divine in the midst of the stream of life. The dividing line does not run between the animal world and man (between the higher primates and *homo faber* lies only a difference of degree). It lies within the human being – a position Scheler defended by a

96 Ibid., p. 157.
97 M. Scheler, *Vom Ewigen im Menschen* (Leipzig 3rd edn, 1933), p. 524.
98 *Apokalypse III*, p. 160.

misunderstanding, so Balthasar thinks, of patristic anthropology, notably Augustine's and, behind him, that of Athanasius, Origen and Irenaeus. Here the mystery of grace is misidentified as the mystery of man himself. Perhaps with the benefit of hindsight into Scheler's biography, Balthasar describes him as now teetering on the brink of a 'defenceless Titanism' that 'thrusts forward into absolute emptiness'.[99]

Scheler's distorted image of the God–man relation could hardly leave unaffected his attitude to Catholic Christianity at large. For Scheler, Christianity is a spiritual power that should rule in the world. It may not have done so hitherto but it has the future of world history at its disposal for the task. Balthasar's hostility to Scheler on this point might just mean that Scheler is a 'Christendom thinker' and Balthasar is not (his post-War essay on the Church in the world, 'The Razing of the Bastions', would show as much).[100] But Balthasar thinks there is more to it than that. Scheler scorns the compromise notion of 'religious culture'. In his Catholic period he is an outright Chiliast, who looks forward to the 'thousand year reign' of the saints on earth, which, at his hands, takes a rather Germanic colouration as the 'continuity of value-goods' between the 'noble', the 'politically heroic' and the 'holy'. The ground of Balthasar's dislike for this – far from ignominious – ideal soon becomes plain. Scheler treats the Christian values, Christian death and the very kenosis of Christ itself as 'the highest forms of a Nietzschean noble humanity'.[101] These sacrifices are for him beautiful overflowings of natural powers. To Balthasar's eyes, Scheler misses the point of Christ's self-emptying which was not, in reality, 'full' at all – except of anxiety, and fear and trembling. It was not natural, but unnatural. It was not heroic, but a matter of sheer obedience. Scheler falsifies the form of the Cross in his own aristocratic manner quite as much as do the bourgeois Christians he excoriates in his prose. But this is just what we might expect from his earlier exaltation into the heavens of the essential core of man as personal spirit.

The way Scheler has spoken of 'insight' in the experience of faith, combined with his understanding of the experience of grace as a 'possession of blessedness', a 'co-looking', strikes Balthasar (in retrospect?) as gnosis in phenomenological clothing leading this philosopher to a kind of deduction of the ideas of revelation, sin, the Saviour, the kenosis, the Church, which goes well beyond the Augustinian 'I believe that I may understand'. Indeed, Balthasar believes Scheler considered phenomenology to be a kind of negative theology which could draw out of worldly being the 'primordial positive divine qualities'.[102] To be sure, Scheler was right to say that sheer formal negation leads to nihilism. But that is not to say negation is the esoteric form of direct vision of the divine. Scheler was not wrong, however, in seeing a connexion between negative theology and something wonderfully positive. The element of no-saying, on Balthasar's (equally personal not to say idiosyncratic) interpretation of the *via negationis*, is all that is dark, mournful, closed and guilty in our attitude *to* the divine Other. This 'to', says Balthasar,

99 Ibid., p. 164.
100 H.U. von Balthasar, *Schleifang der Bastionen. Von der Kirche in dieser Zeit* (Einsiedeln 1952) ET *Razing the Bastions. On the Church in this Age* (San Francisco 1993).
101 Ibid., p. 166.
102 Ibid., p. 169.

lives within the negations of negative theology as a flaming heart that melts all their ice and sets flowing the life-giving waters of the *via eminentiae* whereby we say of God what is superlatively beyond all those negations.

Scheler's understanding of the Fall is seriously off track as well. For Scheler the Fall is an historical event, but it is also inscribed in the very concept of the world. Here tragedy is raised to a false dignity: it belongs with the structure of every possible world. Scheler places man in an 'absolutely tragic situation' where he must fall with the world and rise with the redemption *at one and the same time.* Yet this surely is what we should expect if Scheler confused the Christian attitude with (Hellenic–Germanic) heroics. Balthasar calls the outcome nature's revenge against acosmic personalism.[103] And even more harshly, he speaks of Scheler's 'disenchanting and secularizing of sacral concepts' as a sign, even before disaster struck, that apostasy threatened. Despite the 'serene light' which fell on him from the figure of St Francis, Scheler could not see the intellectual arrogance which allowed him to write as though before him Christian philosophy had never been.

Yet Balthasar writes that it is 'impossible to doubt the reality and depth of his experience of God'.[104] Scheler's dislike of the Scholastic 'proofs' of God's existence stemmed from the way he privileged exemplary causality over against efficient causality: he considered the world an artwork mirroring 'phenomenally something of the spiritual, individual essence of the Artist'.[105] The world's relation to God is not so much that of a product as an *expression*, a term for which he sought and found numerous suggestive synonyms in this connexion. (In his theological aesthetics, Balthasar will say much the same of Francis's disciple, St Bonaventure.) Actually, the way Scheler sets up the religious act and its relation to cognitive activity rules out much (if any) appreciation for a syllogistic 'conclusion' to the existence of God even supposing such a proof were valid. The religious act cannot be 'logicized', since it depends on the self-sacrifice of thinking to the love relationship which alone can register from the human side the divine act of self-revelation – even in creation. All 'evidences' can only be utterly secondary when compared with this initial 'primary revelation'.[106] It is only fair to add, as Balthasar now does, that this holds good in Scheler's 'system of conformity' – of faith and philosophy, that is – only when we are thinking in *the formal perspective of religion*. In *the formal perspective of metaphysics*, by contrast, God figures as a 'boundary concept', *Grenzbegriff*, in the search for the causation of the world in its 'being and being-so'.[107]

Unfortunately, within Scheler's thought as a whole, any real 'conformity' of knowledge and love is quite elusive. Rather is there a schism between 'logos' and 'eros', which leaves Scheler caught 'between ontologism and agnosticism', between – in his vocabulary – 'knowledge of essence' and 'personal knowing'. As Balthasar puts it: 'The possibility of already seeing in the receptive passivity of the knowledge of essence an analogue and

---

103 Ibid., p. 172.
104 Ibid., p. 180.
105 Cited in ibid., p. 175.
106 Ibid., p. 176.
107 Ibid., p. 177.

preamble to religious faith – this radically Augustinian possibility – Scheler in his titanic epistemological absolutism allowed to pass him by.'[108]

Had he not done so, he would have recognized in knowledge a quality of *Hingabe* and therefore of activity – as Goethe did but Husserl did not. Scheler's exclusive emphasis on passivity, anthropologically intolerable as this was, later became, predictably enough, an equally exclusive emphasis on spontaneity, with appropriately unfortunate consequences. Scheler believed we see God only in the light he provides, but, in his unbalanced dislike for Thomas (over against, rather than with, Augustine in these matters), he required the divine light even for a 'basic religious knowledge of the being of the world'. Unless infinite reason illuminates finite reason, Scheler thought, even the distinction of created being from Uncreated cannot be grasped. It is clear, writes Balthasar, that from these positions – where religious love is fulfilled with the love that God is, and the divine ideas are grasped in God himself, only a short step is wanting before we reach the 'self-divinization of man'.[109]

Scheler took it. Had he been more patient, and not sought so early in his Christian experience to translate the grace of God into 'a research object', to grasp phenomenologically the address of the personal God to the personal 'I', things might have turned out differently. In practice he turned the concrete into the abstract, and, refusing to allow that 'absolute supra-temporality, eternity, essentialness' could descend into the 'confusion of temporality, facticity and becoming', ceased to believe that the truth can take on the 'form of a slave' (a very Balthasarian reference to the divine *Abstiegsbewegung* as expressed in the Philippians hymn).[110] The appeal of truth himself – God, and Scheler's own readiness to hear and respond, were exchanged for a 'personless world of essence' and 'spontaneous technique' for its mastery. It rather goes to show that 'even by love to want to be like God is Luciferian'.[111] This too will not be so surprising a judgment for readers of 'Patristik, Scholastik und wir'. In the pride hidden – or not so hidden – in its hubris, Scheler's Christian personalism was, through its own inner dissolution, judged and found wanting.

With 'acosmic love' removed from obedience, the subsequent glorification of instinct might have been predicted. The 'eschaton' of finite spirit cannot leave out a 'moment of potentiality and thereby negativity'. Even in its transcendence of this world is it 'pointed back' to it. In this sense, remarks Balthasar, forging a conscious paradox, when Hegel and Nietzsche announced the disappearance of the finite person whom Scheler had sought 'positively to eternalize', they had got hold of more Christian truth than he had. No matter how pneumatic man may be, for the Gospel he is 'in the world'. This is where Heidegger and Rilke may help us out.

---

108 Ibid., p. 179.
109 Ibid., pp. 179–80.
110 Ibid., p. 181.
111 Ibid., p. 183.

10

❧

From Heidegger and Rilke to Barth

Heidegger and Rilke

Introducing Martin Heidegger (1889–1976) at this point makes anecdotal sense – Heidegger had dedicated to Scheler his study of Kant. Linking Heidegger's name to Rilke's also has a *prima facie* foundation. Without giving reasons, Heidegger wrote, at some point before 1936, that the *Duino Elegies* 'put into poetic form the same thought that I have laid out in my writings'.[1] No justification is offered, so Balthasar offers one himself, and it is typically wide-ranging, both as to idea and as to historical perspective. Rilke unites three questions: about 'things', about God and about 'the possibility of man'. Similarly, Heidegger attempts to enlarge a philosophical anthropology so that, by exploring what is ultimate in human existence (*Dasein*), he can reach the foundations of a general metaphysic. The historical comparison Balthasar proposes for both men is with Hegel. Hegel attempted to synthesize classical German philosophy ('Idealism') with the more existential lucubrations of the poets – figures on whom Balthasar has dwelt at length: Novalis, Hölderlin, Schiller, Goethe and Jean Paul. The aim was to 'render the theoretical something alive in the depth dimension of existence'.[2] The shared task of Heidegger and Rilke was to integrate the contributions of *Lebensphilosophie* and phenomenology with the 'testing' and 'denial' associated with the names of Nietzsche and Dostoevsky. It involved exploring the 'brokenness of finite existence', and that means, for these authors, the brokenness of 'an existence which understands itself (even eschatologically) as referred to the world in its very roots'.[3]

Subjective reports on the fragmented and unsatisfactory nature of experience are not to be treated as flukes, but as reflections of how things are. And this is so in an existence to which – on their account – the language of ultimacy is entirely applicable. 'Transcendence' and 'being in the world' are not alternatives, for the world enables transcendence (thus Heidegger). Such an account of the implications of immanence brings in its train an obvious problem for Christian faith, as Rilke realized when he distinguished his own concept of 'eternalization', over against the Christian, as 'sheerly earthly,

---

1 Balthasar quotes this citation, otherwise unreferenced, from a French study of Rilke: J.F. Angelloz, *Rilke. L'Evolution spirituelle du poète* (Paris 1936), p. 322.
2 *Apokalypse III*, p. 194.
3 Ibid.

deeply earthly, blessedly earthly' in character.[4] When Balthasar comes to write on Barth – whose theology represents the very 'inversion', *Umkehrung*, of these various naturalisms – he is able to specify their contribution more plainly. The structure of spirit, as Heidegger and Rilke describe it, is 'a paradoxical identity of life and death, subjectivity and anonymity, presence in all things and disappearance into all things'.[5]

The meaning of this paradoxical structure cannot be seen from within the 'circle', only from without. Once our perspectives are inverted and we begin to see things, via revelation, from the side of the freedom of God, everything looks different. Heidegger's 'running forward', *Vorlaufen*, towards death and 'authenticity' can recognize itself as a *Vorläufig-sein*, a 'provisional being' towards God, just as our *Zerschellen*, or 'crashing' into nothingness is ultimately into God. Only the 'creative End-situation of 'being addressed [divinely]' can light up the paradox from within and enable us to grasp what finite spirit is and why it is so.

For Balthasar, Heidegger re-thinks Kierkegaard's 'subjectivity' as *Daseins-phänomenologie*, 'the phenomenology of existence'. Rilke develops such a phenomenology in more radical fashion as being in the world, being in time, being transient – and the possible eternalization of transience. Each man has the merit of taking life seriously, come weal or woe. (Rilke called it weighing life 'with the carat of the heart'.) Their 'Yes' to life is not at all the Nietzschean 'Yes', which was to a utopian intensification of life, not to life simply as it is. And so the question becomes, To where does this new 'Yes' lead, now that 'spirit', *Geist*, is submerged in 'being', *Sein*, in the form of 'being-there', *Dasein*? For Heidegger, *Dasein* is far more primordial than knowing or doing. As he wrote in his study of Kant: the metaphysics of *Dasein* is not a metaphysical study of existence. Rather, our subject is a metaphysics that 'of its nature happens *as* being-there'.[6] And just as, for Heidegger, existence is truth, so for Rilke existence is beauty or art. In his little maxim, '*Song* is existence'.[7] Orpheus's going down into death and nothingness makes possible the beauty-character of existence – a key theme of Rilke's late *Sonnets to Orpheus*, to which Balthasar will return. Either way, the metaphysical endeavour takes place as the fulfilment of being-there in its very finitude, placed as this is between being and nothing. And no longer is it a case of *form* threatened by nothingness in the midst of being (as with various writers Balthasar has discussed hitherto). Instead, it is being itself which is nothing-like (*nichtig*). Form's jeopardy has now become a property of the existent itself. Nothingness is not on the margins of life but at its innards – this goes for Rilke too. 'In its innermost heart it feels time and death.'[8] Being-there is as full of holes as a sieve, and as the 'spaces' in between plenary moments suggest to us, we confront in it the 'nothingness of time'.

This raises, says Balthasar, two issues. The first concerns the meaning of such negativity or what he calls 'nothingness as the ground of finitude and subjectivity'. The second asks after the (possible, and if so eschatological)

---

4 Cited in ibid., p. 196.
5 Ibid., p. 323.
6 M. Heidegger, *Kant und das Problem der Metaphysik* (Bonn 1929), p. 221.
7 Cited in *Apokalypse III*, p. 197.
8 Ibid., p. 199.

'totality-being', *Ganzsein*, of being in so frighteningly finite a temporal mode.[9] As his discussion will show, neither question can be adequately answered under the rubric of 'being in the world' – which is how he entitles his initial exploration of the Heideggerian–Rilkeian world-view. That is not so surprising, since the 'method' that corresponds to that 'new view of things' is one of the ever-deepened *repetition of the same* – or what Heidegger himself, in *Sein und Zeit*, famously termed the 'hermeneutical circle'. (Rilke's early poems, in the *Stundenbuch*, say something analogous. They will explore the '"millennial" circling round God'.[10]) Philosophy for Heidegger is 're-remembering' just as for Rilke poetry reawakens childhood, and in each case this is understood as purifying, liberating release from oblivion. Balthasar notes how few motifs are sounded in Rilke's writing: God and death, love and anxiety, the angel and time, transfiguration and jeopardy, more or less sum it up. Rilke repeats these at ever deeper levels, but does not expand them. Balthasar will, in a sense, adopt the same approach. To do justice to Heidegger and Rilke he seeks to capture self-identical themes by a like process, with increasing 'intensity and penetration' as his three chapters proceed. After 'being in the world' he offers, to this end, 'fall and death' and 'creation from anxiety'.

Being in the World

Under that first heading – being in the world – the issue of 'negativity' initially absorbs Balthasar's attention. Heidegger liked to cite Hegel's axiom that 'sheer being and sheer nothing are ... the same'. For them, as indeed for Rilke, the 'inner space' of being is in one sense 'hollow', since, in Scholastic terms, it consists of passive potentiality. But in another sense such 'space' is far from hollow, filled as it is with that contrastingly *active* potency of being which the moderns term 'subjectivity'. Here is a mystery. As what is best known to us, being as such is also the unknown (thus Hegel and Heidegger). Rilke puts it more concretely: the meaning of suffering, love and death is 'not unveiled'. But we *do* have, evidently, even before we start to philosophize, a preliminary apprehension of being – what Heidegger calls a 'pre-ontological' understanding of it,[11] and this can be progressively explored in the course of the philosophical enterprise, so that perhaps – as Hegel thought – the final proposition of dialectics may tell us what 'being' means. Heidegger's approach is not, however, Hegelian, the way of dialectical construction. Rather, as a disciple of Nietzsche, Bergson and Husserl, he understands being as *transcendence*, albeit in a somewhat paradoxical sense which brings before us the famous Heideggerian 'nothingness', *das Nichts*. Insofar as 'being' is 'being-there' – *Dasein*, existence, is literally, after all, *Da-sein* – man as spirit can look over it *de haut en bas*. But such glory has a deep shadow drawn across it. The very same seeming mastery of being draws our attention to our 'possible distance from being', and so to nothingness. Being, so it turns out, is only illuminated when it is penetrated by nothingness. This for

---

9 Ibid., p. 200. Balthasar calls this second area of investigation that of 'the idea of human existence', or 'the essence of existential Platonism'.
10 Ibid., p. 201.
11 Balthasar cites this expression from Heidegger's essay 'Vom Wesen des Grundes', his contribution to the 1929 Husserl *Festschrift*, at ibid., p. 202.

Heidegger is the origin of the ontological 'anxiety', *Angst*, with which existence strikes the human race. Heidegger makes his own Scheler's wonderment that there is something rather than nothing. But he strips it of its
religious raiment, re-clothing it in the more subdued vesture of his own non-
theistic thinking. For Heidegger transcendence, the essence of the subject, is
shot through with nothingness, which 'belongs aboriginally to the ground of
being itself',[12] affecting thereby not only spirit but things. Balthasar is at pains
to show that this same sensibility characterizes Rilke too. His poetic writing,
like Heidegger's (to Balthasar's mind) pictorial thinking, raises the twofold
question, Does man create out of nothing? And, more frighteningly still, Is
nothing what is created in man?

In his exposition of Heidegger's ontology of 'the world', Balthasar stresses
three features, all of which show the Swabian thinker's debt to not only
phenomenology but *Lebensphilosophie* as well. And these are: Heidegger's
sense of the positiveness of finitude, his idea of the essential temporality of
existence, and, more worryingly, his belief in a 'double truth'. The positiveness of finitude suggests Heidegger's place in an apostolic succession of
writers from Bergson and Klages to George and Nietzsche. He emphasizes
the open-ended value of the 'determinate, unique, temporal form' – even as
he considers the 'substance' of this form to be (in the sense above indicated)
'nothing'.[13] For Heidegger a world of forms thus characterized belongs to the
a priori structure of finite knowing which is, therefore, 'subjective' in a
'transcendental' sense: the conditions of possibility of our knowledge are also
the conditions of possibility of objects themselves. This is no assault on truth
since, as Heidegger remarks in *Sein und Zeit*, what is primarily true is *Dasein*
itself, *in* its finitude.[14]

Acceptance of the essential temporality of existence fits naturally here. It is
ruthlessly expressed in Heidegger's Kant book. 'Time and the "I think"... are
the same.'[15] Balthasar maintains that, for Heidegger, 'time is essentially
finitude and therefore history'.[16] This explains how Heidegger can describe
transcendence as *Urgeschichte*, 'primordial history', and how, with huge
repercussions for his metaphysic, he can treat the progressive illumination of
the *understanding* of being as *ipso facto* the ongoing *constitution* of being. This
is an 'historically self-realising, progressive ontology', substituted for the
primacy of the *logos* in thought up to Kant, and incorporating thereby the
entire 'irrationalistic' tradition of the 'philosophy of life' as Heidegger's
immediate predecessors had transmitted it.[17] Here truth becomes finite with
a vengeance.

What, then, of 'double truth' in this regard? By this phrase Balthasar does
not mean the sort of twofold criteriology for the true briefly fashionable in
the Latin Middle Ages – where something might be held for true in philosophy but not theology, and vice versa. Moreover, he praises Heidegger for
'overbridging' the unfortunate duality often found between theory and

---

12 M. Heidegger, *Was ist Metaphysik?* (Bonn 1929), p. 20.
13 *Apokalypse III*, pp. 204–205.
14 M. Heidegger, *Sein und Zeit* (Bonn 1927), p. 220.
15 M. Heidegger, *Kant und das Problem der Metaphysik*, op. cit., p. 183; cf. the claim that the
    'self' is 'in its innermost ground primordially time itself', ibid., p. 187.
16 *Apokalypse III*, p. 206.
17 Ibid.

praxis, as well as that between 'ground' and 'form'. The discovery of truth for Heidegger is 'the metaphysical movement of *Dasein* itself whereby it replaces an original "fallenness" with its own proper "authenticity". This is as much "ethical" conversion as it is "logical" reflection.'

In comparison with Heidegger's near-contemporaries, this view of truth has, comments Balthasar: 'neither the aesthetic character of Bergsonian intuition, nor the ethos-less traits of the Husserlian *epoché*, and if anything comes closest to Scheler's position'.[18] From that position, however, it also differs in that it is a turning to a radically finite truth, indeed to the truth of finitude itself, and thus to the loneliness of *Angst* and decisive orientation towards death. Human solidarity – seen by Heidegger in the mode of fall-enness, thus the cursorily dismissed third person anonymous, *man* – enters this philosophy only with difficulty. In its ethic, 'the root of the ethical is not so much love as solitude'.[19] But Heidegger's account of the contrasting pair fallenness and authenticity becomes really problematic when brought toge-ther with another unhappy couple, this time of Husserlian descent, 'ontic' truth and 'ontological' truth. Here the question of 'double' truth starts to be unavoidable. For Heidegger, as Balthasar explains, 'ontic' truth is that 'truth about existents which is given in direct judgment of things'. By contrast, 'ontological' truth is 'the truth of the being of the existent', and includes a far less clear-cut a priori understanding of how we recognize the existent as such and can refer to being at large. But, as our earlier analysis suggested, this latter *is* Heideggerian 'transcendence'! Hence the great weight Heidegger comes to lay on the 'ontological difference' between beings and being. Hence too Balthasar's criticism that we are dealing here with a potentially perni-cious double-truth account of the real. The way Heidegger reads Kant may enable him to bypass Husserl's anxiety about the facticity of things (as dis-tinct from their 'essence'). But a 'total darkness' nonetheless covers the ground of things, their whence and whither, on Heidegger's bifurcated account.[20] A real rupture opens up in Heideggerianism between essence and existence: essence, *Was-sein*, is related to the truth disclosed in transcendence; existence, *Dass-sein*, to the truth that discloses as transcendence – and so as subjectivity and nothingness. Once again, as so often in the history of post-mediaeval thought, poor old facticity is swallowed up in an a priori. Hei-degger has not sufficiently considered, so Balthasar thinks, the inseparability of spontaneity and receptivity as modes of reason.

Balthasar also finds three terms that characterize Rilke's thought, and they both resemble his trio of Heideggerian key features and yet differ from them. Rilke shows his distance from Idealism and Romanticism not only by the emphasis he places on the positivity of the finitude (Balthasar had already found this in Heidegger), but also in his doctrines of the high value of the unique and, not least, the transient. He is close neighbour to an 'heroic Classicist'.[21] The more Rilke learned to understand his own subjectivity, the more decisively he praised the single, unrepeatable and finite in things. Balthasar indicates the subtlety of Rilke's poetry when he remarks that the

18 Ibid., p. 207.
19 Ibid., p. 208.
20 Ibid.
21 Ibid., p. 210.

less pointed the sensuous contours of things in his writing, the more clearly their 'inner, transcendental borders' stand out, and with that the 'imagistic quality of their essence'. The *Sonnets to Orpheus* show this with immense virtuosity, while the *Duino Elegies* give us its metaphysic, claiming as they do equal and perhaps surpassing significance for finite-temporal form when compared with the eternal and infinite world of the angels. The angel does not know the (similarly) infinite weight of a single irrecoverable moment. Finitude is itself form and beauty: this is the value of 'being in the world'. The 'authenticity of *Dasein*', to use Heideggerian language, is in Rilkean terms the 'fearless affirmation of the radical transience and temporality of being', and that, so Balthasar adds, 'without flight into a Schelerian realm of spirits'.[22] But notice how this is no mere empiricism. Within the horizon of finitude, it is for Rilke the impress of an infinite subjectivity that gives the shape of existence its more than temporal, transcendent worth. Rilke sees death immanent in every moment of life, but not as a negative within the positive. Rather, and here the connexion between the preciousness of finitude and its temporality becomes patent, the negative *is* the positive itself. On Rilke's behalf, Balthasar does not hesitate to speak of the 'ontological identity of life and death'. The 'osmotic traffic between the living and the dead' which occurs in his verse is not an antique survival but the expression of this conviction that 'life is already death and death life'.[23]

But does this not imply – with Heidegger – the identity of being and nothing, and is this not again the 'double' – ontic and ontological – truth? Ontological truth, it is claimed, makes ontic truth possible. But when Balthasar rehearses Rilke's own account of his attempt in *Malte Laurids Brigge* to locate that ontological truth by 'going behind' all things, even death, he finds there a movement *against* ontic being, of such a kind that it merits the epithet 'sacrilegious'. Not mincing words, it is 'Titanic', indeed 'demonic'.[24] Rilke was searching, however, for the strength to live out both truths: the 'truth which *Dasein* is, with all the "honourable things" that come along the road of being, and the truth that it is impossible'.[25]

As the fourth of the *Duino Elegies* has it, these two truths would destroy each other. Man is sundered into two roles, angel and puppet. 'Then there's at least a play! *Dann is endlich Schauspiel.*'[26] Not surprisingly, Rilke sometimes envied the beasts their lot. For them neither subjectivity nor – as a consequence – death was problematic. (The eighth of the *Elegies* points, for the most part, in this direction.) But Balthasar brings forward texts to show this is not necessarily Rilke's final word. Rilke explicitly invited people to read the – to Balthasar, offending – *Malte Laurids Brigge* 'against its stream'. The book's real message was how it is by lack of strength that we 'lose the countless earthly realms' intended for us. Accordingly, Rilke exhorted his correspondents to dig deep, to reach a profounder level of their own nature. The 'I' must in some essential sense 'die', if the 'space of praise' is to be opened up. *That* is the medium in which we can encounter things in their true character,

22 Ibid., p. 211.
23 Ibid., pp. 212–13.
24 Ibid., p. 214.
25 Ibid., p. 215.
26 R.M. Rilke, *Duino Elegies* (trans. J.B. Leishman and S. Spender; New York 1939; 1963), pp. 45, 44.

for now 'receptive spontaneity' and 'spontaneous receptivity' have come together in us. No poet, writes Balthasar, has ever penetrated further than Rilke into the 'mystery of this active-passive medium'. [27] The highest art of subjectivity is to be pure air for things. (Heidegger says approximately the same when he ascribes to the 'nothingness' of *Dasein* the capacity of the existent to come most fully to itself.)

Balthasar finds that in this understanding of finite spirit the two supreme cognitive gains of his entire enterprise in *Apokalypse der deutschen Seele* come together. The first such gain is to understand how the conjoined expression of activity and passivity displays whatever is positive about finitude. (Goethe already knew that, but he had not grasped the 'nothingness' that modifies the substantiality of being.) The second gain is when we see how reality's epiphanic quality – its *Schein* – issues from the 'paradox structure of the world and truth'. (Nietzsche knew that, but drew the falsely sceptical conclusion that subjectivity has no ontological basis, rather than the correct inference that here we meet subjectivity's true ground.) 'Philosophy and the arts' in the German tradition had been unable to decide whether life should be human creation or letting things be in their sheer streaming-forth. Rilke was the first to see how insight and self-forgetfulness are inter-related. Philosophy and the arts had likewise failed to resolve the question, What should be our primal attitude to the world: asceticism or ecstasy? Rilke realized the answer was, really, neither – since both can be obstacles hindering the soul from becoming sheer transparency to the real. We only have to think of love to perceive this, remarked Rilke. Love entails renunciation and fulfilment at one and the same time. Balthasar finds here steps taken towards the overcoming of the pernicious duality of ontic and ontological truth which afflicted Heidegger. In Rilke, their import is as yet unrecognized. But it is there.

Of course that duality could not be surmounted without broadening our consideration beyond the foundations of spirit to those of reality at large, or what Balthasar calls the 'question of the possible wholeness of existence, in relation to its idea'. More briefly – and memorably – this is the 'question of existential Platonism'.[28] For Balthasar, the question of existence is inseparable from the question of idea, *eidos*, form: in a word, ontic truth and ontological truth go hand in hand. Death and nothing are not – *pace* Heidegger – the only horizon in which we live, move and have our being. There is also the 'horizon' of the 'free self-interpretation of being', and here existence goes beyond its givenness – what Heidegger would term the situation of 'thrownness' where *Dasein* finds itself – and confronts the issue of meaning. Such an 'horizon' makes some sort of appearance in Heidegger's Kant book under the rubric of the 'archetypal intellect' or 'originating intuition'. In a freewheeling treatment of Kant's philosophy: this is when pure reason works in receptive rather than creative mode, receiving an object that stands over against the subject within an ontological horizon Heidegger terms 'offering' – or rather, 'coming to be offered', *Angebotenwerden*. Rilke's poetry presents it more strikingly. It is the 'angel'.

Not having received the gift of preternatural foreknowledge, Balthasar could not guess the future development of Heidegger's thought after his time

27 *Apokalypse III*, p. 219.
28 Ibid., p. 222.

of writing. From the vantage-point of 1939, the question he wanted Heidegger to answer was: are you content to let your philosophy be regarded as simply an 'immanent description of finite being in its formal structure' without establishing thereby the 'ground and horizon of truth at large'? [29] If being and nothingness are simply 'abstract extremes' of finite existence then intellectual space remains for an *intuitus originarius* that exceeds sublimely that 'structure'. Balthasar thought Heidegger could develop his philosophy as a kind of analogy-thinking for the God-man relationship, with at its heart the analogy between the absolute and utterly sufficient 'potentiality' of God and the relative 'potentiality', shot through by nothingness, of man. By contrast, in Rilke 'existential Platonism' is not just a possible speculative development. Rather, Rilke's angel is the 'norm of existence', the 'horizon of the transcendent ideal', that being in which the transformation of the visible into the invisible, at which we aim, already fully appears. The angel represents 'the idea of a knowledge without receptivity, without time, a sheer reflexion'.[30] And yet we cannot say Rilke's angel is a final goal for earthly life, any more than was Heidegger's 'originary intuition'. As with Heidegger, the context is simply *this-worldly existence*. Rilke does not reproduce the absolutely open-ended eros of Plato. Around the Rilkean angels too many ambiguities cluster. Are they symbols of Utopia, merely? Are they occasions, simply, for awakening the deeper beauty of the anxious human heart? Are they a 'limit-concept' (as Rilke's own comments sometimes suggest) for the pure achievement of understanding finitude? In Scripture, by contrast, the holy angels are virtually pre-incarnations of God, pseudonyms for God himself.[31] What conclusion should we draw, in this perspective, from the incremental exclusion of the name of God from Rilke's works?

Fall and Death

Moving from 'being in the world' to 'fall [or "decay"] and death', the second of the Heideggerian–Rilkean common themes, is no great distance. The only materials we have for the task of establishing a possible *Ganzsein* or wholeness of being are those we are given in temporal existence. To cancel out time would cancel out guilt – but along with guilt would go the 'I' as well. We soon confront, then, the boundary that is death. Mechanism hardly considers it a problem: what else would one expect than mortality from an aggregation of chemicals? But biologism, and even more, *Lebensphilosophie*, must probe further, alighting maybe, as with Eduard von Hartmann, on the paradox that the highest, the most valuable, integration of life is also the most endangered. Thus for Georg Simmel, figure of the Nietzschean circle to whom Balthasar ascribes a novel 'philosophy of death', individuation and transience go hand in hand.

Yet, as Simmel recognized, this scarcely answers the metaphysical question, Why must the unique die? Spiritually, as biologically, death is the fruit of an entire life, each moment of which is pregnant with its issue. This means that the problem of death is intimately related to the problem of *Ichwerdung*,

---

29 Ibid., p. 225.
30 Ibid., p. 226.
31 Compare the classic Old Testament study by A.R. Johnson, *The One and the Many in the Israelite Conception of God* (London 1942).

the 'becoming of the "I"'. There is a debt here to Goethe who had postulated immortality to the degree that the 'I' emerges. Simmel binds into this what might be called the 'biological' consideration that a *unique* living form will surely enjoy the privilege of abiding existence – life as the 'oyster' bringing forth the 'pearl' of 'inner form' of personal consciousness. Balthasar finds this not particularly satisfactory since it tries to bring together 'two worlds that cannot be united': Idealism and biologism.[32] He has more time for Claudel and Scheler who, he claims, unite an anticipation of Heidegger's 'being towards death' with a realization of the possible felicity of such a condition.

In the *Five Great Odes* Claudel, praising God for making him, as every human being, a finite image of the divine perfection, 'sees' that 'the key which delivers is not that which opens, but that which closes'. Balthasar considers this a re-discovery in specifically Christian terms of the Hellenic insight that limit, *peras*, is essential to meaning. For Scheler, personal death is in itself a non- or anti-value, on which, paradoxically, the positive value of finitude is based.[33] The 'surplus' of spirit over life – that 'spirit' to which so much of what is most dynamic in human thought and action bears witness – cannot be shown without death. As Balthasar cites from Scheler more than once, 'Death is an a priori'. But this is precisely why the person should live continually ' "in the face of" death'.[34] The 'life-curve' runs from the maximally wide to the maximally narrow; the 'spirit-curve' from maximal bonding to the vital powers to maximal freedom from biological instinct. Still, as Scheler insisted, to a person there belongs a body, which is why the 'pictorial thinking' of the Church about the resurrection of the flesh is more profound than contemporary speculation about the survival of mind as some sort of non-spatial point. This remains, however, in Scheler's corpus an undeveloped remark. It can only be expanded, thinks Balthasar, by thinking through what is involved in transcendence *not* over against the 'finite-mortal' creature but rather *of* that same being *but as a whole*. Is this only a matter of seeing ultimacy in a transcendental *tendency*, in a transfiguration of the structure of mortal structure by appropriate *attitude*? Or could there be, as the Heideggerian–Rilkean concepts of *intellectus archetypus* and the 'angel' might lead us to believe, *another horizon for existence than that of death itself*? The closure upon itself of the sphere of essence hardly makes the latter likely, granted guilt, decay, mortality. Not likely – unless we can hope for a lifting of the barriers 'from the other side by sovereignly free divine action'.[35] Even then, though, the first of the two possibilities just mentioned might still have a part to play in a philosophy of man in relation to the ultimate. That of course is the only way, on Christian presuppositions, Balthasar could find some sense in Heidegger's *identification* of finitude with transcendence, time with spirit.

Balthasar's analysis of *Sein und Zeit*, the work which first made Heidegger's name on a European scale, singles out the theme of the truth of existence. *Dasein* wrests (or fails to wrest) its self-understanding from within

---

32 *Apokalypse III*, p. 233.
33 Scheler never completed a planned study of the 'meaning of death', but the *Schriften aus dem Nachlass* I of 1933 contains an important contribution in the essay 'Tod und Fortleben'.
34 Ibid., p. 40.
35 *Apokalypse III*, p. 240.

the horizon of being towards death, thereby allowing its truth to unveil itself, to come out of hiddenness (if indeed, amid the idle curiosity, chatter and ambiguity of the human mass, this actually happens). Fallenness, anxiety, care all point to the exceptional character of the human creature (what other animals exhibit these dimensions?) but not to its possible wholeness. It is indeed axiomatic for Heidegger that as long as existence persists it never reaches totality. *Dasein* is its own possibilities – and therefore its non-being too.

Balthasar asks, Is this a phenomenological description – or is it a meta-physic? Is it a hermeneutic of how existence can understand itself, explore its own dimensions, or is it an interpretation of the existence of the existent as such? (That is, once again, the issue of 'double truth'.) Supposing we allow it the grander claim, to be a metaphysic, Balthasar finds the enterprise unfin-ished. Is *Dasein* the absolute, albeit finite, truth? If so, when in its primal self-determination it renders itself 'actively passive' to the life-field, should we not have to say this *Urakt* is itself originated – and if so by what or whom? Heidegger speaks of 'thrownness'. Is there not then a Thrower? Alter-natively, is *Dasein* something less than the absolute truth? In which case, is not 'thrownness' the sign *par excellence* of its relativity? Balthasar can put the question to Heidegger more sharply, if also more rhetorically: 'What is the ontic? Is it the creation of God or annihilating anxiety?'[36]

So Balthasar turns to Rilke again, on whom the First World War and – in Germany and Austria-Hungary – its revolutionary aftermath wrought a deepening social and cultural pessimism, exacerbated by the new arrivals in Europe of meretricious *Americana*. The fifth and tenth of the *Duino Elegies* orchestrate what are *de facto* Heideggerian themes of the confused inter-mixing of fallenness and authenticity in human life (Rilke's 'circus impres-sions' and the 'city of pain': 'plastered with placards for "Deathless"/ that bitter beer that tastes quite sweet to its drinkers/ so long as they chew with it plenty of fresh distractions'[37]). Now death has clothed itself in the garments of fallenness and is everywhere, taking the social air. But of course, time itself is a dying. Balthasar's exegesis of Rilke is dramatic. For the early poetry, death is at once the 'kernel and the cancellation, *Aufhebung*, of all existence, next to God himself'. Indeed, death is in Rilke's eyes 'the inner-worldly form, *Gestalt*, of God'.[38] Balthasar has already observed how the name of God progressively disappears from Rilke's writing. Now he adds that in the later poems, we hear more and more the note of lament. Rilke begins to sharpen his portrayal of the contours of death, to show not so much its immanence as its boundary-status. That is why in the *Sonnets to Orpheus* the Greek hero can stand for lordship of *two* realms. Yet, as the *Duino Elegies* suggest, this is a *two-in-one* reality. Death is the side of life that is turned away from us.

Man who, when he dies, does so in greater contrast to when he lives than any other creature, is also the one called to save what is precious from out of the 'conflagration of transience'. Or, in Balthasar's more extended effort to capture Rilke's perspective: 'So, then, the human heart, this most fragile of all vessels is really the midpoint of the world, the refuge of things, the point of

36 Ibid., p. 247.
37 R.M. Rilke, *Duino Elegies*, op. cit., pp. 80, 81.
38 *Apokalypse III*, p. 250.

intersection of the roads of the world, as between the reality that passes and the realm of value which is valid and stands, the place of transformation that, itself sinking down, raises everything into the eternal.'[39]

In the *Elegies* Rilke would turn all eyes to the theatre of the heart where truly eschatological changes can be performed. We cannot complete this task on earth, but we must strive to try, doing so by what Balthasar terms a 'self-readying subjectivity that stands open in the unending flight-span of love'.[40] Balthasar appropriately cites the fifth elegy in this connexion.

> Angel: suppose there's a place we know nothing about, and there,
> on some indescribable carpet, lovers showed all that here
> they're for ever unable to manage – their daring
> lofty figures of heart-flight,
> their towers of pleasure, their ladders,
> long since, where ground never was, just quiveringly
> propped by each other, – suppose they could manage it there,
> before the spectators ringed round, the countless unmurmuring dead:
> would not the dead then fling their last, their for ever reserved,
> ever-concealed, unknown to us, ever-valid
> coins of happiness down before the at last
> truthfully smiling pair on the quietened
> carpet?[41]

Naturally, given Rilke's acceptance of the distinction between this world and a 'beyond', his problematic of death and authenticity differs from Heidegger's. By itself, it is true, the mere survival of the soul does not interest him. That the soul sees the (Platonic) archetypes of things, even this does not so much impress him. And the reason is, such a vision is not the eschaton of *this world*, not the transfiguration of its passing realities. Only the fulfilment of the 'deepest remembering holding of the finite-temporal earthly realm' – such as one can occasionally anticipate now in visionary glimpses – is the soul's appropriate destiny. Where Rilke *does* join Heidegger, however, is in his evaluation of suffering, which is the 'depth of existence as negativity and just so as subjectivity its height'.[42] The borders of suffering and desire are permeable the one to the other. Rilke cannot imagine an eschaton where suffering and joy are not coinherent aspects of felicity. Moreover, Balthasar suggests how in the 'ball-game' which recurs in Rilke's imagery the same dialectic of responsiveness and initiative is found as in Heidegger's language of 'throwing' and 'thrownness'. And the same ambiguity attends. Do the two – throwing and thrownness, activity and passivity – bear comparable weight? If the finite is the Absolute they must! But the other possibility lies open: that the finite is *not* the Absolute but stands in relation to it. The ball of our existence is thrown by Another and has behind it – here Balthasar cites a favoured metaphor of St Augustine's – *pondus amoris*, the 'weight of love'.[43]

39 Ibid., pp. 253–54.
40 Ibid., pp. 254–55.
41 R.M. Rilke, *Duino Elegies*, op. cit., pp. 52–53.
42 *Apokalypse III*, p. 257.
43 Ibid., p. 261.

Creation from Anxiety

The last of Balthasar's Heideggerian–Rilkean motifs – 'creation from anxiety' – has already been signalled. What commands the 'dark form of existence', *Angst* or the *Spiritus Creator*? What vis-à-vis the ontological *is* the ontic? Is it merely that whereby 'nothing' eventuates (Balthasar calls this a 'quasi-creation'[44]), or is it the real as issuing from the free gift of God? With Heidegger there is no Husserlian *epochê* or 'bracketing out' of the factual, so the question both can and must be raised. Though Balthasar praises Heidegger for 'having opened our eyes to just how deeply historical finite being intrinsically is',[45] he cannot accept the way Heideggerian *Dasein* would swallow up an account of being. The 'real distinction' between essence and existence which for a Thomist metaphysician such as Balthasar is the key to understanding finite reality in its relation to the infinite reality of God is for Heidegger only a 'tension within an identity' – the identity of 'transcendence' which as understanding is essence, as *Dasein* is existence. By refusing to allow that beyond this anything belongs to the realm of the philosophical properly so called, Heidegger makes the a posteriori in effect a form of the a priori – and thus, for Balthasar, rejoins the Idealism which in principle he rejects.[46] But existence cannot be traced back to identity with essence, existential truth to essential. And, to resolve in his own name the issue of the 'bifurcation of truth', ontic versus ontological, which he believes Heidegger handled so misleadingly, Balthasar writes: 'Existential truth we must call "ontic", for it relates to factual existence in the world; essential truth, by contrast, we must call "ontological", since it thinks back to the grounds of essences in reflection ... upon life.'[47] Heidegger cannot but radically subordinate to the second the first. And this has major anthropological – not to say ethical – consequences. The 'authenticity' of existence is not now found in a relation to the environing world, including care for it, but only through the *Angst* which typifies *Dasein* in its decisive orientation towards death.

Yet Balthasar stresses – writing, to underline this once more, in 1939, and thus without benefit of hindsight – that Heidegger's philosophical enterprise is open to a future Christian development, just as it has, without doubt, a Christian background or past. 'That Christian thinking in very broad measure is co-inspirational for Heidegger is obvious.'[48] Does not Heidegger muse aloud in *Sein und Zeit* that, if a (Christian?) philosophy of divine eternity were to be constructed it should begin from God's 'primordial and "infinite" temporality'?[49] And did not Heidegger, at the end, more or less, of his analysis of Kantian thought, put the question, 'Finitude in existence – can it be developed as a problem without a "presupposed" infinitude?'?[50]

Chiefly the telltale apriorism Balthasar has identified prevents a Christian

---

44 Ibid., p. 262.
45 Ibid., p. 265, n. 2.
46 Thus, for example, Heidegger's pure temporality, however much 'ideally' it may be the archetype of time, 'in fact' needs ordinary, fallen, 'bad' time to render itself possible. Does not this – considered as a pattern of thinking – remind us of the way that in Schelling and Hegel eternity achieved concreteness 'from out of the dark depths of temporality'? Ibid., p. 267.
47 Ibid., p. 269.
48 Ibid., p. 270.
49 M. Heidegger, *Sein und Zeit*, op. cit., p. 427.
50 Heidegger, *Kant und das Problem der Metaphysik*, op cit., p. 236.

interpretation of Heidegger's thought as found in his writings to date, but 'which road he is taking and will take, we know not'. Not then, that is. Meanwhile, even as a torso, Balthasar takes Heidegger's (early) philosophy in its concern with the 'inner face of time' to be the 'novel of the modern soul', the 'most significant new eschatology in philosophical form'.[51]

It says something for his priorities, allegiances, loves, that nonetheless on this key topic (creation or perhaps one should write 'creation') Balthasar allots Rilke three times the space he gave Heidegger. *Angst* also figures prominently in Rilke. Balthasar calls it the 'clay' from which this poet is formed. Anxiety permeates his inner space, but it is creative insofar as his defencelessness permits things to show themselves there 'in their true out-lines'.[52] Balthasar finds in Rilke a gradually intensifying 'identity' of self-surrender, *Hingabe*, and creation, receptivity and spontaneity, all of which, however, are carried by a 'tragic' ground which declares itself in 'anxiety' and might be called God – or, alternatively, death and nothingness. From Rilke's work Balthasar singles out in this regard a trio of themes: the possi-bility – which will prove impossible, in fact – of the 'absolute poet'; the possibility of the impossible, i.e. 'the essence of the poet's tragic existence'; finally, Rilke and Christianity.

'The absolute poet' is an odd term. Balthasar means by it the ideal med-ium of poetic expression were spontaneity and receptivity perfectly to coa-lesce. He finds in the early Rilke of the *Stundenbuch* the claim to be that medium – not in and of his own powers but through a gracious experience of the Russian people and Orthodox spirituality which inspired the decadent, over-refined aesthete with the virtue of humility vis-à-vis the 'boundless space of God and the brotherhood of all things in him'.[53] Despite Rilke's lack of personally appropriated orthodox Christian faith Balthasar can write that never was art more prayerful, nor prayers more formative than in this 'Book of Hours'. Looking back, Rilke compared himself then to a tower whose bell is beginning to ring, likening his poetic creativity to the fermenting of an 'infinite wine for men'. It was not to last, and the reason, thinks Balthasar, is the 'existential contradiction between being the creator and being human'.[54] There is too much Prometheanism, implies Balthasar, in Rilke's project of 'creating' things by 'saying' them. Does the poet have to make the world from the substance of his life? There will be a heavy price to pay: inner rupture between this 'creator' and a human being. Spontaneity and recep-tivity may not so much coalesce as prove mutually subversive, reciprocally destructive. The poet will realize the 'inner shelter' he offers things is too narrow, too alien, owing to the imperfections of love. Guiltily conscious of his own inadequate 'heart-work', Rilke indeed encountered the limits of participation and his poetic capacity to 'make things right'. Possibly, thinks Balthasar, what he met was rather the limit of finitude itself 'which lets no thing arrive at the goal of its idea'.[55] The 'lines which should complete [the

51 *Apokalypse III*, p. 271.
52 Ibid., p. 274.
53 Ibid., p. 276.
54 Ibid., p. 277.
55 Ibid., p. 282.

poet's] picture cannot be projected to their end'.[56] The poet can sing frag-
ments – a stream, a flower, a mirror – but no man is Orpheus enough to sing
the world-rhythm in its entirety. Which is as much as to say we are not God
but at most 'have a part in the great rhythm, the divine creative work'.[57]

If being the absolute poet is impossible, what then is possible, pray?
Balthasar answers, judging from Rilke's example: to be a tragic poet in a way
appropriate to the form of the finite. Rilke grew in humility by accepting a
willed anonymity as the proper poetic stance – an attitude corroborated by
his refusal ever to read anything about his poems or literary status. Rilke
now linked 'distance' to the sublime. Balthasar makes much of one of Rilke's
letters from Muzot, his Swiss retreat in a castle of the Valais, where the poet
speaks of the 'indescribable discretion' which came to define his relation with
God, insinuating that God withdraws the more the closer one comes to him.[58]
'The attributes', wrote Rilke riddlingly, 'become God who is no longer say-
able', and Balthasar is sympathetic enough to find here a 'renewed access to
the full formula of negative theology'.[59]

The painful Parisian period where, poor both literally and figuratively,
Rilke unlearned his earlier more than somewhat hubristic conception of the
poet's task, ended with the realization that the world cannot be 'worked up',
nor 'forms placed before the heavens'.[60] So only *Rühmung*, praising – modified by a sense of the terrible, *Schreckhaftigkeit* – remained. Rilke now realized that *tragedy and completion can be simultaneous*. The transcending of
death (*qua* extinction) in death (*qua* the unilluminated side of life where it
reaches into the infinite), bitter renunciation as ample embrace, the whole set
of mind and heart which made possible the writing in close conjunction of
the *Duino Elegies* and the *Sonnets to Orpheus* – thus lament and praise: what
are we to call this extraordinary combination of attitudes? While recognizing
its closeness to Heidegger's own paradoxes, Balthasar is inclined to answer,
'Tragic Platonism'.[61] The *Elegies* strike time and again the notes of transience
and desire (eros for earth), siting man somewhere between angel and doll,
naming God but once as if to point to God's endless distance from us. But by
writing that to come to love one must take one's distance from the object,
Rilke prompts Balthasar to comment that this single mention shows God is
the true addressee of the *Elegies* at large. The *Sonnets* complement them: these
are poems of transfiguration, longing, beauty, where 'the god' is often named
– a recognition by Rilke, so Balthasar holds, that the poems deal not with 'the
whole God, and yet with something of him'.[62] The term 'complementarity'
does not do justice, however, to the real unity between these two sets of texts.
'The lament of the *Elegies* is praise and comes to its climax in a metaphysic of
acclamatory transformation of the world; the praise of the *Sonnets* is lament
since "only in the room of praising can lament be sung, the nymph of the
wept over source".'[63]

56 Ibid., p. 285.
57 Ibid., p. 286.
58 Cited in ibid., p. 288.
59 Ibid.
60 Ibid., p. 291.
61 Ibid., p. 293.
62 Ibid., p. 294.
63 Ibid., p. 295.

Rilke does not say that death and life are one *simpliciter*. He recognizes, in the spirit of antiquity, the border between them. But the border is opened through 'transcendence and transformation'.[64] This is Rilke's eschatology, and it is filled with the 'Dionysian feeling for the world'.[65] Rilke understood well that this sensibility could not avoid rivalry with its Christian counterpart, to which it stood not shoulder to shoulder but 'eye to eye'. As he wrote to his Polish translator, Witold von Hulewicz, on the meaning of the *Elegies*: the transient forms and their higher significance delineated there must not be taken 'in the Christian sense (from which I more and more passionately withdraw)'.[66] Why 'more and more passionately'? Balthasar's guess is that Rilke sensed the deep incompatibility of his 'definitive affirmation of life and death' with the Christian conviction that there can be no absolute Yes or absolute No to an object which is itself relative, a 'Yes-No', precisely because it is a *creature*.

This brings Balthasar to his final question: Rilke and Christianity, how are they to be inter-related or, at the very least, juxtaposed? For Christ and Dionysus would seem to share a formula which reads: 'life in and through death'. 'Both redeem the world, they do not annihilate it, they transfigure it. And more: both advance upon a final mystery: the self-emptying or rendering self vain of God himself in the vacuity and nothingness of world and time.'[67]

Balthasar calls divine kenosis the 'central event' of Rilke's *Stundenbuch*, his 'Book of Hours'. Rilke portrays the final impotence of God as the locus of both God's 'sweetness' and his 'majesty'. That is why the prayers of this book are such persuasive cantillation. They abstain from all false show, so as to 'kneel before the overwhelming poverty of God'.[68] But what exactly is it in these phrases that Rilke has in mind? Balthasar answers, it is the 'birth and growth of God in the world and its history', which he terms a 'mystical secret' of a comparable depth and truth to the assertion of God's very eternity itself.

Balthasar could point to the patristic evidence for the theme of the 'birth' of the divine–human Christ in believers' hearts. His fellow Jesuit Hugo Rahner (1900–1968) had furnished copious texts on the subject some few years previously.[69] The mediaevals and Baroque spiritual writers played more variations – not least, in the German-speaking world, Angelus Silesius, the 'Cherubinic Wanderer'. But the hetorodox manner in which such notions have been understood in German philosophy has also to be given due weight. For Hegel, for instance, God in himself is insufficiently divine. In the words of one Hegel commentator:

Outside the context of engagement in and with the finite, the divine is not fully realized individuality or self-consciousness ... Actuality has

---

64 Ibid.
65 Ibid., p. 298.
66 Cited in ibid.; I take the translation from Appendix 4, 'The Task of Transformation', in R.M. Rilke, *Duino Elegies*, op. cit., p. 128.
67 *Apokalypse III*, p. 299.
68 Ibid., p. 300.
69 H. Rahner, 'Die Gottesgeburt: die Lehre der Kirchenväter von der Geburt Christi im Herzen des Gläubigen', *Zeitschrift für katholische Theologie* (1935), pp. 333–418.

but a proleptic status on the level of divine immanence and is fully possible only as the term of the complete, and completed, development of the divine infinite in and through the finite. The self-development or self-determination of the divine requires a divine history over and above the metahistory of development on the level of immanence.[70]

Orthodox and heterodox may use the same words, but they will bear very different meanings. To sort out the possible confusion, Balthasar appeals to a court appropriate enough for 'Apocalypse of the German Soul', and this is the understanding of final judgment. From Rilke's depictions of the end, Balthasar can only take away a sense of the 'helplessness of the whole', since how can a God himself in process of becoming allay the anxiety of man, who worries that, in the end, he may miss the goal? Rilke treats the divinity either as a becoming that is not fully being (so how should God guarantee the outcome of creation?) or as a being that engulfs all existence (in which case the world is God's incomplete becoming and the problem recurs). What is this but the 'Dionysian simultaneity of tragedy and fulfilment', and thus the eternalization of ambiguity?[71]

Not surprisingly in these circumstances, Rilkean love is intransitive. It has no object. It neither loves God nor wishes to be loved by him, though it does seek to love as God – which is as much as to say after the fashion of a Titan. This is man willing not to be loved on the ground that he wants to be absolute love and nothing less shall do. To Balthasar this is 'a frightful act of hubris' where the soul consumes its own substance while receiving no nourishment from any 'thou'. Such 'love' would be a living death, the 'grave of the soul'.[72] It is made all the sadder by Rilke's confessions of his own inability to give love in any readily recognizable way. Not that, as Balthasar comments, 'the fusty love of a bourgeois household can be compared with the endless transitivity of the love of God'.[73] Only, thinks Balthasar, at the end of his life – a few days before his death, in fact – did Rilke get a glimpse of the true answer to the prayer of the 'Book of Hours': 'In the end, just make the poor poor again.' (Actually, Rilke's visit to Assisi stimulated an original awareness of what he called 'new poverty'.) Even the 'inner treasure' of love must be offered up in self-stripping if the soul is to give itself over to God. In the Holy Gospels, 'precisely this beoming poor is the immediacy of Christ to the Father on the Mount of Olives'.[74] In humanity's fallen situation there is an altogether desirable *Angst* for whose absence no amount of Rilkean 'praising' can supply.

Yet Balthasar does not want to leave Rilke without gratitude for the gift of symbols through which the poet expressed the 'possible wholeness' of human existence. His friendships with women were parables of that (little did Balthasar know at the time of publishing *Apokalypse* what spiritual friendship with Adrienne von Speyr lay round the corner of the year), as were his encomia of the great abandoned lovers of the past. Yet he also knew the human limitations involved, and so this could be no 'humanly final

70 C. O'Regan, *The Heterodox Hegel*, op. cit., pp. 99, 115.
71 *Apokalypse III*, p. 303.
72 Ibid., p. 304.
73 Ibid., p. 306.
74 Ibid., p. 308.

image'. His flower symbols speak of fulfilment in a 'swaying, weightless love', but this is fulfilment as resignation. Unexpectedly, Rilke's symbolism of blindness takes us further. Balthasar, who had been reading deeply in the works of Origen (c. 185–255), was reminded of the great Alexandrian preacher's teaching on the spiritual senses: sense can be sublimated without rendering us merely sheer spirit. Rilke saw in blind singers what Hölderlin had seen before him: the 'breaking out, all of a sudden, of an inward sun'. But he also saw more than that. It is the combination of such inner illumination with a touching poverty in what concerns this earth's outer show that brings the blind to the 'border of the world'. In the 'Last Poems', this is itself symbolized in night, to which those poems are hymns. These are reminiscences of Novalis, but why sing hymns to night, of all things? Because in night the finite 'I' surrenders to encounter, victorious and definitive, with the however nameless and incomprehensible ultimate 'Thou'. In that context, love cannot be 'intransitive streaming from the heart'.[75] It must come from above.

Recourse to Barth

This entails a real inversion of direction, in fact a *con*version. Concretely, it means Balthasar ends his series of outstanding miniatures with recourse to Karl Barth (1886–1968). The case of Rilke has brought before us the question, what if (our) finite nature is *so* finite that it does not carry within it the preconditions of its own fulfilment? May it be the case that these conditions are not, after all, to hand in a 'world of objective values or ideas' but are to be sought – begged, prayed for – from an 'absolute Freedom'?[76] Perhaps indeed the process of self-realization is inescapably ruptured by discontinuity, and that so deeply, so unbridgeably, that only the freedom of God can throw across a pontoon. When the human is, on all sides, at the end of its tether, there the 'absoluteness of divine freedom' first comes into view. Balthasar's conviction is plain: the deeper the 'de profundis' the higher the 'in excelsis'. This was the only hope, for example, for Stepan Trofimovitch in Dostoevsky's *The Devils*. We cannot assume that dying as such means salvation. There is nothing natural about salvation: God is not part of nature at all. If God exists, he is 'unconfined freedom, self-contentment, unapproachable glory, awesome majesty'.[77] No gradual progress, no humanly measured attainment of norms and laws, can bring us to him. 'If an encounter of man with this absolute freedom comes about, that can only be a radical stilling of the old movement, can only be governed by a wholly new law.'[78]

We cannot *simply* go to God. Direct approach may prove in the end to be distancing. Here Balthasar picks up yet again what is perhaps the main theme of his earliest theological programme in 'The Fathers, the Scholastics and Ourselves'. Any ascent to God not based on his descent to us will probably be self-deification. A bridge must be constructed from God to us, starting on another shore. This is not a higher stage of the human way. It is a

75 Ibid., p. 315.
76 Ibid., p. 317.
77 Ibid., p. 319.
78 Ibid.

break with human ways, and starting again on the way of God. As in that essay, Balthasar does not deny all value to religious humanism. There may be an *element* of graciousness in the 'inclination to Prometheus of the goddess-soul'. Why, even our 'belief in ourselves' can reflect such an element if what we believe in is *ourselves as changed by the grace of God*. But the Serpent's sedulous promise, 'Ye shall be as gods!' rings warning bells.[79] Balthasar goes so far as to say that before God, every voice that speaks of a 'dynamism of exigence' must fall dumb. (This strikes not only at the neo-pagan poets but Blondel and the *nouvelle théologie* men too.) Man is to obey not the call of his own nature, primarily, but the divine gift of faith. Here, Rilke's words, 'And he obeys, inasmuch as he transcends', are true in a wholly new way. What that way is, Balthasar turns to the opening volume of Barth's *Church Dogmatics* to discover. 'Man acts inasmuch as he believes, but that he believes, inasmuch as he acts – that is God's action. Man is the subject of faith. But precisely this, man's being a subject in faith, is bracketed as a predicate of the Subject who is God.'[80] In terms less Barth's and more his own, Balthasar justifies this statement by reference to the extravagant lavishness (*Überschwenglichkeit*) of the revelatory divine action.[81] Here what a Spitteler or a George could call faith is fulfilled through being super-fulfilled. So the law of inversion takes over. Nothing now can be the same again.

In a negative style, Balthasar's reading of Heidegger backs this up. If death is, as Heidegger maintained in *Sein und Zeit*, something more than a biological phenomenon; if it so functions as a boundary for existence that *Dasein* thereby knows itself as more than nature – in fact, as illumined, as spirit; and if in this way existence grasps itself as truth *though only in the manner of* 'an eternal question, an eternal problematic', should we not say that we mortals are less *speaking* than we are *addressed*? We are fundamentally hearers of a word – and in context that can only mean some word of God. Only the word of the Creator can fit the bill, as the word of One who circumscribes both death and existence. That is the explanation of what to Heidegger was inexplicable – 'why death is the *eschaton* of *Dasein*'.[82] Concealed in the Heideggerian understanding of life is a theological a priori: our running towards death and authenticity is a provisional approach to God, our shipwreck in nothingness a shipwreck on God's shore.

So the *Geiststruktur* that Rilke and Heidegger describe – that paradoxical identity of life and death, subjectivity and anonymity, presence in all things and disappearance into all things – must undergo, in this perspective, a corresponding inversion of its own. It must be seen now from the ultimate situation of address by God, where all of these features become hallmarks of creatureliness in its 'aposteriority' and passiveness. Now we know why Nietzsche's ideal man was invisible to him, why Rilke's impossible possibility of the perfect poet was indeed impossible all along. It is God who holds the last word, because he *is* the last word. Balthasar approves Barth's exegesis of Psalm 39.1: 'I laid my hand on my mouth', the mouth of the heart.

In one sense, there are no 'Last Things' for Barth, since God himself is

79 Genesis 3.5
80 K. Barth, *Kirchliche Dogmatik* I/1, (Munich 1932) p. 258.
81 *Apokalypse III*, p. 321, with reference to 1 Corinthians 12.31.
82 Ibid., p. 323.

those 'things' – which, consequently, are not things at all – as Creator, Judge, Redeemer and Reconciler. But in another sense, with the plenary inversion his doctrine represents for our subject, at his hands all theology becomes – rightly, Balthasar considers – eschatology. All theology is teaching about the *eschaton* – or should we write, with the personal adjectival ending, the *Eschatos* – for man, and so the discipline which has hardly had a look in hitherto receives not only a 'co-right to speak' but the decisive voice in Balthasar's search for the 'apocalypse of the soul'.[83] Tracing the odyssey of Protestant eschatology in modern times, from the 'messianic psychology' of liberal biblical scholarship, through the more speculative but still idealistically coloured concept of critical dogmaticians, Balthasar brings out the radicalism of Barth's re-discovery. Barth saw how for the New Testament, and not least, then, its central Figure, final history is quite as significant as ever primordial history could be. The forward frontier of time is also its origin, since all things are grounded proleptically in their end. *Pace* Heidegger, *Dasein* is chiefly historical not insofar as it presses against the border of its own nothingness (that is merely an aspect, which thinking can isolate, of the whole phenomenon), but insofar as it 'receives its frontiers ever anew from authentic Being'.

> Only because God is does the finite receive ever anew its not-being. Only because God is the endless fullness of life can death be a boundary for the finite ... The immanence of death in all finite being only becomes transparent from the standpoint of God's infinite liveliness, where to border yet be distinct is already death.[84]

Touched by the high tension wire of the living God, however, death itself is slain. The 'death of death' is the end of finitude, and so entrance into the sphere of life. In a fashion they could not dream of, Rilke and Heidegger were right.

But now Balthasar has a rather un-Barthian question to put. Is there an 'eros' in the world to which this 'agape' of the prior, descending divine love for man can answer? Is there a 'logos' to the world which unfolds itself in this direction? Evidently, even without the hints dropped in his earliest theological programme in 'Patristik, Scholastik und wir', not to mention the cultural humanism of the youthful essays on music, art and religion, a faithful Catholic theologian like Balthasar would hardly be content with leaving the issue of nature and supernature to one side. In a sense, the 'facts' were not in dispute. Barth could acknowledge all the 'ascending' modes of transcendence which in *Apokalypse der deutschen Seele* the subjects of Balthasar's various literary portraits espoused. Do they amount to a 'dynamic of (natural) existence'? If so, then for Barth that is only because they are the echo of a prior descending revelation. Balthasar wonders if his own 'method' – and content! – in *Apokalypse* has not been hitherto diametrically opposed to Barth's. In this great study has Balthasar not adopted the Scholastic opinion that human intelligence has a 'capacity for all being', and thus the ability, simply on the natural level, to project relative being on to the screen of its absolute source, ground and goal? If so, does he not belong rather in the camp of Barth's celebrated critic Emil Brunner (1889–1966) for whom the

---

83 Ibid., p. 326.
84 Ibid., p. 332.

affirmation in the book of Genesis of man's making to God's image and likeness was a basis for natural theology if not natural mysticism? Balthasar thinks the answer 'less unambiguous' than those remarks make it appear.[85]

In the economy of God, historical man – the only kind of *homo sapiens* we know – has always existed within the *supernatural* order. The eschatological goal of human nature is grace. Factually, which is *not* to say by any kind of necessity, supernature is thus the prime mover of nature. Nature as we in fact know it is embedded in a higher form of being: namely, supernature. Just as in the human being the sensuousness of the body is changed from within through being the dwelling of rational spirit, so too the spirituality of the soul is changed from within by virtue of inhabiting the medium of supernatural grace. This does not prevent that nature which now exists within the graced order from possessing its own functional autonomy – even though such autonomy cannot, without contradiction, be isolated from the wider whole of the natural-supernatural man. Balthasar repeats the point, on which Pope Pius XII's (1876–1958) encyclical *Humani Generis* would focus some few years later: 'this theological a priori in no way cancels out the functional independence of nature'.[86]

Barth's teaching on original sin needs correction here. That sinful man thinks against God does not mean that he fails to think God. Barth draws into the argument an illicit presupposition that created freedom, even when not perverted, and uncreated freedom are somehow competing, at any rate in principle. But this is false. Be the freedom of God and the liberty of the order of grace as sovereign as they may, they will still be 'the innermost freedom even of natural freedom'.[87] This was something which both Hamann and, in less orthodox guise, Hegel understood, and in some manner even Rilke and Fichte surmised. It is the open doctrine of Augustine and Bonaventure, of Nyssa and Aquinas. And here is the answer to Baius – Michel du Bay (1513–1589), the Louvain theologian who claimed God 'had to' engrace his human creature. 'Necessity' is an 'inner-worldly concept', and only an erroneous rationalism gives it a place in the supernatural dealings of God with his creature, in the 'appearing of God's absolute sovereignty'.[88]

And so, to evaluate Barth's own position in these matters, specifically in terms of the key question posed throughout *Apokalypse*'s course. Balthasar will go so far with him as to say that 'Man *de facto*, as alone we know him, is incapable of himself of any final attitude at all, so little is he able to fulfil himself (*sich voll-enden*) without God's revelation. The world as a whole may well have a meaning. Yet, considered in itself, it can have, essentially, no final meaning. The world, factually speaking, is in itself incompletable (*unvollendbar*).'[89] We can certainly consider this one of Balthasar's major conclusions in *Apokalypse der deutschen Seele*, and it is a conclusion that forms a grounding conviction of his mature, post-War, theology.

Of course, the other side of the coin – and this is even more important to recognize – is that God *has* revealed himself and therefore the world *is*

85 Ibid., p. 334.
86 Ibid., p. 336.
87 Ibid., p. 337.
88 Ibid., pp. 337–38.
89 Ibid., p. 339.

'completable'. Balthasar calls this 'the *prius* of God in relation to everything worldly', and it brings in its train a certain discontinuity between the world and the world's last destiny. So far as religion in general is concerned – the religion that is not the religion of the Incarnation, the religion of revelation – only God can say what light if any falls on it from his side, and where and to how great a degree it is spiritual darkness. That is not merely learned ignorance. As Balthasar points out, with acknowledgements to Barth, from the *telos*, the goal of the world – Jesus Christ – we can look back, or around, and find 'images and signs from before him, or even after him'.[90] God's hiddenness, by which in his righteous anger he responds to human sin, is not his last word to the world. Yet the need to examine those 'signs and images' *christologically* shows that no more is the revelatory to be excogitated from the world's side. As Barth puts it in his customary frank fashion, to say we receive the Holy Spirit is to recognize we do not have the Holy Spirit. Balthasar is inclined to be generous to Barth when the latter describes mysticism as 'esoteric atheism' and atheism, for that matter, as 'popular mysticism'. Basically, he thinks, Barth hardly goes further than St Paul in the latter's declaration that God has sealed all under sin so that he might have mercy on all.[91] Moreover, Barth's dictum confirms Balthasar's own conclusion to his discussion of Nietzsche: atheism is the concrete form of a unilaterally negative theology. By the same Barthian token, Balthasar insists that we should resist the temptation to consider the 'paradoxical unity of life and death' theme in Rilke and Heidegger an anthropological, preambular sketch of the christological mystery. From anthropology to Christology there is no passage. Only in the reverse direction is movement possible. The systematic interpretation of the concrete image of man must set out from Christ – and Balthasar claims he did just that by means of his twin tropes – 'Prometheus', 'Dionysus' – even though, in so doing, he did not give divine revelation its proper name. 'Our studies count as a pre-school of conversion.' The lesson they teach is conversion's 'secret beginning'.[92]

Balthasar warns against thinking the Barthian revolution amounts to a personal victory for theological resentment against all that is self-assertively glorious about the world. The highest anthropological values are in no way denied. What is denied is simply that they are a point of attachment – the famous *Anknüpfungspunkt* of the Barth–Brunner debate – for divine revelation. If these amount to a 'capacity for revelation' one might as well ascribe to a drowning man, lifesaved by a strong swimmer, so Barth remarked tartly, a 'capacity for salvation' likewise.

That is not to say Balthasar has no doubts concerning the Barthian position. He wants to revisit the question of how the 'reverse irradiation from the *telos* of Christ on to the world in its totality' should be conceived. He is not convinced Barth has grasped fully the 'relatively independent role of human nature and the world within the *de facto* order of revelation'.[93] But this is a secondary question. On the primary question, that everything should be seen from that revelation's perspective, he is with Barth all the way. In Balthasar's

90 Ibid., p. 340.
91 Romans 11.32.
92 *Apokalypse III*, p. 342.
93 Ibid., p. 345.

own resolution of that 'secondary' (but certainly not negligible) question: the same reality which, seen 'from below', philosophically, one might call the self-transcendence (towards God) of our natural spirit can legitimately also be interpreted theologically, 'from above', as the antecedent donation of the Holy Spirit. Actually, since the period of his commentaries on the Letter to the Romans, Barth's own thought, so Balthasar considered, was moving in this direction too.

Dialectical – Dionysian – Theology

Balthasar distributes Barth's theological career under two headings: 'Dionysian theology' and 'the theology of Christ'. He is not so well-disposed towards the first. He enormously admires the second. Barth's earlier dialectical period he places under the sign of Dionysus owing to its anti-Idealist, Existentialist stamp which – as with Kierkegaard – considers truth available only through an 'infinite movement between two impossible extremes'.[94] For the early Barth, revelation is an impossible possibility. Man can neither do with it nor do without it. And as for God, for him to show himself to man is the same as for him to declare he is wholly other than man. How could such 'communication' be non-dialectically thought? To the eyes of this Barth, to understand religion as a 'worldly possibility' is the *real* 'original sin', it is turning God's address into discourse of my own, using his grace as instrument in my own defence against him. And this is no exceptional incident but the very mode in which the world at large – human culture generally but above all religious culture – now stands to God. *Above all* religious culture, since as Barth put it, 'No human gesture is in itself more questionable, more precarious, more dangerous than the religious gesture.'[95]

In the ambiguity of death, the 'abyss of man's lostness opens up to him, and his boundless inadequacy'. How can new life bloom amid this ruin? 'Salvation' means the resurrection of the dead, whether or not here and now I happen to be alive. The world of the resurrection would be a world where everything I am now, fractured, problematic, suffering (indeed Balthasar goes so far as to say, on Barth's behalf, everything with which I am identical as a subject), is taken from me, and everything with which I am non-identical is given to me. This is the utterly novel 'synthesis' which takes place by anticipation in the grace of faith. Such a shift of identities is another reason for calling this theology 'dialectical'. To live so is to live, in terms St Paul would have recognized, not 'by the flesh' but 'by the Spirit'. This is even now the Parousia, *futurum resurrectionis*, God's eschatological presence in our spirit.

Balthasar considers the view that this is Schelling revivified, the Schelling who in his 'daimonic-Promethean self-salvation in the movement of faith into an infinitely liberating Beyond' took as his formula 'Hell as the basis of Heaven'.[96] But like all Idealists, and despite the seeming difference of standpoint in the later philosophy, Schelling thinks 'upwards', 'from the abyss to the heights'. Barth thinks 'downwards', 'from the eternally existing God'. Barth's dialectical theology is more like an 'existential Platonism',

---

94 Ibid., p. 347.
95 K. Barth, *Der Römerbrief* (Munich 5th edn, 1929), p. 112.
96 *Apokalypse III*, p. 351.

where the concepts of participation and dependence are key, original sin replaces declination from the Idea, and for Platonic *anamnêsis* is substituted the groaning of the creature for the lost glory of the children of God.

Still, there is a Schellingian – and hence Idealist – dimension. Non-identity with the divine – the fall into temporality where *So-sein* and *Da-sein* fail to coincide: that, understood existentially, is for the Barth of *Romans* the curse of our creatureliness, the root of sin. The same dark notes are struck in both 'systems': the pre-temporal fall of the *An-sich* which is creation in God to the *Für-sich* of a cosmos outside him. For Barth, 'existence is being-in-God in that form of identity which Schelling accepted as between God and the arche-types'.[97] To know God 'face to face' is not, for *this* Barth to know analogously as I am known but to know self-identically with God. And meanwhile the shadow of the abyss, and therefore sin and Hell, is only graciously covered up, not removed: when God creates, positing things outside himself, he must in a sense produce Hell, albeit a Hell in which his grace can take effect. What saves Barth from Idealism is his insistence that the judgment of grace is not in 'the eternally-simultaneous moment' but, rather, in 'eschatological history', the history of God's descending grace.[98] Even so, there remains a doubt as to whether Barth simply 'believes' what Schelling 'sees'.

It may strike readers of the later Balthasar (and his critics) as curious that a major sticking point here is Barth's notion of the 'irreversibility' of God's gracious election of man. Has Barth not heard the Christ speak 'in infinite affliction of the eternal darkness [of the lost]'?[99] We can remember that, on any responsible version of his mature thought, Hell plays a notable part in Balthasarianism: the Hell of Christ's descent, the – at any rate finite and possibly infinite – Hell to which the damned after Christ go, and the defi-nitely unending Hell where their sins are 'deposited' in utter distance from God. But really, for the Barth of the dialectical theology, the Hell that eschatological grace abolishes is the world in its 'irredeemable ambiguity'.[100] Barth accepts from the magisterial Reformers assurance of salvation, but not – far from it! – double predestination. From his Catholic standpoint, Bal-thasar considers this a view of faith which finds no room for hope; it is faith as prematurely anticipated Heaven. By contrast, Barth's reworking of the doctrine of predestination in a christological mode – it is Jesus Christ who is supremely the Elect One, the rest of us only in our relation to him – Balthasar gratefully accepts. That gives yet another twist to the concept of theological 'dialectics' – and one which will remain with Barth, as first the 1936 study 'God's Gracious Choice', part of the series *Theologische Existenz heute*, and subsequently the later volumes of the *Church Dogmatics* will show.

To Balthasar's mind, the Barth of the dialectical theology was still too indebted not only to the Idealist tradition but, in its wake, to non-dogmatic forms of Protestant theology, and notably to Wilhelm Herrmann (1846–1922), who had sought to make the act of faith a sheer experience of createdness and freedom for God, with no mixture of objectivity of truth-claim that could bring it into confict with science or scholarship. Balthasar finds the early

97 Ibid., p. 355.
98 Ibid., p. 356.
99 Ibid., p. 357.
100 Ibid., p. 359.

Barth a similar exponent of a theology of experience, who pushes the heights and depths of religious experience to an infernal extreme in order that the whole might be an experience of the 'dark madness of grace'.[101] By asserting that grace has no affinity with special 'experiences', using here one rather narrowly defined German term, *Erlebnis*, Barth hopes no one will notice he is still working with 'experience' in the sense of a much broader German term, *Erfahrung*. Balthasar would take the opposite tack. He advises Barth to leave behind definitively the experiential *starting-point* of Herrmann's theology and yet admit, when practising the theological discernment of the Christian life in its *progression*, the possibility of signs or symptoms of the working of grace in discrete experiences, as did the founder of Balthasar's Order, St Ignatius Loyola, in his *Spiritual Exercises*.

As it is, the early Barth's teaching remains under the banner of Dionysus, since the eschatology it offers 'is not redemption from this world but virtually a transfiguration of its painful ecstasy'.[102] Considered as Christian thought, only the 'majestic Barthian concept of God' saves it from collapse. It is proof that Idealism means not just the secularization of the Reformation but, on occasion at least, the midwife that helped it to better understanding. The dialectical Barth is the 'self-understanding of Luther in the mirror of Schelling', seeking as Schelling had, to construct a 'philosophy of the mystery of love in being' which would lead back to Luther. And Balthasar's question is:

> Whether this dialectic really corresponds to the law of inversion which would give God honour and freedom, and make depend all inner-worldly necessity on the unique 'necessity' of God's disposing and measuring, or whether the creature, its problematic, its fragmentedness, are not themselves transposed Prometheus-like into the heavens – whether a Christian 'confidence' which time and again employs the accents of 'identity' is really still *Christian* confidence at all.[103]

Indeed, Barth himself has given his own answer.

Barth's Mature Thought – the 'Theology of Christ'
So we come to Barth's second theological period, as Balthasar would assess it, the time of 'the theology of Christ'. In the writing of the *Church Dogmatics* it did not take Barth long to warn against certain of his own earlier comments on the 'tragic' character of the God-world relationship in *Romans*.[104] What blew out of the water Barth's earlier ocean-going construction, with its – as Balthasar would see it – 'abstract dialectic' and view of the eschaton from the side of 'the human being and the Dionysian tension of his fate', was, quite simply, Barth's discovery of the real Jesus Christ, the God–man, as Chalcedon permits us to describe him, in his objective, historical facticity.[105] From 1929 onwards, Barth's subjective preoccupation with human 'nothingness' is more and more displaced by objective concern with the kenosis of God in Jesus Christ.

---

101 Ibid., p. 362.
102 Ibid., p. 364.
103 Ibid., p. 365.
104 Notably at K. Barth, *Kirchliche Dogmatik* I/2 (Zollikon–Zurich 1938), p. 55.
105 *Apokalypse III*, p. 366.

The Creed, so Barth realized, does not find it necessary to expatiate on sin and death before confessing the saving work of Christ. And the reason is that light falls from Christ on to these negative realities, rather than the other way round. His self-emptying is the primary mirror in which we can see our emptiness for what it is for the first time. In this way, the *Ecce homo* gives us the 'true apocalyptic image of our soul'.[106] The kenosis, which first reveals the abyss in which we stand, also closes it. Of course sin is separation from God. But only God can measure what that means. The Saviour's cry from the Cross, 'My God, my God, why hast thou forsaken me?', is the measure involved. Thus the importance of that text from St Mark's Gospel[107] which would mean so much later to Balthasar and his mystical co-worker Adrienne von Speyr, was first drawn to his attention by the Barth of the *Church Dogmatics*.[108] It can hardly go without comment that Barth links to it not only the Passion and Death but also the Descent into Hell. Meanwhile, the 'law of inversion' invites us to find ourselves in him: 'For he shows us ourselves, as we are, and at the same time lifts us up above everything that in ourselves we are.'[109] Human destiny is in an altogether novel way taken up into God's act. All talk of dialectics, tangents, diacritical points is now swept aside as mere 'Kierkegaardianism'. No human experience can be decisive here, nor even a privileged locus. God's action embraces all human possibilities alike, and in a strange way the attempts of such modern writers as Bergson and Klages, Nietzsche and Scheler, Heidegger and Rilke, to overcome the rationalism and spiritualism of the ancient philosophy of spirit, are found to be justified thereby. The baptism of an infant without reason or sensibility could have no meaning for the Barth of *Romans*. But now all is changed, since are we not all children of Adam for whom Christ died? The divine action touches as much bodies as souls – here we have a clue to Balthasar's pronounced interest in the objective, sacramental physicality of God's way of salvation and his looking for inspiration, along those lines, to that great patristic hammer of the Gnostics, St Irenaeus of Lyons. What is distinctive of Balthasar's own thought, even at the early date of these remarks on the later Barth, is the twofold conviction that, first, the ground of that 'sacramental structure' is the kenosis of Christ, and, secondly, that this 'sacramental event of salvation' brings about an immanence of the divine in human subjectivity. Balthasar will be a theologian, after all, of the mystical life, and not merely of the social rituals of the Church.

So the conclusion of his essay on Barth in *Apokalypse der deutschen Seele* sums up in advance much that is to come.

First of all: faith is essentially faith in the divine Flesh-taking. It is God's self-disclosure in a worldly form – a *Gestalt*: thus the key term of the theological aesthetics takes a first bow on the stage.[110] The true faith is always sacramental faith: it is faith in the divine presence and saving action in a worldly sign – Christ, the Church, and the sacraments in the narrower sense.

But secondly, the sacramental 'space' of the visible Church is itself

---

106 Ibid.
107 Mark 15.34
108 Ibid., p. 367, with reference to K. Barth, *Kirchliche Dogmatik* I/1, op. cit., pp. 80–81.
109 *Apokalypse III*, p. 368.
110 Ibid., p. 370.

conditioned by the 'structure' of divine action in Christ. Just as Jesus had no
hypostasis – no personalizing centre – save that of God the Word, so from her
innermost being the Church is forbidden to act vis-à-vis Jesus Christ in a
freedom of her own. The Lord's humanity was expropriated into the service
of God, just as the Church's corporate subjectivity must be in the service of
her Head – which means, above all, a *kenotic* Head. On the Cross, with the cry
of anguish from the Son to the Father, when God seems most incomprehensible – seems in quite appalling fashion, in fact, the 'hidden God' of Job
and the Psalms of David, the Father actually gave his final 'Yes' to human
salvation, thus revealing his ultimate Glory, which is his groundless Love.
The Resurrection of the Lord does not reverse the Passion, where the Flesh-
taking came to its climax. The Resurrection makes the Passion transparently
visible for what it is. Here we have *in nuce* so much of Balthasar's essay on
the Easter Triduum, *Mysterium Paschale*,[111] and the closing, New Testament
volume of *Herrlichkeit*: well-titled in English *The Glory of the Lord*.[112]

Though philosophy can never do this justice – another theme of Balthasar's 'Theology of the Three Days' – one can see in this radiant light embers
of truth glow in the writers Balthasar has discussed in this phenomenal
survey. Such as: Schelling's insight that the greatest distance from God and
the greatest intimacy with him may be closer neighbours than we think; or
Hegel's conviction that in the suffering of the Son God's greatest 'seriousness' makes its appearance; and even Heidegger's identification of the
Absolute with the most utterly finite. But none of these thinkers can
encompass the real. None knows the Christ of orthodoxy, in whom alone is
the *eschaton* realized. As Balthasar's later 'theological logic' will maintain,
reading the world-compass aright can only be done from a christological
central point.

Then thirdly, this 'objective vision of the saving history' must be subjectively appropriated, made our own. And here it is to our vast advantage
that our freedom need meet no *conditions to encounter* the divine descent; it
can be and is defencelessly open to God. At the same time – and here a
metaphysic suited to the scriptural revelation cannot be avoided, God's
effortless pre-eminence over all creation makes possible his own immanence
in finite being – even if the extraordinary extent of this immanence is made
known only in Christ. The greeting of these two freedoms, and their co-
operation, does not amount to the 'works righteousness' so dreaded by
Luther. On the contrary, this is grace in its purest form (Balthasar will later
call it 'nuptial'). Here Barth learned well an Augustinian-Thomist lesson:
God's freedom dwells, energizing, in our own. (Balthasar is surprised that
Barth could not see the application to the Mariology of the Church.)

'From dialectic to sacrament': for Balthasar, that phrase sums up Barth's
journey.[113] Unfortunately, it was not quite followed through to the end.
Balthasar notes for future reference – and his massive post-War book on
Barth will explore this[114] – two themes in particular dear to Catholic divinity

---

111 H.U. von Balthasar, *Mysterium Paschale. The Mystery of Easter* (ET Edinburgh 1990).
112 Idem., *The Glory of the Lord. VII. Theology: The New Covenant* (ET Edinburgh and San
    Francisco 1989).
113 *Apokalypse III*, p. 379.
114 H.U. von Balthasar, *The Theology of Karl Barth. Exposition and Interpretation* (ET San
    Francisco 1991).

where justice is not yet done. The 'obediential potency' of nature to grace and the 'analogy of being': these concepts, Balthasar believes, are increasingly presupposed and even expressed in Barth's work, despite the continued way Barth polemicizes against Catholicism on their account. Such notions of how all nature is *disponible* in relation to grace, all finite being in communion – albeit in a dissimilarity more striking than the similarity – with its Creator, are needed by Barth for a consistently sacramental theology which takes as its axis the union of divinity and humanity in Jesus Christ. The action of God cannot be sundered from the being and disposition of its instruments. Only relics of his erstwhile dialecticism prevent Barth from seeing this patent fact.

Barth rediscovered the sovereignty of God. For those readers of Balthasar who have listened with him to voices from Lessing to Heidegger, Barth can be the herald of God's Word in a fashion calculated to strike as well as seduce. Balthasar's admiration and even love urge him on where he thinks Barth fails us. Is Barth not *restricting* the freedom of God when he denies it can be 'possessed', even (asks Balthasar) in an 'authentic, loving resting in self-surrender', in 'living away from self'?[115] Is Barth not *reducing* the force of revelation when, influenced perhaps by the Expressionism of Nietzsche's last disciples, he takes the imagistic dimension of the saving economy to be as much the sign of God's absence as of his presence (since between interiority and expression a great gulf is fixed)? Both mistakes conspire in an ecclesiology which too often resembles Scheler's acosmic community of spirits for its own good. Even in so central a topic of his dogmatics as the theology of time, too exclusive a contrast between sinful time and God's time suggests that, so long after the commentaries on the Letter to the Romans, Barth's world is still in danger of 'breaking apart into God and Counter-God'.[116] Yet rightly, Balthasar ends on a positive note. Significantly, it concerns apocatastasis and the hope for universal salvation. Though we have no access to the subjectivity of grace other than through Christ and the objectivity of his revelation, nevertheless the kingdom of God's love, which has now taken root in the nature of man in Jesus Christ, surely extends beyond all visible bounds. That is not the worst *entrée* to the final topic of *Apokalypse*: revelation's parables in the extra-revelatory world.

115 Ibid., p. 387.
116 Ibid., p. 390.

11

❦

Myth, Utopia, Kairos

In *Apokalypse der deutschen Seele* Balthasar has brought before us a parade of figures representing different styles of would-be transcendence. He briefly recapitulates what he regards as the two complementary series which bring us most immediately to his conclusion. The first of these series moves from 'life' to 'spirit'. Starting out from Bergson's sheer 'life', we encountered an 'unfriendly border', the *Geist* of Klages. Various attempts at compromise among the poets of 'life' lead to the insight that between life and intelligence a positive tension reigns. To begin with, the accent lies on the worldly aspect of spirited understanding but in the 'wrestling match' between Nietzsche and Dostoevsky the supra-worldly, religious aspect comes to the fore. In its course we realize that a 'No!' to life can also be a higher 'Yes!' Thus the first series issues in an awareness of the *judgment* to be passed on mind or spirit.

In the second series, the movement is, rather, from 'spirit' to 'life'. In Scheler *Geist* is 'divinized', but in such a fashion as to be isolated and emptied of power, as spirit and life fall tragically apart. Heidegger 'takes up the consequent impotence and turns it on its head', calling nothingness positive, and identifying time with spirit and finitude with inwardness. Now Rilke is needed to free the description of human life from so cramped a condition. Giving great space in this regard to 'praise', *Rühmung*, he actually finds 'night' to be his 'last word', the best formula for 'throwing open the crucial seal of spirit's createdness'.[1] Barth's achievement is to see in all this the theological a priori at work. Neither life nor spirit are absolute. Indeed, their tension is the sign of their relativity. Finite existence will not reach its own truth, its *eschaton*, until it grasps itself as addressed by God. *Boundaries* are not to be feared, as with Klages, for here above all is the locus of the truth of *Dasein*. 'As Kant, Goethe and Heidegger in different ways realised, existence is ec-centric. It is at this decisive frontier that history is fulfilled.'[2]

Balthasar notes something interesting. The 'life' series runs from a (rather naïvely evolutionistic) concept of history to a concentration on an inner moment – even, in Nietzsche and Dostoevsky in their religious moods, *over against* a sense of the future meaning of the world. The 'spirit' series runs in the opposite direction: from a concentration on the inner moment to a

---

1 *Apokalypse III*, p. 392.
2 Ibid.

rediscovery of the importance of time in the (Heideggerian) 'deeper, more spiritual idea of the historical'.[3] But the decisive frontier Barth has in mind is 'even more primordially the source of all history'. The line of inner history and the line of outer history do not coincide but they must, surely, converge in that life and spirit are not separate realities in man and so must ultimately have one single destiny. 'If Barth's theological a priori is thought through to the end, if God in his kenosis really becomes man (and does not just address man from an unreachable other shore), then this alone is where definitive history happens, at this decisive point of encounter.'[4]

What Balthasar has traced in the history of mentalities in the period he studied was the way that, at the end of Idealism, and the beginning of *Lebensphilosophie*, the destinies of the individual on the one hand, corporate humanity on the other, fell apart. Here at last this disjunction can be overborne as outer, evolutionary history and inner spiritual history come together in the 'midpoint' of the divine–human history of God incarnate. Clearly enough, Balthasar's own later theology of history – both in the book of that title and in his essay collection *Man in History* – take their origins from this discovery.[5] Now in one sense, this is a rediscovery of the unitary eschatology of the Middle Ages. But in another sense the 'final eschatological attitude of present-day man' has – or can have – a 'richness and tension' unknown in the (patristic or) mediaeval period, owing precisely to the turbulent succession of modern philosophers and poets with something to say on the matter whose *periplus* – this was no straightforward voyage – Balthasar has charted.

Myth

Balthasar wants to consider this 'midpoint' in three perspectives, indicated by the three constitutent words of this chapter's title: 'myth', 'Utopia', 'kairos'. Like a number of theologians, however ill-advisedly, Balthasar wants to reclaim the word 'myth' – or perhaps, to avoid some, at least, of the negative connotations of the English term, we should use the form 'mythos' – for an orthodox purpose. Balthasar wants to use it for the 'final form of finite truth' where finitude, sensuousness and historical temporality come together. By 'Utopia' he means the human perspective that looks from the here and now towards an historical horizon farther than that of evolutionism or any sort of sociological projection. The more such a perspective is aware of the theological a priori the better it will understand its own task of pointing to history's 'absolute' bounds. Finally, 'kairos' – the term is taken from the New Testament Greek for a (key) moment – 'takes the midpoint in possession', making its own the descending history of God and the ascending history of man that, by his grace, rises to meet him. At that 'kairos', revelation and Utopia meet.

'Myth', then, ought to signify a unique form of creaturely truth, though only too often what it means in actual usage is well-placed doubt about it. Even in Nietzsche, who sought to rehabilitate it, it can have that overtone,

---

3 Ibid., p. 393.
4 Ibid.
5 H.U. von Balthasar, *A Theology of History* (ET New York and London 1963); idem. *Man in History* (ET London and Sydney 1967).

though with Scheler, Heidegger, Rilke and, especially Karl Jaspers, the phenomenalism which affected Nietzsche's thinking is gradually eliminated until in Jaspers we are dealing with a real 'synthesis of philosophical-mythical thought'.[6] For Balthasar what this means in great part is the over-coming of Cartesianism, whose exclusive preference for clear and distinct ideas could hardly coinhabit with mythopoeic expressions of truth. Super-natural revelation does not abrogate mythopoeic truth. It fulfils it. (This will be the theme of much of the volume of Balthasar's theological aesthetics that deals with the 'metaphysics of antiquity'.[7]) This is only what we might expect if supernature appeared to us – as in Christ it did – in the form of kenosis: that is, a divine sanctioning of finitude as such. For Hegel, such religious, mythopoeic thinking needs to be 'overcome' in pure philosophy. But the Christian, Balthasar responds, knows that, on the contrary, it is to be guarded as the definitive access to the truth, an access rendered eternally valid in the God–man. But of course, such custodianship, precisely by the way it privi-leges not only the infinite but also the finite pole of truth, must concern itself with the latter's dimensions of 'nothingness' and 'seemingness'. In an almost untranslatable passage: 'The eternalisation of the space of mythical truth is at the same time the eternalisation of the empty space that reduces to nothing, inasmuch as, considered as seeming, this space is shot through by the eternal appearing of God – just insofar as it is the inconspicuous place of the infinite epiphany of the Infinite.'[8] The beauty of Barth is that he saw how this was so.

Not that Balthasar wishes entirely to underwrite Barth's ontology, his account of the mystery of being, which is too inclined to make the divine apocalypse not so much the fulfilment of the finite as its cancellation. That could have unpleasant implications for Barth's story of the mystery of love, rendering it a 'tragic-heroic struggle with a self-enclosing existentiality'. Surely the transfigured flesh is to *travel* to heaven – not be forcibly removed there like Ganymede! In working out what Balthasar terms an 'historical ontology' we should try to do better than this, for 'the mystery of being is the kernel of primordial history'.[9] Rejecting the traditional metaphysical patri-mony, nineteenth- and early twentieth-century European thinkers have wandered between undesirable watering-places – monism, 'limitless plur-alism', and – most frequented, if also, after the century's turn, most rejected – historicism. The desire to hold together in some way, as yet unrealized, eternal 'value' and finite 'appearance' prepared the way for a profounder concept of the historical and so – this is the implication – for a recovery of the mythic. (So with Nietzsche, for example, applying to the historical process the twin mythopoeic concepts of 'the moment' and 'the eternal return' is meant to bring out the essence of what it is that process constantly carries.) Historicism – the merely empirical understanding of historical process in naïve objectivity – is, at least in certain quarters,[10] 'interiorized' so that a new concept of history can step forth. History may be a polymorph but it must also be *thought as a whole* – which is why the call for a new mythic

6 *Apokalypse III*, p. 395.
7 H.U. von Balthasar, *The Glory of the Lord IV. The Realm of Metaphysics in Antiquity* (ET Edinburgh and San Francisco 1989).
8 *Apokalypse III*, p. 395.
9 Ibid., p. 396.
10 Balthasar mentions in this connexion Dilthey, Rickert, Troeltsch, Wobbermin, Scheler.

interpretation of history by the school of Stefan George is justified. Of course, despite George's flight from the Third Reich to Switzerland (in part, to avoid embarrassing compromise with the Party and State), some commentators might find the valid outcome of those aspirations in the Fascist view of history. For his part, Balthasar finds it in Barth.

Here the in-depth categories needed are not merely applied to life, as with Nietzsche, nor even, as with Heidegger, to that *Dasein* of which it can be said that 'nothing' truly 'happens'. In Barth finite existence attains to the status of myth because Barth is concerned with *what God makes of the empty question of man*. The question is existential, the God who would answer it – in one of Barth's favourite names for the divinity – *Concretissimum*, the 'Most Concrete', so here we have, most concretely, divine entry into the human question. We have it, in fact, in Christ through whom 'the Christian philosophy of history reaches a universal-mythical historical understanding'.[11] In that understanding – where the two chief approaches to the historical Balthasar traced with Herder's assistance in the opening chapters of *Apokalypse* come together – the richness of the concept of myth in its inner dimensions unfolds. Axiologically, the 'moment' when God and man meet is truly a world-historical event, for the Source of history can make itself transparent, in the midst of history, in a sign. And this means that teleologically, the divine–human Eschaton holds the pivotal place in 'world apocalypse' too: the long but – we can now say, with assurance – goal-directed process of world history as a whole. That must include the history of nature, of peoples, of culture, as Herder included them. Catholicizing Barth, Balthasar declares that, since grace surrounds all nature open to spirit, grace 'really becomes world-historical truth', not least in that place whence human beings have their roots – community.[12] And that means the Church as the motherly mediatrix of the mystical union of human beings in the mystery of their single destiny.

Utopia

What, then, of 'Utopia', the far future of the race? When one adds together the ideas of creation and community in the context of End-directed thinking, not the least likely residue of the process is Socialism. Socialist ideology, pressed far enough, becomes a pursuit of transcendence of a utopian kind. Marxism, by attempting to use the tools of this world to smash through the kingdom of the world to a novel kingdom of freedom (there is a rather remarkable formal resemblance there to Barth's early project), is not only eschatological but (hopelessly!) Utopian as well. With Eduard Bernstein (1850–1932) and the Marxian revisionists there begins the demythologization of the Socialist vision, the fight for a non-'catastrophic' version of social change. The 'pathos of a profane eschatology' yields pride of place to the revolution of technology. Utopian thinking now moves elsewhere, to Scheler who claimed to foresee the dying out of capitalistic man as blood starts to speak louder than gold, an antithesis which in *Von kommenden Dingen* Walter

11 *Apokalypse III*, p. 403.
12 Ibid., p. 404.

Rathenau (1867–1922) raised to the level of *Lebensphilosophie* in his appeal to 'the way of the will'.[13] Immediately after the First World War Utopian writers in Germany sought 'a this-worldly paradise' by sheer future-oriented inspiration, eschewing science and scholarship as essentially 'retrospective'. As the lyric poet and essayist Ludwig Rubiner (1881–1920) declared, 'Everything that has been is false', and 'We are doing everything for the first time.'[14] Here the goal, comments Balthasar, is 'an ever purer self-creation' to which matter is an obstacle – hence Rubiner's description of it as 'original sin'.[15] In the Marxist tradition of materialism, however dialectical – as with Lev Trotsky (1879–1940), whom Balthasar also cites – that would hardly be said. But then the 'real [read "material"] paradise' Trotsky sought requires at any rate a 'sketch of an apocalypse', and how is that to be forthcoming? It means, as with the unplaceable Russian thinker Nikolay Fedorov (1828–1903) the unmaking of death. For Fedorov the resurrection of the dead is an accessory tool in the 'physical-chemical-physiological methods' to be used for this outcome.[16] Balthasar also has to consider the spate of 'practical-political' revisionings of civil life which early twentieth-century novelists offered, by way of continuing Enlightenment-type Utopian thinking. While in England, as he notes, that would importantly include H.G. Wells (1866–1946), in Germany these were writers broadly of the Expressionist school, and all of them in one way or another had to face the fact that a trans-mundane world is hardly portrayable in terms of nature. That is why they constantly rub shoulders with irrationality, which in Fedorov's case means a secularized transcendent miracle.

Socialistic and Utopian elements are combined in Ernst Bloch's *Geist der Utopie* of whose hostility to being (over against value) Balthasar speaks severely as 'the enchanted memory of an evil dream'.[17] The answer to Bloch's dystopian projections Balthasar finds in Joseph Winckler's 1921 story 'The Chiliastic Pilgrimage' where, with increasingly disastrous effects, a king gathers the suffering millions in a pilgrimage to all quarters of the earth until in the icy conditions of the Arctic night all that remains of Paradise is 'Utopian will'.[18] The king lets them go home, each to build a paradise with the knowledge gained of what 'man' betokens. But the *Novelle*'s conclusion reminds Balthasar too sharply of Voltaire's (1694–1778) in *Candide* – 'we must cultivate our garden' – which for a theologian of the *eschaton* will scarcely suffice. Is it possible to renew Utopian thinking without falling into Bloch's (and others') fatal disassociation of 'I' and world? Perhaps it depends who the 'I' is whose self-realization is sought. In George Lukács' (1885–1971) *Geschichte und Klassenbewusstsein*, the 'I', as befits a Marxian literary critic, is that of man's social consciousness which finds its fulfilment through class consciousness, notably proletarian, in history, the ultimate point being the transformation of the world.[19] Consciousness that fails to discern this objective has undergone self-alienation and fallen into the 'fetishism' of

13 W. Rathenau, *Von kommenden Dingen* (Berlin 1915).
14 L. Rubiner, *Der Mensch in der Mitte* (Potsdam 2nd edn, 1920), pp. 85, 151.
15 *Apokalypse III*, p. 409.
16 Ibid., p. 410.
17 Ibid., p. 413, with reference to E. Bloch, *Geist der Utopie* (Berlin 1923, 2nd edn, 1923).
18 *Apokalypse III*, p. 414, with reference to J. Winckler, *Chiliastische Pilgerzug* (Berlin 1921).
19 G. Lukács, *Geschichte und Klassenbewusstsein* (Berlin 1922).

hypostatizing 'things'. But though the bourgeoisie are for Lukács the chief culprits, and Socialist revisionists hardly fare better at his hands, he finds himself forced to substitute for the empirical consciousness of the proletariat an ideal awareness of his own, Marx-inspired, construction. For Balthasar, this is a poor basis on which to posit the possibility of a 'capacity to be whole'. Here too empiricism and Utopianism, being and value, remain sadly apart.

Despite the many pitfalls, the final intentions of Utopian thinking become decipherable – and realistic – in Christianity, by which Balthasar means not a Christianity that has become naturalistic or positivistic but one with a *Wunder*, both 'marvel' and 'miracle', to set against the pagan Utopias' own. Balthasar thinks of Vasily Rozanov's (1856–1919) statement of a passionately anti-ascetic and this-worldly thesis in 'Apocalypse of our Time'. There the veneration for earth in Soloviev and (to a more marked degree, Dostoevsky) is taken all the way, and, by a reversal of Marcionite dualism, the Father-Creator of the Old Testament is preferred to the Redeemer-Son of the New. 'Preferred' is putting it mildly, for in Rozanov's apocalypse, mankind is to be made new as the 'ghost of the Christ-shadow perishes'.[20] But Rozanov knows that all is in vain. 'What would the earth have become without the Church?' Without the dark 'counter-sun' he cannot live: he cannot live without the Christ who 'reveals himself only to tears'.[21] Though Rozanov appears to haver, he recognizes the religious meaning of Utopian contradiction. In other words, he 'uncovered the theological a priori in Utopian Socialism', something that, Balthasar thinks, could have happened only in Russia, the 'country of classic Utopia'. This paved the way for the scholarly treatment of the same theme in Karl Mannheim's study 'Ideology and Utopia', which explicitly traced the Utopian schemes and thinking of the modern West, including that of Marx, to Christian roots.[22] But the negative judgment on Russian Utopianism is also a like judgment on Russian Christianity. When, in the steps of Ivan Karamazov, Rozanov calls the Russian monastery a perfect integral Christendom his meaning is ironic, since it is the Russian village that feeds the monk as everyone else. The contribution of Utopian Socialism is its 'eternal claim of right' against a church that has turned away from the world. Humanity by its nature is one, and it is in this unity that it has been redeemed and glorified. Thus speaks Balthasar, disciple in such matters of Henri de Lubac (1896–1991). But he also adds: 'And where Socialism places itself in the wrong is where it fails to understand that the freedom of man coursing toward its realisation is sustained by a divine Freedom – and where too it does not grasp that the "emptiness" Christ brings is no alien transcendence but the emptiness of nature itself which in the dying of God is filled to the brink.'[23]

Which brings him neatly to his last topic, 'kairos'.

20 *Apokalypse III*, p. 419.
21 Cited in ibid.
22 K. Mannheim, *Ideologie und Utopie* (Bonn 1929)
23 *Apokalypse III*, p. 422.

Kairos

What Balthasar would learn from Socialism (though in fact had caught from de Lubac) is that 'humanity is as a whole so very much a unity that even its temporal development cannot be a matter of indifference to noumenal history'. That could also be put more theologically, from the standpoint of revelation, something he now proceeds to do.

> The dynamism immanent in humanity and conditioning its evolution is no longer adequately separable from the supernatural dynamism furnished by the self-revealing God, and that very much holds true where the history of humanity is in process of becoming the history of the mystical body of the incarnate God.[24]

There can be, and often is, too crude a dividing line drawn between 'authentic', 'divine', 'eschatological' or 'primordial' history on the one hand, and 'vulgar history' on the other. To consider, as any account of 'kairos' must do, the 'meeting point of the great lines of the world', is inevitably to encounter the issue of the 'mystery of iniquity' whose presence and activity Balthasar's investigations of the issues at stake between Nietzsche and Dostoevsky revealed. If there is to be talk of a conjunction of Dionysus, as the immanent God, with Christ as the appearing of the transcendent God, let it be understood that in Dionysus lies hidden the *mysterium iniquitatis* too often misinterpreted as divine immanence. With its emphasis on free creativity, Socialistic eschatology may in fact be aiming at the Antichrist, replacing the God-man with the Man-god.

In this context, Balthasar takes from the Evangelical Lutheran theologian Paul Tillich (1886–1965) the thought that the idea of kairos, in its developed form, is born of debate with Utopians.[25] 'Kairos' means the possibility of understanding some 'moment' in the perspective of the Absolute and thus being able to turn it, even in its fracturedness, towards the Eternal. The French Jesuit spiritual theologian Jean-Pierre de Caussade (1675–1751) had called that, long before Tillich, 'the sacrament of the present moment'. But Tillich, reacting against the excessive negativities of the early Barth, had added an important nuance which Balthasar finds useful. To see something as a kairos does not mean having to subvert it in its natural metaphysical character – as what Balthasar calls a 'form-content relation'. Kairos does not exclude logos. Natural knowledge remains valid, though when placed before the Absolute by kairos-thinking a question arises about its further significance. All Christian thinking entails both logos and kairos, or, if one prefers, truth and decision. This discovery would be of some importance for his attempt to conjoin ancient, mediaeval and distinctively modern attitudes towards truth in the opening volume of his theological logic, 'Truth. The Truth of the World', his next major publishing project after *Apokalypse* was safely completed.[26] It helps to show how that largely philosophical first volume is in fact and from the start oriented towards its theological

24 Ibid.
25 P. Tillich, *Kairos und Logos* (Darmstadt 1926).
26 H.U. von Balthasar, *Wahrheit. Wahrheit der Welt*, op. cit.

successors 'Truth of God' and 'Truth of the Spirit'.[27] Balthasar emphasizes that this is not meant to call into question the objectivity of knowledge. If the act of knowing were to become questionable, there would be no stable sands on which decision could build. What is called into question by the 'decision character' kairos lends to logos is not the possibility of objectivity but the temptation of thinking to become an absolute, a law unto itself. Appropriately to the title of the present study of the early Balthasar, theological student of philosophy and the arts, he declares: 'Kairos as decision is creative, it is the abiding openness of time for the eternal seed.'[28]

But if creative decision is integral to the kairos, then when decision goes awry what we find in such 'moments' is 'Luciferian counter-spirit, demonry', not freedom under grace. That can most readily happen when the immanent is turned into a false transcendent. This is why Balthasar does not support a tendency he discerns in Tillich to absolutize the creaturely in those 'moments'. Certainly, there must be some sort of unification of, on the one hand, the Barthian idea of a 'crisis' finding 'axiological' application at every moment with, on the other hand, the 'Greek' (presumably, New Testament) notion of a 'right time' and indeed 'fullness of time'. Tillich's way of achieving this unification is – for lack, presumably, of a metaphysic and fundamental theology adequate to the task – scarcely more than magic. Might the Russian Orthodox thinker Nikolay Berdyaev (1874–1948), who also makes use of the concept of *kairos*, do any better?

Compared with Tillich, so it turns out, more contextualization is needed. Balthasar approaches Berdyaev via the latter's root metaphysical concept – that of freedom whose prominence in his corpus is surely owed to his reading of Schelling. *Urgeschichte*, primordial history, is an act of freedom on the part both of God and of man. For Berdyaev, nature lies essentially open to the 'sphere of freedom' which at its innermost core is also creativity. Berdyaev's freedom is unique: above the distinction of subject and object, beyond the grasp of categories metaphysical or theological, it can only be experienced in a 'mystical touch'. Balthasar calls it *Liebes-Leben*, 'love's life', and with a reference to the pre-Socratic philosophers of ancient Greece, considers it a new Heracliteanism. Creating is its give-away sign. For Berdyaev the key couplet in Christian analysis is not nature vis-à-vis supernature but nature (body and soul) vis-à-vis spirit which for him means personality. Personhood means participation in mystical communion, the ultimate ground of which is the Eternal Humanity of the (pre-incarnate) Logos. A community in origin is reflected in a community in act and aims at a community of destiny or fate.[29] There must be, then, an inner continuity between the history of individuals and of humanity at large. Since the depth of individual spirit and corporate spirit are the same, world history can open to the individual as '*anamnêsis* and self-knowledge'. On this basis, Berdyaev finds two factors in the formation of historical consciousness: memory and creative freedom, as spirit develops from a 'naïve-organic' stage through one

---

27 Idem., *Theologik II. Wahrheit Gottes* (Einsiedeln 1985); *Theologik III. Der Geist der Wahrheit* (Einsiedeln 1987).

28 *Apokalypse III*, p. 424.

29 Seeing this as typically Russian, Balthasar finds in it the reason why a number of Russian writers have difficulty with the doctrine of Hell. Its rejection is 'always socially grounded in the impossibility of knowing one's fellow-humans as eternally lost', ibid., p. 427.

of 'distancing' (with which Berdyaev would associate not only the Enlightenment but also phases of dominance of historicism and nationalism) to a
phase of self-transparency where spirit recognizes the historical character of
being, and returns from the phenomenon to the noumenon which it itself is.
This is as much as to say that, for all its debts to Eastern Orthodoxy and the
wider Christian tradition, Berdyaev's remains a Dionysian mode of
apocalyptic.

Digging further, Balthasar uncovers strata not only Schellingian but even
Gnostic in Berdyaev's vision of time. From the potentialities of an irrational
Urgrund God and the human world arise together, the first eternally active
but consumed by longing for 'another', the second free but only capable of
fulfilment in God. The ground of human freedom remains 'a darkness prior
to good and evil';[30] in freedom's graceless birth evil is unavoidable. In God,
however, freedom is *aufgehoben*, both cancelled and elevated, and becomes
the 'necessity of love'. But precisely here is where Christ meets the universal
need. 'As a free man, he is already born in God, and all freedom outside God,
since it mirrors his archetype, is in its fall still graciously surrounded. So evil
can be purified, when it turns to God.'[31]

Balthasar calls this 'the tragedy of freedom'. It is for Berdyaev the primal
history and the meaning of being. Berdyaev is not interested in the forgiveness of sins, thus manifesting the imperfect penetration of his thought by
the Gospel. He is only interested in the annihilation of sin in the transfiguring
of human nature. True, the restoration of all things cannot be made accessible
to rational enquiry. But it can be an ethical imperative: that each one should
be saved for the sake of all.

For Balthasar, Berdyaev 'forces the great eschatological lines of the
world's happening to converge in the unity of kairos'. 'The opposites of
noumenal and phenomenal history, of individual destiny and the fate of
humankind, of revelation and *anamnêsis*, of religion and creative development, are shown to be [merely] provisional. Christ himself comes together
with Dionysus.'[32]

Naturally, those final words are ironic and disapproving. Ultimately, we
are faced here with an 'impersonal metaphysic' where freedom derives from
a chaotic abyss, love remains a drive, and creation is 'Dionysian outbreak'.
What Berdyaev worships is 'not the majesty of God, but the dark majesty of
human freedom enthroned in the heart of God'.[33] Berdyaev's freedom knows
neither humility nor judgment.

Much more briefly, and by way of a coda, Balthasar considers a third
philosophy (after Tillich and Berdyaev) to originate from Barth with a special
interest in the theme of kairos. This is the far less well-known Erwin Reisner's study sub-titled 'Foundation of a Christian Metaphysic of History', for
which history is the 'fall of sin and the way to judgment'.[34] This sounds

---

30 N. Berdyaev, *Die Philosophie des freien Geistes. Problematik und Apokalyptik des Christentums*
    (Tübingen 1930), p. 188.
31 *Apokalypse* III, p. 428.
32 Ibid., p. 429.
33 Ibid., p. 430.
34 E. Reisner, *Die Geschichte als Sündenfall und weg zum Gericht. Grundlegung einer christlichen
    Metaphysik der Geschichte* (Berlin 1929).

hopeful, up to a point. But treating as the original form of the human the 'I–thou' relation of man and woman joined by the circumincession of love, itself realized through divine presence, Reisner regards the advent of the 'it' (*das Es*) in the emergence of referring discourse as at once the sign of sinful aversion from God and the beginning of time and history. 'The whole development of history is nothing other than the phenomenal expression of the Fall as such.' World-judgment, accordingly, is not a contingent trans-cendent act, but the 'end-point of the inner logic of the Fall itself, the fruit of the entire history'.[35] This is historical time as the ceaseless depotentialization of plenary being in the direction of emptiness and death. In a cosmic kairos, what for Heidegger or Barth was an orienting attitude towards death or judgment becomes the very method of the philosophy of history. For Reisner, Paradise is essentially forgetting. True remembering can only issue, for him, from revelation, where God's address does not abolish the road to noth-ingness but changes its meaning, establishing the hope that with annihilation comes also salvation. In context, the Incarnation can hardly be other than an 'embarrassment'. Christ's kenosis is inadequate to the greater kenosis of time and sin, and Balthasar compares Reisner's Saviour to the impotent Wotan at the close of *Götterdämmerung*.

How, then, *should* we think of kairos? In answering this question, Bal-thasar brings his study to a close. We have seen how Berdyaev placed sig-nificant moments of time on an ascending line – a way of divinization of the earth, while Reisner situated them by an opposite tack – on a road to noth-ingness. This 'contradiction of world-historical dimensions' may remind us of a comparable antinomy discovered by Heidegger and Rilke: negativity is positivity, annihilation is transfiguration, or, in Pauline terms: 'as dying and behold we live'.[36] Could we not say, then, that the outreach of existence – between life and spirit, between existential truth and ideal truth, earth and heaven – which gives human life its full truth and its 'final' attitude has the shape of a crucifixion? Mythopoeically or – what amounts for Balthasar to the same thing – concretely, a *crossbeam* emerges from the contradictions he has surveyed both in volume I of *Apokalypse* (on the tensions of Idealism) and in volumes II and III (on those between nature and spirit). He brings forward texts from the ancient and mediaeval divines – Origen, Augustine, Bona-venture – for all of whom only the Cross unites, kairos-like, the length and the breadth, the height and the depth of the world and human affairs. So 'Christ gives the world its form and its law, inasmuch as he lives on the Cross what the Cross imagistically expresses.'[37] And within this shape, 'Pro-metheus bound' and the 'crucified Dionysus' can be allotted their place. All Idealism was an exchange with Christianity. But what decisively dis-tinguished it from Christianity was the Prometheanism which made man – and not the incarnate One – the mediator between God and the world. Such hubris, however, is also the 'ground of the form of the Cross'. Christ is Saviour 'for Prometheus', by which Balthasar means, I take it, that only divine kenosis can draw the sting of human pride. As for the figure of Dionysus, he 'stands already in temporality, finitude, death', and in his

---

35 *Apokalypse III*, p. 431.
36 2 Corinthians 6.9.
37 Ibid., pp. 434–35.

purest forms he grasps his final task which also points on to Christ: to overcome the hero in the form of the child. That means ultimately the little one of Bethlehem and Nazareth whose manger–crib looks to the Cross.

Of course it will always be an affront to reason to say of the death by crucifixion of one man in a corner of the Roman empire that it 'precondi- tioned and determined not only the entire course of world history but, more deeply, the interiority of every single human being, and indeed their entire ontological structure'.[38] But this is what Christian philosophy takes as its cognitive goal, and rightly. And if the assertion at the heart of that enterprise is true, then all thinking, which inevitably takes place in a creation where nature is only a relatively autonomous reality now existing in the higher medium of grace, must in some way or another come up against a boundary relevant to its claim. Volumes II and III of *Apokalypse* have depended in one way or another on the classic distinction – present in Heidegger and Barth as in ancient and mediaeval thought – between existence and essence. In recognizing this 'real distinction', ancients and moderns are at one. Finite truth is caught between being so (essence) and being there (existence). It is, we can say, the truth of a being that is in tension, in movement, on the way. Now: 'when the humanised God lifts this truth onto the divine level, he is this truth only insofar as he is beforehand the way, and so is an extended (*ausgespannte*) existence, a life ...'[39] whereupon, as in the opening of the second volume of the theological logic, Balthasar cites the Gospel according to St John: 'I am the way, the truth, and the life'.[40] Factual, finite being is in its innermost character *weghaft*, 'on the way', or, in a word, 'historical' – which means in turn that the historical is in *its* innermost character ontological, *seinshaft*.

It is perfectly possible that, say, Nietzsche, Heidegger and Rilke under- stood a good deal of the truth of being while recognizing almost nothing of the truth of history. The latter was the rock on which most Promethean and Dionysian thinkers suffered shipwreck. If German thought, in either manner, has one single most prominent *Leitmotiv*, it is surely that of *becoming*, the potentiality of being – understood over against the Scholastic notion of being as sheer actuality, pure act. What such German minds failed to see was that the form of becoming – which indeed is the 'form of the world' – is itself poised between two kinds of potentiality: positive, active potentiality and negative, passive potentiality. There is a difference between the super- becoming (one might even write the 'super-nothingness') of God, and the genuinely impotent nothingness found in creaturely becoming. (This is why man cannot be the mediator or the Absolute that Prometheans want him to be!) If we look again at the bipolarity of essence and existence we might realize that in their non-unity they point on to a 'wholly other' that is no longer simply de facto reality.

The truth of being has its deepest foundation in the relation of essence- and-existence to God. And because God is beyond both essential and exis- tential truth, he is at once highest objectivity and highest subjectivity, at the same time being *par excellence* and history *par excellence*. That is why being

38 Ibid., p. 435.
39 Ibid., p. 436.
40 John 14.6. Cf *Theologik II*, op.cit., pp. 13–16.

can be 'dialogical'. The truth of finite being is historical – and that means, ever new because directed to the God who is himself 'ever-new, always-unreckonable, ever-surprising'. This conceptualization of God will return, much developed, in the final volume of Balthasar's theological dramatics.

Of course if ontology is historical, then the claims made by Christian philosophy for Incarnation and (especially) Atonement begin to look more feasible. Revelation proposes to us the Cross of Christ as the centre of world history. Thought can also propose it – granted the theological a priori of the supernatural order – as belonging with 'finite being's most formal ontology'.[41] 'The space of truth in which the creature wanders is as such to its very foundations the space of sin and the space of redemption. And therefore the "emptiness" of this space is at one and the same time the nothingness of creaturehood, the satanic nothingness of sin and the divine nothingness of the kenosis of Christ – and so is kairos.'[42] In this case, the relation of the individual soul to God will have the same form as that of the 'total soul', all humanity in its spiritual search, from which Balthasar draws the inference that the same intermeshing of axiological and teleological eschatology the individual knows (the Word of God can strike me at any moment but does so supremely at the hour of my death) will apply *mutatis mutandis* to human history at large.

The sheer scale of human history, pre-history and – who knows? – future history daunts the interpreter. But he or she can at least say that, up to the present time, the whole ascent of humanity – which is, let it be emphasized, a real ascent – is more deeply a falling. That is owing not only to the transience of its forms, which come into being and pass away again, but also to the fact that this terrific 'offering of time to the throne of eternity' is 'subverted through and through by revolt against Eternity'.[43] Nor is this unpredictable. When time runs ashore on the banks of the Eternal, there is not only a 'natural drama' but a 'drama of redemption' which implies, then, sin, and therefore Fall.[44] Immeasurable cosmic evolution is paralleled by the invisible dying of the world. Evolution produces more – and 'higher' – material for conflagration. 'The more radical transfiguration follows the more radical death.'[45] This Heidegger and Rilke saw (as had Kierkegaard before them). What they did not know was that this is no mere cosmic law, but the 'primordially historical law of the God-man'. It was and is the plan of God for 'the fullness of time, to unite all things in him, things in heaven and things on earth'.[46]

How does this vision differ from the mediaeval synthesis from which *Apokalypse* started, with its integration of cosmic, individual and corporate eschatology? Not at all, save in one respect which in a sense changes everything. The mediaevals could only put forward that integrated eschatology as a theologoumenon, a theological assertion. 'No comprehensive philosophical insight could round off this belief.'[47] But now, equipped with a

41 Ibid., p. 438.
42 Ibid., p. 439.
43 Ibid., p. 440.
44 Ibid., p. 441.
45 Ibid.
46 Ephesians 1.10.
47 *Apokalypse III*, p. 441.

philosophy of history and – what is more – an historical ontology, endowed with a thanatology and an existential interpretation of truth (all of these Balthasar has developed in dialogue with the major figures of his book), we have at last a 'worldly and human basis and breadth' on which to proceed. Balthasar resumes the thinking about theological culture and method of 'Patristik, Scholastik und wir' when he concludes that we have not 'returned' to the beginning (by an act of straightforward *ressourcement*), going back to the sources of the patristic and mediaeval theological world. Rather, we have let the source itself travel with us down the centuries, gathering the flawed yet invaluable wisdom of the (largely neo-pagan) moderns, sharpening and broadening the Christian intellectual thrust. Here too the Christian lives from how he dies, germinating inwardly in the seed (that metaphor again!). And this inner germination is – here Balthasar looks ahead to the theological aesthetics – the entry of God's glory into the outspread world.

In fact, Balthasar's last word is more a premonition of the theological dramatics. He has already reintroduced the comparison of both natural and supernatural life with the drama. From the circle of the *Lebensdichter*, he returns to Hugo von Hoffmansthal and his 'Kleine Welttheater' with which now to end. Wittingly or not, all players take their part in this theatre. The world clothes them for their parts yet they are immediate to the 'master of the play'. Each player has the freedom to play his role ill or well (that is how good and evil arise). But only the play-master can see the issue of all inter-action, the meaning of the whole. This we must let be. In this context: 'Gnosis is the anti-Christian attempt to "understand" in man "angel and doll", freedom and essence, grace and nature in a secret point of unity.'[48] Instead, the world must be *played* – though, of course, each player tends to think he or she is the centre of the drama at large. Balthasar praises Hofmannsthal's conception and its realization, this world that 'knows itself as aesthetic play and yet does not know: in how much deeper a sense is it a play!'[49] Beauty, freedom, truth all appear (these are the key terms of, in series, Balthasar's own aesthetics, dramatics and logic) but it is in the dialogue between Wis-dom and 'the beggar' that the breakthrough in 'Kleine Welttheater' takes place – a breakthrough via 'decision' to the 'essential, higher dialogue'. During Wisdom's prayer the beggar is smitten by divine grace in a Damascus Road experience – which is how freedom comes to understand itself aright, and existence to find its truth for the first time. The beggar sees that the ultimate deed is not *to be done*. Instead, it *has been done*. Henceforth, souls that do not seek in their clothing (which is simply worldly) the ground of apoc-alypse can go forward to be powerfully changed, re-formed, though in no way is this an Idealistic reversion to the merely impersonal. Balthasar finds in the kiss for the ground (the 'cornseed's rest') of the beggar the redemption of the 'intoxicated chthonic kiss' of Dostoevsky and the 'melancholy kiss' of Rilke. Lament becomes song, tragic perseverance is liberated, and in letting go lies hope. The beggar brings the Dives figure, 'Reich', with him in his death, so that even in the solitude of judgment where all are separate there is a wonderful 'showing of the unity of destiny, like a golden chain'. Wisdom entreats the transcendent angel not to say 'never' to the rich man, and the

48 Ibid., p. 443.
49 Ibid., p. 445.

angel points to the place far below where in fact he is kneeling. *Apokalypse der deutschen Seele* leaves its very last words to Hofmannsthal's angel:

> Up then! Go before the Master's face!
> Prepare yourselves for enormous light.[50]

50 Cited in ibid., p. 449.

12

❧

The Tasks of Catholic Philosophy in Balthasar's Time

The Outcome

The outcome of this Herculean effort of reading and reflection – Herculean for students of Balthasar and not just for the man himself! – is to be seen scattered through the rest of Balthasar's *oeuvre*, at dozens of points where he takes up questions raised by these writers, corrects their answers in the light of revelation, and makes *some* use of their overall conceptual tool-box. In these ways he is thinking alongside them, though more than not over against them, guided by Scripture, the Fathers, and the mediaevals, notably as interpreted by his three most important mentors: Henri de Lubac, Karl Barth, Adrienne von Speyr.

But in another sense the outcome was more focused and specific. It was to be his 1946 essay, 'On the Tasks of Catholic Philosophy in our Time'. After all, Balthasar had tried to come to terms – on behalf of revelation, of the Judaeo-Christian tradition of understanding the world – with the philosophy of the modern and contemporary periods. In a sense, the huge effort of *Apokalypse* was leading up to this summary piece. Looking ahead to it will help connect this fourth instalment of my 'Introduction to Hans Urs von Balthasar' to a fifth and final book in this series.

Balthasar had come to see Idealism as the arrival point of a long drawn-out fragmentation of the plenary Christian eschatology of the Middle Ages and before. Kant's posing of the problem had proved emblematic. To synthesize personal being with eternity was beyond the capacity of the founder of 'transcendental' philosophy to achieve. In a way this very failure successfully gave voice to the tragic aspect of the human condition (without the self-revealing God). The truth of man's own being is inaccessible to his very own faculties. The attempt of Hegel, most impressive of the 'objective Idealists', to resolve the problem contained some valuable elements, and notably Hegel's insistence that the fullness of objective spirit is only possible through sacrificial abandoning of self – accomplished in religion. But all is vitiated by the replacement of divine freedom with divine need or necessity. Hegel's God needs finitude so as to recognize himself: for this 'God' Christ's sacrificial suffering is a logical necessity, not the marvel of his loving liberty. The upshot of Idealism, which Balthasar placed under the sign of Prometheus, is fairly plain. The two poles of human life, earth and the eternal, could not be brought into a higher synthesis leaving intact the primacy and freedom of love – divine and human.

Existentialism, placed under the sign of Dionysus, rejected all system-building, and sought instead to elaborate a phenomenology of finitude. By comparing and contrasting Nietzsche and Dostoevsky, Balthasar found the Dionysus myth – the tragic acceptance of life as it is, here and now – a way only to a dialectic of contradiction. The vitalist forms of the Dionysian approach which emerged at the end of the nineteenth century, through the exploration of temporality as of the essence of finitude (from Bergson to Heidegger), make an important discovery. It is indeed in the dimension of such temporality that the drama between human and divine freedom will be played out. The ending of *Apokalypse* with the work of Barth, who redis-covered both the eschaton and the dogmatic Christ, points towards the only resolution possible. It is found in the Resurrection of the Crucified. As one student of Balthasar's early writings has noted: 'The emergence of the theological a priori is for Balthasar an anthropological necessity even more than it is a theological one.'[1]

Balthasar's Jesuit cousin Peter Henrici, himself a philosopher by training, in an essay on 'The Philosophy of Hans Urs von Balthasar', remarks correctly that Balthasar always sees philosophy in the light of revelation.[2] Not that for Balthasar philosophy is itself an understanding of revelation (that would be theology). Rather is it what Henrici calls 'a conscious and unconscious approach to revelation' – or, after the Incarnation when the universal claims of the Gospel become known, a turning away from it, alas.

Catholic Philosophy's Tasks

Balthasar's long essay, 'On the Tasks of Catholic Philosophy in Our Time' belongs more or less to the controversy over *la nouvelle théologie*.[3] It was stimulated by the criticism made of his study of Gregory of Nyssa by the Toulouse Dominican Michel-Marie Labourdette, a strong Thomist in the line of the successive quasi-official commentators on Aquinas in the Thomistic school: Capreolus, Cajetan, John of St Thomas. What worried Labourdette was that the Jesuits in France seemed to want to replace Thomas as both theology and philosophy by a combination of Greek patristics and modern philosophy. Labourdette thought he saw just this agenda in Balthasar's study, subtitled as it was 'Essay on the Religious Philosophy of Gregory of Nyssa'. The book deals with the distinction between existence and essence in the framework of a set of philosophical themes – becoming, love, the image – not obviously pre-eminent in Scholastic thought. What could this be, asked Labourdette, except a covert attack on the Scholastic heritage? It is true that *Apokalypse der deutschen Seele*, had Labourdette read it, gives few signals

---

1 R. Sala, *Dialettica dell'anthropocentrismo. La filosofia dell'epoca e l'antropologia cristiana nella ricerca di H. U. von Balthasar: premesse e compimenti* (Milan 2002), p. 402.

2 The Philosophy of Hans Urs von Balthasar', in D.L. Schindler (ed.), *Hans Urs von Balthasar: His Life and Work* (San Francisco 1991), pp. 149–67, here at p. 163.

3 'Von den Aufgaben der katholischen Theologie in der Zeit', *Annalen der Philosophischen Gesellschaft der Inner Schweiz* 3.2–3 (1946–1947) pp. 1–38; cited below is the English translation: 'On the Tasks of Catholic Philosophy in our Time', *Communio* 20 (1993), pp. 147–87.

Balthasar had been studying Scholastic philosophy in Bavaria, chaperoned from afar by Przywara, though there are occasional references there to Thomas. (In my exposition of Balthasar's mammoth text, I have been at pains to show how a 'Thomasian' metaphysical engagement is more sub-terraneously pervasive than the small number of explicit allusions would suggest.) In 1941, in the first edition of his Maximus book, Balthasar had unwittingly fuelled Labourdette's anxieties. Writing about his patristic trilogy on Gregory, Maximus and Origen, he said that Gregory could provide a point of encounter with Existentialist philosophy; Maximus with the problems of German Idealism, and Origen to just about all the main controverted issues of contemporary Catholics. In the essay, 'On the Tasks of Catholic Philosophy in our Time', Balthasar implicitly answered Labourdette's charge that behind all this was a flight from Thomas and the Thomist tradition.[4]

How, then, did he see in this essay the relation of philosophy and theology, crucial as this is to the making of his theological logic? He explained that he understood Christian philosophy as philosophizing within faith and with a view to theology. Although at the First Vatican Council, the Catholic Church clearly distinguished between the natural and the supernatural orders, that should not be taken as licensing a total autonomy for the natural man. 'Even if nature has its own regular laws and reason its own evidential character, still these laws and evidential characters can never appear as a final authority over against grace and faith. Their autonomies remain relative and stand as such always at the disposal of the final authority which belongs to the divine revelation, and to its plans and directives.' As Christ is Lord even of the laws of nature which he is able to break when 'his work and the glorification of God require this', so too his Church, mandated by him, 'takes captive all the thoughts of men in order to place them at the service of Christ'.[5] For a Christian, all reason lies at the disposal of faith.

That was to take a particular option within a debate about how Christians should practise philosophy which went back beyond *la nouvelle théologie* to the 1920s and 30s. It was an issue that divided Thomists among themselves. On the whole, high and dry Thomists – sometimes called Thomists of the strict observance – thought that philosophy should be accorded more autonomy than this job-description suggests, though they agreed its resources also needed to be put to service in the understanding of revelation as well. Gilsonian Thomists, following in the steps of the historian of mediaeval philosophy (but also philosophical practitioner) Etienne Gilson, were more inclined to say philosophy at Christian hands never abstracts completely from faith even if this is only a matter of the interests on which such philosophy concentrates. For Balthasar, the real achievement of Christian philosophy was a spiritual and indeed a Christocentric one. Acquainted as now we are with the grand lines of *Apokalypse der deutschen Seele* we shall not be surprised by how he describes that achievement. It consisted in the opening of all finite philosophical truth towards Jesus Christ by purifying

---

4 See for the background and *déroulement* of this controversy, A. Nichols, OP, 'Thomism and the *nouvelle théologie*', *The Thomist* 64 (2000), pp. 1–19.

5 H.U. von Balthasar, 'On the tasks of Catholic Philosophy in Our Time', with a reference to 2 Corinthians 10.4–5.

philosophical ideas that had originated outside the Church and transposing them to the new context of Christian thought. This is what his own recent patristic monographs – on Origen, Nyssa, Maximus – had been showing.

Balthasar emphasizes, then, how:

> The material separation of the two spheres of reason and faith, as this is demanded by the Vatican Council, does not in any way prevent the recognition of their *de facto* inter-connection in the concrete world-order as this in fact exists from Adam onwards and as indeed it was determined from primeval times in the plan of God's providence.[6]

The *sign* of this is the way that, from Plato and Plotinus to Hegel, Nietzsche and Bergson, philosophers have made demands of the *entire human person* – and not of his or her theoretical reason alone. The pupil is called on to practise decision, to be ethically committed in an ultimate sense, and this for a Christian 'cannot be cleanly separable from the other total decision ... the decision for God' or, concretely, 'for Christ and for his Church'.[7] More than this: 'all truly living philosophy outside Christianity lives from a theological *eros*' (this is the 'theological a priori' of *Apokalypse*), and: 'It is only through this *eros* that it has the power to move and to draw others into the same disposition of seeking orientated towards what is ultimate.'[8]

This is why the greatest Christian philosophers are those who have maximally appropriated the theological enterprise and not the philosophical alone. 'Wherever Catholic philosophy is alive, the *eros* of thought propels it outward, over the penultimate sphere of the objects of philosophical thought, into the sphere of the personal divine Logos.'[9]

Readers of *Apokalypse* will not be taken aback when Balthasar expresses himself optimistically about the latent possibilities of useful encounter between such Christian philosophy and early or mid-twentieth-century movements like *Lebensphilosophie* and Existentialism as well as what he terms, vaguely enough, to be sure, the 'modern spirit of history'. But the justification offered for this optimism in 'On the Tasks of Catholic Philosophy in our Time' is instructive. *Post*-Christian philosophical thought, he avers, only develops 'truly intellectual passion' when the 'Christian-theological element' appears there in secularized form. Accordingly: 'The truly Christian philosophy is animated very frequently by the passion to retrieve this secularized theological material which has lost its way and to bring it back to its true form.'[10]

To reclaim the neglected theological, or at least supernatural, impulses in secular or secularized philosophy is an aspiration that joins together all the major philosopher–theologians of the Church from Clement to Newman. To secularize the theological in the name of philosophy typifies those thinkers who, regrettably, have betrayed their task. The last of these Balthasar names is his great disappointment among the intellectual stars of his lifetime, the once Catholic Scheler.

6 Ibid., p. 152.
7 Ibid.
8 Ibid., p. 153.
9 Ibid., p. 154.
10 Ibid., p. 155.

As Balthasar sees it, the Catholic philosopher has two chief tasks. And the first of these is 'breaking open' finite philosophical truth 'in the direction of Christ'. As he explains: 'Just as the archetype of the revealed truth, the Son, is true because he eternally opens himself to the infinite Father, so *a fortiori* all the finite truth of this world can establish itself as truth only by opening out onto the mystery of God.'[11] How otherwise would the Fathers have used the term 'philosophia' for the 'Christian act of thinking of the revealed truth'? This means taking the analogy of being seriously. It also means accepting that, since the form of worldly being is not homogeneous but 'polar' (shades of Przywara), the infinite truth of the uncreated Trinity will need 'innumerable forms of expression of worldly truth' even to begin to do it justice. What would otherwise be stigmatized as syncretism is entirely in place here. Thomas is a good example of such manifold quarrying by the doctors. 'The fragment or stone that they pick up may come from the bed of a Christian stream, or of a pagan or heretical stream, but they know how to cleanse it and to polish it until that radiance shines forth which shows that it is a fragment of the total glorification of God.'[12]

Predictably enough, Balthasar finds modern German philosophy to be particularly well-disposed to this treatment. Idealism is unthinkable without Christianity, though he sympathizes with those who prefer out-and-out negation of the faith to this 'Christian-anti-Christian amalgam'.[13] The same is true of the 'philosophers of life' and, more recently, the philosophers of existence.

The second chief task of the Catholic philosopher, Balthasar terms 'the art of clarifying transpositions'. This means 'translating' the *philosophia perennis* (Balthasar has by no means abandoned that concept) into multiple new languages. This is a task of diffusion rather than, as was the case with its predecessor, gathering. Balthasar's selection as his prime example of the Belgian Jesuit Joseph Maréchal, with his 'bold attempt to translate Kantian transcendentalism into the modality of scholastic ontology', would probably have confirmed the Toulouse Dominicans' worst fears.[14] Not that Balthasar is breezily optimistic about just how readily this sort of transposition can be carried through. The task requires great discernment ('test everything' was one of his favourite New Testament commands). Some philosophical idioms are simply not worth the effort of troubling oneself about (he instances the 'artificially polished system of Sartre's nihilism'[15]). Though the Catholic philosopher cannot pretend he stands 'absolutely on the same level as the non-believing philosophers', for this would be untrue,[16] he ought not to be a self-conscious know-all. He should submit himself to the labour of understanding alien manners of thought.

But then Balthasar changes tack. None of this, he asserts, would bear any fruit unless Catholic thinkers hold on to key elements of Christian Scholasticism – notably the Scholastic doctrine of the transcendentals and the real

11 Ibid., p. 157. Translation slightly amended.
12 Ibid., p. 159.
13 Ibid., p. 167.
14 Ibid., p. 161. Balthasar claims, however, that Kant has not only been supremely well understood by Maréchal but also 'applied and overcome', ibid.
15 Ibid., p. 162.
16 Ibid., p. 164.

distinction between essence and existence, the 'fundamental constitutional structure that permeates finite being'.[17] That he meant what he said is strongly hinted already in *Apokalypse*. It would become still plainer later, in 1947, on *Wahrheit*'s appearance. There the theme of the mutual indwelling of the transcendentals is prominent as is the notion of participation, dear to more Platonically minded Thomists. Other motifs in the book, like the idea of truth as unveiling and the truth of being as sheltering, sound a more Heideggerian note. This will be, of course, in the context of the Trilogy, the first volume of the theological logic.

A Coda on Thomas

It is noteworthy that in Balthasar's *oeuvre* where so many major and even comparatively minor figures of Christian thought are delineated, often in great detail, no sketch of Thomas Aquinas and his thinking is ever drawn. But Henrici (like the present author) judges Aquinas to be covertly present through *Apokalypse der deutschen Seele*, informing Balthasar's judgments on the writers he assesses, even if this is only really explicit at two points, when Balthasar is discussing Hegel and Barth. (These are, however, the two giants who, so to speak, define from the extremes the Germanist tradition in Balthasar's eyes.) Nor is it just that Thomas is the sole thinker expressly cited in *Wahrheit*; the quantity of references is also impressive. Most evidential of all, though, in Henrici's opinion, is the way 'On the Tasks of Catholic Philosophy in our Time' pivots on Thomas and that in three respects.

First, there is Aquinas's great ontological breakthrough, the distinguishing of *esse* from *essentia*. By understanding *esse*, the act of existence, as the fullness and perfection of all that is real and yet, outside God, a non-subsisting fullness and perfection, which is the gift of Another, God himself, Thomas combined a doctrine of the contingency of all finite things with an affirmation of their ontological richness. Secondly, pivotal for Balthasar is Thomas's account of the natural desire for the vision of God. By nature, a man cannot be definitively fulfilled without it. Yet no human being has a claim on it. Thirdly, Thomas was a theologian who sought to understand all metaphysics as ordered towards theology. Of course, there is also a more general intellectual likeness between Thomas and Balthasar: both received with reverence the vast treasury of Tradition and tried to order its precious contents. In the volumes of the theological aesthetics on metaphysics, ancient and modern, Henrici's report that Balthasar remained deeply influenced by Thomas's distinction between essence and existence is fully borne out. Balthasar treats that distinction as the greatest discovery of Christian metaphysics, and the single most important key to all reality.[18]

These 'Thomist' convictions would remain with Balthasar until the end of his life. We can corroborate that claim by reference to a piece Balthasar threw off in 1984, just four years before his death. The title of an article he chose for his contribution to a multi-authored volume of Francophone essays, *Pour une Philosophie chrétienne*, shows that his basic approach, as described by Henrici,

---

17 Ibid., p. 185.
18 Cf. A. Nichols, OP, *The Word Has Been Abroad*, op. cit., pp. 142–47 for an account of how Balthasar sees Thomas as the climax of Christian metaphysics.

remained stable.[19] In Balthasar's own words, that approach was 'Regaining a Philosophy from the Starting-point of Theology', and the substance of the essay deals with St Thomas on the question of the natural desire to see God. Balthasar criticizes all modern attempts to abolish, by transcending, the distinction between nature and grace. They can only lead, he says, to a position like that of Meister Eckhart who treats the eternal emanation of the Logos from the Father as coincident with the emanation of the world from God. Balthasar stresses in this regard what he calls the central paradox of St Thomas's thought. At once we see Thomas's position as Balthasar's chief court of appeal in this general area. The central paradox he identifies is that, for Thomas, the natural desire for the vision of God belongs to a spiritual nature created by God which, without being able to make any claim to grace, is ordered to a uniquely supernatural end unattainable, however, except by God's free gift. The Fathers of the Church had always believed this. But Aquinas was the one to make it explicit. This is of course Henrici's second pillar of Balthasar's debt to Thomas, and the way Balthasar formulates it shows, unsurprisingly, that he accepts de Lubac's correction of Cajetanian Thomism while also accepting the Dominicans' criticism of the unguarded manner in which de Lubac had made that correction. Faced with the early modern approach which de Lubac criticized for saying grace elevated man only extrinsically, not intrinsically, and the later modern approach for which the purpose of God's free revelation appears to be the securing of the natural end of man, he could only say, A plague on both your houses.

What has happened in the intellectual history of the modern West, Balthasar says, has been an attempted absorption of grace into nature by an effective incorporation of theology into philosophy with as both cause and consequence the secularization – whether thorough-going or half-hearted – of Christianity. What we have from Descartes to Heidegger is a secularized theology, or as he puts it 'a philosophy which only remains thinkable against the background of a Christian pre-history'.[20]

That is very much the line taken by the founder of the recent movement 'Radical Orthodoxy', John Milbank, in his extraordinarily ambitious work, *Theology and Social Theory*.[21] As if in refutation of those who have sniffed at Balthasar's corpus and reject it as infected by Hegelianism, Balthasar calls Hegelian thought the worst possible example of this tendency which turns the doctrine of the Trinity into a mere description of 'the fundamental structure of mind or spirit'.[22] In a sense, though, adds Balthasar, we might say that modern humanity *has* grasped the Thomist paradox – but only implicitly. When among the German Idealists we suddenly see the emergence of Faustian man or among the French Existentialists 'man in revolt', what is this but a tacit confession that man cannot achieve his God-given end by his own inner resources?

Anyhow, for his own part, Balthasar proposes to regain Thomas's essential paradox from – as his title has it – a theological departure point. If

19 'Regagner une philosophie à partir de la théologie', in *Pour une philosophie chrétienne* (Paris and Namur 1983), pp. 175–87.
20 Ibid., p. 180.
21 J. Milbank, *Theology and Social Theory. Beyond Secular Reason* (London 1990).
22 'Regagner une philosophie à partir de la théologie', art. cit., p. 181.

we bear in mind that for theological doctrine the human creature has its own intrinsic structure, since it is made according to God's image and likeness, and yet at the same time the world is created not for humanity but *in Christ*, we should appreciate the fact that the gift of grace both strengthens and deepens human freedom in its autonomy (thus confirming man's inherent structure as spirit) and also gives the human being a fuller participation in the intimate being of God (thus confirming the primacy of the Mediator, Jesus Christ, in the creation covenant). On this basis we can find a way back to the basic truth of philosophy from the theologian's angle. And this truth is that, in Balthasar's words:

> the *donum* of grace enriches and liberates the *datum* (nature) in such a way that the latter is equipped for far-seeing thought (*la pensée clairvoyante*).[23]

---

23 Ibid., pp. 183–84.

13

꧁꧂

A Very Summary Conclusion

What then, in the last analysis, is the importance of Balthasar's early philosophical writings? Taken in their entirety – of which, of course, *Apokalypse der
deutschen Seele* forms the lion's share, they furnish evidence for his conviction
that in *die Neuzeit*, the modern age, the venerable human 'measure', product
of the fruitful marriage of ancient civilization with the Gospel, has collapsed.
Despite the very real advances of modernity when it comes to evaluating the
concrete, the particular, the historical, the measuring rod has snapped and
we are left with two monstrosities: either the impossible *Übermensch*, the
bearer of a 'non-metaphysical transcendence',[1] or the deplorable *Unter-
menschen*, the sub-human, robotic workers and consumers of the mass
society. Both of these 'visions' are in fact dystopias, and not, as their cham-
pions would have it, Utopias at all. But precisely this development forces the
reflective to look elsewhere – to look outward and upward. Sooner or later,
they will ask about the 'metahistorical measure of man'.[2] That is why Balthasar wanted to be clear about the relation between worldly humanism and
supra-worldly humanism – to be clear, that is, about the Christian measure of
man. Titanism destroys the human; anarchic freedom condemns us by its
hubris to ills unlimited. The best paganism always knew that man was
'girdled by an ultimate measure that gives him his being and his spirit'.[3] I am
thought, therefore I am.

That points us to the truth that nature is created for something beyond
nature. It is created for grace. The order of nature has no final independence,
since, just as it was founded in the total plan of God in Christ for the world,
so it will be fulfilled there. And that means, further, that, in the last analysis,
nature can only 'disclose its inner lawfulness inasmuch as it is consciously
integrated in, and ordered to, the higher law of Christian revelation'.[4] The
solution of the human 'problem' lies in the inexhaustible truths of the Trinity
and the Incarnation which Balthasar's later theology, in the Trilogy, and
beyond it, will lay out. The form of the Trinity, its divine *Gestalt*, is the

1 R.J. Hollingdale, 'Introduction', in *A Nietzsche Reader* (Harmondsworth; Penguin 1977),
p. 11.
2 Balthasar, 'Christlicher Humanismus', *Gloria Dei* 4.1 (1949–1950), pp. 37–48, and here at
p. 37.
3 Ibid., p. 38.
4 Ibid., p. 40.

fullness of life and love. This is what the Incarnation brings home to us, and bestows on us. And only so can humanity have sufficient reason by which to endure and enjoy.

Index of Names

Ambrose 26
Angelico, Fra 171
Anselm 73, 122
Aquinas, *see* Thomas Aquinas
Aristotle 3, 28, 36, 38, 102
Arnold, M. 33
Athanasius 26
Augustine 26, 27, 38, 75, 117, 155, 202, 213, 222, 240

Baader, F. von 123, 130
Bach, J. S. 6
Baius, *see* Bay, M. de
Barlach, E. 186
Barth, K. 19, 20, 31, 120, 142, 176, 188, 189, 198, 219–29, 231, 232, 233, 234, 237, 240, 241, 245, 250
Basil 26
Bay, M. de 222
Becher, J. 184
Beer-Hofmann, R. 144
Beethoven, L. van 6
Béguin, A. 8
Benson, R. H. 182
Berdyaev, N. 167, 171, 238, 239, 240
Bergson, H. 39, 133, 134, 135–9, 141, 144, 145, 187, 190, 191, 193, 205, 206, 227, 231, 246, 248
Bernstein, E. 234
Bloch, E. 180, 235
Blondel, M. 146
Böcklin, A. 139
Böhme, J. 81, 119
Bonaventure 201, 222, 240
Boyle, N. 107
Brandes, G. M. C. 156

Brockes, F. 182
Brod, M. 186
Brown, R. 71
Brunner, E. 221, 223
Bülow, C. von 3

Cajetan 246
Capreolus 246
Catherine of Siena 138
Caussade, J. P. de 237
Chrysostom, *see* John Chrysostom
Claudel, P. 146, 147
Clement of Alexandria 248
Coleridge, S. T. 33
Columbus, C. 56
Congar, Y. 24
Copleston. F. 69
Cooper, A. A. 55
Cyril of Alexandria 26

Daniélou, J. 18
David, King 227
Dehmel, R. 182
Derleth, L. 187
Descartes, R. 43, 136, 194, 251
Dessauer, F. 180
Diesel, E. 181
Dilthey, W. 139
Dominic 25
Dostoevsky, F. 132, 154–78, 179, 187, 190, 219, 231, 236, 237, 243, 246

Eckhart, Meister 251
Empedocles 87, 88, 89
Engels, F. 129
Eriugena, *see* John Scotus Eriugena

255

Fedorov, N. 235
Fénelon, F. de S. de la M. 197
Feuerbach, L. 75, 128
Fichte, J. G. 37, 54, 57, 59–67, 69, 70,
    74, 80, 92, 93, 109, 111, 112, 114,
    124, 127, 130, 133, 135, 194, 222
Fischer, M. 182
Francis of Assisi 34, 138, 197, 201
Freud, S. 139, 144, 145, 147

George, S. 134, 140, 141, 144, 145, 146,
    147, 148, 150, 182, 193, 206, 234
Gide, A. 147
Gilbert, W. S. 28
Gilson, E. 247
Goethe, J. W. von 36, 57, 58, 59, 90,
    91, 98–108, 110, 113, 114, 115,
    120, 124, 127, 133, 136, 175, 193,
    194, 203, 209, 211, 231
Gregory of Nyssa 117, 246, 248
Guardini, R. 156
Günther, A. 30, 36
Hamann, J. G. 46–7, 48, 222
Hardenberg, F. L. von, see Novalis
Harnack, A. von 26
Hartmann, E. von 180, 210
Hartmann, N. 139
Hauptmann, G. 185
Hebbel, C. F. 126–8
Hegel, G. F. W. 6, 35, 58, 69, 70, 76,
    92, 109, 114–23, 124, 127, 129,
    130, 133, 142, 157, 158, 174, 180,
    197, 202, 203, 205, 217, 222, 228,
    233, 245, 248, 250
Heidegger, M. 43, 94, 98, 99, 111, 133,
    139, 141, 152, 188, 189, 202,
    203–19, 220, 223, 227, 228, 231,
    233, 234, 240, 241, 242, 246
Henrici, P. 246, 250, 251
Herder, J. G. 34, 46, 47–50, 55, 99, 100,
    101, 111, 115, 191, 234
Herman, M. 148
Herodotus 5
Herrman, W. 225, 226
Hesse, H. 185
Hofer, C. 183
Hoffmann, E. T. W. 125
Hofmannsthal, H. von 134, 139, 141,
    143, 145, 146, 147, 148, 149, 151,
    152, 187, 243, 244

Hölderlin, C. F. 57, 82–90, 101, 109,
    114, 124, 127, 203, 219
Huch, R. 182
Hulewicz, W. von 217
Hume, D. 193
Husserl, E. 134, 190, 192, 193, 194,
    195, 202

Ibsen, H. J. 127
Ignatius Loyola 30, 59, 226
Irenaeus 21, 227

Jaspers, K. 161, 186, 233
Jean Paul, see Paul, J.
Jeremiah 89
Joachim of Fiora 42
Joan of Arc 246
Job 228
John, evangelist 12, 27, 70, 78, 83, 89,
    167
John Chrysostom 26, 132
John Scotus Eriugena 42
John of St Thomas 246

Kafka, F. 179, 193
Kant, I. 11, 30, 37, 50–4, 55, 57, 60, 65,
    90, 93, 96, 98, 102, 112, 127, 130,
    135, 157, 165, 193, 197, 203, 204,
    206, 209, 231, 242
Keyserling, H. 145, 148, 149
Kierkegaard, S. 11, 12, 23, 105, 120,
    125, 126, 129–32, 134, 145, 156,
    204, 224
Klages, L. 134, 140–3, 144, 145, 187,
    193, 206, 227, 231,
Kleist, H. von 57, 112, 125
Kraus, K. 183, 193

Labourdette, M.-M. 246, 247
Ladner, G. 138
Lagerlöf, S. 182
Leibniz, G. W. 43, 55, 70, 99, 101, 115,
    153, 154
Lessing, G. E. 45–6, 49
Lewis, C. S. 39
Lorrain, C. 121, 161, 171
Lubac, H. de 29, 42, 236, 245,
    251
Lukács, G. 235, 236
Luther, M. 43, 226, 228

Mannheim, K. 236
Maréchal, J. 249
Maritain, J. 43, 136, 137
Mark, evangelist 227
Mary, Blessed Virgin 22, 67
Marx, K. 236
Maximus 3, 247, 248
Migne, J. P. 18
Milbank, J. 251
Murdoch, I. 146

Neumann, R. 186
Newman, J. H. 10, 20, 33, 199, 248
Nietzsche, F. 4, 34, 37, 39, 66, 82, 89,
    115, 125, 126, 129–32, 133, 134,
    139, 140, 143, 146, 147, 154–78,
    179, 180, 181, 187, 190, 191, 198,
    199, 202, 205, 220, 227, 229, 231,
    232, 233, 234, 237, 241, 246, 248
Novalis 36, 57, 79–82, 83, 101, 109,
    114, 124, 180, 203, 219

Origen 26, 219, 240, 247, 248

Paul, apostle 14, 27, 42, 78, 137, 138,
    167, 223, 223
Paul, J. 57, 91, 109–13, 120, 203
Pascal, B. 151
Peter, apostle 56, 178
Picard, M. 183
Pius XII 222
Plato 12, 36, 85, 102, 140, 146, 210, 248
Plotinus 63, 74, 119, 135, 137, 248
Proclus 6
Przywara, E. 19, 20, 31, 40, 247

Rahner, H. 217
Ramuz, E. F. 182
Rathenau, W. 234–35
Reisner, E. 239, 240
Rembrandt 12
Richter, J. P. F., *see* Paul, J.
Rilke, R. M. 43, 107, 127, 133, 134,
    139, 141, 147, 148, 151, 189, 193,
    202, 203–19, 220, 222, 223, 227,
    231, 233, 240, 241, 242, 243
Röttger, K. 183
Rozanov, V. 236
Rubiner, L. 235
Runge, P. O. 79

Sartre, J.-P. 249
Scheler, M. 9, 10, 133, 134, 146, 147,
    180, 181, 187–202, 203, 206, 207,
    227, 233, 248
Schelling, F. W. J. von 36, 37, 59,
    69–78, 80, 95, 98, 111, 114, 116,
    119, 120, 124, 128, 129, 133, 191,
    224, 225, 226, 228, 238
Schiller, J. C. F. 15, 54–7, 84, 90–8, 99,
    100, 102, 109, 114, 120, 229
Schlegel, A. von 57, 125
Schlegel, F. von 57, 58, 76, 125
Schleiermacher, F. D. E. 126
Schmidt, J. K. 125
Schopenhauer, A. 112, 125, 128, 129,
    130, 140, 180
Schreyvogel, F. 182
Schrijver, G. de 37
Schumann, R. 125
Shaftesbury, Lord, *see* Cooper, A. A.
Shestov, L. 156
Silesius, A. 217
Simmel, G. 43, 133, 139, 140, 210, 211
Simon, U. 110
Socrates 130, 131
Soloviev, V. 182, 236
Sonnenberg, F. von 125
Spengler, O. 43, 140, 196
Speyr, A. von 218, 225, 247
Spinoza, B. 70
Spitteler, C. 134, 140, 141, 144, 146,
    150, 187
Staël, Mme de 33
Sterne, L. 109
Sternberg, L. 186
Stirner, M., see Schmidt, J. K.
Strähler, G. 180
Strauss, R. 6, 134
Stravinsky, I. 6–7
Swedenborg, E. 51
Sychrava, J. 55

Taylor, C. 72
Teresa of Avila 25, 139
Tertullian 21
Thérèse of Lisieux 34, 82
Thomas Aquinas 10, 19, 28, 29, 34,
    35, 36, 66, 117, 122, 124, 142, 175,
    176, 246, 247, 250, 251
Thucydides 5

Tieck, L. 125
Tillich, P. 237, 238, 239
Tolkien, J. R. R. 39
Tolstoy, L. 12
Trakl, G. 184
Troeltsch, E. 139
Trotsky, L. 12
Turner, J. M. W. 13

Ulitz, A. 182, 186

Valéry, P. 147
Verdi, G. 6
Voltaire 235

Wackenroder, W. H. 125
Wagner, R. 3, 89, 126, 128–29, 167
Wells, H. G. 140, 245
Werfel, F. 149, 152
Wilde, O. 147
Winckler, J. 145, 235